FROM MYCENAE TO HOMER

by the same author

GREEK THEATRE PRODUCTION

FROM MYCENAE TO HOMER

T. B. L. Webster

Professor of Greek
University College · London

LONDON 1958
METHUEN & CO LTD
36 ESSEX STREET · STRAND · WC2

FIRST PUBLISHED 1958

The royalties on the sale of this book will be given
to the Michael Ventris Memorial Fund c/o
Architectural Association, 35 Bedford Square,
London W.C.1

CATALOGUE NO. 6044/U

© 1958 T.B.L. WEBSTER
PRINTED IN GREAT BRITAIN BY
JARROLD & SONS LTD. NORWICH

CONTENTS

ILLUSTRATIONS

PLACED AT THE END

15 Mycenaean krater from Enkomi. Nicosia, Cyprus Museum. *Photograph: Medelhavsmuseet.*

16*a, b* and *c.* Steatite vase from Hagia Triada. Crete, Heraklion Museum. *Photographs: Heraklion Museum and Warburg Institute.*

17 Mycenaean krater from Aradippo, Cyprus. Paris, Louvre, AM 876. *Photograph: V. Karageorghis.*

18 Mycenaean krater from Cyprus. London, British Museum, C 391. *Photograph: British Museum.*

19 Impression of ring from fourth shaft-grave, Mycenae. Athens, National Museum. *Photograph: German Archaeological Institute.*

20*a* and *b.* Attic Geometric oenochoe, Battle for the ships. Copenhagen, National Museum, 1628. *Photograph: National Museum.*

21 Attic Geometric amphora, Funeral. Athens, National Museum, 804. *Photograph: German Archaeological Institute.*

22 Attic Geometric krater, Funeral. Athens, National Museum, 990. *Photograph: German Archaeological Institute.*

23 Attic Geometric amphora, Funeral. Athens, Agora Museum, P 4990. *Photograph: American School of Classical Studies.*

24*a* and *b.* Attic Geometric kantharos. Copenhagen, National Museum, 727. *Photograph: National Museum.*

25*a* and *b.* Attic Geometric oenochoe, Aktorione-Molione. Athens, Agora Museum, P 4885. *Photograph: American School of Classical Studies.*

26 Attic Geometric amphora, Centaurs. Copenhagen, Nationa Museum, 7029. *Photograph: National Museum.*

27 Attic Geometric jug, Herakles and the Stymphalian birds. Copenhagen, Ny Carlsberg Glyptotek, Inv 3153. *Photograph: Ny Carlsberg Glyptotek.*

28*a* and *b.* Attic Geometric oenochoe, Shipwreck. Munich, Antikensammlungen, 8696. *Photograph: Antikensammlungen.*

29 Attic Protogeometric amphora. Athens, Kerameikos Museum, Inv. 576. *Photograph: German Archaeological Institute.*

30 Attic Protogeometric krater. Munich, Antikensammlungen, 6157. *Photograph: Antikensammlungen.*

ACKNOWLEDGEMENTS

Acknowledgements are due first to my wife and Professor Martin Robertson for reading my manuscript and Dr. Michael Coffey for reading my proofs. I have removed many errors as a result of their scrutiny; for those that remain I alone am responsible.

Many people have given me information, photographs, or permission to publish and I should like to express my gratitude to the following: H. Biesantz, G. Bing, C. W. Blegen, N. Breitenstein, P. Courbin, H. Diepolder, P. Dikaios, G. Dontas, Ch. Dugas, A. Frantz, R. Higgins, V. Karageorghis, Chr. Karouzos, E. Kunze, D. Levi, N. Platon, V. Poulsen, L. Talcott, O. Vessberg, as well as to the American School of Classical Studies, the French and Italian Archaeological School, and the German Archaeological Institute in Athens, and the Warburg Institute in London, the National Museum, the Agora Museum, and the Kerameikos Museum in Athens, the museums at Delos and Heraklion, the Cyprus Museum at Nicosia, the National Museum and Ny Carlsberg Glyptotek in Copenhagen, the Medelhavsmuseet in Stockholm, the Antiken Sammlungen in Munich, the Louvre in Paris, and the British Museum in London.

I have learnt a great deal from the discussions at the Linear B Seminar at the Classical Institute of the University of London, which started meeting at the beginning of 1954 under the chairmanship of Professor E. G. Turner. Michael Ventris was an active member and his discovery was the origin of the Seminar as of this book. The debt which I owe to him will be obvious to my readers; it is owed not only to a scholar but to a friend. Now that he is dead I can only offer this book with all its imperfections as a tribute to his memory.

T. B. L. WEBSTER

October, 1957

CHRONOLOGICAL TABLE

The absolute figures in the left-hand column are a
general indication rather than precise dates.

2000 M.M. II	Kamares vases Earliest frescoes, Knossos		Old Babylonian literature
	BEGINNING OF LINEAR A		
1750 M.M. III	Knossos, Priest-King relief Snake goddess		Earlier archive at Alalakh Mari tablets
1600 L.M. I	H.T. Harvester vase (fig. 16)	Mycenae, New Grave Circle; shaft-graves (figs. 3–5, 19)	
1450 L.M. II	H.T. Sarcophagus (fig. 6). Isopata ring (fig. 13). Knossos, throne room. Palace Style vases	Mycenae, ring from Acropolis treasure (fig. 10)	Later archive at Alalakh
	LINEAR B: KNOSSOS TABLETS		
	Destruction of Knossos		
1400 L.H. III A (L.M. III)	Phaistos seal (fig. 12)	Mycenae, Megaron frescoes; Lion Gate	Hurrian poetry. Ugaritic poetry. Hittite relations with Ahhiyawa. Mycenaean vases from Cyprus (figs. 15, 17, 18)
1300 L.H. III B	Pylos frescoes (figs. 8, 9)	Delos ivories (fig. 2). Athens, ring from Agora (fig. 11)	Mycenaean vases from Cyprus (fig. 14)
			Mycenaean settle- ment at Ugarit. (1230) Sack of Troy
L.H. III C		Mycenae, Warrior vase (fig. 7)	Destruction of Boghazkeuy, Ugarit, and Alalakh
	Pylos tablets (fig. 1) Mycenae tablets		

1200	Sack of Pylos and Iolkos.	Destruction of houses outside the citadel, Mycenae. Attack on Athens.	
	Expulsion from Messenia	Melanthos' arrival in Athens	
	SUB-MYCENAEAN		
1100	Sack of Mycenae. Settlement of Samos	Defence of Athens (Kodros).	
	PROTOGEOMETRIC		
	Ionian migration	Nucleus of Ionian League and beginning of Panionia	
1000	LATE PROTOGEOMETRIC (figs. 29–30)		
	Settlement of Chios by Amphiklos		
900	PURE GEOMETRIC (figs. 31–4)		
	Ionian capture of Smyrna. Introduction of alphabetic writing. Hektor of Chios	Widening of Ionian League	Bronze tripods in Ithaca
			Greek pottery at Al Mina
760	ELABORATE GEOMETRIC (figs. 20–2; 24–5; 27–8; 35–6)		
	Hero cults in Greece	Eumelos of Corinth	Cretan shields (fig. 37)
	Iliad and Odyssey. Earliest inscribed pottery at Athens and Ischia	Agamemnon of Kyme	
725	LATE GEOMETRIC (figs. 23, 26)		
	Arktinos of Miletos. Hesiod	Lesches of Mitylene	Ionian imports into Ithaca
700	EARLY PROTO-ATTIC		

INTRODUCTION

Michael Ventris' decipherment of Linear B in 1952 proved that Greek was spoken in the Mycenaean world. This fact had long been suspected by archaeologists and, to quote two outstanding examples, Nilsson had maintained that much of Greek mythology was Mycenaean in origin and Miss Lorimer claimed that Homer's knowledge of perishable Mycenaean objects came from a poetic tradition which went back to the time of the shaft-graves of Mycenae. On the linguistic side, Bowra had shown the probability that words common to the Homeric poems and Arcado-Cypriote came to both from Mycenaean Greek.

Ventris' discovery not only confirmed these views but provided a considerable mass of varied material in the tablets recovered from the Mycenaean palaces (even the houses in which the tablets were found at Mycenae were probably outhouses of the palace). In reviewing the great work, *Documents in Mycenaean Greek*, in which Ventris and Chadwick described the discovery, discussed the picture of the Mycenaean world which the tablets give, and translated and commented on a large selection of tablets, I tried to point out the consequences which follow from reading these documents:[1]

'Because they are written in Greek, they tell us a great deal about the Greek language half a millennium and more before Homer. Because they record Mycenaean civilization in Mycenaean terminology, while Homer was writing in Ionian Greek at the beginning of the *polis* civilization, they show, when joined with other evidence, how much in Homer is Mycenaean; and where we can say that these Mycenaean elements cannot have survived till Homer's time, they tell us something of the poetry which bridged the gap. Because many of the personal names are known from mythology, which was already supposed to go back to Mycenaean times, they pose the question of what Greek mythology was already existent. Because they give us the names of Greek gods then worshipped, they make a new assessment of the earliest Greek religion and

[1] *Antiquity*, 31 (1957), 6.

its relation to Minoan religion desirable. Because they prove that Mycenaean civilization was a Greek-speaking civilization, they show also that Mycenaean art is Greek art; except for a comparatively small number of imports, objects of art on the mainland from the Shaft-Grave period and in Knossos at least from the middle of the fifteenth century must have made sense to their Greek-speaking owners and must have been explicable in Greek terms. Because Linear B is derived from Linear A, communication between Greeks and Minoans is proved, and the Greek occupation of Knossos (and probably many other parts of Crete, as the tablets and Idomeneus' contingent suggest) is likely to have been followed by the borrowing not only of script but also of stories, and by the borrowing not only of art techniques and forms but also of the ideas conveyed by those forms, since here Greek and Minoan artists were working side by side and could communicate with each other. Because Asiatic words were found in the tablets, we can suppose that the Mycenaean out-stations in Ugarit and the port of Alalakh were to some extent bilingual (and the Hittite correspondence shows that verbal communication between the Greek world and the Hittite world was possible); we can therefore surmise that Eastern stories entered the Mycenaean repertoire, but there is no reason to suppose that Eastern works of art which found their way to Greece carried their interpretation with them, except on the possible occasions when the artist himself travelled; when Mycenaean artists on the mainland were inspired by imported works of art, their interpretation would be a new Greek interpretation, which need bear no relation to what the Eastern artist meant. Because the Mycenaean palaces used tablets and the tablets can now be read, Mycenaean civilization becomes comparable with other civilizations which used tablets at this time.'

The possibility of drawing a picture of Mycenaean civilization from its documents and not only from archaeology (which continues to provide more and more material), the linguistic evidence that Mycenaean Greeks were in contact with the East, and the determination of Mycenaean Greek as a stage which can be distinguished in the development of the Greek language have come at a time when knowledge of the contemporary Eastern world is both fuller and more accessible to the classical scholar than it has ever been before. This is partly due to recent discoveries and partly to the number of reliable and convenient translations (often with text indices) which have been issued in the last few years. It is therefore now possible to see Mycenaean civilization against contemporary civilization and form some opinion of the contacts between the Greek world and the Near East. By seeing the Greeks against this background we can measure more clearly than ever before the achievement of the Greeks in leaping out of this context to become the founders of modern civilization.

Ventris' decipherment has also shown the state of the Greek language in the Mycenaean Age, and philologists have been able to sketch three stages of Greek language corresponding to three stages of Greek civilization – Mycenaean, between the fall of the Mycenaean palaces and about 900 B.C., 900–700 B.C. Historically these three stages correspond to the Mycenaean period, the period which covers the Dorian invasion and the Ionian migration, and the period in which some degree of prosperity has been regained and the classical city state was beginning to take shape. In art the three periods are termed Mycenaean, Sub-Mycenaean and Protogeometric, and Geometric. In art alone we have a full and continuous series linking the Mycenaean Age with the time of Homer, and we can appreciate that the difference between Sub-Mycenaean and Protogeometric constitutes a major revolution in style. We can see this revolution happen in Athenian pottery, and as pottery was a major art and Athens was the centre through which the refugees of the Mycenaean settlements passed on their way to Ionia, this revolution must be given its full importance.

The purpose of the present study is to use our new knowledge to describe Greek art and poetry in these three periods within the limitations imposed by the title, 'From Mycenae to Homer'. Mycenae is interpreted widely as Mycenaean civilization in its contemporary setting; Homer means the *Iliad* and the *Odyssey*. This limits my subject in several ways. First, I have been particularly concerned with the stories which are told or alluded to in the *Iliad* and the *Odyssey*, and I have not attempted to deal with the whole range of Greek mythology; the stories included in the *Iliad* and the *Odyssey* are numerous enough. Secondly, Hesiod, Eumelos, and any other poets (or poems) that may be dated in the eighth century are only mentioned in so far as they have a bearing on Homer; they are not considered for themselves in their own setting. Thirdly, I am not concerned with what happened to the *Iliad* and *Odyssey* after the eighth century. A great deal of careful scholarship has been spent, is being spent, and will be spent on the difficult subject of the transmission of the *Iliad* and the *Odyssey*.[1] For a general study of this kind our texts of the *Iliad* and *Odyssey* can be accepted as substantially faithful reproductions of the poems as they were composed.

The literature of the subject is vast, and I can only claim the normal acquaintance which accrues during twenty-five years of lecturing on Homer. I am much more indebted to others than my footnotes can show, particularly to books like Murray's *Rise of the Greek Epic*, Bowra's *Tradition and Design in the Iliad*, Cauer's *Grundfragen*, and Nilsson's *Homer and Mycenae*, which have been part of my Homeric thinking for a very long time. One other essential source is even harder to define: as an undergraduate I was fascinated by the balanced composition of Attic Geometric vases and with the more general question of the interrelation between poetry and art. Myres' discussions, which started in the late twenties in Oxford, of the parallel between Geometric vases and Homeric composition struck me as extremely revealing. I think that he tried to push the parallelism into too great detail and I think that he was too preoccupied with bilateral symmetry, which is only one kind of Geometric composition; but that he pointed to an essential element in eighth-century poetry I have no doubt at all. Just before the war Schadewaldt's *Iliasstudien* demonstrated what I should call the dynamic pattern in the *Iliad* (particularly the references forward and the references backwards) as Myres sought to demonstrate the static pattern. Of post-war books I need only mention here Miss Lorimer's great codification of archaeological knowledge in *Homer and Mycenae* and most recently Ventris and Chadwick's *Documents in Mycenaean Greek*.

A most useful account of Homeric scholarship in the last fifty years is given by Dodds, Palmer, and Miss Gray in *Fifty Years of Classical Scholarship*, edited by Platnauer in 1954. Recent works are brilliantly assessed by Lesky in his reports in the *Anzeiger der Altertumswissenschaft*. A very full bibliography of works on Homer or connected with Homer but excluding archaeology is given by Mette in the first volume of *Lustrum*. A bibliography of *Mycenaean*

[1] For a discussion cf. J. A. Davison, 'Peisistratus and Homer', *T.A.P.A.*, 86 (1955), 2f.

Civilization covering publications from 1936 to 1956 has been compiled by Miss Moon and issued as *Bulletin Supplement no. 3* of the Institute of Classical Studies in the University of London. Current bibliography on Linear B appears in *Minos* and in *Studies in Mycenaean Inscriptions and Dialect*, published by the London Institute of Classical Studies. New archaeological discoveries are reported annually in *Archaeology in Greece* (a supplement to the *Journal of Hellenic Studies*) and in other journals, particularly in *TO ERGON*, published by the Greek Archaeological Society.

In my footnotes I have used in the main for periodicals the abbreviations adopted by *L'Année Philologique*. Certain other abbreviations may conveniently be listed here. In quoting inscribed tablets I have used, wherever this is not otherwise clear, a prefix of two capital letters to indicate their place of origin: AL for Alalakh, KN for Knossos, MA for Mari, MY for Mycenae, PY for Pylos, TH for Thebes, UG for Ugarit. Other abbreviations which I have used frequently are as follows:

C.V. for *Corpus Vasorum Antiquorum*.
Desborough for V. Desborough, *Protogeometric Pottery*.
Docs. for M. G. F. Ventris and J. Chadwick, *Documents in Mycenaean Greek*.
Gesch. for M. P. Nilsson, *Geschichte der griechischen Religion*.
HB. for C. H. Gordon, *Homer and the Bible*.
HM. for H. L. Lorimer, *Homer and the Monuments*.
K. for W. Kraiker and K. Kübler, *Kerameikos: Ergebnisse der Ausgrabungen*.
K.i.B. for F. Winter, *Kunstgeschichte in Bildern*.
Matz for F. Matz, *Kreta, Mykene, Troja*.
MMR. for M. P. Nilsson, *The Minoan Mycenaean Religion*.
MP. for A. Furumark, *The Mycenaean Pottery: Analysis and Classification*.
NET. for J. B. Pritchard and others, *Ancient Near Eastern Texts*.
PM. for Sir Arthur Evans, *The Palace of Minos at Knossos*.
RGPT. for A. W. Persson, *The Religion of Greece in Prehistoric Times*.
SCE. for E. Gjerstad and others, *The Swedish Cyprus Expedition*.
SG. for G. Karo, *Schachtgräber von Mykenai*.
Stubbings for F. J. Stubbings, 'Mycenaean pottery of Attica', *Annual of the British School of Athens*, 42 (1947), 1f.

I

RECORDS OF SOCIETY IN
THE SECOND MILLENNIUM

The Mycenaean palaces of Greece like the Minoan palaces of Crete and many palaces in the Near East kept their records on clay tablets. Inscribed tablets from Knossos and other Cretan sites have been known for many years. Blegen discovered tablets (fig. 1) when he found an unknown palace some seven miles north-east of Navarino Bay at Pylos in 1939; this was followed, after the war, by his further discoveries at Pylos and by Wace's discoveries at Mycenae. Ventris' decipherment of the script known as Linear B has made it possible to read the tablets written in this script from Knossos, Pylos, and Mycenae, and compare them with tablets in other languages. Thus we have an entirely new kind of material for the comparative study of Mycenaean civilization, written texts from the fifteenth-century palace at Knossos, from the thirteenth-century palace at Pylos, and from thirteenth-century houses at Mycenae. These houses may very well have been the houses of palace officials rather than private houses in the normal sense, so that palace records can be claimed from Mycenae as well.

Comparison with tablets of other civilizations not only illumines dark passages in the Mycenaean tablets themselves, but also shows what elements of Mycenaean civilization were common to other civilizations and what were the divergences. The Mycenaean tablets are records which can be put alongside contemporary Eastern records, just as Mycenaean art and architecture can be compared with contemporary Eastern art and architecture. The juxtaposition has yet a third purpose: to establish what kinds of record have survived from other sites but are lacking from Knossos, Pylos, and Mycenae. If records are largely alike, the civilizations which produce them are likely to have large common elements. If some kinds of record are missing, the reason must be sought.

The Mycenaean records that can be read are written in Greek.

The earliest of them, if the date can be trusted, are the fifteenth-century tablets from Knossos. The script in which they are written is derived from an earlier script known as Linear A, found at Knossos, Hagia Triada, and some other sites in Crete. The earliest datable tablets in this earlier script belong to the eighteenth century, and the script went on being used outside Knossos until the end of the fifteenth century. The language recorded in Linear A (and *a fortiori* in the still earlier Cretan pictographic script) is not Greek, and it is natural to assume that it was the language of the pre-Greek population.[1] Many of the tablets seem to be lists of men working in the palace and elsewhere, and others are inventories of grain, figs, olives, wine, oil, and pots, like many of the Linear B tablets. But the scribes of Linear A used a different system of weights and measures from Linear B; Bennett[2] has suggested that the origin of this may lie in Egypt, whereas the Linear B system points rather to Anatolia. For our purpose we can only say that Mycenaean records are the descendants of earlier Minoan records, and that both have analogies with Eastern records.

Another early script, which has resemblances to Linear A and B and perhaps derives from A, is the script found in Cyprus and known as Cypro-Minoan.[3] Most of the inscriptions are on vases and other small objects and run from the sixteenth century down into the classical period, but two longer tablets (of the thirteenth century and later)[4] were published in 1953, and the second of these, which was found in a temple, may possibly be in verse. An earlier fragment (of the late sixteenth century)[5] has been discovered more recently. These inscriptions cannot yet be read, but it is interesting to find that an alphabet analogous to Linear B was used for writing texts (as distinct from records) in an island which certainly had Mycenaean settlements, if it was not actually part of the Mycenaean kingdom.

[1] Cf. Ventris and Chadwick, *Documents in Mycenaean Greek* (=*Docs.*), 31; G. P. Goold and M. Pope, *Preliminary Investigation into the Cretan Linear A script*, Cape Town, 1955; A. Furumark, *J.d.I.* (forthcoming); C. H. Gordon, *Antiquity*, 1957.

[2] *A.J.A.*, 54 (1950), 222.

[3] See most recently O. Masson, *R.A.*, 47 (1956), 26f.; *B.C.H.*, 81 (1957), 6f.; P. Meriggi, *Athenaeum*, 34 (1956), 3f.; V. and J. Karageorghis, *A.J.A.*, 60 (1956), 351.

[4] P. Dikaios, *Antiquity*, 27 (1953), 103f., 233f.

[5] P. Dikaios and M. Ventris, *Antiquity*, 30 (1956), 40f.

Tablets from many places in the East can however be read, and of these places the most interesting are those which are known to have been in contact with the Mycenaean world. Ugarit on the sea-coast of Syria near the modern Latakia was a kingdom of considerable importance from the eighteenth till late in the thirteenth century, and had a flourishing Mycenaean settlement[1] in the thirteenth century. The French excavators of the enormous palace have discovered countless clay tablets including letters to other kings, juridical and economic documents, as well as poetry. The poetry was written in the Ugaritic language but most of the documents quoted were in Akkadian. All are in alphabetic cuneiform except two recently discovered which are written in a local variant of Cypro-Minoan. Different kinds of documents were found in different offices, and nearly all the poetry was found in the temple of Baal; the possibility of a similar separation of documents at Mycenaean sites must be remembered. The foreign contacts of Ugarit included Egypt, the Hittites, Carchemish, Byblos, Beirut, Sidon, Tyre, and (according to very probable interpretations) Cyprus and Crete.[2] Forty miles north of Ugarit was the port of the inland kingdom of Alalakh; both the port and the capital were excavated by Woolley, who judges that 'it is likely enough that there was a colony of the sort' (like the Mycenaean colony at Ugarit) 'at Al Mina, the port of Alalakh through which imports from the Aegean world come'.[3] In Alalakh itself inscribed tablets were found, mainly from two separate archives, one of the eighteenth and the other of the fifteenth century. They fall into the same general divisions as the records from Ugarit, but literary texts were not found, although a few religious texts, found together in a single place, and three lexicographical texts suggest that there may have been literary texts in another archive. More important than either of these were the Hittites, whose capital was at Boghazkeuy, about a hundred miles east of Ankara. Here there was, of course, no Mycenaean settlement, but a Mycenaean seal was found in the excavations,[4] and the identification of Ahhiyawa, a

[1] F. H. Stubbings, *Mycenaean Pottery from the Levant*, 71; C. F-A. Schaeffer, *Syria*, 31 (1954), 63; O. Masson, *Ugaritica*, III, 227f.

[2] Crete cf. C. F-A. Schaeffer, *Ugaritica*, I, 53; *Syria* 31 (1954), 38. Cyprus cf. J. Nougayrol, *C.R.A.I.*, 1955, 141f. on no. 18, 114.

[3] *A Forgotten Kingdom*, 157. Cf. on comparative chronology of Eastern and Aegean sites, J. Mellaart, *A.S.*, 7 (1957), 55f.

[4] See Laroche, *Minos*, 3 (1953), 8.

power with whom the Hittites were in contact from the early fourteenth to the late thirteenth century, with Mycenaean Greeks, whether in Asia, the islands, or Greece itself, has now been generally accepted.[1] The law code has already been fruitfully compared with the Mycenaean tablets by Palmer,[2] and other points of contact will be noted in their place. Outside the range of close Mycenaean contacts is the vast mass of Sumerian, Babylonian, and Akkadian cuneiform tablets from the area of the Euphrates, which can only be quoted for particular purposes. Something will be said of the literature at a later stage. Here however the kingdom of Mari (which lies on the Euphrates some fifty miles below its junction with the Khabur) should be mentioned, because the letters between the King of Assyria and his son, the King of Mari, and the letters between the Kings of Mari and their various administrators show how a kingdom actually worked early in the second millennium, and provide some explanation for the bare lists of men and things which survive from other sites. Finally, the Mycenaeans were also in contact with Egypt, but the organization of Egypt is perhaps too unique and too specialized to be of much use for our problem.

The records[3] may be examined from two points of view. One is the point of view of the palace: what was worth recording? The other is our own: what do the records tell us of the general structure of society, of the parallels between different societies, and particularly of those elements of civilization which are likely to have been remembered and transmitted by poetry? This survey is an attempt to combine both points of view and is divided into the following main headings: grades of society; the labour force

[1] O. R. Gurney, *The Hittites*, 46 ff.; F. H. Stubbings, *Mycenaean Pottery from the Levant*, 110; R. Crossland, *Proc. C. A.*, 50 (1954).

[2] *Transactions of the Philological Society*, 1954, 37 f.

[3] The following editions are the basis of this survey and their numeration is used: Knossos, Michael Ventris, *The Knossos Tablets*, London, Classical Institute, 1956; Pylos, E. L. Bennett, Jr., *The Pylos Tablets*, Princeton, 1955; Ugarit, J. Nougayrol, *Le Palais royale d'Ugarit*, Paris, 1955; Alalakh, D. J. Wiseman, *The Alalakh Tablets*, London, British Institute at Ankara, 1953; Mari, A. Parrot and G. Dossin, *Archives royales de Mari*, vols. I–VI, Paris, 1950–4. Where necessary to distinguish the tablets from different sites, I have prefixed KN (=Knossos) etc. to the numbers. The Mycenaean tablets mentioned will be found translated with commentary in M. Ventris and J. Chadwick, *Documents in Mycenaean Greek*, Cambridge, 1956 (abbreviated below as *Docs.*).

and its operations; the land, its produce and goods made from its produce; war; offerings to the gods. It must be remembered that the primary object is to show the points of agreement between the documents from different sites rather than to bring out the divergences. The picture must be constructed from short records of details and necessarily makes difficult reading. But the detail must be given as it is our only evidence; it has the further value of revealing the niggling bureaucracy of these palace civilizations, which contemporary and later poets ignore.

The head of the Mycenaean State was the King. I use this word to translate the Greek *wanax*. The Mycenaean *basileus* – the classical Greek word for king – was a much less important person, and I shall distinguish him by writing him king with a small *k*. *Wanax* in classical Greek (except in high poetry depending on Homer) was only used of gods, and similarly the Mycenaean word for his land, *temenos*, was later only used for land sacred to the gods. In Pylos the Commander of the Army also had a *temenos*.[1] This means that both of them were in some sense divine, and this divinity survives in Homeric terminology – Zeus born, Zeus nurtured, dear to Zeus, honoured like (or as) a god, etc. Eastern Kings also had divinity or near-divinity. So on the ivory panel of a fourteenth-century couch from Ugarit[2] the King is shown drinking from the breast of the goddess – he is goddess-suckled, and on Alalakh seal impressions the Kings of Alalakh and Yamkhad are called 'beloved of (the god) Adu'.[3] So also according to Gurney[4] the Hittite Kings during the imperial age (from 1460 onwards) were called 'Hero, beloved of the god (or goddess)'.

The King had a household. The Pylos tablets mention the King's armourer, the King's potter, and the King's fuller, titles for which parallels could easily be found in the East. Palmer[5] has identified as the King's companions or 'counts' the *Eqeta*, who appear in Pylos and Knossos as grandees of noble family, and as military commanders with chariots, uniforms, and male and

[1] PY Er 312 (*Docs.* no. 152) is the essential text. For royal land in Ugarit cf. 12.33, 16.151, in Mari cf. iii. 3, v. 73.

[2] C. F-A. Schaeffer, *Syria* 31 (1954), 55; and on the theme cf. Gordon, *Homer and the Bible*, sect. 42.

[3] AL 7, 433–4.

[4] *The Hittites*, 65. Cf. Marinatos, *Studies presented to D. M. Robinson*, 1, 126f.

[5] *T.Ph.S.*, 1954, 51. Cf. *Docs.* 121. Chief references: PY An 519 etc.; Sa 790; An 607; Eb 847; KN Ld 571; As 821; B 1055.

female slaves. Together they must have formed something like the Hittite Great Family.[1] The tablets from Ugarit show something of the machinery of promotion into the higher ranks; the King gives a man certain territories, and (1) he assumes 'the duties of the sons of the Queen', or (2) he is placed among the Counts of the Queen; he is free and the Mayor will not enter his house, or (3) he is placed among the Charioteers.[2] I have chosen these three examples out of a considerable number of texts for various reasons. First, they show various different ranks which the men receive and which carry with them different duties or services to the King. Secondly, when the men are promoted, they are made 'free' from the duties of their former rank; the word is the same as that used for freeing a slave; and in the same way in Pylos[3] the King 'frees' certain materials from duty. Thirdly, the promotions are accompanied by a gift from the King, and in return the man promoted takes on himself new services and also makes payments in silver.

Many of the precious objects recovered from Mycenaean sites must have been gifts. Finley[4] in discussing the world of Odysseus (which in this respect is purely Mycenaean) says 'there was scarcely a limit to the situations in which gift-giving was operative'. Gifts covered what we should call fees, rewards, prizes, and sometimes bribes; the successful suitor gives the largest 'gifts of wooing' and receives a counter-gift in the dowry; the whole of diplomacy was conducted by gift exchange. One set of tablets at Pylos[5] has the heading: 'What Pu-ke-qi-ri saw when the King appointed Sigewas *damokoros*', and lists decorated jugs, boiling pans, tripod cauldrons, fire-tongs, etc., and furniture, tables, chairs, and footstools, inlaid with ivory, coloured glass, gold, and precious stones. Parallels for the objects have been noted from Mycenaean sites, Egypt, and Ugarit.[6] It is not clear whether 'when the King etc.'

[1] Gurney, *The Hittites*, 67.

[2] References: UG (1) 16.204, (2) 16.348, (3) 16.132. For the chariotry at Ugarit cf. 12.34.

[3] PY Na 334, with discussion, *Docs.* 298.

[4] *The World of Odysseus*, London, 1956, 70; cf. for Egypt, Breasted, *Ancient Records*, e.g. II, 22.

[5] PY Ta 711 etc.; cf. *Docs.* 332f.; Palmer, *Minos*, 5 (1957), 58.

[6] Cf. R. Higgins, *B.I.C.S.*, 3 (1956), 39. For Ugarit cf. above. For Egypt, the tomb of Tutankhamen, and Breasted, *Ancient Records*, I, 534; II, 32, 390, 436.

merely gives the date for an inspection of the royal treasure or whether these are the actual gifts given when Sigewas was appointed. In any case the machinery of gift exchange is attested in the tablets by the adjective 'for guests' applied to clothes at Knossos.[1] Many of the precious objects listed in the tablets are likely to be gifts.[2] Such gifts can be quoted from all the Eastern collections of tablets, and I restrict myself here to two examples. In Ugarit[3] the wedding gifts of the Queen Akhatmilku consisted of jewellery, gold vessels, clothes and pieces of stuff (like clothes 'for guests' at Knossos), couches, chairs, and footstools incrusted with gold, ivory, and lapis lazuli, bronze vessels and implements including cooking-pots and tongs (as on the Pylos tablets quoted). The Mari tablet[4] in which the King describes the appointment of the mayor of Ia-il (a parallel to the *damokoros* of Pylos) is broken, but the appointment seems to have been accompanied by a gift of silver and sheep. The largest gift of all is a town or towns. In Homer[5] Agamemnon proposes to give Achilles seven cities of Messenia, whose inhabitants would honour him as a god, and Menelaos had hoped to settle Odysseus in a city in his kingdom. In the same way Alalakh[6] in the eighteenth century was given as a present by Abban to Yarimlim, who was duly installed as ruler, and later the King of Ugarit[7] gave a town with its tithes, its customs, and its offerings to Karkushuh and the lady Apapa and the sons of the lady Apapa.

The grades of society cannot be defined too precisely, because the boundaries between them were fluid and a man could move or be moved from one grade to another, as we have seen in Ugarit, and the emphases were different in different localities. But broadly I think it would be true to say that below the immediate entourage of the King comes first a nobility, which receives its lands from the King, and then the towns or villages with a mayor and elders, with whom the craftsmen and agricultural workers are registered. An obvious local difference is that in Ugarit, which was probably the most highly developed as a commercial civilization, the craftsmen appear to have been organized in corporations which held

[1] KN Ld 573–4, 585 (*Docs.* no. 215).

[2] E.g. PY Ta 641, Tn 966 (fig. 1); KN K tablets; V 280 (noted as '*not* feudal dues') cf. Lejeune, *B.S.L.*, 52 (1956), 199.

[3] UG 16.146, cf. 16.61; AL 409; cf. 363, 419 (furniture).

[4] MA i. 119.   [5] *Iliad* 9, 149; *Odyssey* 4, 174.

[6] AL 1.   [7] UG 16.276; cf. also MA iv. 11.

land.[1] But in Ugarit also, as we have seen, the man who is placed among the Counts of the Queen is thereby freed from the jurisdiction of the Mayor, which seems to agree with the general structure that I have sketched.

In the Hittite law code the distinction between the men of feudal service whose land reverts to the King and the craftsmen whose land reverts to the village is clear, but arrangements were also made for passing from one grade to the other. Palmer[2] has found the same essential distinction in the Mycenaean tablets, where 'settlers' land' (*Ki-ti-me-na*), held by men, who in respect of the feudal dues which they pay are called *te-re-ta* (*telestai*), is distinguished from common land (*Ke-ke-me-na*), which is held from the village or *damos*, and its holders are described as *Kamaewe*, etc. Here too the boundaries are fluid and it is both possible (*a*) for a noble to hold common land as a private portion, and (*b*) for a shepherd or a fuller to hold a portion of settlers' land.[3] It is probable that the settlers were or included the men who owned the chariots (in so far as the chariotry extended beyond the Counts). There are two indications of this. One is that on the Pylos order of battle tablets[4] the men who are named seem to be chariotry as distinct from foot-soldiers; they consist of others besides the Counts and some of their names recur on a census list,[5] which includes the Counts but seems to be restricted to a fairly high level of society. The second is the occurrence of the word *opa* on the Knossos chariot tablets;[6] *opa* seems to be a word for a feudal due, and it looks as if some of the settlers at least were required to provide chariots, horses, corselets and helmets, garments and sheep, as part of their service. The word also occurs in connexion with arrows, rams, cloth, wheat, and

[1] Cf. Virolleaud, *Syria*, 21 (1940), 123 f. *Su-qo-ta-o ko-to-na* (PY Ea 109 etc.) has been interpreted (*Docs.* 134) as 'land of the Swineherds' but the singular is equally possible, and I think rather of a Royal Swineherd (like Eumaios in the *Odyssey*).

[2] *T.Ph.S.*, 1954, 37 ff. The essential texts are PY En 609 etc. for settlers' land and the Ep series for common land. They are discussed in *Docs.* 232 ff. Cf. also Bennett, *A.J.A.*, 60 (1956), 103 f.; Adrados, *Emerita*, 24 (1956), 353 f.

[3] Cf. (*a*) PY Ep 301/8 f.; (*b*) PY Ea 71, Eo 269.

[4] PY An 654/14 gives the distinction between infantry and chariotry.

[5] PY Sn 64 and An 218 are parts of a single list; cf. *Docs.* 175 ff.; M. S. Ruipérez, *Minos*, 4 (1956), 146.

[6] E.g. KN Sd 0403, Sf 0420; cf. *Docs.* 168.

oil[1] (at the *opawoneia*, headquarters of those who pay *opa*); and this gives some idea of the range of feudal dues. With some misgivings I use this word feudal as a convenient way of describing the paying of dues and services to the palace in return for privileges and possessions.

The first class in the Pylos census list is called *basileuontes* (performing the function of kings) and includes two men, who are called *Koreter of Timitija* and *Koreter of Iterewa*. I think we may regard them as the mayors of these villages or towns and suppose that there were at least three words for mayor – *basileus*, *koreter*, and *damokoros* (the appointment of a *damokoros* by the King was mentioned above). For the *basileus*[2] we have considerable evidence; twelve are known in Pylos, they have a *basileia* (house) and a *gerousia* (council of Elders), and they supervise the allocation of bronze to smiths at three villages or towns. The *Koreteres*[3] (or in two cases the *damokoros*) of towns or villages are noted as contributing gold, bronze from the temple for arrows and spears, oxen with calves, and possibly hides. Normal contributions are recorded under the name of the town alone; when instead 'the mayor of X' appears, this probably marks a special contribution for a special occasion. These mayors are men of great importance, as their position on the Pylos census list shows. They personally rank somewhere near the level of the Counts. So in the Mari archives[4] the mayor and elders of a village appear before the local governor to assure him that a rumour which has reached the King of Mari is a pure lie. In Alalakh the mayor is reckoned among the chariotry of one village, although he does not himself own a chariot, and the elders receive distributions of grain and oil.[5]

A number of census lists from Alalakh, according to Wiseman,[6] give the inhabitants of villages arranged in three classes in ascending order; he describes the lowest (*hupshu*) as a semi-free

---

[1] Arrows KN Ws 1704; rams: C 50, Dm 1184; cloth: L 695; wheat: E 971; oil: Fh 339. Cf. also KN As 821, where men are contributed. PY Ea 805 gives a contribution in return for being free of *opa*; is this a case of degrading, cf. Eb 294? PY Sh 736 gives helmets and corselets.

[2] Note particularly PY Ae 889, An 616, Jn 431; cf. KN As 1516.

[3] Note particularly PY Jo 438, Jn 829, On 300; cf. KN Ch 902, V 865.

[4] MA iii. 73.   [5] References: AL 138; 271; 322.

[6] *Op. cit.*, 10; cf. particularly AL 131 (including a doctor, 2 carpenters, a singer, and 3 herdsmen); 136 (13 of 42 *hupshu* have no ox); 138, noted above.

class of serf, the next higher class includes the craftsmen, and the highest class are the chariotry. The Pylos census list is a classification of the high class corresponding to the chariotry of Alalakh. The big land tablets of the En and Ep series give the details of the land holders of a particular town, subdivided into holders of settlers' land and holders of common land. The area of settlers' land is given at the beginning (the area of the common land may have been lost); and after each holder an amount of corn is given, which may be the tax; similarly the vineyard holders of a village in Alalakh are listed with their plots and the total tax to be paid by the village.[1] But we have nothing from Pylos or Knossos quite like the class census lists at Alalakh; the nearest are certain summaries which give totals of two classes in a particular place: thus at Pylos in a grain total *telestai* and *kamaewe* (workers of the common land) are listed in parallel and at Knossos *telestai* and carpenters at Aptara are noted together.[2]

The palaces also kept detailed records of the available labour force, of the rations which it was given, and of the operations on which it was engaged. On one occasion the King of Mari told the governor of Terqa to inspect the men of his district; he swore in inspectors in every town and they wrote down the names of the men; the tablets were then copied and sent to Mari.[3] This gives the background of the Mycenaean lists which survive. Some are nominal rolls with nothing to say what the people are.[4] Sometimes there is an indication of place, often with the addition of a man's name, the man for whom they have been working, who provides them for an unspecified task, or who owns them.[5] But many of the lists specify that the men are craftsmen, and these lists are sometimes nominal roles with the crafts appended and sometimes summaries of craftsmen at particular places.[6] The crafts are very numerous: the following list merely gives those that are common to the Mycenaean sites and Alalakh or Ugarit[7] – doctor, priest, goldsmith, carpenter, smith, cook, herdsman, potter, tailor, weaver, measurer of grain.

Both in Pylos and Knossos the labour force includes large

[1] AL 207.   [2] PY Ec 411; KN Am 826.   [3] MA iii. 19.
[4] E.g. PY An 192; KN As 1519; UG 15.09; AL 169–71.
[5] E.g. PY An 172, 340; KN As 40; AL 146, 162.
[6] E.g. PY Ae 574; An 39, 298; Vn 865; KN As 1517; B 101; V 56; cf. UG 15.172; AL 220, 227.
[7] Alalakh see Wiseman, *op. cit.*, 158f.; for Ugarit, *Palais royale*, iii, 232f.

numbers of women, and associated with them men, girls, and boys.[1] The place at which they are is sometimes given; they often have ethnics and sometimes are described as captives or slaves. They are sometimes described as having certain skills, for the most part connected with making textiles, dealing with grain, doing the housework. In Knossos we have some evidence that the younger women were trained by the older women. In Pylos (on the Ad tablets) men and boys are described as 'boys of the X women' and they seem to be listed for some particular purpose since defaulters are indicated. Both in Pylos and Knossos some groups of women, girls, and boys seem to have a connexion with the land, but what connexion is not clear; possibly these groups of women and their dependents were allotted land as were the corporations in Ugarit. Tritsch has compared these tablets with a tablet from Ugarit, which lists a number of women, girls, and boys as in the houses of different citizens of Ugarit; the numbers in each house range from one boy to three women, three boys, and five girls; on the edge they are all said to come from Alashia (probably Cyprus).[2] This again seems to be a list of foreign women with their children, and here the palace has distributed them in various houses. When the King of Mari demands a labour gang of boys and girls from the governor of Terqa, the governor sends men to the villages to raise them;[3] here, as often, the correspondence of Mari gives an explanation for the lists which we know from other sites. They are a labour force at the disposal of the palace, and their memory (though diminished) survives in the great palaces of the *Odyssey*.

We hear occasionally of special operations in Pylos: 'rowers to go to Pleuron'[4] is not necessarily a naval order. 'Builders to build'[5] does not sound like a large operation; twelve in all are to go to four different places. They are perhaps specialists like the master mason demanded from Mari by the King of Assyria.[6] From Ugarit we[7] have an instruction to eight towns to supply each a number of days' work on the reconstruction of another town.

---

[1] PY Aa; Ab (with rations); Ad; Ae 303, 629, 634; An 199, 292, 607; Vn 1191; Wa 114; KN Ak, Ap, Ag. cf. *Docs.* 155 ff.

[2] UG 11.857, *Syria*, 21 (1940), 247 f.; F. J. Tritsch, *Minoica* (forthcoming).

[3] MA iii. 39.   [4] PY An 1 (*Docs.* no. 53).

[5] PY An 35; KN Am 601 seems to be a *corvée* of some sort (*Docs.* nos. 41 and 34 respectively).

[6] MA ii. 2.   [7] UG 11.836, *Syria*, 21 (1940), 130.

The distribution of bronze to smiths[1] in different localities in Pylos is recorded with the amount given to each smith and the number of unemployed smiths; the local *basileus* (as noted above) sometimes checks or guarantees the amount. The Alalakh tablets[2] also record copper distributed to smiths, but note in addition that it is to be used for making baskets or arrowheads; and the King of Assyria[3] sent copper to Mari to be made into nails by the local craftsmen. A report from Pylos that the wood-cutters in two places are delivering 150 axles and 150 spars to the chariot factory may be compared with Ugaritic texts on the delivery of wood for making arms, and a note of wood delivered to the carpenters for the construction of wagons in Alalakh.[4] We may add here, also from Pylos,[5] a list of wooden objects made, a list of vessels received from men (perhaps mayors) in various places, and a note of pieces of ivory; to set beside this rather slender evidence of Mycenaean manufacture Alalakh provides a record of sixty-four business houses and their produce; they include smiths, leather workers, joiners, and cartwrights. It is likely that in Alalakh and Ugarit manufacturers bulked much larger than in Pylos and Knossos; but we have no records (except perhaps the single tablet noted above) for the considerable manufacture of pottery which we know took place at Pylos, and Mycenaean pottery was exported far and wide.

Something has already been said about land tenure and the division between royal land, settlers' land, and common land as it is observable in the various other places. The produce of the soil was taxable, and was inspected: at Pylos[6] Axotas, who must surely be a palace official, is recorded as inspecting the crop in five areas. The amounts of grain against the individual holdings may well, as has been suggested, be an assessment of the tax to be paid, and some of the grain figures for places under Knossos should be so interpreted as distinct from much larger figures glossed 'harvest'.[7] An Alalakh tablet[8] records that 640 *parisi* of emmer and 100 of vetches, the produce (rent or tax) of the territory of Alama, is owed by the village inhabitants. In Pylos and Knossos two words

[1] PY Jn series (*Docs.* 352f.).   [2] AL 397, 401, 402.   [3] MA ii. 1.
[4] PY Vn 10; UG ap. *Syria*, 31 (1954), 25; AL 422, cf. 425.
[5] PY Vn 46; Vn 130; Va 404, 482; AL 227.
[6] PY Eq 213; cf. Pn 30; Un 267; Wa 917; cf. *Docs.* 268.
[7] KN. tax: e.g. F 157; harvest: e.g. F 852 cf. for Egypt, Breasted, ii, 871.
[8] AL 42.

– *apodosis* 'payment' and *ophelos* 'deficit' – show what tablets certainly refer to tribute to the palace. From these words some idea can be formed of the range, if not of the amount of the contributions. Olive-oil[1] is a 'payment' at Lyktos in Crete. A Pylos tablet records a distribution of wine to the nine towns, and Ugarit provides the opposite picture of twelve towns providing the palace with 148 jars of wine.[2] One series of Pylos tablets (Ma) records a tribute of mixed products including hides, honey, and possibly flax; payment and deficit (or last year's deficit) are recorded, and in many towns the smiths are exempted. They also (with certain other classes and individuals) have free allowances of boxes (perhaps of made-up flax), which are recorded under towns and individuals in another series (Na); we may compare a label from Ugarit 'clothing given to knife-holders'; a considerable deficit of boxes of flax required from various towns is also recorded in Pylos.[3] Payments of spices are recorded in the Knossos Ga tablets.

Records are also kept at Pylos and Knossos of animals – horses, asses, deer, cattle, sheep, goats, and pigs.[4] The lists often give owner, place, and herdsman; sometimes however the animals are listed under towns and shepherds only. Similar lists are found in Ugarit and Alalakh.[5] The occurrence of 'deficit' both in Knossos and Pylos shows that many of these tablets are records of tribute to the palace; a list in Ugarit[6] gives the towns as supplying oxen as well as wheat and wine. Lists from Knossos which give both sheep and wool are probably records of shearing, and the 'deficit' sign in the Dk tablets shows the deficiency in the amount of wool provided, and in the Dl tablets deficiencies both in sheep and wool; there is a standard relation between the total amount of wool including deficit and the number of sheep. A note from Alalakh[7] may be compared: '8 talents, 1,800 (shekels' weight) of wool plucked by Kipugga from 308 wool-bearing sheep. 2,700 shekels of wool are no good'. A functionary of the King of Mari[8] complains that the King's instructions to shear the sheep in his district cannot be carried out, because he has not sent enough men

---

[1] References: KN Fh 349; cf. PY Gn 1184; KN Uc 778; UG 16.257; AL 320, 322.

[2] References: PY Vn 20; UG 10.045, *Syria*, 21 (1940), 123 f.

[3] References: UG 11.799, *Syria*, 21 (1940), 123 f.; PY Nn 228; cf. *Docs.* 289 ff.; Lejeune, *R.E.A.*, 57 (1956), 9 ff.; *Études Mycéniennes*, 237 ff.

[4] Cf. *Docs.* 195 ff.   [5] E.g. UG 16.155, 16.274, 16.294; AL 333 ff.

[6] UG 10.044.   [7] AL 361.   [8] MA v. 67.

to do the shearing; the sheep have been washed and the men and women weavers, who have been assembled to work the wool, are idle. Mari again gives the background.

Women spinners, combers, and wool workers are recorded for Pylos.[1] In Knossos[2] the women workers are sometimes labelled after the kind of cloth on which they work. I have already noted the special cloth for gifts, the cloth for the Counts, and the fact that cloth could be part of a feudal due. The main headings of the lists, cloth, clothes, and wool, are found also in Ugarit and Alalakh.[3] The word *chiton* (shirt) is common to Knossos and Ugarit, and was presumably borrowed by the Greeks at this time. In Knossos (and its surrounding towns) the women produce the cloth to a schedule: the familiar terms 'deficit', 'payment', and 'allotment' occur,[4] and one tablet gives an equation between wool and textiles.[5]

The palace also records war material delivered and amounts in store. We have records in a standard form from Pylos of helmets and corselets, and various tablets from Knossos record the existence of helmets, corselets, and armoured shirts.[6] The Knossos Sc series gives names of men with horses and chariot and in addition either corselet (of two types) or ingots (for armouring shirts). Tablets were found in Ugarit[7] which record scale corselets; the scales have also been found in quantity. The lists of chariotry from Alalakh, which note whether they possess chariots or not, and the list of chariotry at Bekani in the neighbourhood of Ugarit have already been mentioned.[8] Knossos lists chariots in various stages of manufacture, and wheels.[9] There are also records of swords, spears, and arrows: one tablet notes two lots of 6,010 and 2,530 arrows, and the numbers may be compared with the 1,500 copper arrowheads made by the smiths at Alalakh or the 4,000 shekels of copper for arrowheads noted on a seal impression at

---

[1] Spinners: Aa 89; combers: Ab 578; wool workers: Aa 762. Cf. *Docs.* 313 f.

[2] Ak 638, *enereja* (from *eneron*); Ap 629 *tu* (short for *tunano*).

[3] UG 15.135, 16.187a; AL 357–9.

[4] KN L 473, 728; Lc 535; cf. L 641.   [5] L 520.

[6] References (cf. *Docs.* 360 ff.): PY Sh; KN G 5670 (helmet and corselet), J 693 (armoured shirt), L 7514 (armour for shirts), K 740 (corselet), V 789 (corselets and helmet attachments).

[7] *Syria*, 31 (1954), 25.   [8] References: UG 12.34; AL 128 f.

[9] KN Sd, Se, Sf, So (cf. with the last PY Sa). Cf. Chantraine, *Minos*, 4 (1956), 50 f.; Lejeune, *R.Ph.*, 29 (1955), 147 f.; 30 (1956), 175 f.

Alalakh.[1] It is possible that the goats and horns listed in the Knossos Mc tablets were used in making bows and bowstrings. The number of arrows suggests that archers were by no means unimportant in the Mycenaean age, and they may have been second only to the chariotry as they clearly were at Ugarit and Alalakh.[2]

Records of actual operations are rare. The 'rowers to go to Pleuron' from Pylos need not be on war service, but a larger list of oarsmen, of which the preserved figures add up to 443 and the total probably reached 550, may well be operational.[3] The men are entered in groups ranging from 3 to 40 in number. Some of the groups have place-names or ethnics and these are sometimes subdivided into Settlers and Aftersettlers (or perhaps they might be called resident-aliens on the analogy of the Homeric *metanastes* and the classical *metoikos*), but two of the groups come after a proper name in the genitive and are therefore 'dependents of X' or 'Y'. One group has a trade name, *pokutai*; and a figure of 126 ropes is included with the men. In the shorter list the men are grouped under five places. These may be compared with the tablet from Ugarit which gives a naval operational strength in the form 'Ship belonging to B' etc.[4] From Pylos also we have a series of tablets[5] headed: 'Thus the watchers are guarding the coast' (or 'The watchers are not released from the coast'). Each section is headed 'Command of X at Y', and the heading is followed by a list of personal names (possibly the chariotry, as suggested above); these names are followed by groups of infantrymen (ranging from 10 to 70), sometimes with an ethnic and/or a place or sector, and the section ends 'and with them the Count MN'. The only parallel I have noticed are the lists of small, special forces from Alalakh,[6] which are composed of a small number of charioteers, a number of warriors with the names of their villages, and attendants.

[1] KN Ra, R series (particularly R 0482); AL 227, 401. On the figures given in *Docs.* (352 and 356), 4,000 shekels of copper would make 22,000 arrowheads. Large numbers of arrowheads were found in a tomb near Pylos by Marinatos, *das Altertum*, 1 (1955), 144f.

[2] UG *Syria*, 21 (1940), 123f., no. xi; AL 183 etc.

[3] Shorter: PY An 1; longer: PY An 610. Cf. *Docs.* 183ff.; J. Kerschensteiner, *Münchener Studien zur Sprachwissenschaft*, 9 (1956), 37f., reaches a higher total, by including the *ko-ni-jo* 126 (without the man ideogram).

[4] UG 8279, *Syria*, 18 (1937), 167; V. Burr, *Klio Beiheft*, 49 (1944), 121ff.

[5] PY An 657 etc.; *Docs.* 188ff. Mühlestein now interprets the word translated 'command' as 'ship' (*die Okatafeln von Pylos*).   [6] AL 180, 182.

Religious offerings are on the whole too specialized for comparison. In Knossos monthly offerings were made of oil to various deities, of honey to various deities, and of some metal to Potnia.[1] The monthly offerings of barley and sesame oil in Alalakh may be compared.[2] The offerings recorded at Pylos seem rather to have been for particular occasions.[3] The most impressive is the offering of gold vessels and men and women to gods in various shrines; here we may perhaps compare Yarim-Lim's dedication of an incrusted statue and silver vessels in Ishtar's temple when he was installed King of Alalakh.[4] On the same occasion he offered goats, lambs, pots of oil, mannah, and honey – mixed offering of the fruits of the earth such as we find made to Poseidon at Pylos – wheat, wine, a bull, ten cheeses, a fleece, and honey.[5]

Such a survey, based on a very large number of detailed and fragmentary documents, is necessarily unsatisfactory. But it may serve to show that the range of the records in Pylos, Knossos, and the Eastern sites is much the same, and that quite often particular documents or classes of document can be closely compared. Undoubtedly Ugarit and Alalakh were more concerned with manufactures than Knossos or Pylos, and silver by weight was already for them performing the function of money, whereas, as far as can be seen, in the Mycenaean centres no such standard existed. But against these differences must be set the similarities of a palace keeping minute records of every department of life in war and peace, of a divine or at least god-like King at its head surrounded by court officials, who were partly military leaders and partly administrative officials, of a wider circle of nobility owning large estates worked by their tenants, a nobility some of whom formed the chariotry, while some were the mayors of the towns and villages, and were responsible for the craftsmen and landworkers in their districts. All grades were held together by the services which they paid to the palace and by the gifts, which came from the palace particularly when promotions were made by the King; gifts and counter-gifts were also the cement of relations between kingdoms. Thus the records fully agree with the

---

[1] Reference: KN Fp series, Gg series, Oa 7374. Cf. *Docs.* 303 f.
[2] AL 309 ff. Grain offerings in Egypt: Breasted, II, 171.
[3] PY Cn 3, Cn 608 are phrased as instructions.
[4] PY Tn 316; AL 366, cf. 413; cf. also for Egypt, Breasted, I, 500.
[5] AL 126; PY Un 718; cf. PY Un 1189, Cc 665; cf. *Docs.* 280f.

material remains in showing that the rich, elaborate, and highly centralized Mycenaean civilization was much more akin to contemporary Near Eastern kingdoms than to the city states of archaic and classical Greece.

In spite of the likenesses two differences are interesting. We do not even know the Mycenaean word for scribes, although elsewhere they advertise themselves proudly; they appear in the census and ration lists of Alalakh, and of the tablets from Ugarit used in this survey more than sixty are signed by scribes, some of whom give also the name of their father or teacher; in Mari 'the scribes have organized the daily labour for a canal' and 'clever scribes' are sent to the capital to carry out a census and a land-survey.[1] Yet if Mycenaean writing was handed down from fifteenth-century Knossos to thirteenth-century Pylos and Mycenae with extraordinarily little change of form, it must have been a traditional craft, and the Mycenaeans showed no reticence about the names of crafts. It is possible that some other craft-name such as 'herald', which is found in Pylos, covered the activity of the scribes. It is tempting to argue that writing itself was not regarded so highly as in the East.

The other difference is the absence of literary texts, letters, and juridical texts from Mycenaean sites, although, as has been said, longer and more continuous texts are found as near as Cyprus. There are several possible reasons for this absence which must be considered. Two possibilities are so obvious that they prevent us from asserting confidently that the Mycenaeans did not possess such texts. They may have been written on clay and stored apart from the documents which have been found. We have noticed that in Ugarit the poetic texts were stored in the temple instead of the palace, and that the palace archives were divided according to subject. There is always the possibility that stores of other kinds of documents at Knossos or Pylos escaped the conflagration which baked and preserved the tablets that have been discovered; what has survived is in fact not a selection of all sorts of material but a remarkably full collection of some sorts of material – very full on sheep and chariots at Knossos, a nearly complete account of the land tenure of one of the nine towns of Pylos, etc. The other possibility is that another material, such as papyrus or skin,

---

[1] References: Wiseman, *op. cit.*, 159; *Palais royale d'Ugarit*, III, 236; MA vi. 7; i. 60.

was used for documents which the Mycenaeans themselves wished to preserve. There are two reasons for supposing this. One is that the forms of the letters, which survived so remarkably unchanged through the centuries, are much easier to make with a pen or a brush than with an incising tool, and it is difficult to believe that they would not have been simplified if they had only or primarily been used for inscriptions on clay. The other reason is Marinatos' observation that a clay sealing at Knossos shows very fine lines on the back which look as though it had been attached to a papyrus document.[1] It has been noticed that, except for the monthly offerings in Knossos and possibly the *damokoros* tablet,[2] if that in fact gives a date, the records are undated and therefore consolidated records may have been made on another material instead of on clay as in Babylon; against this must be set the fact that the big Pylos land tablets[3] are consolidated records, compiled from brief tablets, many of which survive.

It is then possible that other kinds of texts existed and have perished. Poetry we shall have to consider later more fully; here a caution may be expressed; in the East poetic texts have been found in temples and writing schools. We have them partly because scribes practised writing them, partly because they were needed for recitation at religious festivals. We do not know whether either of these needs existed in the Mycenaean age; we might even go further and say that the absence of reference to scribes makes the existence of developed writing schools unlikely and that we have no evidence that Mycenaean festivals were accompanied by the kind of recitation or song which required a written text. But it is equally true that we have no evidence against the existence of recited poetry.

Linear B, as we have it, is only used for internal palace records, which would probably be read by the scribes who wrote them. A very little adaptation, notably the recording of all double consonants and final consonants, would make the script precise enough to be read without difficulty by scribes in other palaces.

For the moment we can only say that the Mycenaeans had an adequate script for recording poetry, if they needed it, and for

[1] *Minos*, 1 (1951), 40; cf. also the discovery of sealings from the same seal in different places.
[2] PY Ta 711. Cf. *Docs.* 113 f. with two possible additions from Pylos.
[3] PY En, Ep series.

written correspondence between the Mycenaean palaces and between the Mycenaean palaces and places outside the Mycenaean world. Two points suggest the existence of such a correspondence. If the King of the Hittites wrote to the King of Ahhiyawa, the King of Ahhiyawa must surely have been able to reply; moreover the letter from the King of the Hittites to the King of Ahhiyawa about troubles in Lycia and the Homeric letter from the King of Argos to the King of Lycia, recommending Bellerophon as an expendable brigand,[1] sound extraordinarily like the Eastern and Western ends of the same story. The second point is the likeness of the script wherever Linear B is found; it may be argued that one reason for this similarity is the use of Linear B for correspondence between Mycenaean Kings, and some such medium of communication would clearly be convenient if there is any truth in Homer's picture of a Mycenaean world knit together by allegiance to Agamemnon and capable of undertaking an overseas expedition on a large scale.

The third general kind of text which we lack is the juridical text, whether individual contracts and rulings or collections of generalized rulings such as the Babylonian code, the Hittite code, or the edict of Harmhab of Egypt. Again the answer may be the chance of survival, whether such texts were written on clay and have been lost or were written on some more perishable material. Certainly the orders for coastal defence and instructions for sacrifices, the detailed description of chariots, the long summary of land tenure with its notes of default and disagreement, prove the possibility and even the likelihood that there were Mycenaean juridical texts. We can say at least that Homer preserves the picture of the King as appointed by Zeus to dispense justice, as he did in the East. The Homeric phrase 'preserve the rulings from (i.e. given by) Zeus' naturally reminds us of Hammurabi of Babylon, who is depicted receiving his laws from the god of justice.[2] Rather similar is the picture on a ring from Mycenae,[3] which shows a goddess instructing a King. In Homer[4] Minos of Crete is described as 'the familiar friend of Zeus', and in the Underworld he gives *themistes* to those who ask him for rulings.

---

[1] *Il.* 6, 168.

[2] The stele is reproduced by H. Frankfort, *Art and Architecture of the Ancient Orient*, 59, pl. 65; cf. *NET*, 163 ff.

[3] Cf. below p. 53, n. 7. [4] *Od.* 19, 178; 11, 568.

Themistes are the rulings which the King preserves and from which he selects for the particular case. The same word is used once in Homer and at least twice on the Knossos tablets for a feudal due, which is a particular kind of royal ruling. The dues were recorded as we have seen. Perhaps the juridical rulings too were recorded in some form, so that the King and his household and his successors knew them. Such records were *themistes*, and the King chose one which applied. The word for choose is *krinein*, the word which comes to mean simply 'judge'. The development of meaning is clear if it originated in the choice of an applicable ruling from among the recorded rulings. This however is conjecture; Homer gives us evidence enough that like other rulers of the second millennium the Mycenaean King was also the dispenser of justice.

2

MYCENAEAN ART IN ITS SETTING

Comparison of the tablets has suggested that Mycenaean civilization was one of a number of co-existing civilizations which communicated with each other, and had much in common, while preserving strong local differences. The furniture tablets from Pylos[1] describe inlaid tables, chairs, and footstools of a kind which can be paralleled from Egyptian and Asiatic as well as from Mycenaean sites. Such precious objects were given as presents over the whole Aegean area, as we have seen; and the memory of them lingered in Homer, sometimes as gifts like the boar's tusk helmet[2] or Agamemnon's breastplate,[3] and sometimes as possessions like the couch of Penelope[4] 'inlaid with ivory and silver, with a footstool growing out of it, made by the artist Ikmalios', which provides the clearest analogy to the chairs and footstools in the inventory from Pylos. The decoration of the Pylos chairs and footstools – helmets, running-spirals, sea-shells, birds, heifers, men, lions, griffins, horse, octopus – can be paralleled on Mycenaean works of art, but some of the materials, particularly ivory and gold, and two of the themes, lions and griffins, were foreign to the Minoan-Mycenaean world.

Carved and engraved ivories, used for the most part for decorating furniture and boxes, are a good starting-point for a first appreciation of the international character of Mycenaean art. A magnificent set, partly carved in relief, partly engraved plaques (fig. 2), was found at Delos,[5] and they are dated by the excavators to the late fourteenth or early thirteenth century. The excavators suggest that they come from a throne, which will then have been made a little earlier than those recorded on the Pylos tablets, and a little later than the couch from Ugarit, noted in the preceding chapter. The carvings include a warrior equipped with boar's tusk

[1] Ta 711 etc. = *Docs.* no. 235 f.; cf. above p. 12.
[2] *Il.* 10, 261 ff.   [3] *Il.* 11, 19 ff.   [4] *Od.* 19, 55 ff.
[5] Delos Museum B7069–112: H. Gallet de Santerre and J. Treheux, *B.C.H.*, 71/2 (1946–7), 148 f.

helmet, body-shield, and thrusting-spear (fig. 2), combats of animals – lions against deer and ox, griffin against deer, griffin against lion, papyrus flowers, columns. Again the material must be foreign; lions and griffins point outside the Mycenaean world, and the papyrus flowers directly to Egypt. This throne was apparently a famous and revered work of art, which survived until the shrine of Artemis was rebuilt in the eighth century, when it was buried in the foundation deposit of the new shrine. Much ivory from furniture was also found at Mycenae, including a heraldic pair of sphinxes,[1] again a foreign theme, found in a house, which also contained Asiatic faience vases and an Egyptian alabaster vase. A round ivory box,[2] from a fourteenth-century tomb in Athens, is decorated with two griffins attacking a herd of deer. The material was certainly imported, ultimately from Syria, but lions, griffins, and sphinxes had long been in the repertoire of Mycenaean artists in all materials by the date of these ivories, and it may even be that we should see an influence back from the Aegean in the griffin on the twelfth-century ivory panel from the Egyptian governor's palace at Megiddo, as we certainly should in the Minoan-Mycenaean goddess seated between goats on the lid of a box from the port of Ugarit.[3] It is difficult in some instances to decide whether what we have is an imported object, the work of a travelling artist, or the work of a local artist inspired by foreign models.

The inlaid dagger blades[4] from the shaft-graves of Mycenae (fig. 3) are another interesting example of this internationalism. They date from the late sixteenth or early fifteenth century and their style is Cretan; the technique of metal inlay is also found on the fourteenth-century cup with bulls' heads from Dendra,[5]

---

[1] A. J. B. Wace, *B.S.A.*, 49 (1954), 240, pl. 38c.

[2] Athens, Agora Museum B1511: T. L. Shear, *Hesperia*, 9 (1940), 286, fig. 27; P. Demargne, *Crète Dédalique*, 194, pl. III.

[3] H. Frankfort, *Art and Architecture of the Ancient Orient*, 154, pl. 148A and 150, and P. Demargne, *loc. cit.*

[4] Athens, National Museum: Karo, *Schachtgräber* (=*SG*), pl. 91, 93–94 (nos. 747, 765, 394–5); Matz, 96; *K.i.B.* 84/11, 84a/2, 3, 87/7; Lorimer, *HM*, 140, fig. 1; H. Frankfort, *B.S.A.*, 37 (1937), 113; A. W. Persson, *New Tombs at Dendra*, 178; A. H. Evans, *Palace of Minos* (=*PM*), III, pl. 20 etc.; W. Lamb, *Greek Bronzes*, pl. 1–3. Cf. the newly discovered dagger blades from Pharai in Achaea and from near Pylos, *TO ERGON*, 1956, 88 ff.; *Antiquity* (1957), pl. 4–7.

[5] Athens, National Museum: A. W. Persson, *Royal Tombs at Dendra*, 48 cf. Schaeffer, *Enkomi-Alasia*, I, 379. Cf. also *B.S.A.* 51 (1956), 121.

but not later. A memory of this kind of decoration is preserved
in Homer when he describes the shield of Achilles and the use of
different metals to colour the scenes, but he includes tin and
kyanos, which were not so used, and his Hephaistos makes preparations more suitable for working iron;[1] poetry must therefore
have preserved some description of an object decorated with
metal inlay. This technique of metal inlay is first known from
Byblos in the nineteenth century, and then centuries later on a
metal belt from Boghazkeuy, on dagger blades from Egypt and
Mycenaean sites, and on vases from Dendra and Enkomi in
Cyprus. One of the dagger blades from Mycenae has two cats
leaping out of a papyrus thicket and seizing ducks; this is a Nile
scene, but the cat in the thicket has two ancestors:[2] one is a
fresco of the seventeenth century from Hagia Triada in Crete
with a cat stalking a pheasant, and the other a cat in a papyrus
thicket from a Twelfth Dynasty Egyptian tomb. It is difficult to
know whether the cat on the dagger blade comes direct from
Egypt or through the mediation of Minoan art. On another
dagger blade from Mycenae a crested griffin is seen at full
speed; a couchant crested griffin of very similar type and similarly
inlaid is seen on the contemporary battle-axe of King Aahmes of
Egypt. The technique of inlaid metal is Syrian, and the crested
griffin (like the female sphinx) is Syrian. Perhaps we should think
of a great Cretan artist who worked first in Syria and then in
Egypt and then came on to Mycenae, but that may be too simple a
solution.

The ivories and the dagger blades give striking examples of the
international characteristics of art in the second millennium. Here
only a brief account can be given of Aegean borrowings. Aegean
loans are less interesting except in so far as they provide further
evidence of intercommunication. The inlaid metal belt[3] from the
Hittite capital of Boghazkeuy is decorated with a spiral pattern
which is believed to derive from the Aegean. A gold bowl[4] from
Ugarit has Aegean running-spirals, and the lions take a flying leap
on to their victims as on many Aegean monuments. The running-
spirals surrounding the frescoes[5] at Mari have also been derived

[1] *Il.* 18, 468 f.; cf. D. H. F. Gray, *J.H.S.*, 74 (1954), 3, 12.

[2] Hagia Triada, Heraklion Museum: *K.i.B.* 85/13; *Mon. Linc.*, 13, pl. 10;
Matz, 48. Cat from Beni Hasan: L. Curtius, *Antike Kunst*, 137, fig. 110.

[3] Frankfort, *Art etc.*, 132. [4] Frankfort, *Art etc.*, 150.

[5] Frankfort, *Art etc.*, 61.

from the Aegean. At Alalakh the decoration of a particular group of thirteenth-century pottery[1] is thought to have been inspired by a single piece of fifteenth-century Cretan pottery, which had been preserved as a treasure. An Egyptian fresco[2] of the early fifteenth century shows a cup being brought as a gift to the King of Egypt; it is shaped like the Mycenaean gold cups from Vapheio and decorated with bulls' heads like the cup from Dendra. Thus all the places which have been quoted in the preceding chapter because their tablets provide parallels with Mycenaean tablets also show Aegean influence in art.

In the other direction much influence on Aegean art has been seen both from Egypt and from Asia. We have already mentioned lions, sphinxes, griffins, papyrus flowers, the technique of metal inlay and the technique of carving ivory. The planning of Minoan palaces round a courtyard seems to have come from Asia with later refinements from Egypt; and into this Minoan plan the independent *megaron* of the Mycenaean palaces was an intrusion.[3] The eighteenth-century palace of Yarim-Lim at Alalakh was decorated with true frescoes like the Cretan frescoes (whereas the Egyptian walls are decorated in tempera on dry plaster), and the methods of construction are the same as those at Knossos; the excavators maintain that Yarim-Lim's palace antedates the Cretan examples by more than a century, and therefore believe that architects and painters were invited to Crete from Asia to build and decorate the palaces.[4] But if the technique of Minoan fresco decoration is Asiatic, the influence of the naturalistic style of the Egyptian Twelfth Dynasty cannot be denied; the cat fresco[5] from Hagia Triada has already been cited, and on the earliest surviving fresco[6] from Knossos the saffron-picker is now known to be not a boy but a monkey, introduced presumably from Egypt. As later with the metal inlay, the relationship between Asia, Egypt, and the Aegean is here triangular. It is certain that many themes were borrowed by Aegean art from Asia and Egypt: the master of animals, the mistress of animals and snakes, antithetic pairs of

[1] Woolley, *A Forgotten Kingdom*, 156.

[2] Furumark, *Op. Arch.*, 6 (1950), 223f.; *K.i.B.* 87/2; Matz, 75.

[3] A. W. Lawrence, *B.S.A.*, 46 (1951), 81ff.; B. Schweitzer, *ibid.*, 160ff. The Megaron itself is known much earlier at Troy and Beyce Sultan.

[4] Woolley, *A Forgotten Kingdom*, 76f. The same claim is made by the excavators of Beyce Sultan, *Anatolian Studies*, 6 (1956), 118.

[5] Cf. above p. 29, n. 2.   [6] Heraklion Museum: *PM*, 1, 265, pl. 4.

animals, groups of lion tearing bull, are known from Sumerian art of the third millennium. Egyptian parallels have been quoted for the so-called cup of Nestor and the goddess with the floral crown from the shaft-graves at Mycenae, and Syrian parallels for the goddess with a mirror on the ivory mirror-handle from the Tomb of Klytemnestra.

The evidence for internationalism in art is overwhelming. It is less clear how often borrowing the form also involves understanding the content. This is a difficult problem, which is unlikely to find a completely satisfactory solution. It is easy to think of modern instances where art forms have been borrowed and given an entirely new meaning: Japanese prints have greatly influenced Western painting but this influence brought no ideas with it. On the other hand Britannia on the English penny was modelled on Roma and was originally meant to carry this reminiscence. In discussing ancient art different interpreters are likely to draw the line differently. Perhaps the admitted tendency of Mycenaean artists in the course of years to reduce natural forms to their abstract elements, so that their origin is no longer recognizable, and they become elements of design which can be recombined with other elements, may be regarded as evidence that these artists are unlikely to have borrowed meanings as well as artistic forms or at least that they forgot the meanings very quickly. I think we may start from two propositions: first, that the borrowing artist and his customer give the borrowed form the most obvious meaning that it can bear, and that therefore a foreign meaning is only borrowed if the symbolism is clear. My second proposition is more important for the next chapter than for this: it is quite simply that literary borrowing and artistic borrowing are likely to be entirely independent of each other. If we find reason to suppose that a Mycenaean artist has borrowed an Eastern form and given it an entirely new meaning, his ignorance of the meaning of his original does not in the least imply that a Mycenaean poet could not have understood a poem from the same place at the same time and borrowed its theme for his own song. A poem cannot travel unless it is understood; a work of art may travel because it is beautiful or curious.

With these propositions in mind we may look again at some of the works of art for which borrowing has been suggested. The groups that show a god or goddess as master or mistress of animals have an obvious meaning, and the only question is what name the Mycenaean artist would give the deity represented. That monsters (griffins and sphinxes) and strong animals (lions and lionesses) are symbols of the gods' power or more concretely ministers who put that power into effect, is also obvious. If the King is divine or semi-divine, as Mycenaean Kings like their Eastern counterparts were, then these ministers of god protect him. The griffins on either side of the throne at Knossos,[1] the griffins and lionesses (fig. 8) on either side of the throne at Pylos,[2] and the lions above the gateway at Mycenae[3] are all borrowed from the East; they represent the divine protection of the divine Kings in exactly the same way as the lions in front of the Hittite King's palace at Boghazkeuy,[4] and they find an echo in the gold and silver dogs which Hephaistos made to guard the palace of Alkinoos, deathless and ageless through all time.[5] The lion may be the King himself, as the minister of god or simply as a strong animal. On one of the carved stone stelai[6] from the shaft-graves in Mycenae (fig. 4) a warrior is shown driving his chariot over a recumbent foe and beneath him a lion pursues an animal. Persson interprets this 'as a pure pictograph, in translation: "the prince pursues his enemy as the lion his prey"', and gives Egyptian parallels both in art for the prince driving over his recumbent foe and in literature for the equation of the prince with a lion. The interpretation is undoubtedly right,[7] but the symbolism is so obvious that there is no reason to suppose any knowledge of Egyptian literature in the Mycenaean artist. Similarly the King of Mari after a successful campaign describes himself as 'the wild bull among kings'.[8] A silver vase[9] from the shaft-graves shows a siege and in the water at the bottom a head is seen which Persson believes to be a hippopotamus (fig. 5). If this is right, the artist

---

[1] Curtius, *Antike Kunst*, 41, fig. 24; *PM*, IV, fig. 895; Matz, 31.

[2] Blegen, *A.J.A.*, 60 (1956), pl. 40.

[3] *K.i.B.* 93/11; Wace, *Mycenae*, 22; Dirlmeier, *Rh. Mus.*, 98 (1955), 36.

[4] O. R. Gurney, *The Hittites*, pl. 9.   [5] *Od.* 7, 91 f.

[6] Athens, N. M.: *SG.* pl. 7 (1427); *K.i.B.* 86/1; Lorimer, *HM*, 140, fig. 3; Persson, *New Tombs*, 186; Cf. however Mylonas, *A.J.A.*, 55 (1951), 134.

[7] On a stele from the new Grave Gamma the human victor and his victim flank a pair of lions devouring an animal (Mylonas, *Ancient Mycenae*, fig. 45).

[8] Dossin, *Syria*, 32 (1955), 1 f.

[9] Athens, N. M.: *SG.* pl. 122 (481); *K.i.B.* 90/3; Forsdyke, *Minoan Art*, pl. 7; Lorimer, *HM*, 142, fig. 4; Persson, *New Tombs*, 181; Matz, 93–94.

must again have known an Egyptian model, but the Mycenaean prince will have related the picture of the siege to some achievement of his own and have regarded the animal as a sea monster.

Two other works of art from the shaft-graves have been connected with Egyptian art by Marinatos. He has shown convincingly that the cup,[1] long called the cup of Nestor, has nothing to do with Nestor's cup as described in the *Iliad*.[2] It is not a drinking cup but a libation cup, and the birds on the handles are not doves but falcons. It is a special libation cup like the one which Achilles brought with him from home for libations to Zeus.[3] So far all is well, but Marinatos argues further that the falcons are copied from Egyptian Horus falcons, which is possible. He believes that the Mycenaean princes who were buried in the shaft-graves fought with the Egyptians against the Hyksos and brought Egyptian gold and Egyptian ideas with them; the cup is therefore the King's cup and the falcons symbolize the King, as in Egypt they may symbolize Pharaoh as the son of Horus. This seems to me rather an intriguing possibility than a probability. Marinatos goes still further in interpreting an elaborate gold and silver pin[4] from the third shaft-grave, the head of which is modelled into a goddess in Minoan dress, holding two curved objects in her hands; she supports on her head volutes, terminating above in three pairs of branches, which curve round and down to end in papyrus flowers and fruits, and three erect papyrus flowers. From Egyptian parallels, the volutes and the canopy can be interpreted as 'millions of years of joy', the papyrus flowers as the Northern land and the papyrus flowers with fruit as the Southern land, and the two curved objects in the goddess' hands as another symbol for lands; the whole then means: 'Countless joyful years to the Kingdoms and to the Royal Houses of Crete and Mycenae.' Here again we are asked to accept far more than a simple borrowing of Egyptian themes. We are asked to believe that the complicated and far from obvious symbolism of Egyptian art was understood and translated into Mycenaean terms so that what had meant Upper and Lower Egypt now means Crete and Mycenae.

[1] Athens, N. M.: *SG*. pl. 109 (412); *K.i.B.* 87/3; Lorimer, HM, 334, fig. 48; Sp. Marinatos in *Festschrift B. Schweitzer*, 11.

[2] *Il*. 11, 632f. [3] *Il*. 16, 226f.

[4] Athens, N. M.: *SG*. pl. 30 (75); Matz, 90; Curtius, *Antike Kunst*, 11, 14, fig. 17; Nilsson, *Minoan-Mycenaean Religion* (=*MMR*), 367; Sp. Marinatos, *B.S.A.*, 46 (1951), 102f.

A similar difficulty arises with Persson's interpretation of Aegean rings.[1] He interprets them as a vegetation cycle, and in fact there is much to be said for assigning different scenes to different times of year, as the tree, which is often shown, is given varying amounts of foliage. What seems to me questionable is how far an admitted parallel with an Eastern work of art involves also a parallelism of cult or myth beyond what is represented in the actual scene. To take two examples, the goddess with the mirror appears on a ring from Mycenae,[2] on an ivory mirror-handle from the tomb of Klytemnestra,[3] and on a wooden mirror-handle from Dendra.[4] Persson finds the origin in Syro-Hittite reliefs and cylinders; he supposes that the mirror is a solar symbol and that it was used in some magic rite to make the sun shine. This may be true of the Eastern originals, but I do not feel clear that we need suppose that the Mycenaean goddess needed the mirror for any other purpose than her own adornment. On another ring[5] from Mycenae three persons in long skirts holding branches in their hands approach a shrine; Persson has observed that they show no sign of female breasts, which are always clearly seen in contemporary Aegean art. He says that they are obviously meant to be eunuchs, and refers to the self-mutilation practised in the cults of Cybele and Attis. I think that the most we can say is that the Mycenaeans possibly had cult dances in which men wore female dress. The peculiar stiff robe with slanting bands, which is worn by Hittite Kings[6] and in the sixth century by the Megabyzos at Ephesos,[7] is also worn by a man with an Oriental single-bladed axe and by a man leading a griffin on two seal stones from Vapheio;[8] this coincidence tells us nothing about Mycenaean cult but only that the artist had seen Hittite works of art, and used his knowledge to embellish a figure whom we should probably recognize as a god.

[1] *Religion of Greece in Prehistoric Times* (=RGPT), 32 f. On Minoan-Mycenaean seal stones generally see the recent work of H. Biesantz, *Kretisch-Mykenischer Siegelbilder*, Marburg, 1954.

[2] *K.i.B.* 92/10; Persson, *RGPT*, no. 6; Nilsson, *MMR*, 351.

[3] Wace, *Mycenae*, fig. 55–56; Demargne, *La Crète Dédalique*, 193.

[4] Persson, *RGPT*, 44, fig. 7; *Royal Tombs*, 96, fig. 71.

[5] *K.i.B.* 91/7; Persson, *RGPT*, no. 13; Nilsson, *MMR*, 180.

[6] E.g. Frankfort, *Art etc.*, 127, fig. 54, pl. 130B, 133B.

[7] *J.H.S.*, 71 (1951), pl. 35.

[8] *K.i.B.* 94/4; Persson, *RGPT*, 146, fig. 27; Nilsson, *MMR*, 159; *PM*, IV, fig. 341, 343C.

A more difficult case is the sarcophagus (fig. 6) from Hagia Triada in Crete.[1] The style puts it in the late fifteenth or early fourteenth century, the time when the Greeks were already installed in Crete. It is decorated with two main bands and two small panels. In one of the main bands a procession with a flute-player moves towards an altar, at which a bull and other victims are being sacrificed; the altar is before a sanctuary, in which a tree stands; near the altar a pillar rises crowned by a double axe, on which a bird perches. On the other main band a lyre-player and a woman with baskets move to the left towards a third woman, who pours liquid into a big mixing bowl set between two columns surmounted by double axes and birds; three men, two carrying animals and one a boat, move to the right towards a stepped altar with a tree behind it; behind the tree a male figure stands at the door of a tomb. The two small panels have each a chariot carrying two persons; one of the chariots is drawn by griffins. Much has, of course, been written on this sarcophagus, and some of the details will concern us later. But the central problem has been put and solved succinctly by Nilsson:[2] 'The libation and probably also the animal sacrifice are parts of the divine cult; on the other hand all analogies and all customs of other peoples would indicate that the paintings on the sarcophagus must refer to the deceased who was laid in it. I see only one way out of this dilemma, and that is to suppose that the dead was deified and consequently worshipped in the forms of the divine cult.' Nilsson further argues that the dead man must have been a Mycenaean and not a Minoan, because, whereas there is no evidence for any kind of pomp or circumstance in Minoan burials, great Mycenaeans were at this time buried in beehive tombs, in which they lived on as Heroes; he regards this picture of the dead man receiving divine honours as a Cretan equivalent.

This explanation is convincing and particularly interesting now that we know also from the tablets that something like divine honours were paid to the King in Mycenaean Greece.[3] Moreover some of the details – the animal offerings, the vessels containing liquids, the basket of fruit (which might perhaps be cheeses) – the

[1] Heraklion Museum: Matz, 46; *K.i.B.* 91/12, 92a; Persson, *New Tombs,* 160 ff.; Nilsson, *MMR,* 425 ff.; *Geschichte der griechischen Religion* (=*Gesch.*), 1, pl. 10; *Docs.* 282; Eitrem, *A.E.,* 1954, 30f.

[2] *MMR,* 438.   [3] Cf. above p. 11.

sheepskins worn by the worshippers have been compared with the offerings made to Poseidon on a Pylos tablet.[1] But the question of foreign influence must again be faced. All interpreters have pointed out Egyptian elements in these pictures: the robes of the worshippers, both the skin dress with a tail and the long dress with a stripe of different colour, the boat carried as an offering, the figure standing before the door of the tomb, all have convincing Egyptian parallels. There are two possibilities; either the artist has painted ceremonies which were in fact a fusion of Egyptian and Minoan cults, or the Cretan artist faced with the demand for a suitable picture to place on the sarcophagus of a dead Mycenaean, who was honoured as a god, borrowed from Egyptian pictures of processions to tombs and joined this honouring of the dead to a Minoan cult scene. But if we cannot say for certain that Cretan cults for the dead were influenced by Egyptian cults for the dead, we can say that reverence for the mighty dead was a characteristic common to both Egyptian and Mycenaean civilizations, and that the Cretan artist (or some predecessor of his whose work we have lost) knew exactly where to go for an Egyptian model which would express the ideas he was asked to express.[2]

In his interpretation of the sarcophagus from Hagia Triada Nilsson assumes that Minoans and Mycenaeans differed essentially in their ideas of the dead. There is, therefore, within the wider question of traffic in artistic forms and ideas between the Aegean world on the one hand and Asia and Egypt on the other, a narrower question of the traffic in artistic forms and ideas between the non-Greek-speaking Minoans and the Greek-speaking Mycenaeans. Enough is known of the Linear A script to prove that the language for which it was used was not Greek; this script takes the language back to the eighteenth century (how much earlier we cannot say) and it was preceded by the earlier Cretan hieroglyphic script, which was presumably used for recording the same language. Linear B is derived from Linear A and must have been devised by scribes who were bilingual. The two languages evidently co-existed for some time, since Linear A survived outside Knossos at least until the end of the fifteenth century

[1] Un 718. The parallels are pointed out in *Docs*. 281f.
[2] At the time of the shaft-graves the Mycenaeans evidently experimented with embalming, cf. Schliemann *apud* Persson, *RGPT*, 11, fig. 2.

(and Crete is regarded by Homer[1] as an island of many languages).
We may therefore suppose that the Greek-speaking lords of Crete
could find out what Minoan artists meant and that borrowing of
ideas could go hand in hand with borrowing of art forms. It is, of
course, true that the Mycenaeans who settled in Ugarit and
Alalakh may have known what was represented on works of art
produced there, but there is no reason to suppose that they
transmitted the interpretations as well as the works of art themselves to Greece, even if, as I hope to make plausible, they also
transmitted local stories home. But the situation in Crete was
entirely different; there the Mycenaeans were rulers of a land
which had developed its own beliefs and found a brilliant expression for them in its art. The Mycenaeans took over the artists
just as they took over the scribes, and the occurrence in classical
times of Greek gods and heroes with non-Greek names is some
evidence that ideas as well as art forms were taken over. We must
suppose that like the art and the script these ideas spread beyond
Crete to the rest of the Greek world. But we must also suppose
that wherever possible the gods or heroes would be given Greek
names, although here and there a name survived, particularly in
Crete, because it was too holy to be lost; examples are Hyakinthos,
Diktynna, Eileithyia, Athena.[2] It is probably impossible for us
now to sort out precisely which ideas the Mycenaeans took over
from the Minoans, but sometimes we may be able to trace an
artistic representation in Crete back beyond the earliest likely date
for the Mycenaean occupation, and these were presumably originated or at least transmitted by the Minoans. The essential fact
however which has been established by the decipherment of Linear
B is that Greek was the language of the rulers of Knossos in the
fifteenth century, that many Cretans then had Greek names, and
that they worshipped Greek gods. We are therefore compelled to
consider Greek interpretations not only for works of art produced
on the mainland of Greece, but also for works of art produced in
Crete during the period of Greek overlordship. Nilsson may be
right in saying that the sarcophagus of Hagia Triada (fig. 6) was
made by a Minoan artist to express the ideas of a Mycenaean
master. In most cases we cannot detect a clash between Mycenaean
content and Minoan form; we can only say that works of art owned
by Mycenaean masters were intelligible to them and therefore

[1] *Od.* 19, 175 f.   [2] Cf. Nilsson, *MMR*, 556, 511, 521, 489.

we must find a Greek interpretation for them where we can. We have representational art from the Middle Minoan II period to the Mycenaean IIIc period, roughly from 1900 to 1100 B.C. The art of the mainland of Greece from the time of the shaft-graves (the sixteenth century) must be interpreted as Greek; so must the art of Crete from at least the middle of the fifteenth century (late Minoan II). It is not so clear where the line should be drawn for earlier Minoan art, but it seems safe to assume that Middle Minoan is pre-Greek and to consider on their merits works of Late Minoan I (1550–1450); the earlier part of this period is contemporary with the shaft-graves, and many of the works in the shaft-graves may have been imported from Crete; in the later part of the period Crete may have been already under Mycenaean rulers.

Before considering the content of Mycenaean art something must be said about its style. It is easy to distinguish a naturalistic element borrowed from Crete from a formalistic element inherited from Middle Helladic and to trace a gradual desiccation of the naturalistic element, which is dominant at the time of the shaft-graves, until the jejune formalism of Sub-Mycenaean is reached. The general development may be so viewed, but when looked at from nearer at hand the development seems far less regular. In the first place Cretan art itself has a strong decorative element, which can be seen at a date too early for Mycenaean influence. The naturalistic style in Crete itself seems to be a breakaway from an earlier decorative style, which is beautifully exemplified by the formal designs on Kamares vases of Middle Minoan II.[1] The change to naturalism can most easily be seen in pottery, but is probably due to the influence of fresco painting, to some extent, as we have seen, inspired by Egyptian models. Crete was therefore not accepting anything alien when the potters of Knossos produced the so-called Palace Style,[2] probably under mainland influence in Late Minoan II. Secondly, Mycenaean art shows a quite unexpected new realism in the Warrior vase[3] (fig. 7) and the Warrior stele,[4] which are dated at the earliest in the late thirteenth

[1] E.g. *K.i.B.* 84, 6–8 (6 = Curtius, *Antike Kunst*, pl. 6; 7 = Forsdyke, *Minoan Art*, fig. 4); Matz, 70.

[2] E.g. *K.i.B.* 84/13 (= Curtius, *Antike Kunst*, fig. 36); Matz, 72; *B.S.A.*, 47 (1952), 264, fig. 10.

[3] Athens, N. M. 1426; *K.i.B.* 90/15–16; Matz, 109; Lorimer, *HM*, 146, pl. 3, 1; Furumark, *MP*, 452; *B.S.A.*, 39 (1939), 70.

[4] Athens, N. M.: *K.i.B.* 90/13; Lorimer, *HM*, 148, pl. 2, 2; Furumark, *MP*, 453.

century and more probably in the twelfth. Thirdly, a strong conservatism of various kinds may be observed. Sacred objects continue to have the same shape. Deities continue to be represented in the same form. Subjects of frescoes are echoed from palace to palace, and the repetition carries with it some of the style of the original. Some crafts, such as ivory carving and seal-cutting, have a strong conservatism of their own and only superficially reflect the change of style. Pottery perhaps is the clearest guide and survives in greater quantity than any other kind of work of art, but even pottery also is open to alien influences, to the influence of frescoes[1] and possibly textiles[2] in its decoration and to the influence of metal vessels in its shape.[3] But when all these reservations have been made, the following general scheme is not grossly misleading. The period of the shaft-graves (late sixteenth to early fifteenth century) was a period of naturalism, in which Cretan influence was extremely strong on the mainland. Nilsson[4] has compared the Roman conquest of Greece and the corresponding cultural conquest of Rome by Greece. From before the middle of the fifteenth century the love of formal decoration became strong, and from now on the mainland rather than Crete was the initiator in design; but the subjects remained largely the same as in the preceding period. When we think of this period, we think perhaps first of the so-called Palace Style vases,[5] which are found and were manufactured both on Crete and on the mainland, and of the triglyph frescoes from Knossos and Orchomenos[6] and the repetition of the same pattern on a smaller scale in ivory from Mycenae and in alabaster from Tiryns.[7] Of the subjects of representational art more will be said later, but it may be noted here once more that the fifteenth-century throne[8] at Knossos is flanked by griffins and the thirteenth-century throne[9] at Pylos by griffins and lionesses (fig. 8). This is a single instance of continuity in palace decoration for which other examples will be quoted. The

---

[1] Cf. Forsdyke, *Minoan Art*, 10; Furumark, *MP*, 452.

[2] Cf. V. Karageorghis, *A.J.A.*, 60 (1956), 147f.

[3] Cf. F. H. Stubbings, *B.S.A.*, 42 (1947), 60f.   [4] *MMR*, 21.

[5] Crete: cf. above p. 38, n. 2. Mainland: e.g. Athens N. M. Kakovatos: *K.i.B.* 85/5–6; Lorimer, *HM*, 21f. Dendra: Persson, *New Tombs*, fig. 47, 77. Mycenae: *K.i.B.* 85/1; Wace, *Mycenae*, fig. 59–61; Matz, 111.

[6] Knossos: *K.i.B.* 92/5. Orchomenos: *K.i.B.* 80/3; Matz, 82.

[7] Mycenae: *K.i.B.* 79/7; Matz, 80. Tiryns: *K.i.B.* 79/8.

[8] Cf. above p. 32, n. 1.   [9] Cf. above p. 32, n. 1.

continuity of the style of writing in Linear B is a parallel in another material. The term 'Palace Style' should be kept for the distinctive style of the late fifteenth century and particularly for its pottery; but it may sometimes be useful to speak of 'Court Style', when referring to this continuity in the art of the great palaces. It is true that the later examples from the third Mycenaean period lack something of the rounded juiciness of their predecessors, and Demargne has described this change very well in discussing the ivory box with griffins from Athens.[1] But these works still recognisably belong to the naturalistic tradition, whereas in the mass of pottery formalism has gone much further. Stubbings[2] has clearly summarized the general tendency in discussing the Mycenaean pottery of Attica: 'In Late Helladic III (1400–1100) Minoan influence in Greece has ceased, and there is a mainland reaction on Crete – a reaction that had begun in L.H. II. Broadly speaking the Minoan spirit is one of freedom and somewhat florid naturalism, the Helladic of restraint and formalism. Design in the L.H. III period shows a constant development towards the formal and abstract, a tendency which continues almost uninterrupted till the Geometric period. Little is added in L.H. III to the heritage of Minoan design, but Minoan motifs are gradually reduced to strictly stylized forms.' Distinct from both of these but almost unique are the paintings on the Warrior vase from Mycenae (and on the Warrior stele,[3] which is possibly from the same hand). In this picture soldiers leave their home and advance towards the foe. Both the idealization of the Court Style and the formalism which can be seen in the figure scenes of contemporary vases[4] are absent: here are the men, one feels, who met the Dorian invasion, and whose descendants succeeded ultimately in transmitting Mycenaean culture to Ionia and to Homer.

The subjects of Mycenaean art interest us chiefly because they may also have been subjects of Mycenaean poetry. Some of the objects found in Mycenaean sites are imports. But imported works of art must often have been given a Greek interpretation, and in the case of Cretan imports, as we have seen, there is always the

---

[1] Cf. above p. 28, n. 2.   [2] B.S.A., 42 (1947), 69.
[3] Cf. above p. 38, nn. 3 and 4.
[4] E.g. from Mycenae, the bull-leaper, Lorimer, HM, 229, pl. 16, 3; from Tiryns, chariot and warriors, Lorimer, HM, 149, fig. 9; Åkerström, Op. Ath., 1 (1953), 12, with reconstruction of chariot vase and more examples.

possibility that the original meaning was translated into Greek. Therefore even for imported works of art a Greek interpretation may be justifiable; works of art produced on the spot are now known to have been produced for Greek speakers, and the tablets prove that they worshipped Greek gods; presumably therefore some Greek divine mythology was already in existence, as well as the heroic mythology attested by the proper names (discussed in a succeeding chapter). Interpretation is seldom certain, but at least possibilities can be suggested, and the tablets give us for the first time a list of deities who certainly were worshipped by the Mycenaean Greeks.

The gods are sometimes shown in human form, sometimes in aniconic form, sometimes in both together. The rather clumsy term 'aniconic form' is here used loosely to cover a number of rather different things: the god appears as a bird; the god may reside in a tree or a stone; the double-axe or the 'horns of consecration' mark places where the god may be expected to come. The origin of the double-axe or the 'horns of consecration' is not clear and they do not survive the Mycenaean age; both go back into the Middle Minoan period, and last into the late Mycenaean period so that it is likely that the Mycenaeans adopted them from the Minoans. Horns of consecration surmount a model shrine in the so-called Shrine of the Dove Goddess[1] at Knossos (Middle Minoan II) and beautiful bronze double-axes (apparently Middle Minoan III) were found in the cave at Arkalokhori.[2] Both can be seen again on the late Hagia Triada sarcophagus.[3] But it is more important that a double-axe was erected on a stone base[4] on the citadel of Mycenae. It seems to me likely that it was a symbol of royal as well as divine authority because the King was himself divine. The very early Shrine of the Dove Goddess in Knossos gets its modern name from the birds sitting on columns in a terracotta model of a shrine. The birds are the epiphany of the goddess. A model shrine made of gold leaf,[5] with two birds alighting on horns of consecration on the roof, was found in one of the

[1] *PM*, I, fig. 166; Nilsson *MMR*, 87, 331; *Gesch.* pl. 11/2. They may have been originally Anatolian, W. R. Lamb in *Anatolian Studies*, 6 (1956), 91 f.

[2] *PM*, IV, fig. 290; Nilsson *MMR*, 60, 197; *Gesch.* pl. 9/1. Cf. *B.S.A.*, 51 (1956), 132.

[3] Cf. above p. 35, n. 1. [4] Nilsson *MMR*, 218; *Gesch.* pl. 3/3.

[5] Athens, N. M.: *SG.* pl. 18, 27 (26, 242–4); *K.i.B.* 92/6; Nilsson, *MMR*, 173, 331; *Gesch.* pl. 7; on bird epiphanies cf. Jessen, *A.A.*, 1955, 281 ff.

sixteenth-century shaft-graves of Mycenae, but in another was found a nude woman made of gold leaf[1] with a bird on her head; at this date then the artist portrayed the goddess anthropomorphically but said at the same time that she appears as a bird. On the Hagia Triada sarcophagus also (fig. 6) the birds sitting on the double-axes are divine epiphanies; in the small scenes the goddesses in the chariots are represented in human form. Homeric comparisons of the gods to birds[2] ultimately go back to these epiphanies. Our Homer may have thought of a goddess as moving *like* a bird, but a Mycenaean poet would have thought of her appearing *as* a bird. The god might settle in a tree or a stone, and trees and stones were worshipped because the god might come there. Many references to sacred stones and trees survive from the classical period: for instance Eros at Thespiae was worshipped in this form,[3] Helen was worshipped as Dendritis (i.e. a tree goddess)[4] in Rhodes, and when Andromache's father was killed, 'the mountain nymphs, daughters of aegis-bearing Zeus, planted elm trees round his tomb'.[5] This reminds us of the tree which stands between the altar and the tomb on the long panel of the sarcophagus[6] from Hagia Triada (fig. 6). In the *Iliad* the tree in which the nymph or goddess resides has become the tree which the nymph planted. Both trees and stones are very common on Mycenaean and Cretan seal rings; they are marked as holy by some sort of enclosing wall or shrine.[7] Again the goddess often appears beside her tree: on the ring[8] from the Acropolis treasure of Mycenae (fig. 10) the goddess sits beneath her sacred tree and in front of her is a small cairn on which a worshipper is standing; this is, I believe, a sacred stone, whether it belongs to her or to another divinity. In all these cases the Mycenaean seems to be somewhere between a stage in which birds, trees, and stones are

---

[1] Athens, N. M.: *SG.* pl. 27; *K.i.B.* 92/3; Nilsson, *MMR*, 333; *Gesch.* pl. 23, 3–4; Matz, 90.

[2] E.g. *Il.* 7, 59.

[3] Pausanias, 3, 19, 10, cf. sacred stone and grove at Delphi; olive and salt spring on the Acropolis at Athens, etc.

[4] Pausanias, 9, 27, 1.   [5] *Il.* 6, 419.   [6] Cf. above p. 35, n. 1.

[7] E.g. *K.i.B.* 91/11; Nilsson, *MMR*, 256, 277; *Gesch.* pl. 13/5; Persson, *RGPT*, no. 4; *PM*, III, fig. 93.

[8] Athens, N. M: Matz, 52; *K.i.B.* 92/2; Nilsson, *MMR*, 347, 264, 281, 412; *Gesch.* pl. 17/1; Persson, *RGPT*, no. 22; H. Thomas, *B.S.A.*, 39 (1939), 80, pl. 28e.

gods, and complete anthropomorphism in which gods in human form have birds as attributes or trees and stones which are sacred to them; and in popular belief this double view lasted long after the time of Homer.

We must try, however tentatively, to give names to these Mycenaean gods. On the ring from the Acropolis treasure from Mycenae (fig. 10), which seems to belong to the late fifteenth century, the goddess sits beneath her tree, holding three poppy heads on long stalks. Behind her a small worshipper picks fruit from the tree; in front, another small worshipper stands, as I think, on a small cairn; above her a double-axe seems to stand on a base, and at the top the sun and moon above two wavy lines. The goddess is approached by two large worshippers, the second of whom brings flowers; above her is a small figure with figure-of-eight shield and spear. The edge behind the worshipper is decorated with six animal heads, which are presumably the remains of sacrifices, perhaps nailed up in the precinct – to this practice the Mycenaean affection for *boukrania*[1] (ox skulls) as a decoration is presumably due. Persson holds that we have here a graphic picture of the great shrine at Mycenae: at the foot of the sacred tree is seen the epiphany of the tree goddess, whose poppies, as he notes, were connected in classical times with Demeter; we have the sacred cult symbols, the double-axe on its base, the shield on its standard, half anthropomorphized by a head and an arm; the celestial bodies suggest that the sun and moon were connected with the cult. We now know that Demeter was worshipped in Pylos[2] in the thirteenth century, and Wace suggested that the ivory group,[3] which was discovered on the Acropolis of Mycenae and may have fallen from the shrine above, represented Demeter, Kore, and Iakchos. That the goddess of the ring is Demeter is therefore very probable, and her shrine was in all probability near the base with the double-axe which has been already mentioned.[4] Perhaps she is also the goddess with the floral crown of the gold pendant from the shaft-graves.[5] Much later, the little terracottas representing two types of standing goddess, standing or seated

[1] Cf. e.g. the inlaid cup from Dendra, p. 28; Pylos tablet, Ta 711 = *Docs.* no. 235.

[2] PY En 609 = *Docs.* no. 114; cf. *Mélanges Déonna*, 531.

[3] Athens, N. M.: Wace, *Mycenae*, 87, fig. 101/3; *J.H.S.*, 59 (1939), 210, pl. 14; Nilsson, *MMR*, xxiv, 313, n. 20; Mylonas, *Ancient Mycenae*, 62.

[4] Cf. above p. 41, n. 4.   [5] Cf. above p. 33, n. 4.

goddess with a child, or two standing goddesses with a child which are found in Mycenaean tombs at many sites, may represent Demeter and Kore and Iakchos (if that is the right name for the child);[1] but Mylonas' new interpretation of them as divine nurses is also possible, in which case the child will be Dionysos. Finally, Demeter may be recognized in a Sub-Minoan idol[2] with poppy-heads round her forehead-band from Gazi in Crete.

The tiny armed figure on the ring from the Acropolis treasure at Mycenae was rightly compared by Persson with the painted limestone tablet[3] also found in a room in the Acropolis of Mycenae. Now that we know that Athena was worshipped in the fifteenth century at Knossos,[4] nothing prevents our identifying the goddess with the shield on the tablet and the figure on the ring as Athena.

The ring also shows the sun and the moon with two wavy lines beneath them. The heavenly bodies appear several times in Mycenaean art and earlier in Minoan art.[5] On the ring sun and moon appear above the two wavy lines, which Schliemann interpreted as the sea and Persson as the firmament; a more elaborate canopy with dots and branches separates the sun from the procession to the seated goddess (Hera?) on the contemporary great gold ring from Tiryns.[6] On a gold ring from Thebes[7] the sun appears above a single wavy line; below a man worships a goddess outside her shrine. Attractive as Schliemann's interpretation of the wavy line is, it seems more likely that it marks off the sky from the earth and therefore represents the firmament. Because it segregates the sun (and moon), neither sun nor moon are to be identified with any of the figures below. Three rings however may perhaps

[1] E.g. K.i.B. 92/12–13; Nilsson, MMR, 304; Lorimer, HM, 366; Furumark, Chronology, 86, 130; Poulsen, Delphi, 61, fig. 9; G. E. Mylonas in The Aegean and the Near East, 110f., pl. 15.

[2] Heraklion Museum: Nilsson, MMR. 100; Gesch. pl. 14/5; Matz, 59.

[3] Athens, N. M.: K.i.B. 92/11; Nilsson, MMR, 344, fig. 156; Gesch. pl. 24/1; Lorimer, HM, 434, pl. 1; PM, III, fig. 88.

[4] Kn. V 52 = Docs. no. 208.

[5] E.g. bronze tablet from Psychro (L.M. I): Nilsson, MMR, 171; Gesch. pl. 7/2.

[6] Athens, N. M.: Matz, 52; Nilsson, MMR, 147, 348; Gesch. pl. 16/4; Persson, RGPT, no. 24; Higgins, B.I.C.S., 3 (1956), 39, fig. 1; Docs. 333, fig. 21; PM, IV, fig. 385.

[7] Nilsson, MMR, 179, 347.

be interpreted as showing a male sun god. One is said to come from near Sestos.[1] A woman on the left worships a male god, who stands in front of a sacred enclosure in which is a tree; the sun blazes out between them. On the other two the sun itself is not shown, but a small male god, who may be the sun, appears in the sky holding a bow. One comes from Knossos[2] but probably belongs to the period of Greek occupation; the general scheme is the same, but in the doorway of the sacred enclosure stands what may be a lamp, and if so could be used to invoke the sun. The other probably comes from Greece.[3] The female worshipper again is on the left; on the right a woman bends over a jar, which stands next an elliptical stone in front of a leafless tree; above, the small male god with bow and arrow (?) and to his right an eye and ear. The eye and ear show, I think, that the male god is the sun god: 'Sun, who seest all things and hearest all things.'[4] The leafless tree shows that it is winter; the woman is mourning over someone who is buried in the jar. This is undoubtedly a vegetation ritual, lamentation at the end of winter which results in the coming of spring. A Greek might find two myths, one nearer and one farther from the intention of the ritual. Demeter mourning for the dead Persephone, or Pandora with her jar – and whatever she has become by the time of Hesiod, Pandora's name shows that she was once a goddess of the fruitful earth. The sun god in Homer is usually called Helios but sometimes Hyperion, or both together. Ventris[5] has suggested that Hyperion may be restored on two Knossos tablets. Our sun god, as distinct from the sun, may therefore be Hyperion. The moon goddess was called Mene at Knossos;[6] for her we have no Mycenaean record of a human form with another name.

The sun god has a bow, because he shoots out his rays; the master of animals has a bow, because he shoots animals; the god

[1] Nilsson, *MMR*, 266; *Gesch*. pl. 13/2; Persson, *RGPT*, no. 20.
[2] *K.i.B.* 91/9; Nilsson, *MMR*, 256, 283; *Gesch*. pl. 13/4; Persson, *RGPT*, no. 15.
[3] Oxford, Ashmolean Museum: Nilsson, *MMR*, 342; *Gesch*. pl. 16/5; Persson, *RGPT*, no. 1. Biesantz, *Kretisch-Mykenische Siegelbilder*, 114f., doubts its genuineness.
[4] *Il.* 3, 277.
[5] *Docs.* 7, 309 on KN E 842. He suggested to me privately that in KN V 52 (*Docs.* no. 208) the possible '*u*' at the end of the first line may begin Hyperion.
[6] Cf. *Docs. loc. cit.* on E 842, Gg 717.

of healing has a bow, because he shoots diseases into his enemies. Here is a connexion between three gods, who in classical times were all Apollo. In Mycenaean times the sun god was Hyperion and the god of healing was Paieon,[1] who still preserved his individuality in Homer. If Apollo already existed (and of this the tablets tell us nothing), he may perhaps be identified with the master of animals, just as his sister Artemis, who is attested on the Pylos tablets,[2] is the mistress of animals; but the case for Dionysos Zagreus as the master of animals has recently been argued by Kerenyi. The Minoans already had a master and mistress of animals, who were so alike that they might easily be interpreted as brother and sister.[3] In Mycenaean times a male between two lions on a gem from Kydonia[4] may be paired with a female between two lions on a gem from Mycenae.[5] Seal impressions from Knossos[6] show a man worshipping a goddess with a bow or spear; she stands on a cairn on which two lions rest their front paws; on the far side is a shrine with horns of consecration. This 'mother of mountains' may be Artemis or some Cretan goddess whom the Greeks may have identified with Artemis. The mistress of animals on a seal[7] from Knossos (with griffins) and on a seal[8] from Mycenae (with lions) has wavy lines above her head and above them the double-axe. If the wavy lines are bows, which in this context seems the most likely explanation, she again should be Artemis. The earliest figure which might be identified with Apollo (but a pre-Greek Apollo) is the master of birds on a Middle Minoan gold pendant,[9] who has the same bows represented behind him. We should perhaps also see Apollo (or Hermes,

---

[1] KN V 52. [2] E.g. Es 650. Kerenyi, *S.O.* 33 (1957), 127.

[3] E.g. the Middle-Minoan seal impressions from Hagia Triada (Nilsson, *MMR*, 355; *Gesch.* pl. 18/6) and Knossos (Nilsson, *MMR*, 354–5; *Gesch.* pl. 18/2 and 4); *PM*, III, fig. 324a–325.

[4] *K.i.B.* 93/9; Nilsson, *MMR*, 357; *Gesch.* pl. 20/4; Demargne, *La Crète Dédalique*, 290; *PM*, IV, fig. 391 bis.

[5] Athens, N. M.: *K.i.B.* 93/2; Nilsson, *MMR*, 358; *Gesch.* pl. 20/5; *PM*, IV, fig. 598b.

[6] *K.i.B.* 93/1; Nilsson, *MMR*, 353, 387; *Gesch.* pl. 18/1; *PM*, III, fig. 323a; Matz, 52.

[7] Knossos: Hood, *B.S.A.*, 47 (1952), 272, no. III (20).

[8] Mycenae: Wace, *Chamber Tombs*, no. 515/31; Nilsson, *MMR*, 226 ff., 361; *Gesch.* pl. 21/1.

[9] British Museum: Nilsson, *MMR*, 367; *Gesch.* pl. 21/4; Marinatos, *B.S.A.*, 46 (1951), 115; Higgins, *B.I.C.S.*, 4 (1957), 27.

who is attested in the Pylos tablets) in the fresco at Pylos[1] with a figure in a long robe seated on a rock playing a lyre (fig. 9); his divinity is shown by the bird flying beside him, which is his epiphany, but we may wonder whether some such scene mis-understood gave rise to the myth of Orpheus. If he is Apollo, we may recognize Apollo and the Muses in a terracotta group (L.M. III) of a long-robed lyre-player and three dancing women from Palaikastro in Crete.[2] The long robe, which he wears on the Pylos fresco, is not unlike the long robe of the man with the griffin on the Vapheio ring;[3] both the robe and the griffin suggest that he too is Apollo.

We noticed that in the Shaft-Grave period a goddess could both be represented as a dove and as a nude woman with a dove on her head.[4] Who is she? She must be the same as the naked seated goddess found at Delphi, a terracotta of the L.H. III period.[5] A dove goddess appears twice on the Pylos tablets according to the most likely interpretation of her name.[6] In classical times she would certainly be Aphrodite, as would also the goddess with the mirror, of whom several Mycenaean examples have been noted.[7] It seems to me at least possible that a Minoan dove goddess kept her individuality in Mycenaean times but was later identified with Aphrodite. The tablets record several goddesses whom we cannot easily identify. Diwija and Posidaeja are related to Zeus and Poseidon, and Iphimedeia is known as a bride of Poseidon in Homer.[8] It is possible that some of these goddesses are springs, and this interpretation is particularly attractive for the Pylos tablets[9] which record offerings to two Wanassai and Poseidon; the names of the two 'Queens' may have been Posidaeja and Iphimedeia. Nilsson speaks of Poseidon calling forth the springs in connexion with the Arcadian Great Goddesses, and the story

[1] Blegen, A.J.A., 60 (1956), pl. 41. Picard, R.A., 48 (1956), 78 interprets as an illustration of Od. 3, 270f., but the bird shows that the singer is divine. On the possibility that Orpheus himself was Mycenaean cf. Böhme, Orpheus (reviewed Guthrie, Gnomon (1954), 303).

[2] Heraklion Museum: Nilsson, MMR, 109; PM, III, fig. 41; Lawler, A.J.A., 44 (1940), 106.

[3] Cf. above p. 34, n. 8.   [4] Cf. above p. 42, n. 1.

[5] Delphi Museum. Nilsson, MMR, 305; Gesch. pl. 16/3.

[6] Py Tn 316; Un 1189; Docs. pp. 125f., 288.

[7] Cf. above p. 34, nn. 2–4.   [8] PY Tn 316; Od. 11, 305.

[9] L. R. Palmer supposes that wo-no-so-i, is a miswriting for wa-na-so-i (Minos, 5 (1957), 91). Cf. Nilsson, Gesch. 151.

of Amymone belongs to the same circle of ideas. It is tempting to interpret the gem (fig. 11) from the Agora at Athens[1] as Poseidon leading forth two Spring goddesses: a man with a stick, which divides into three parts at the end, is leading two women, who are attached to him by a rope.

Poseidon may perhaps be seen again in the figure driven in a chariot over the waves with a sea monster behind on a vase (fig. 14) from Cyprus of the thirteenth century.[2] In the highly stylized pictures of Mycenaean vases of the fourteenth and thirteenth centuries it is impossible to distinguish between mortals and gods, and the distinction is likely to be unclear at a time when the King and Army Commander were themselves in some sense divine. Many of the chariot scenes represent nobles going out to war, as the close conjunction of the chariots with warriors shows.[3] Schaeffer[4] has made the very attractive suggestion that a picture on a vase from Ugarit, which shows an enormous bird chained in front of the chariot, may represent a mythical expedition to capture a monster which guarded gold. A chariot drawn by griffins on a thirteenth-century vase from Cyprus[5] can only be conveying gods, as also in one of the small scenes of the Hagia Triada sarcophagus.[6] In the next chapter[7] I shall suggest that the chariot of Hera in the *Iliad* goes back to a Mycenaean poem inspired by a Hittite original. I think therefore that the same Mycenaean description of Poseidon ultimately inspired both the vase from Cyprus and the late description in the *Iliad*:[8] 'he started to drive over the waves and the monsters gambolled beneath him'. I should be inclined to suppose also that a chariot driving past a palm tree over flowery ground[9] is a fourteenth-century picture of Apollo arriving in Delos, possibly from the land of the Hyperboreans.

[1] Athens, Agora Museum, J5: *Hesperia*, 4 (1935), 319, fig. 7; Nilsson, *MMR*, 40; *Gesch.* pl. 26/4; Persson, *RGPT*, 101. Too little is left of the M.M. III coloured relief of the Priest King at Knossos (*K.i.B.* 91/5; Matz, 33; Pendlebury, *Palace of Minos*, pl. 5) to say whether this is a Minoan ancestor of the Agora gem or not. For the trident cf. *SG*. pl. 102 (515).

[2] Stockholm, Enkomi, II, 33. *SCE*, pl. 121; Schaeffer, *B.S.A.*, 37 (1937), 222; Furumark, *Op. Ath.*, 1 (1953), 53, fig. 3e.

[3] Cf. below p. 56 ff.

[4] *B.S.A.*, 37 (1937), 223 f.; Furumark, *Op. Ath.*, 1 (1953), 53, fig. 3 f.

[5] British Museum C397: *CV.* pl. 7/1; Schaeffer, *B.S.A.*, 37 (1937), 228, fig. 25; Furumark, *MP*, 296.

[6] Cf. above, p. 35, n. 1.   [7] Cf. below p. 85.   [8] *Il.* 13, 27.

[9] Stockholm, E. 3, 257; Furumark, *Op. Ath.*, 1 (1953), 53, fig. 3a.

Another vase from Cyprus[1] shows in front of the chariot a man with a pair of scales (fig. 15). Nilsson sees in him Zeus, as the steward of war, the holder of the scales, by which the death of Hektor was decided.[2] Björck however regards him as a man taking an omen before the chariot sets out. Tiny gold scalepans with butterflies on them were found in the third shaft-grave at Mycenae.[3] It is difficult not to see a reference here to the weighing of souls; and yet the symbolism of the soul as a butterfly cannot be reconciled with the view that the dead man lives on in his tomb, which was clearly held by those who buried their dead with such a wealth of precious objects. But such inconsistency in beliefs about the dead is common. The butterfly scales may then allude to the divine decision which had decreed that the king buried here should die. And this act of weighing attributed to the divinity may have had its origin in a human method of taking omens, as Björck suggests. We have however, as far as I know, no Greek evidence for this method of divination, whereas, as Nilsson saw, the bare phrase 'steward of war' shows that the idea of Zeus holding the scales was established before the date of our *Iliad*. It still seems to me therefore more likely that the figure with the scales on the vase from Cyprus is Zeus weighing the destinies of the man in the chariot. Zeus is attested on the tablets,[4] but there is, as far as I know, no other early picture of him, unless the seal impression from Knossos[5] with a child beneath a horned sheep is an allusion to his youth. The story of Zeus and Europa was evidently known on the mainland in the fourteenth century as blue glass plaques with a woman (or rather a goddess) riding on a bull were found at Dendra.[6]

The discovery of Dionysos' name on a Pylos tablet[7] and of the Lady of the Labyrinth on a Knossos tablet[8] led Professor Kerenyi[9]

[1] Nicosia, Enkomi 71.1; *SCE*, pl. 120; Nilsson, *MMR*, 34; *Gesch.* pl. 25/1; Schaeffer, *B.S.A.*, 37 (1937), 220, fig. 10; Björck, *Eranos*, 43 (1945), 58; Furumark, *MP*, 437.

[2] *Il.* 19, 223; 22, 209, cf. 8, 69; 16, 658.

[3] Athens, N. M.: *SG.* pl. 34 (82); *K.i.B.* 86/8; Nilsson, *MMR*, 46; *PM*, III, fig. 100; Matz, 91.   [4] PY Tn 316, etc.

[5] Nilsson, *MMR*, 540; *Gesch.* pl. 26/6; *PM*, III, fig. 326; Matz, 54.

[6] Persson, *Royal Tombs*, 65; Nilsson, *MMR*, 36; *Gesch.* pl. 26/7. Cf. terra-cotta, Mylonas in *The Aegean and the Near East*, 112.   [7] PY Xa 102.

[8] KN Gg 702.2, interpreted by Palmer, *B.I.C.S.*, 2 (1955), 40.

[9] 'Herkunft der Dionysosreligion', *Arbeitsgemeinschaft Nordrhein-Westfalen*, Heft 58; cf. also E. Coche de la Ferté, *Bull. des Musées de France*, 11 (1946), 10.

to find a cult of Dionysos with its bulls, its wine, its women, and its snakes in Minoan Crete. The Lady of the Labyrinth is the goddess Ariadne, for whom Daidalos (himself a god, I think, in Crete) made a dancing place;[1] she was the bride of Dionysos, who was stolen by Theseus and killed by Artemis on the representation of Dionysos,[2] a story which has its parallel in the legend of Apollo and Koronis. The canonical story of Theseus and the daughter of Minos would then be a later version, which tended to depress Ariadne from the divine to the heroic level and leave Dionysos alone as the god of maenads and wine. The theory is extremely attractive; and if it is accepted, a number of links between Minoan-Mycenaean art and later pictures connected with Dionysos become apparent. The ecstatic dances on many Minoan-Mycenaean rings (fig. 13) will then be the ancestors of the dances of maenads (with or without satyrs) which are known in classical art. The march of the harvesters on the steatite vase (fig. 16) from Hagia Triada[3] with the dancer 'breaking through the marching files and exchanging impolite remarks with the men whose solemnity he disturbs' is, as Forsdyke has seen, an ancestor of classical comedy; in fact the stooping dancer who interrupts is linked with comedy by a chain of figures intermediate in time. Another pointer forward to drama is the bearded frontal head between two wild goats on a seal stone (fig. 12) from the necropolis at Phaistos.[4] The detached human head is unique, and Nilsson argues that the artist has extended the use of a motif (in this case the head of a sacrificed animal, e.g. a *boukranion*) beyond its original and proper significance. It is much easier to suppose that it is a mask (in classical Greek art, the earliest frontal heads can be traced to the influence of masks). The bearded mask is more likely to be a daimon than a deity, but the association with goats suggests Dionysos; this then is an ancestor of the classical satyr like the phallic terracotta daimon from Larissa.[5] If the Mycenaean Dionysos and his Minoan predecessor was connected with goats like the classical Dionysos,

[1] *Il.* 18, 590.

[2] *Od.* 11, 324; cf. Hyginus, *Astronomikon*, 2, 5; Kunze, *Ol. Forsch.*, 11, 178.

[3] Heraklion Museum: Matz, 67; *K.i.B.* 89/5; Nilsson, *MMR*, 160; *Gesch.* pl. 17/3; Forsdyke, *J.W.I.*, 17 (1954), 1f.

[4] Nilsson, *MMR*, 234.

[5] Möbius, *A.A.* (1954), 209f. Hood (*J.H.S.*, 76 (1956), Suppl. 30) reports phallus-like objects from a Middle-Minoan deposit at Knossos. Perhaps cf. also *PM*, 1, fig. 93a.

he is to be recognized riding in a chariot drawn by goats on a gem from Lyktos,[1] and standing in the horns of consecration between a winged goat and a 'genius' (a kind of being to be defined later) with a ritual jug on a seal stone of Spartan basalt from Kydonia;[2] both gems are Cretan and were probably carved in the early fifteenth century; therefore Mycenaean influence is possible, but this is more likely to have been the Minoan god. But it is difficult not to connect the gem from Kydonia with a gold ring from Mycenae[3] showing a goat, a tree, a man, and an enclosure surrounding a sacred tree and a sacred stone. If the fact that the man touches the tree compels us to interpret him as a worshipper rather than as the god Dionysos, the presence of the goat suggests still that tree and stone were sacred to Dionysos. Dionysos may also be seen in the man between two goats on a seal which was apparently used to seal a pottery store in Mycenae.[4]

In the Minoan cult Ariadne, as has been said, was probably as important or even more important than Dionysos. On a gold ring (fig. 13) from Isopata near Knossos[5] four women dance in a meadow by sunlight (represented by the eye); two snakes are above their heads, whether they are meant to be on the ground or thrown about between them; a tiny goddess appears to them. It is natural to identify the goddess who appears to these 'maenads' with the well-known faience figures from the Central Palace sanctuary in Knossos.[6] Is she then Ariadne and the Lady of the Labyrinth – or rather her Minoan predecessor, since the figures are Middle Minoan? There is one difficulty, and I doubt if it is fatal. Nilsson regards the snake goddess as a house goddess, and the bell-shaped idols,[7] who either have snakes wrapped round them or are found with sacred vessels decorated with snakes, seem to have nothing to do with ecstatic dances. In later Greek practice the snake is associated both with maenads and Dionysos and with the house cult and Zeus. These two functions of the

---

[1] Lorimer, *HM*, 312, fig. 40; *PM*, IV, fig. 803.

[2] Nilsson, *MMR*, 148, 358; *Gesch*. pl. 19/4; *PM*, IV, fig. 392.

[3] Nilsson, *MMR*, 258; *Gesch*. pl. 13/1; Persson, *RGPT*, no. 10.

[4] *J.H.S.*, 74 (1954), 171, pl. 10b; *Docs.*, 331.

[5] Nilsson, *MMR*, 279, 322; *Gesch*. pl. 18/3; Persson, no. 8; *PM*, III, fig. 38.

[6] *K.i.B.* 85/12; Nilsson, *MMR*, 84, 311; *Gesch*. pl. 15; Matz, 60, 61.

[7] E.g. from Gournia (L.M. I): Nilsson, *MMR*, 80, 311; *Gesch*. pl. 1; from Gazi (Sub-Minoan): Nilsson, *MMR*, 100; *Gesch*. pl 14/4; from Katsamba (L.M. III B): Hood, *J.H.S.*, 76 (1956), Suppl. 29.

snake were probably quite distinct in Minoan Crete too, but this would not prevent the goddess of the dance being included in a shrine which also held or primarily belonged to the goddess of the house, just as in Gazi a goddess with poppy-heads on her crown shares the shrine with a goddess who has birds on her head. It may be that the two faience figures from the Palace sanctuary in Knossos are neither two aspects of the same snake goddess nor snake goddess and votary but two goddesses, the snake goddess of the palace and the goddess of the maenads. If this separation is right, it is probable that the snake goddess of the palace became known to the Mycenaeans as the Lady of the Labyrinth and the goddess of the maenads as Ariadne. The fact that the goddess of the maenads was worshipped in the palace would make it possible to identify her with the daughter of Minos. Two rings, one from Tiryns[1] and one from Crete,[2] show a man and woman and a ship; two other rings,[3] both from Crete, show a woman alone in a ship. The first two have naturally been connected with Theseus and Ariadne, but all four must be considered together. Persson has given Egyptian and Babylonian parallels for a divine boat in which a goddess alone, or a goddess and a god may sail, and notes that Dionysos still has a ship in the cult of classical Athens. That the Cretan rings show the departure or arrival of a goddess of vegetation alone or with her consort is likely enough, and it may well be that the scene with goddess and consort would be interpreted by the Greeks as Ariadne's departure with Theseus; this interpretation certainly cannot be excluded for the Tiryns ring, found on a Greek site but having obvious Minoan ancestors.

The name 'genius' is given to the curious monsters who sometimes attend on gods. Their chief characteristic is a long snout and a scaly back which ends in a kind of tail, but they walk on their hindlegs like humans and use their forelegs like human arms. The Dionysos from Kydonia[4] stands between a genius and a winged goat; the seated Hera of the ring from Tiryns[5] receives a

[1] Nilsson, *MMR*, 38; *Gesch.* pl. 26/5; Persson, *RGPT*, no. 25; *PM*, IV, fig. 926.

[2] Nilsson, *MMR*, 39; *Gesch.* pl. 26/3; Persson, *RGPT*, no. 26; *PM*, IV, fig. 923; Marinatos (*B.C.H.*, 57 (1933), 227) interprets as the voyage of Menelaos and Helen to the Elysian Fields.

[3] (*a*) *K.i.B.* 90/6; Nilsson, *MMR*, 269, 350; *Gesch.* pl. 12/6; Persson, *RGPT*, no. 27; *PM*, IV, fig. 919. (*b*) Persson, *RGPT*, no. 28; *PM*, IV, fig. 920.

[4] Cf. above p. 51, n. 2.   [5] Cf. above p. 44, n. 6.

procession of four genii with jugs. Here they are a substitute for human worshippers, as when they water sacred branches on a gem from Vapheio[1] or various holy objects on glass plates from Mycenae;[2] but when a genius stands between two lions on a gem from Mycenae[3] he is a substitute for the god himself. They do not represent the power of the god like the griffin, sphinx, or lion; they do not appear in isolation like the centaurs on a gem from Argos.[4] Probably the Greeks called them *daimones*, in the sense in which the word is used in the *Odyssey* and by Hesiod for the watchers who report the sins of men;[5] but there is one class of being which occupies very much this position in the classical world, mostly human and partly animal, sometimes playing the part of human worshippers and sometimes serving as the representative of the god, the satyrs who form the *komos* of Dionysos. The satyrs may be a survival of a much larger class of intermediate beings from the Minoan-Mycenaean periods.

The Mycenaean king was given divine honours in his lifetime. Griffins protected his throne and lions his gate. His gods had their shrine in his palace. When he died, he was buried in his sumptuous tomb to which divine honours were paid; and if he died abroad, a sacred stone was buried instead of him, so that, like a god, he could take up residence in it and benefit his countrymen.[6] One ring from Mycenae[7] may be added to the representations of the divine King. A goddess sits on a stool in front of what I take to be a sacred cairn; in front of her stands a man built to a smaller scale with a sceptre (rather than a spear, as it has no head) in his hand. The difference in scale shows that they are neither two divine beings (Persson) nor two mortals (Nilsson),

---

[1] *K.i.B.* 94/16; Nilsson, *MMR*, 146; *Gesch.* pl. 7/4; *PM*, IV, fig. 378.

[2] *K.i.B.* 94/19; Nilsson, *MMR*, 146, 256; *Gesch.* pl. 22/5; Wace, *Mycenae*, 44, fig. 67 a–b; *PM*, IV, fig. 379–80.

[3] *K.i.B.* 94/15; Nilsson, *MMR*, 359; *Gesch.* pl. 20/7.

[4] Nilsson, *MMR*, 37, fig. 4; *Gesch.* pl. 26/2.

[5] *Od.* 17, 485; Hesiod, *Op.* 122 ff.

[6] 'Menhirs' at Dendra: Persson, *Royal Tombs*, 73, 108; Nilsson, *MMR*, 600; *Gesch.* pl. 25/2.

[7] *K.i.B.* 92/7; Nilsson, *MMR*, 351; *Gesch.* pl. 17/2; Persson, *RGPT*, no. 21; Forsdyke, *J.W.I.*, 15 (1952), 19; *PM*, III, fig. 324. Cf. also the fourteenth-century vase from Aradippo (Cyprus) in the Louvre (fig. 17) with (*a*) a man with spear and rod approaching a seated goddess, (*b*) three men with spears approaching a seated goddess: Louvre *AM* 676: *B.C.H.*, 31 (1907), 232, no. 6; Furumark, *MP*, 444.

but a goddess and a mortal (Forsdyke). Persson interprets their gestures: 'it is as if the goddess had accepted a promise from the lesser god'. If however he is a mortal, he may be a King, who is here shown pledging himself to serve the goddess in return for his sceptre; this in its way would be parallel to the Eastern picture of Hammurabi receiving his laws from the god of justice. The King in turn proudly receives a priest and his acolytes on a steatite vase from Hagia Triada.[1]

Various forms of divine worship are represented in art, and many of these have been already noted in discussing the gods and goddesses who receive the worship. Except for the Hagia Triada sarcophagus most of the objects quoted have been rings, but both the dances and the processions occur on frescoes too. A dance of women in a grove surrounded by crowds of men is one of the subjects of the Minoan miniature frescoes of the third Middle Minoan period at Knossos.[2] The cup-bearer[3] of Knossos is part of the Procession fresco, and more figures in a similar procession are seen on a steatite vase from Knossos,[4] where they are climbing a staircase under horns of consecration. Later and on the mainland a feminine counterpart can be seen in the woman with a bottle from the fresco at Thebes,[5] the woman with a jug from the fresco at Tiryns,[6] and the procession to the seated goddess from Pylos.[7] Now we have a text for these processions, as Ventris has seen: a tablet in Pylos[8] reports or orders the carrying of golden cups and bowls by men to gods and by women to goddesses in various shrines. It is not certain whether games in general and bull-jumping in particular should be included in divine worship; but these sports seem to have taken place in the special theatral areas or in the central courts of the Cretan palaces, and it is far more likely that they were a form of honour to the gods of the palace like the festival games of classical Greece than that they had no religious significance. Whether the bull-jumping had originally in Crete a

[1] Heraklion Museum: Matz, 66; *K.i.B.* 89/8; Forsdyke, *Minoan Art*, pl. 8; *J.W.I.*, 15 (1952), 13 f.

[2] Persson, *RGPT*, 50, fig. 11; *PM*, iii, pl. 18; Matz, 37.

[3] *K.i.B.* 91/3; *PM*, ii, 4, pl. 12; Matz, 38; Furumark, *MP*, 71 n. 8.

[4] *K.i.B.* 91/2; Nilsson, *MMR*, 183; *Gesch.* pl. 3/1; *PM*, iii, fig. 37.

[5] Lorimer, *HM*, pl. 28/1.

[6] Lorimer, *HM*, pl. 28/2. Cf. Matz, 105. Reusch argues that the frieze when complete had at least ten women (*A.A.* (1948–9), 239).

[7] Blegen, *A.J.A.*, 59 (1955), 31.   [8] *Docs.* no. 171 = PY Tn 316.

further religious significance, we have not the evidence to say. The series of representations stretches from Minoan Crete in the sixteenth century to a Mycenaean vase of the thirteenth century.[1] On the early Cretan frescoes[2] the ladies of the court watch both the games and the bull-jumping and on the late fifteenth- or early fourteenth-century frescoes from the Ramp House in Mycenae[3] women spectators of acrobatic displays and bull-jumping are also shown. Perhaps the duels of men with swords on the frescoes from Pylos[4] should also be reckoned as sports rather than warfare and find an echo in the duel of the funeral games of Patroklos.[5]

Bull-jumping alone is shown on the early Toreador fresco[6] from Knossos and the late Mycenaean fresco from Tiryns:[7] the toreadors are of both sexes and the feat most frequently represented is the somersault over the back of the bull. The details of this and other feats can be seen from seal stones and rings, two of which were found in a Mycenaean tomb at Asine, which is possibly the Ri-jo of the Pylos tablets.[8] The Mycenaean palaces have no obvious place for the sport, and it might be thought that bull-jumping was a Minoan practice which was not adopted by the Mycenaeans, since neither Homer nor any other early Greek author has any reference to it, and there seems to be no demonstrable link between Minoan bull-jumping and the bull-fighting practised in Christian times in Asia Minor and Thessaly. Then, if the story about Theseus and the Minotaur has any connexion with bull-jumping, it means that Theseus stopped the practice, and may mean therefore that the Greek occupiers of Knossos stopped the practice; it is certainly possible that the Athenian girls and boys had been designed for toreadors and that the Minotaur was the Cretan King, enveloped in the ritual cult dress,

[1] Cf. above p. 40, n. 4. On boxers cf. V. Karageorghis, *Syria*, 34 (1957), 90f.

[2] *K.i.B.* 89/1; Nilsson, *MMR*, 174; *Gesch.* pl. 6; Forsdyke, *Minoan Art*, pl. 6; *PM*, III, pl. 16, fig. 143. On the place represented cf. Graham, *A.J.A.*, 61 (1957), 255.

[3] Lorimer, *HM*, pl. 27/2; Wace, *Mycenae*, 64, fig. 98.

[4] *A.J.A.*, 59 (1955), 31.

[5] *Il.* 23, 798f. Mylonas argues that funeral games were already a Mycenaean institution, *A.J.A.*, 52 (1948), 77.

[6] Pendlebury, *Palace of Minos*, pl. 13; *PM*, III, fig. 144; Matz, 51.

[7] *K.i.B.* 89/2: cf. also Mycenae, Tomb of Atreus, *PM*, III, fig. 133, 135–7 (British Museum).

[8] *Docs.* 182; Persson, *RGPT*, fig. 16; cf. *PM*, III, fig. 154, 158. Cf. also terracotta in Princeton, F. F. Jones, in *The Aegean and the Near East*, 124.

the bull's hide, and wearing the bull's mask.[1] If bull-jumping stopped with the Mycenaean occupation of Crete, then the bull-jumping on Mycenaean frescoes, vases, and rings is an artistic echo of the bull-jumping on the Knossos frescoes and has no relation to contemporary performance. The Mycenaean vase and the Asine rings may well be reflections of the frescoes, and we shall have then further to suppose that frescoes which have not survived were their models, since the exact positions of the jumpers do not occur elsewhere. If it cannot be shown that the late bull-fights of Ephesos and other places go back to the early period of Ionian history, in which case it could be argued that bull-fights were imported by the Mycenaean colonists but had unaccountably vanished from all intervening literature and art, we must suppose that frescoes of bull-jumping (and copies of them on rings) were part of the court style which the Mycenaeans took over. They were acceptable because they were intelligible, but bull-jumping, unlike boxing and other sports, was not described in poetry because it was not practised. The sport however gave rise to three different stories. One is the story of Theseus and the Minotaur. The second is the story of Herakles' capture of the Cretan bull; the capture of the bull is the preliminary to the games and is shown on the two gold cups from Vapheio.[2] The third is the story of Theseus and the bull of Marathon; the end of the games is the killing of the bull by breaking its neck[3] and in one version Theseus kills rather than captures the bull. There are two points of interest if this interpretation of the bull scenes is accepted. One is that a practice which the Mycenaeans discontinued gave rise to three myths about Greek heroes. The second is that Mycenaean Kings continued to have their palaces decorated with pictures of a Minoan sport which they no longer practised, because such decoration was part of the grand manner which their ancestors had taken over from the Kings of Crete.

The palace at Tiryns also had frescoes of men setting out in a chariot with boys holding their hounds[4] and of the final scene

[1] Persson, *RGPT*, 98. Cf. Pendlebury, *Studies presented to D. M. Robinson*, I, 1841; Cook, *Zeus*, I, 491 f. A sixth-century terracotta from Cyprus (*SCE*, II, pl. 233, no. 809) shows a man putting on a bull's mask. Could this be a survival of a Bronze Age rite? I owe my knowledge of this to Dr. O. Vessberg.

[2] *K.i.B.* 88, 1-4; Forsdyke, *Minoan Art*, pl. 9; *PM*, III, fig. 123-7; Matz, 64-5. [3] Persson, *RGPT*, fig. 23; *PM*, III, fig. 162-4.

[4] Lorimer, *HM*, 362, fig. 51; *PM*, IV, fig. 565, 804; Matz, 104.

in a boar hunt when the boar is surrounded by hounds and has
already been hit by throwing-spears.[1] The boar hunt already
occurs on a Middle Minoan dagger blade, on which a man receives
the charging boar with his spear;[2] and on a gem from Vapheio[3]
a man thrusts his spear into the boar's forehead; but there seems
no reason to doubt that each is an illustration of contemporary
sport; and a poem about such a hunt lies somewhere behind the
account of Odysseus' slaying of the boar on Parnassos.[4] At first
sight the gem from the shaft-graves at Mycenae[5] could also be a
contemporary illustration of a deer hunt, but Persson has pointed
out that the composition with an archer shooting a deer from a
chariot probably goes back to Eastern or Egyptian models. Nor
can the lion hunt (fig. 3) on the inlaid dagger blade[6] be a contemporary illustration, since lions were unknown in the Peloponnese
or in Crete. The artist may have been to Syria, as suggested above;
he was certainly acquainted with Eastern models, but equipped
his men with figure-of-eight and tower shields to please his
customers. Whether Minoans and Mycenaeans met lions on their
travels or only knew them from works of art and Eastern poetry,
they were deeply impressed with this lordly beast and its combats
with other animals, which appear on the dagger blades, on one of
the stelai from the shaft-graves (fig. 4), and on gems. The lion
appears beside the griffin or instead of the griffin as the divine
protector of the King, and I have quoted above[7] Persson's interpretation of the lion pursuing an animal on the stele as a kind of
simile of the action depicted over it, the prince driving his chariot
over his foe. He also interpreted the magnificent seal stone from
Dendra[8] with a lion tearing a bull's neck as symbolic of the
triumph of Mycenae over Crete. Here he has moved to another
kind of symbolism – the heraldic animal which represents the
State; the lion is the King of Mycenae; Herakles as Eurystheus'
vassal wears the lion skin, and his battles with local wild beasts

[1] Matz, 102; cf. with contemporary vases Åkerström, *Op. Ath.*, 1 (1953),
18f.   [2] *PM*, III, fig. 62.   [3] *PM*, IV, fig. 551.

[4] *Od.* 19, 428f. Cf. the fourteenth-/thirteenth-century vase, Louvre *AM* 675,
B.C.H., 31 (1907), 232, no. 7; Furumark, *MP*, 442.

[5] *S.G.* pl. 24 (240); *K.i.B.* 87/5; Lorimer, *HM*, 311, fig. 38; Persson, *New
Tombs*, 186; *PM*, IV, fig. 564; Matz, 90.

[6] Cf. above p. 28, n. 4.   [7] p. 32.

[8] *The Royal Tombs at Dendra*, 121ff.; *Dragma*, 380 ff. Cf. the vase from
Enkomi, *SCE*, pl. 118/7 (E18S50).

symbolize the victories of Mycenae over these localities. The theory is seductive, and the early existence of heraldic animals is likely, but for the Dendra ring, which may well have been the royal seal, the simpler symbolism is more probable, the King can worst his foes as the lion worsts the bull. These examples in any case suggest that Mycenaean poetry like contemporary Eastern poetry had animal comparisons.

It is impossible to say whether two of the early rings and gems from the shaft-graves[1] with men fighting with swords and figure-of-eight shields are duels (as suggested for the late pairs of swordsmen on the Pylos frescoes) or battles, but the third (fig. 19) with four combatants in a 'rocky glen' must be a battle. From this kind of fighting the Homeric description of Ajax derives. All three stelai (fig. 4) from the shaft-graves[2] have a warrior in a chariot and his opponent on foot, and show that the lords of Mycenae put their trust in chariots, as Homer and the later Pylos tablets confirm. The most interesting of the battle scenes are the siege scenes. Little can be made of the battle on one of the early frescoes from Knossos,[3] but it shows that battles were already painted in Minoan Crete; Evans saw spearmen throwing their spears upwards, but they may rather be slingers, whirling their slings round their heads. The next chronologically is the silver vase (fig. 5) from the shaft-graves.[4] An attack is being made on a town from the water. The attackers wear Mycenaean helmets. At the bottom are swimmers and the animal identified by Persson as a hippopotamus but which is more probably a sea monster. The hill is defended by slingers and archers, and by spearmen with tower shields; women watch from the walls, and just beyond them is a grove of trees (one remembers Andromache's fear that the Greeks might succeed after three attempts in entering Troy by the fig tree, 'where the citadel is most easily scaled and the wall is weakest').[5]

[1] SG. pl. 24. (a) K.i.B. 90/5; Lorimer, HM, 142, fig. 5; (b) K.i.B. 90/10; Lorimer, HM, 142, fig. 6; (c) K.i.B. 90/4; Matz, 90; Lorimer, HM, 140, fig. 2. Cf. the seal impressions from Hagia Triada, PM, IV, fig. 456; and the ring recently found at Tragana Pylos, J.H.S., 76 (1956), Suppl. 16; B.C.H., 80 (1956), 285.

[2] (a) above p. 32, n. 9; (b) K.i.B. 86/2; Lorimer, HM, pl. 24, 1; (c) Lorimer, pl. 24/2.   [3] PM, III, fig. 45.

[4] Cf. above p. 32, n. 9. Cf. also silver vase, SG. pl. 128–31 (605), attackers with body-shields and boar's tusk helmets in hilly landscape.

[5] Il. 6, 433 f.

The Mycenaean archer disembarking from a boat and shooting upwards, presumably aiming at a defender on the rampart, whom Miss Lorimer has identified on a fifteenth-century fragment of a steatite vase from Knossos,[1] might belong to the same scene. Later fragments of fourteenth-century frescoes from the Megaron at Mycenae[2] show a Mycenaean warrior falling off the wall while ladies look on from the palace windows. Persson aptly compares Egyptian historical scenes, which may well have provided the original model for the artist, including presumably the hippopotamus if such he be; but obviously this tells us nothing of the place where these sieges took place. The warriors and horses on further fragments from the Megaron[3] belong to the same scene, as is shown by the occurrence of a chariot horse above the falling warrior: the chariot and foot battle is evidently regarded as going on outside the besieged town. The scenes are reflected on vases: on a rather earlier Mycenaean vase (fig. 18) from Cyprus[4] ladies in windows frame a chariot; on a rather later vase fragment from Tiryns[5] where the grand manner of the frescoes has been highly stylized, a chariot is preceded by two warriors with raised spears and followed by two marching warriors. The palace at Pylos[6] also had a fresco with a scene of mass slaughter, which seems to have been part of a Mycenaean siege of a hill town. It is clear that the storming of a citadel was part of the repertoire of palace frescoes inherited from the Minoans, and Mycenaean Kings felt it enhanced their dignity to have such a scene on their walls. How alike these scenes were our fragmentary evidence fails to tell us, but the palace spectators are common to the silver vase and to the Megaron, the archer on the Knossos steatite vase seems to fit in the scene on the silver vase, and if the falling warrior comes from an Egyptian model he is likely to go back to the earlier version. Whether the scenes derive from a single model or not, from the time of the silver vase the attackers are identifiable as Mycenaeans. The story

[1] Lorimer, *HM*, 279, fig. 35; *PM*, III, fig. 59.

[2] Lorimer, *HM*, pl. 12, 3; Persson, *New Tombs*, 188; *PM*, III, fig. 48; Rodenwaldt, *Fries des Megarons*, Halle, 1921 (with useful reconstructions but excessively early dating).

[3] Lorimer, *HM*, pl. 27, 1; Wace, *Mycenae*, fig. 99b; Matz, 109.

[4] British Museum, C 391; *CV*. pl. 6/9; *K.i.B.* 96/8; Furumark, *MP*, 445; V. Karageorghis, *J.H.S.*, 77 (1957), 269. Another vase also from Enkomi may well illustrate a naval expedition, *SCE*, pl. 121/3 (E 3.262).

[5] Cf. above p. 40, n. 4.   [6] *A.J.A.*, 60 (1956), 95.

of the siege of a citadel by the sea was therefore a Mycenaean story, a story which was presumably sung by Mycenaean poets.

The scene of the siege was painted in the Court manner and belonged in Mycenae to the Megaron, which was not constructed before the late fourteenth century and was still standing when the Palace was sacked. The late thirteenth- or early twelfth-century Warrior vase[1] (and the stele which echoes the picture on one side of the vase) is, as was noted above, something quite new (fig. 7). These are Mycenaean warriors represented with no trace of idealism in the clothing and equipment of their own day. The likeness between the rows of attacking spearmen on the stele and on the vase may be due to their being the work of the same school or to dependence from a common original. The latter seems to me more likely. However that may be, Miss Lorimer is surely right in seeing on the vase two stages in the same story: on one side six warriors march out with provision bags on their spears leaving a woman lamenting behind them. On the other side the foe advance with raised spears to meet them. Here again we feel that there is a story behind these scenes; the lamenting woman has sent them to their doom or knows that it is inevitable, but whether the part she plays is that of Kassandra or Eriphyle or Meleager's wife we cannot say.

We cannot tell whether she is Kassandra or Eriphyle or Kleopatra, and in Mycenaean art as in later Greek art we are often faced with this kind of problem because the artist has not given us the additional information which is necessary to fix the scene in a particular legend or myth. We can very often say that the artist has represented a mistress of animals, but whether she is Artemis or Athena or Diktynna or some quite different goddess he seldom tells us, although his contemporaries in that particular place would know. Modern critics can easily destroy any particular interpretation of an early work of art in terms of myth or legend, but this does not prove that it did not represent some myth or legend to contemporaries. The idea of representing scenes from everyday life is a modern idea, and our approach to ancient art is dangerously conditioned by our knowledge of the camera, the one-sided efficiency of which we expect our artists to emulate. The artist of the Warrior vase (fig. 7) (or of the fresco behind the Warrior vase, if such is to be assumed) tells us that an expedition

[1] Cf. above p. 38, n. 3.

went out and a woman knew it would be disastrous, whether she had sent them out or not. Such a story is much more likely to be a story in poetry than a contemporary event; the interesting thing is that the artist has brought the warriors' equipment up to date and the woman wears contemporary clothes instead of the Minoan dress of the court manner. This however is exactly what we believe the poet does too; the warrior like Ajax, who never wears a corselet because he originally had a body-shield and often retains it, is the exception.

It is a pity that we have not more evidence to trace out the long series of siege scenes, which run roughly from the seventeenth century to the late thirteenth, to see where and when similar changes occurred. But we cannot, I think, be wrong if we suppose that there was a very old story about a siege of a city by the sea in which not only the attackers but the defenders and their women were interesting. It is likely that the Mycenaeans took the story over from the Minoans and that the attackers then became Mycenaeans. If a Mycenaean King attacked a city and commanded his poet to sing of his achievements, his poet would tell the new story in the framework provided by the old because he had no other framework. He would change the names, bring the equipment and organization of his own side up to date, and introduce a few new exploits, but he would not know much more than this, and the new poem would be a blend of history and legend. Some such process happened to the old story when the Mycenaeans captured Troy VII A.

Modernization of this kind only affects stories on the human level, and among them only stories which are subject to this kind of change. The divine stories which we have detected are with some exceptions unlikely to have changed, at least within the Mycenaean period. Hermes or Apollo singing alone, Apollo singing among his Muses, Apollo's journey to Delos, Poseidon driving his chariot over the sea, Zeus with the scales of man's destiny, Zeus in his infancy suckled by an animal, Zeus as a bull carrying off Europa are stories or bits of stories which need show no development or change. Other stories like Poseidon leading forth the springs, or the King receiving instruction from a goddess, only survived in a modified or attenuated form after the Mycenaean period: Poseidon makes a spring for the Danaid Amymone, and Minos is said to have been a 'familiar friend of

Zeus'.[1] More interesting are the cases where one suspects that one can see the birth of a classical myth. We can perhaps detect two distinct procedures, although they may be confused with each other. One is the misunderstanding of a work of art. The vegetation goddess mourning over the burial pithos under the leafless tree became the first woman, Pandora, opening the box of evil things, or the god singing with the bird which shows that he is a god became Orpheus charming the birds, or the god and goddess sailing in a divine boat became Theseus and Ariadne. But in this last example the new interpretation also belongs to the other procedure, which may be very loosely termed political interpretation. The Minoan goddess of wild dances and her consort became the Greek Ariadne and Dionysos. But gradually the Greeks made new interpretations which suited the new political situation. For Ariadne there are two main versions: either she deserted Dionysos for Theseus or Theseus deserted her and Dionysos found her. In either case Dionysos remains the god and Ariadne sinks to mortal status as the daughter of the Cretan King, and can only rise again with the help of Dionysos (in the second version). Similarly the bull games of the Minoans and their representation in pictures, which continued to be painted in Mycenaean palaces and copied on Mycenaean seal rings, were the origin of three myths, which are political in the sense described: Theseus liberating the Athenian captives and slaying the Minotaur, Theseus and the bull of Marathon, Herakles and the Cretan bull. The Mycenaean occupation of Crete gave rise to the stories, for which Minoan art provided the material, and they glorify a Greek hero.

Mycenaean art tells us something of the subjects of Mycenaean poetry, and, as we shall see later, its evidence can be combined with the evidence of the tablets and of Homer to illustrate the setting of the stories. It also shows us five different types of performance. The wild dances must have been accompanied by song (fig. 13). The dancer on the Harvester vase[2] and his interlocutor are undoubtedly speaking, and the interchange is accompanied by a rattle (fig. 16). The lyre-player and the three women from Palaikastro,[3] whether they are Apollo and his Muses or not,

---

[1] *Od.* 19, 178.

[2] Cf. above p. 50, n. 3. On Cretan dances, generally, cf. L. B. Lawler, *Studies presented to D. M. Robinson,* I, 23 f.   [3] Cf. above p. 47, n. 2.

are certainly a solo singer and a chorus of dancers. A lyre-player accompanies the libation and a flute-player the sacrifice on the Hagia Triada sarcophagus[1]; the celebrants must surely sing as they perform the ritual (fig. 6). Finally Hermes or Apollo with his lyre[2] on the fresco in Pylos is a solo singer (fig. 9). These are all types of performance which survived in classical Greece.

[1] Cf. above p. 35, n. 1.   [2] Cf. above p. 47, n. 1.

3

EASTERN POETRY AND MYCENAEAN POETRY

Much Eastern poetry survives from the Mycenaean period and earlier, but no tablets containing literature have been found on Mycenaean sites. I have argued above[1] that absence of literary tablets cannot be used as an argument for absence of written poetry. Mycenaean art, as we have seen, gives strong indications of the existence of Mycenaean poetry of several kinds, and further indications will be discussed in the next chapter. If the general picture of a common Eastern Mediterranean culture with strong local differences is correct, Mycenaean poetry may have had a general likeness to contemporary Eastern poetry. If many similarities with Homer can be shown,[2] the question arises whether these similarities are due to recent acquaintance with Eastern poetry or to Homer's inheritance of Mycenaean poetry. The possibility of recent borrowing cannot, of course, be excluded at any rate for the poetry of Asia Minor. It is certain that Ugaritic poetry was known to the Phoenicians, and the *Odyssey* seems to show knowledge of Phoenician traders of recent date. That Hittite poetry in some form could have been handed down in Asia Minor and reached the Greeks through Lydian or other intermediaries is certainly possible. It is more difficult to see how

[1] Cf. above p. 23 f.

[2] Recent works on connexions between Early Greek and Eastern poetry include: A. Lesky, *Anz. Wien. Ak.*, 1950, 148; *Saeculum*, 6, 35; C. H. Gordon, *A.J.A.*, 56 (1952), 93; *Minos*, 3 (1955), 126; *Riv. Stud. Orient.*, 24 (1955), 161; *Hebrew Union College Annual*, 26 (1955), 43 (= HB); F. Dirlmeier, *Rh. Mus.*, 98 (1955), 20; T. B. L. Webster, *Minos*, 4 (1956), 104; G. Germain, *Genèse de L'Odyssée*; L. A. Stella, *Il Poema di Ulisse*. This last came out after I had sent my article to *Minos* and I should like to record here my far-reaching agreement with it as well as my indebtedness. Cf. also R. D. Barnett in *The Aegean and the Near East*, 212 f. C. H. Gordon, *ibid.*, 136 f. F. Dornseiff has republished his papers in *Antike und alter Orient*, Leipzig, 1956.

knowledge of Egyptian literature could have reached the Ionians at any date early enough for our Homer.

If the possibility of late borrowing cannot be denied, neither can the possibility of early borrowing. We know places where borrowing could have happened, we know foreign words which were in fact borrowed in the second millennium, and we can point to memories of the East in the second millennium which have survived in our Homer. We are concerned primarily with Ugarit, the Hittites, and Egypt. Egypt will prove to be the least important and the evidence is here least satisfactory. Strong Egyptian influence on Minoan and Mycenaean art is undoubted, but is not in itself enough to prove that stories were communicated; nor is the established fact that 'during the reign of queen Hatshepsut (early fifteenth century) an embassy from Crete visited the Egyptian court at least on one occasion'.[1] Yet we have two pieces of evidence from Knossos which point to a closer connexion. A man in Knossos in the fifteenth century was called Aigyptios,[2] just as an Athenian in the sixth century was called Amasis and a man in thirteenth-century Pylos was called Aithiops.[3] A fresco from Knossos[4] shows a young Cretan officer leading black troops. At this time the Cretan officer would have been Greek speaking like his contemporary Aigyptios. Greek pottery of this date and earlier has been found in Egypt as well as Minoan pottery.[5] It is therefore perfectly possible that Odysseus' story[6] of the Cretan raid on Egypt, which resulted in the Cretan's acceptance by the King of Egypt, is a Mycenaean memory of the fifteenth or fourteenth century, and Menelaos' reference[7] to the riches of Thebes, from where he brought back two silver baths (like those recorded on the Pylos tablet, illustrated in fig. 1), cannot be later than the early fourteenth century. Miss Lorimer suggests the possibility of a small commercial Mycenaean settlement in Tell-el-Amarna, which was the residence of the Egyptian king for roughly the second quarter of the fourteenth century; that would provide direct and certain contact. It seems to me far less likely that the Cretan officer on the fresco is leading a troop of mercenaries as a

[1] Furumark, *Op. Arch.*, 6 (1950), 239.
[2] KN Db 1105 (+1446); *Docs.* 136.
[3] PY En 74/11 etc.; *Docs.* 99. [4] *PM*, II, pl. 13 = IV, fig. 869.
[5] For all this cf. Lorimer, *HM*, 85 f.; Stubbings, *Mycenaean Pottery in the Levant*, 56, 90, 102 f. [6] *Od.* 14, 257 f. [7] *Od.* 4, 125 f.

reinforcement against an invasion by mainland Greeks[1] than that the fresco is a memory of some Cretan who did service in Egypt like the Cretan of Odysseus' story; such a Cretan might well have brought back stories and ideas as well as riches. He might also have brought back the Egyptian word for sword.[2]

In Ugarit, as we have seen,[3] a Mycenaean settlement is almost certain, and a similar settlement is thought likely at the port of Alalakh; from Alalakh no actual literary texts survive but this whole area formed a cultural unity. And for this area we also have linguistic evidence. Before the decipherment of the Mycenaean tablets Albright[4] had pointed out that the place-name Byblos must have come into Greek before 1200 B.C. when the pronunciation changed from Gubla to Gubal, and that Tyre and Sidon must have become Greek words at a time when their initial letters were still distinguished in Phoenician, at least before 1000 B.C. The tablets now prove that the words for gold, *chiton*, lion, cummin, and cyperus had already been borrowed from Semitic in Mycenaean times and therefore presumably from this area. Foreign spices may have been imported in the Canaanite jars found at several Mycenaean sites. The inhabitants were probably called Phoenicians by the Mycenaeans since they used 'Phoenician' in various forms to denote a spice, a colour, and a fabulous monster.[5] The discovery of a Cypro-Minoan tablet in Ugarit[6] may show that the chief intermediaries between the Mycenaeans in Ugarit and the mainland of Greece were the Mycenaeans in Cyprus. A route for communicating stories was open, and Menelaos' visit to the King of the Sidonians, who gave him a silver krater made by Hephaistos, is likely to be a Mycenaean memory.[7]

One contact with Asia Minor, which cannot yet be accurately assessed, may have been extremely important. If the Minoans were, as seems likely, an Asiatic people, Minoan Crete, as was suggested in the last chapter,[8] was a source not only of artistic inspiration but also of Asiatic ideas and stories. If the suggestion that their language was related to Hittite can be proved, they would provide a direct channel for Hittite stories and ideas to reach the

---

[1] Furumark, *Op. Arch.*, 6 (1950), 260.   [2] *Docs.* 348.
[3] Cf. above p. 8.   [4] Albright, *A.J.A.*, 54 (1950), 165 f.
[5] Cf. *Docs.* 135–6, etc. On Greek words in Semitic see Gordon, *HB*, 50 f. On Canaanite jars, V. R. Grace in *The Aegean and the Near East*, 81.
[6] Schaeffer, *Syria*, 31 (1954), 63 f.
[7] *Od.* 4, 615 f.; cf. Lorimer, *HM*, 80.   [8] Cf. above p. 9.

Mycenaeans. Without this another good channel is indicated by the Hittite texts which mention Ahhiyawa.[1] A Hittite queen was banished to Ahhiyawa. A prince of Ahhiyawa was sent to the Hittites to learn about chariots, or a Hittite chariot master was sent to Ahhiyawa to teach him. A god of Ahhiyawa was fetched to cure the Hittite king. Whoever the king of Ahhiyawa was (and it is of no importance for our problem whether he should be located in Mysia, Rhodes, Crete, or Mycenae), he must have been an Achaean, and a channel by which Hittite stories could have reached Mycenaean courts is established. Mycenaean contact with the Hittites is proved by finds in Boghazkeuy, and Homer seems to have preserved some memories of the Hittites in this period, the fourteenth and thirteenth centuries. The story of Bellerophon[2] is the most interesting. His warlike excursions from Lycia seem to have some connexion with the troubles in Lycia about which the king of the Hittites wrote to the king of Ahhiyawa, and the Chimaira may perhaps be a fourteenth-century Hittite monster. Memories of the Hittites have also been seen in the Halizones from Alybe, which is in the neighbourhood of the Hittite capital, in Priam's campaign against the Amazons on the river Sangarios, and in the Ceteians who followed Eurypylos.[3]

Routes can thus be provided for early and late borrowing (except for late Egyptian borrowing). At the moment we are only concerned with early borrowing. It will be shown that the manner of Eastern poetry has many parallels in Homer, and this comparison may lead to useful inferences about the manner and performance of Mycenaean poetry and about its preservation in Homer. By itself however this would show that Mycenaean poetry was a local variant of Eastern Mediterranean poetry (just as we have seen that Mycenaean civilization and Mycenaean art is a local variant of Eastern Mediterranean civilization and art), but not that Mycenaean poets borrowed Eastern themes. The evidence for early borrowing can only be convincing if it can be shown either that certain borrowings are so essential to the *Iliad* and *Odyssey* that they must have been very early if not original elements of the

---

[1] Cf. above p. 10, n. 1.

[2] *Il*. 6, 168f., cf. C. M. Bowra, *Homer and his forerunners*, 38; F. J. Tritsch, *Actes du Ier Congrès de F.I.E.C.*, 279.

[3] *Il*. 2, 856; 3, 184; *Od*. 11, 521, cf. Bowra, *loc. cit*.; Lorimer, *HM*, 64, n. 2, rejects Alybe, but (454) accepts the Sangarios story. On identification of Telephos with Hittite Telepinus see Barnett, *loc. cit*., 219.

story,[1] or that certain borrowings were already in the story when it was told in the pre-migration period, during which the mainland Greeks had little or no contact with the East.

Eastern poetry must now be more clearly defined.[2] Included under this heading are: first, the small amount of Egyptian prose which is relevant; secondly, Sumerian poems known from texts of the early second millennium but sometimes much earlier in conception; thirdly, Akkadian poems, which survive partly in Old Babylonian versions of the early second millennium and partly in Assyrian versions of the ninth to the eighth century (sometimes both versions and an earlier Sumerian version have been preserved and give valuable evidence on the process of expansion); fourthly, Hittite poems, which can be dated before the destruction of the capital in 1225 but may be considerably earlier (the two most important texts for our purpose are Hittite versions of Hurrian originals of at least the early fourteenth century); fifthly, Ugaritic poems dated to the second quarter of the fourteenth century (but the stories again are likely to be much older). No intermediaries other than the Hittites (including possibly the Minoans) and the people of Ugarit are needed between the Mycenaeans and the Akkadians and Sumerians, because the stories which are essential for our purpose were taken over from the Sumerians by the Akkadians, from the Akkadians by the Hurrians, and from the Hurrians by the Hittites and in one case certainly also by the people of Ugarit. I have called these works poems because they are metrical; Akkadian verse according to Speiser[3] was normally a unit of two distinct halves with two beats in each half; Hittite verse according to Güterbock[4] had a 'normal' line with usually four stresses and about twelve to seventeen syllables, with occasional shorter and longer verses; Ugaritic poetry according to Ginsberg[5] falls into kola, of which there are normally two but sometimes three to a stich. There seems no reason to suppose that any of these metres had the precision of the Homeric hexameter, but neither should we expect that the Homeric hexameter had been far

[1] E.g. Achilles and Patroklos, Odysseus' wanderings.

[2] Most of the material is conveniently collected in J. B. Pritchard, *Ancient Near Eastern Texts*[2], 1955 (=*NET*). I have used also H. G. Güterbock, 'Song of Ullikummi', *Journal of Cuneiform Studies*, 5 (1951), 135 f.; 6 (1952), 8 f., and G. R. Driver, 'Canaanite myths and legends', *Old Testament Studies*, 3 (1956), which give parallel text and translation.

[3] *NET*, 60.   [4] *Song of Ullikummi*, 7 f.   [5] *NET*, 129.

developed in the Mycenaean age, although it is probable that Greek poetry was already composed in double short rhythm.[1]

Poetry in the second millennium was composed for a particular kind of society, the main lines of which were described in the first chapter. In many essential aspects Mycenaean social structure can be compared with other contemporary East Mediterranean societies. The divinity or near divinity of the ruler in these societies had important effects on both the subjects and the style of poetry. Because the ruler was a god or near a god, divine and human characters are inextricably mixed. Even in official records the gods may take part in the king's operations.[2] In one Sumerian poem Gilgamesh, the king of Erech, engages in an apparently historical battle with Agga of Kish, but in another he fights with the monster Huwawa.[3] In an Ugaritic poem at the bidding of the god El, his father, who appears to him in a dream, King Keret marches to Tyre and Sidon, besieges Udum and wins its princess as his wife; then the gods attend his wedding. The geography seems to be real and the siege itself may be historical. This interchange between gods and men is familiar in Homer and was no doubt characteristic of the poetry of the Mycenaean period when Kings were still divine. For Homer himself the relationship is a thing of the past, because 'the men of today', being lesser men than the heroes, are also further removed from the gods, and the relationship between the gods and heroes has also been modernized, so that the actions of the gods can often be explained in rational terms.[4] From the old relationship arise a number of situations which are common to Eastern poetry and Homer: for instance, protection of a hero by a god, appeal for a hero by a god to a higher god, affront to a god by a hero, appeal against a hero by a god to a higher god, divine council to deal with an appeal. Thus it is easy to provide Eastern parallels for the scenes between Achilles and Thetis, or Athena and Odysseus (Gilgamesh and Ninsun, Keret and El), Thetis and Zeus (Ninsun and Shamash), Diomede and Aphrodite, or Odysseus and Kalypso (Aqhat and Anat, Gilgamesh and Ishtar), Helios and Zeus in the *Odyssey* (Ishtar to Anu, Anat to

[1] See below p. 92.

[2] Stella, 196 quotes Hittite and Egyptian instances. Barnett, *op. cit.*, 216 notes that a Hittite god made a Hittite King invisible in battle, cf. *Il.* 3, 380 etc.

[3] *NET*, 44f., 48f. Huwawa may represent a political enemy, cf. Barnett, *op. cit.*, 223f.

[4] Cf. recently W. Kullmann, *Das Wirken der Götter*, 1956; cf. below p. 291.

El); the divine councils in the *Iliad* and *Odyssey* may be compared with the divine councils in the Akkadian Gilgamesh epic, the Hittite song of Ullikummi, and the Ugaritic poem about Baal. It is extremely likely that such situations occurred in Mycenaean poetry, reflecting a similar relationship between god and man, and we can only say that they were borrowed from Eastern poetry if there is something unique about a particular situation or if a series of situations in a Greek epic strikingly echoes a series in a single Eastern epic.

Particularly in councils and in visits gods and men behave in a stately way which may confidently be supposed to reflect the behaviour of the great courts of the time. We have then to ask whether court formalities also affected the language of poetry. In all these poems and in Homer repetitions are frequent, whereas in later Greek poetry they decrease so clearly that there is no doubt that Homer marks the end of an epoch in this use. The different types of repetition may be due to various causes, and their preservation or extension may be due to some quite different cause, such as the poet's convenience, a cause which will however cease to operate when the audience ceases to enjoy the manner. For the moment let us consider the possible origin of different types of repetition. Court formalities are certainly one source: a guest must be offered a chair, food, and drink, whether Athirat visiting El in the Ugaritic *Baal* or Hermes visiting Kalypso in the *Odyssey*;[1] if he is in a hurry, he will refuse like the sun god when he visits the storm god in the Hittite *Song of Ullikummi* and like Patroklos when he visits Nestor in the eleventh book of the *Iliad*. In the divine council both in the *Song of Ullikummi* and in the first book of the *Iliad* the other gods get up when the great god enters.[2] But although court etiquette may prescribe a set form of action, this need not always be described in the same form of words, although it is not unnatural that this should be the case. Sometimes however in real life the repetition of the same words or the repetition of the same general structure with different words for details is essential. God or divine King must be addressed by the right title, and these titles, as Stella[3] has pointed out, are found both in official or religious documents and in poetry; obvious instances in poetry are in Sumerian 'Gilgamesh, lord of Kullab', in the

---

[1] Gordon, *HB*, sect. 60. [2] Lesky, *Saeculum*, 6, 49.
[3] Stella, *op. cit.*, 17, 20, 67, 108, 163.

Hittite *Song of Ullikummi* 'Kumarbi, father of the gods', 'the sun god of heaven' (once extended by adding 'the land's king'), 'the storm god, Kummiya's king' (twice extended to 'Kummiya's brave king'), in Ugaritic poems 'Baal, rider of clouds', 'virgin Anat' (both these occur in two different poems), 'Aqhat hero', 'Danel from Repha, hero from Hyrny', in Homer 'Zeus, father of men and gods', 'Agamemnon, King of men', 'Menelaos, dear to Ares'. Though the compulsion of religion is absent, men have their correct title in Mycenaean official documents: 'the Count Alektryon, the Eteoklean', 'Hektor, slave of god', 'Pekita, fuller of the King'. This kind of title survives in Homer in 'Nestor the Nelean', 'horseman Oeneus'. The title is one type of what is usually called the noun-epithet formula, and we may pause to ask whether other noun-epithet formulae may have a similar origin. The earth is frequently dark in the *Song of Ullikummi* and Achilles is frequently swift-footed in Homer, although neither dark nor swift-footed can be described as titles. Originally the compulsion is perhaps the same as in the titles: just as to be lord of Kullab is the essential characteristic of Gilgamesh, so darkness is the essential characteristic of earth and swiftness of Achilles, whether at the moment they are exhibiting this characteristic or not. So a Chinese painter said:[1] 'the flowers and fruits must move in the wind and be sprinkled with dew; the birds should flutter and the animals run. The spirit must be taken from the real things.'

Before invoking this principle of unique and right expression further, let us look at another instance where poetic practice is modelled on real procedure (the influence of Mycenaean military orders, religious reports, and inventories on poetry will be considered below).[2] When the King of Carchemish wants to communicate with the King of Ugarit, his scribe writes down the message in a set form:[3] 'Thus the King of Carchemish. To Anmistamru, King of the land of Ugarit, say: Greetings to you. As for the judgment etc.' The message itself is in the actual words of the King, as he dictates it to his scribe. Only the opening words 'Thus etc.' are the words of the scribe. Essentially the same form had been used long before by Samsi-Addu, the King of Assyria, to his son Iasmah-Addu, the King of Mari. The beginning of one letter may be quoted:[4] 'To Iasmah-Addu say this.

---

[1] Tung Chi Chang ap. Siren, *The Chinese on the Art of Painting*, 142.
[2] Cf. below p. 97 ff. [3] UG 16.03. [4] MA i. 21.

Thus Samsi-Addu, your father. On the subject of the Telmunite messenger of whom *you have written to me* in these terms: "he entered the house of a merchant . . . and *somebody beat him*. Therefore I *have not up to today sent him to you*." This is what *you have written to me*. Suppose *somebody beat him*. Cannot he ride a donkey? You *have not up to today sent him to* me, Why? etc.' The sender's name, Samsi-Addu is here put inside the message so that the whole represents the message which he dictated to his scribe. The six groups of italicized words indicate three repetitions, each of two or more words in the original. Within the message sent is an exact quotation of a message received from the addressee, and this is framed by the repeated 'you have written to me'; this framing is common in early Greek poetry and is usually known as ring form. The other two repetitions are quotations from the message received which have been introduced into the text of the new message.

These last two repetitions, which pick up the words of the previous message in answering it, are like the repetitions found constantly in poetry, where the answer is phrased in the words of the question or the carrying out of an order is phrased in the words of the order. Instances are very common in Eastern poetry and Homer; Odysseus asks his mother,[1] 'What fate of low-laying death overcame you? Was it long *disease* or did Artemis the *archeress visit you with her kindly arrows and slay you*?' And she answers 'Neither did the keen eyed *archeress visit me with her kindly arrows and slay me* in the palace nor did any *disease* come upon me such as takes life from the limbs by hateful wasting away.' In the Ugaritic poem *Keret*[2] the god El advises Keret in a dream: 'In a bowl of silver pour wine, honey in a bowl of gold. Go up to the top of the tower; bestride the top of the wall'; when he woke up, 'in a bowl of silver he poured wine, honey in a bowl of gold. He went up to the top of the tower, bestrode the top of the wall.' The passage is in fact much longer than this; the transposition of the verbs from the second person imperative to the third person of the past tense makes no difference to the scansion of the lines. I think we may go further and suppose that the visit scenes already mentioned are similarly described in the terms in which the successive operations are ordered, but here the poet only gives the

[1] *Od.* 11, 171f.
[2] *NET*, 143, ll. 72–76, 165–8; Driver, *Keret* 1, ii, 18–22; iv, 1–4.

description and not the operation order. Richardson[1] proposes a similar origin for the Homeric typical scenes of landing, sacrificing, arming, etc.: 'these sequences of operations suggest dependence on a laconic and adjectiveless code of directives'. Two such directives may be quoted from the Pylos tablets: first, the military operation order already mentioned,[2] and secondly, an instruction for ritual offerings.[3] This runs: 'Pylos: perform a certain action at the place Pa-ki-ja-ne, and bring the gifts and bring those to carry them. To the Mistress: one gold cup, one woman.' This is repeated four times for different places and different divinities. In poetry instructions for such offerings to different gods would be repeated in the same terms, and the description of the offerings being made would also be given in the same terms.

Eastern poetry like Homer (with the significant exception of the Bellerophon story) never mentions writing. In real life, as the correspondence shows, the King dictates his message to a scribe who writes it on a tablet; the tablet is carried by a herald to the addressee, who reads it with the aid of another scribe. In poetry the King speaks his message to a herald, and the herald goes on his way and repeats it word by word to the addressee. It is not wholly fanciful to say that in the absence of writing the terms of speaking take the place of the correspondence formulae and become similarly stereotyped. A passage from the *Song of Ulli-kummi* is worth quoting in Güterbock's translation:[4]

'Kumarbi to Impaluri began to speak: "O Impaluri! The words which I speak to thee, to my words (thine) ear hold inclined. Into (thy) hand a staff take, upon thy feet as shoes the swift winds put, and to the Irshirra (gods) go, and these strong words before the Irshirras speak: 'Come. He calls you, Kumarbi, the gods' father, to the gods' house. But the matter about which he calls you (?), that ye know not (?). Now come promptly. . . .'" When Impaluri the words heard, into (his) hand the staff he took, upon his feet the shoes he put. And forth he travelled, Impaluri, and to the Irshirras he came. And

[1] L. J. D. Richardson, *Hermathena*, 86 (1955), 54f.

[2] PY An 657 etc.; *Docs.* 188f., cf. above p. 21.

[3] PY Tn 316; *Docs.* 284f., with the interpretation of Meriggi and Palmer this becomes a report instead of an order.

[4] *Op. cit.*, 21, cf. *NET*, 122.

Impaluri the words to the Irshirras again began to speak: "Come. He calls you, Kumarbi, the gods' father. But the matter about which he calls you, that ye knew not. Now hurry, come!".'

The herald Impaluri repeats his master's message word for word as though he had brought a tablet. He is told to take a staff and put on shoes, and the same words (with the omission of 'the swift winds') describe his doing it; in a later passage of the same poem the action exactly corresponds with the order; in two earlier passages the same action is described in the same words, once with and once without 'the swift winds'. The order seems therefore to be a standard command to take the road, and the action of taking the road with shoes and staff is described in the same terms, whether the command has been given or not. The phrases used for speaking are also repeated. At the beginning of the passage quoted 'Kumarbi to Impaluri began to speak'; this form 'A. to B. *began to speak*' recurs six times in the poem; a longer form 'A. to B. *again began to speak*' is used fourteen times; and a yet longer form 'A. the *words* to B. *again began to speak*' occurs later in our passage and once elsewhere in the poem. Yet another variant 'A. to B. *the words began to speak*' recurs three times. Thus the poet (like the letter writer) had a standard introduction and could vary its length for the space available. In Ugaritic also the line (or rather kolon) translated 'he (she, or they) lifted up his voice and cried' recurs five times in *Baal* and four times in *Keret*; neither the gender nor number affect the scansion nor the copula 'and', which can be added at the beginning if needed for the sense. Other Ugaritic formulae which Gordon has noted as having analogies in Greek are, 'and here's something more I will tell thee', and 'scarce hath the word left his mouth; his speech left his lips'.[1] A further formula in Hittite 'A. to his own mind began to speak' has parallels in Akkadian, Assyrian, Egyptian, and Greek to introduce a soliloquy, or rather to introduce a description of the speaker's thoughts, which are represented as a soliloquy.

The examples so far quoted do not stray far beyond the usage of real life. Operations conducted under orders are described in the terms of the orders. The formulae for speeches are an extension of the formulae for correspondence. But in the noun-epithet formulae the range is, as we have seen, extended from titles of gods, Kings,

---

[1] Cf. Gordon, *A.J.A.*, 56 (1952), 93.

and ordinary men to 'swift-footed Achilles' and 'the dark earth', and here the principle seems to be that unique and right expression should be used on all or most occasions. This may account for repetitions for which no explanation can be found in court practice. A seven-line description of hell in the Akkadian Gilgamesh epic recurs in the Descent of Ishtar,[1] and here it is reasonable to suppose that the poet was used to repetitions, and therefore thought it sensible to repeat a description which had already proved successful. Many other instances of this analogical extension could be found.

In his account of formulae which have parallels in Greek Gordon noted two others. One is the formula for a new day in the Gilgamesh epic:[2] 'With the first glow of dawn'. This, like the Homeric line 'when early-rising rosy-fingered dawn appeared', has the quality of a refrain, but of a refrain used to introduce a new section of the poem, describing the events of a new day. Its use implies the use of refrains in other poetry, probably hymns and cult songs. The second kind of formula Gordon calls the literary device of climaxing a number by a higher one.[3] He quotes examples from Ugaritic poetry, and others can be found in Assyrian and Hittite: thus in the *Song of Ullikummi*[4] 'And before Ea's first door five times he bowed, but before the inner door five times he bowed. But when before Ea they arrived, before Ea fifteen times he bowed.' Here as in the refrains the origin seems to be in poetry itself, in the desire to have two or more lines which are closely similar but slightly different in content. The technique is particularly clear in the short kola of Ugaritic poetry:[5] 'Sixty-six towns he took, seventy-seven hamlets, of eighty-eight he became lord, of ninety-nine'.

So far we have spoken of various compulsions which account for repetitions in Eastern poetry; their survival in Homer suggests that they were also characteristic of Mycenaean poetry. Titles of gods, Kings, and men must be given correctly, and in a courtly world the principle of correct expression may be extended further. Royal correspondence is highly formal, and this formality is extended beyond the messenger scenes of poetry to the formulae used for introducing speeches. Similarly operations are reported

---

[1] *NET*, 87, VII, iv, 33–39 = 107, 4–10.
[2] *NET*, 88, 93, 94.   [3] *HB*, § 178 ff.   [4] *NET*, 124; Güterbock, 41.
[5] *NET*, 134; Driver, 101.

in the terms of the operation order, whether the operation order itself is given or not, and this technique is extended to other descriptions, which have no such operation order behind them. These compulsions all derive ultimately from the court of the King, and it is reasonable to suppose that the court in turn enjoyed such formality in poetry. Another kind of influence – the influence of hymns and the influence of poetic rhythm – may account for the 'refrains' and the climaxing (with other such phenomena). Yet other compulsions may come from the conditions of performance and the conditions of recording this poetry, and we have to ask whether we have any evidence for either of these things, and whether, if so, this affects our view of Mycenaean poetry.

The texts of Eastern poetry come in the main from temple libraries, palace libraries, writing schools, and in the case of Egyptian texts certainly from tombs. When they have reached these depositories, they cease to be interesting to us except in so far as they were used for recitation. They were copied and re-copied by carefully supervised scribes, whose names are often appended, and might be read by a very small number of literate people, but the poet in no sense wrote for a reading public. The information about scribes comes from Egyptian, Akkadian, Assyrian, and Ugaritic colophons. Thus the Akkadian Atrahasis epic was written by Ellit-Aya, the 'junior' scribe, in the eleventh year of Ammisaduqa (late eighteenth to early seventeenth century);[1] the Assyrian Gimil-Ninurta poem was 'according to its archetype written and collated. Script of Nabu-rihtu-ushur, the apprentice, member of the academy of Nabu-aha-iddin, the courtier. For the perusal of Qurdi-Nergal';[2] the Ugaritic *Baal* was 'written by Elimelech the Shabnite . . . Donated by Niqmadd, King of Ugarit' (second quarter of the fourteenth century).[3] Once the tablet was written, its recopying was no doubt subject to the same shortcomings as are found in any other manuscript tradition, but this does not concern us. We are however concerned with its use for performances.

A Sumerian tablet speaks of scribing as 'the mother of recita-tion',[4] and the Akkadian Creation Myth was recited on the fourth

[1] *NET*, 105.   [2] O. R. Gurney, *Anatolian Studies*, 6 (1956), 159.
[3] *NET*, 141; Driver, 115.
[4] British Museum, Sm 61, quoted by C. J. Gadd, *Teachers and Students*, 1956.

day of the New Year festival.[1] The Hittite myth of Illuyankas has two versions:[2] the first is introduced as 'the cult legend etc. they no longer tell' and the second 'This is the way in which X. told it later'; after a considerable break which seems to have contained another legend the document ends 'Thus it is found on the tablet. I have told the holy saga as it is found there.' This seems to give evidence of recopying but also of recitation, since 'they no longer tell' and 'told it later' surely refer to the use of the tablets for reciting. Three of the Ugaritic poems contain instructions to the performers. In *Baal*[3] 'Go back to the passage when the servitors were sent' is carefully marked off by ruled lines from the text and is a clear instruction to repeat a stock passage. *Aqhat* also has an instruction to repeat on the edge of the tablet.[4] *Shacher and Shalim*[5] has a rubric marked off by ruled lines: 'Seven times shall it be recited to the lute, and the ministers shall respond etc.'. Thus the tablets were certainly used for recitations, and these recitations presumably kept to the text of the tablet.

We have also some evidence for the poets. Two works listed in the catalogue of Assurbanipal's library at Nineveh (seventh to eighth century) have against them the note 'from the mouth of X'. This suggests that they were dictated by the poet. According to Gurney[6] Hurrian passages in Hittite texts are introduced by 'the singer of the land of Hurri sings as follows', and both the Kumarbi myth and the Ullikummi myth[7] are called 'Songs' on the tablets; one begins 'let there listen the gods of heaven' and the other 'I will sing'. These are songs therefore, and must have been recorded by dictation. Similarly the Ugaritic *Nikkal* begins 'I sing of Nikkal' and *Baal* was 'dictated by Attani-Puruleni, chief priest, chief shepherd'.[8] Thus we have some evidence for what in any case we must assume that the poets dictated to the scribes, but no evidence that the poet himself was a scribe. He was a singer, who could dictate his songs to the scribe, and probably also a reciter, that is a singer who learnt his song from the tablets read to him by a scribe.

The first question to be asked is whether the existence of this trio – singer, scribe, reciter – influenced the form of poetry. We

[1] *NET*, 60; Cornford, *Principium Sapientiae*, 231 f. [2] *NET*, 125.
[3] *NET*, 134; Driver, 99. [4] *NET*, 155; Driver, 67.
[5] Driver, 121. [6] *Hittites*, 124. [7] *NET*, 120, 121.
[8] Driver, 125, 115; *NET*, 141.

have spoken of various compulsions which gave Eastern poetry its repetitive character. Is there yet another here? Dictation to a scribe writing a difficult script must have been a slow business and might be helped by repetitions (the Ugaritic colophons show that repeated passages were sometimes omitted). Dictation from a difficult script would be similarly aided by the formal character of the text, and learning by heart would be greatly aided. As poetry was in fact dictated, recorded, and recited, it is possible that what was called above analogical spread of repetitions (where they cannot be regarded as conditioned by contemporary practice in real life), was partly due to the difficulties of dictators, scribes, and reciters. The manner survives (although in some significant ways modified, as will be shown later) from Mycenaean poetry to our Homer. Linear B is a difficult script; but until literary texts in Linear B are found, we cannot claim this compulsion also for Mycenaean poetry.

These Eastern poems, as long as they were kept within the palace or temple, whether they were read by a small royal or priestly public or recited at festivals or copied and recopied by scribes, remained fixed except in so far as any form of transmission implies a certain amount of corruption and emendation. But we have texts of the same story from different places or from the same place but of different dates, and these later texts show far more expansion and variation than any scribal tradition could cause, even if the tradition involved also translation into another language. Here we see poets at work and a completely different kind of transmission, in which the main lines are preserved and the manner may remain the same, because the new poet also is working in the same kind of courtly circle, but incidents and details are handled with complete freedom. Such transmissions were made from Sumerian to Babylonian, from Babylonian to Hurrian and to Assyrian, from Hurrian to Hittite, Ugaritic, and Phoenician, and, I think we can say, from Hittite, Ugaritic, and Phoenician to Mycenaean Greek. The routes by which Eastern stories (including Egyptian) could have been transmitted to the Mycenaeans have already been considered; whether transmission in fact took place, and whether it took place in the Mycenaean period has to be argued for each particular case, and acceptance or rejection of any one instance does not involve accepting or rejecting any other. There is moreover an additional interest in noting what happened in the earlier, well documented Eastern stages of the transmission, because it may be expected that similar alterations will have been made in the five hundred years which separate our Homer from the ,Pylos of the tablets.

Four Sumerian poems[1] about Gilgamesh survive – Gilgamesh and Agga, Gilgamesh and the Land of the Living, the Death of Gilgamesh, Gilgamesh and the Huluppu Tree. The first, as we have seen, contains elements at least of historical fact; the second and fourth are mythical; the third may be regarded as a mixture of myth and history. The fourth survives partly in a Sumerian version and partly in an Akkadian translation, which appears to be a scribal translation and not a poet's adaptation. Nevertheless it forms the twelfth tablet of the Akkadian Epic of Gilgamesh,[2] which was composed late in the second millennium. The other eleven tablets contain the latest adaptation in the straight line of descent from the Sumerian Death of Gilgamesh. Earlier are the fragments of an Old Babylonian version from the first half of the second millennium, a Hurrian version of the early fourteenth century, and a slightly later Hittite version.

Comparison with the Sumerian version shows the same outlines: the association of Gilgamesh and Enkidu, the journey to the cedar forest, and the fight with Huwawa. The relationship of Gilgamesh and Enkidu has changed between the three Sumerian poems in which Enkidu appears and the Old Babylonian version: they had been master and servant, they have become friends. From Gilgamesh's first resolve to the death of Huwawa only 170 lines are needed in the Sumerian version: Gilgamesh appeals to Utu, makes his axe, crosses the mountains, fells the cedar and sleeps; he arms himself; Enkidu tries in vain to dissuade him; he fights with Huwawa and at the last moment pities him, but Enkidu persuades him to kill Huwawa. The Akkadian version, as given in *NET*, is put together from pieces of the Old Babylonian, Hittite, Hurrian, and Assyrian versions, so that any exact computation of length is impossible. In Tablet III of the Old Babylonian version Gilgamesh makes his resolve and Enkidu tries to dissuade him (the dialogue has clear reminiscences of the Sumerian but comes much earlier in the story); Gilgamesh makes his preparations, then consults the Elders who try to dissuade him. But he appeals to Shamash (this is the new position for the appeal to

[1] *NET*, 44f., 47f., 50f., 97f.　　　　　[2] *NET*, 73f.

Utu which opened the Sumerian version); then he arms himself and the Elders entrust him to Enkidu. This whole passage occupies about 300 lines. The Assyrian version takes up with a shorter version of the Elders' second speech and follows with a visit to Ninsun, the mother of Gilgamesh, who prays for him to Shamash the sun god; this version is very broken and originally contained at least 300 lines. Tablet IV gets the two heroes to the forest; in Tablet V Gilgamesh sleeps, then fells the cedar (again the Sumerian order seems to have been changed), and battles with Huwawa; again Enkidu counsels against sparing Huwawa. Thus the same stretch of the story takes some 1,200 lines instead of 170; the main expansion seems to have occurred between the Sumerian and the Babylonian version, and some incidents have been switched to different positions to make the story more effective.

Tablet VI opens with Gilgamesh in his glory wooed by Ishtar, whom he rejects (so in the Hittite *Ullikummi* she fails to win Ullikummi, and in Ugaritic *Aqhat* Anat fails to win Aqat). She persuades Anu to send the bull of Heaven against Gilgamesh, and the bull is killed by the pair. In Tablet VII Enkidu dreams that the gods in Council have decreed his death. Before he dies he dreams of his arrival in the House of Darkness. In Tablet VIII Gilgamesh laments Enkidu. In Tablet IX he sets out to find the secret of life from Utnapishtim and visits the Scorpion man and his wife, and pushes on to a marvellous garden. In Tablet X, for which again Old Babylonian, Hurrian, and Hittite, as well as Assyrian fragments survive, he is consulting the ale-wife Siduri, and she sends him on to Urshanabi (Sursanabu) the boatman of Utnapishtim. The Old Babylonian version is demonstrably the same but more economical in words and repetitions than the Assyrian. Gilgamesh takes the boat and reaches Utnapishtim. In Tablet XI Utnapishtim tells him the story of his own escape in the ark, and then tells him how to find the plant of new life, which he duly finds and a serpent steals. Tablet XII, as noted above, is a translation of the Sumerian story of Gilgamesh and the Huluppu Tree: Enkidu is sent to bring up the magic drum-stick and drum from the Nether world, but is seized by the gods there; his spirit is allowed to talk to Gilgamesh.

Utnapishtim's story in Tablet XI has its own rather complicated ancestry. A fragmentary Sumerian tablet[1] tells how Ziusudra,

[1] *NET*, 42.

King of Shurippak, standing by a wall, was told to build a house-boat to save 'the name of mankind and the seed of vegetation' from the deluge. After the flood Utu the sun god brought his rays into the giant boat, and Ziusudra sacrificed to him and was finally transferred to live as a god 'in the land of crossing, the land of Dilmun, the place where the sun rises'. Ziusudra of Shurippak becomes Atrahasis (the very wise) in the Akkadian Atrahasis epic[1] and Utnapishtim in the Gilgamesh story, where Utnapish-tim describes himself as living in Shurippak (11) and is later called Atrahasis (190). The Atrahasis epic survives in two Old Baby-lonian fragments, written in the late eighteenth to early seventeenth century, and two Assyrian fragments. The stories in all the versions are closely parallel. Ziusudra received his news and instructions through a wall. In the Old Babylonian Atrahasis the god Ea says 'Wall, hearken to me, Reed hut, guard well all my words! Destroy the house, build a ship' and in the Assyrian version of Gilgamesh Utnapishtim quotes Ea's words as 'Reed-hut, reed-hut, wall, wall, Reed-hut, hearken, Wall, reflect. Man of Shurippak, son of Ubar-Tutu, Tear down house, build a ship.' This is an expansion of the normal kind between two versions. Utnapishtim goes on with his story, dividing the days by the formulae 'with the first glow of dawn', which had already been used earlier of Gilgamesh's travels. He builds the boat according to instructions; the flood comes; the boat settles on Mount Nisir; sacrifice is made to the gods, and Ea persuades Enlil to allow Utnapishtim to become like the gods and to reside far away at the mouth of the rivers. From the point of view of poetic technique it is interesting to observe that a separate Sumerian story, which survives as a separate story in Old Babylonian and in Assyrian, is built into the Gilgamesh story as a cautionary tale told to Gilgamesh. Utnapishtim begins 'I will reveal to thee a hidden matter' and ends 'Who will for thy sake call the gods to Assembly that the life which thou seekest thou mayest find?' In the same way in the ninth book of the *Iliad* Phoenix introduces the Meleager story as a cautionary tale to warn Achilles. Gilgamesh's journey to Utnapishtim was already an element of the Old Babylonian version, but we have no way of deciding whether there Utnapish-tim did more than tell Gilgamesh how to get the magic plant, or whether already at that stage he told the story of the deluge.

[1] *NET*, 104.

Gilgamesh's fights with the monster Huwawa and the Bull of Heaven have many parallels in Greek legend, particularly in the stories of Herakles and Perseus: Huwawa has a strong facial resemblance to the Gorgon.[1] It is certainly possible that such stories came into Greek mythology from the East, which provided many examples. Many scholars have also pointed out connexions between the Gilgamesh story and Homer's *Iliad* and *Odyssey*. If a sufficient number of parallels exist, borrowing is likely; and if they are deeply embedded in the structure of the Greek poems, the borrowing is likely to be early and in fact Mycenaean. In the *Iliad* the relationship of Achilles and Patroklos may be compared with the relationship of Gilgamesh and Enkidu, and the relationship of Achilles and Thetis with the relationship of Gilgamesh and his mother, the goddess Ninsun. The two passages in the *Iliad* which come closest to the Gilgamesh epic are both in the eighteenth book. When Gilgamesh visited Ninsun to tell her of his resolve to seek out Huwawa,[2] Ninsun raised her hands to the sun god Shamash and said: 'Why, having given me Gilgamesh for a son, with a restless heart didst thou endow him? And now thou didst affect him to go on a far journey to the place of Huwawa, to face an uncertain battle, to travel an uncertain road.' This is surely the tone of Thetis in the *Iliad* (18, 54): 'Ah! wretched me, who have born a hero to misery, I bore a son who was blameless and strong . . . as long as he lives and sees the light of the sun, he is grieved.' When Enkidu died, Gilgamesh lamented him:[3] 'like a lion he raised up his voice, like a lioness deprived of her whelps. He paces back and forth before the couch'; and later, like Achilles, he prepared an elaborate burial for his friend. In the *Iliad* (18, 316) the Achaeans lamented Patroklos all night; Achilles began the lamentation, laying his murderous hands on the breast of his friend, groaning deeply like a bearded lion, whose whelps have been stolen by a hunter. The parallel between the two similes is striking, but the parallel between the double relationships is more striking. Achilles is unique in the *Iliad*; he is the only hero who is unthinkable without his mother and his friend. If this double relationship was inspired by Gilgamesh, it seems to me likely that the borrowing took place very early.

The case for supposing that the *Odyssey* was influenced by the

---

[1] Cf. T. P. Howe, *A.J.A.*, 58 (1954), 109.　　　　[2] *NET*, 81.
[3] *NET*, 88.

Gilgamesh poem is rather different. Here Germain finds 'un enchaînement semblable d'épisodes que certains traits rapprochent'.[1] The beginning of the two poems prompts us to look further: 'He who saw everything to the ends of the land, who all things experienced, considered all' is not unlike the man who 'saw the towns of many men and got to know their way of thinking'. It is, of course, in Odysseus' story to Alkinoos that this theme is developed. Germain sees a first likeness in the Laistrygones (*Od.* 10, 81 f.), who live far away, where the paths of day and night are near, and the wife of the King is as big as a mountain; they have something in common with Gilgamesh' Scorpion man and his wife, who live far away across difficult seas and guard the gate of the mountain which keeps watch over sunrise and sunset. They however pass Gilgamesh on to a magic grove in which the ale-wife (if that is the right translation) lives. She is the Circe of the story, who sends him farther on his way and points out the difficulty of the journey: 'only the valiant sun god crosses the sea and in between are the Waters of Death that bar its approaches'. Circe however (as Calypso after her) tries her wiles on Odysseus, like Ishtar much earlier in the Gilgamesh poem, and, like Ishtar there too, can turn men into animals. For the journey to Utnapishtim Gilgamesh has to build a boat, just as Odysseus builds a raft on Calypso's island[2] (this is the kind of disturbance of the order of incidents which we have already noted within the tradition of Eastern poetry itself). Utnapishtim supplies the information that Gilgamesh needs, just as Teiresias supplies the information that Odysseus needs. But Teiresias is quite different from Utnapishtim, who has become like the gods and resides far away at the mouth of the rivers. Teiresias is a shade, who has to be summoned by a special ritual; but again the passage of the Nekyia (11, 204f.), where Odysseus tries to embrace his mother and she tells him the lot of the dead, and the similar passage in the *Iliad* (23, 97f.), where Achilles tries to embrace the shade of Patroklos, have a parallel in the twelfth tablet: 'the spirit of Enkidu, like a windpuff, issued forth from the nether world. They embraced and kissed each other', and then Enkidu tells Gilgamesh of the

[1] *Op. cit.*, 422; cf. also 342 ff., 414 ff.; cf. also Stella, *op. cit.*, 200 f., 210, 215 f., 220 ff.

[2] *Od.* 5, 234. I do not feel certain of Germain's very ingenious comparison of the raft with Egyptian rafts (*op. cit.*, 399 f.).

horrors of the after life. For our Homer, who knows cremation, the shades are so unsubstantial that embrace is impossible.

The striking correspondences are all in Odysseus' tale to Alkinoos, which undoubtedly includes many other elements and has been in the course of time completely altered in tone: Odysseus is in search of Ithaca, not rejuvenation. But it certainly seems possible that far behind our *Odyssey* lies a Mycenaean borrowing of the Gilgamesh poem. A possible route for such borrowing lies as we have noted through the Hittites, and it is therefore interesting that two other parallels with Hittite poetry have been noted in the *Odyssey*: one is the small but convincing comparison made by Lesky between the description of Atlas in the first book (52) with the giant Upelluri in the *Song of Ullikummi*. The other is Stella's[1] comparison of Odysseus' triumph over the suitors with a Hittite story of King Gurpanzah, who with his bow killed sixty princes and seventy barons at a banquet and recovered his wife; in the Mycenaean period, as we have seen, the bow was highly thought of and such borrowing is much more likely then than later.

The description of Atlas in the first book of the *Odyssey* is one of many allusions in Homer to what may conveniently be called the Creation myth. Schadewaldt[2] has pointed out that Homer like Hesiod had an old source, which dealt with the foundation of Zeus' rule, and that the incidents, which appear scattered through the *Iliad*, complete each other, as is the case with other incidents drawn by Homer from old stories. An old source common to Homer and Hesiod means a source in pre-migration poetry, and therefore in all probability a Mycenaean source. The Akkadian Creation myth[3] is itself the remodelling of a Sumerian myth, in which Apsu and Tiamat quarrelled and Ea imprisoned Apsu. When the Babylonians became supreme, the Babylonian god Marduk was introduced and destroyed the older Tiamat and her monsters. The Hurrian myth[4] adds a further generation, the Hurrian storm god Teshub, who defeated his predecessor Kumarbi and then had to do battle again with Kumarbi's son, the stone man Ullikummi. This story is preserved for us by the Hittites; they also had two versions of the battle between the storm

---

[1] *Op. cit.*, 146.   [2] *Iliasstudien*, 118.
[3] *NET*, 60; cf. Cornford, *Principium Sapientiae*, 225 f., 239 f.
[4] *NET*, 120, 121 (cf. Güterbock, *Song of Ullikummi*).

god and the dragon Illuyankas,[1] who has clear reminiscences of Tiamat. We have two Phoenician versions. In the Ugaritic *Baal*,[2] Baal succeeds the older god El, who is identified in another text with Kumarbi, and by the help of his sister Anat is established after defeating Yamm, the god of the sea, and Mot, the god of death. This is only the last stage, but Beirut[3] had a Phoenician version of the whole Hurrian-Hittite myth. It is preserved by Eusebius, who quotes Philo for it; Philo translated it from Sanchuniathon whom he dates 'before the Trojan war', because he had found the King of Beirut, who 'accepted the history' in the King lists; the form of colophon which Philo quotes is so like the colophon of the Ugaritic *Baal* (quoted above pp. 76f.) that there is no difficulty in the early date; Beirut is known to have been in correspondence with Ugarit (cf. above p. 9), and scholars have noticed coincidences between the names of the gods in the Beirut version and the names occurring in the Ugaritic *Baal*.[4] In the Beirut version the quarrel between husband and wife, which is in the first generation in the Sumerian myth, is shifted into the second generation; the emasculation of his father by El (=Kumarbi) is performed by a special implement, like the special implement used to cut through Ullikummi's legs; the storm god Baal succeeds peacefully. Thus as the story wanders through the centuries to different places it is not only expanded but incidents change their places, as in the Gilgamesh story.

Hesiod's version agrees in general with the Phoenician version, and Kronos (=El) uses a special knife or sickle[5] to emasculate Ouranos; but the latter stages where Zeus battles with the older gods are more like the Hurrian myths and the Hittite story of Illuyankas. Homer also refers to these later stages in the *Iliad* – the deposition of Kronos (8, 479; 14, 274), the battle of the giants (5, 385, cf. *Od.* 11, 308), the blasting of Typhoeus (2, 782); the magnificent description of Hera's chariot (5, 722) when she goes out to fight recalls the preparation of battle wagons when the storm god and the other gods go out against Ullikummi.[6] Zeus in particular sometimes behaves in the *Iliad* more crudely than we expect: in the fifteenth book (18) he reminds Hera how he had

[1] *NET*, 125; cf. P. Walcot, *C.Q.*, 50 (1956), 198f.
[2] *NET*, 129; Driver, 72.   [3] Text in Müller, *F.H.G.*, III, 566.
[4] Cf. Driver, *op. cit.*, 12f., 15ff., 19, 101.
[5] Nilsson, *B.S.A.*, 46 (1951), 122f.   [6] *NET*, 123f.; Güterbock, 33f.

hung her up in the clouds with two anvils attached to her feet, and thrown down to earth any god who tried to set her free; this is perhaps a reminiscence of Marduk[1] splitting Tiamat like a shell-fish and setting half of her up as the sky, but these passages also remind us of the violence in the Ugaritic *Baal*,[2] when Baal smashes Yamm with two maces or Anath threatens to beat up elderly El. When Zeus deposed Kronos, Hera took refuge with Okeanos, the father of the gods, and mother Tethys (14, 200); now she says, these two are quarrelling. They are Apsu and Tiamat of the Akkadian story, and the Akkadian (or rather Sumerian) pair quarrelled because Apsu wanted to destroy all the younger gods, who made so much noise. In the deluge story this desire of the gods to destroy their own creations becomes a desire to destroy men, and in the Atrahasis epic a series of such destructions is devised, flood, famine, and pestilence. An echo of this story is found in the *Cypria*, where Gaia begs Zeus to destroy men because they are so heavy on her, and thus Zeus was persuaded, instead of using fire and flood, to destroy men partly by the Theban war, and partly by the Trojan war. In the *Iliad* this attitude of Zeus to mankind appears quite often, for instance:[3] 'he turned aside and sat apart from the rest, glorying in his strength, looking upon the city of the Trojans and the ships of the Achaeans and the gleam of bronze, and the slaying and the slain'. This is not so very far from the wholesale slaughter perpetrated by Anat in the *Baal*.[4]

The Ugaritic *Keret*[5] also has a claim to be considered among the stories which may have been borrowed very early. We have seen that the Mycenaeans had a siege poem, in which evidently the ladies of the palace played a part, since they are represented; and that this was an old story which was possibly taken over from the Minoans. Gordon has argued that the hero of the Keret story is a Cretan. Whether this equation is accepted or not (and it is, of course, possible that the story and its hero were transplanted to Ugarit) the parallel which he draws with the background of the *Iliad* is startling enough. The poem opens with Keret in utter misery because 'his lawful wife surely went away, his rightful spouse whom he had got with a bride gift did depart'. He falls

---

[1] *NET*, 67. [2] *NET*, 131, 137; Driver, 83, 91.

[3] *Il.* 11, 80; cf. 8, 51; 20, 22; 21, 289. Cf. Kullmann, *Philologus* (1955), 167f.; *Wirken der Götter*, 20f. [4] *NET*, 136; Driver, 95.

[5] *NET*, 142; Driver, 28f.; Gordon, *Minos*, 3 (1955), 126f.

asleep and in a dream is visited by El, who tells him to besiege Udm and demand the King's daughter, Huray. This is duly done, and after a preliminary attempt to buy Keret off the King surrenders his daughter, and the gods attend the wedding. The subsequent fortunes of Keret do not concern us. Gordon assumes that Huray was Keret's original wife who was won back, but this does not seem clear from the text. At least we can say that Keret's wife had abandoned him and he was bidden by a dream to besiege a town to get a wife. That such a poem could have inspired the story of Helen of Troy is clear (it was an act of poetic genius to identify the wife who had deserted with the woman to be won from the town), and from the frescoes we know that the Mycenaeans had a siege poem, perhaps inherited from the Minoans, in which the ladies of the palace played a part. The plight of Keret at the beginning of the poem recalls the description of Menelaos in Aeschylus' *Agamemnon* (410f.): even the dream is there, but Aeschylus has converted it into a deceitful vision of Helen. The substitute statue (416) may well be old as in the story of Protesilaos (but there the statue is a substitute for a dead man like the statue of Enkidu in the Gilgamesh epic, and not for a departed woman). Aeschylus may have drawn on the *Cypria* here, and the *Cypria* may go back to a very old source; that Menelaos' misery was described in the *Cypria* we know, because someone tried to tempt him with wine (fr. 13, Allen). The attempt of the besieged King to buy Keret off may have an echo in Paris' offer to restore what he took from Menelaos with interest, an offer which is made and indignantly refused in the seventh book of the *Iliad* (363 ff.). The marriage attended by the gods has its parallel in the marriage of Peleus and Thetis, which was told in the *Cypria* (as well as in other Greek stories such as Kadmos and Harmonia); this would again be the transference of an incident to a quite different place in the story. Thus it may well be that the whole story was borrowed in Mycenaean times, remodelled later by a genius, and so became in time part of the background of the *Iliad* and the foreground of the *Cypria*.

The last source for early borrowing which need be considered is Egypt. Late borrowing, as has been said, is extremely unlikely owing to the slow resumption of contact with Egypt. The evidence for a contact which might have permitted a borrowing of stories has been given already. The suggestion often made that the

Odyssey owes something to the story of Sinuhe or to the story of Wen-Amon seems to me entirely without foundation. The story of the shipwrecked man[1] has a better right to consideration. The shipwreck is the result of a sudden storm; the hero is the sole survivor, and survives by clinging to a plank, like Odysseus after his companions had eaten the cattle of the sun (12, 403 f.). The Egyptian was washed up on an island and slept under over-arching bushes like Odysseus when he arrived in Phaeacia (5, 475 f.). The island is a magically rich land ruled by a serpent, who tells him that finally a ship will carry him away laden with presents but the island will vanish in the waves. It is certainly possible that this story, which is dated in the beginning of the second millennium, lies in the far background of our *Odyssey*, and features survive both in Odysseus' first shipwreck and Calypso's island, and in his second rescue from the sea, and his treatment in the magic kingdom of Alkinoos and the subsequent disaster to that kingdom. It has also been suggested that the strange story of Proteus, the king of seals, is an Egyptian story;[2] Proteus is described as an Egyptian, and the paradise which he promises Menelaos has been compared with Egyptian descriptions of the after life. This seems the more likely as Menelaos' other memories of Egypt seem to be early. The mention of 'fair Rhadamanthys' in this paradise may show that the story came through a Cretan intermediary; Odysseus also pretends to be a Cretan when he tells an early story of Egypt.[3] Another possibility which should at least be mentioned is that the light-hearted treatment of the gods in some Egyptian stories[4] may have influenced, for instance, Hera's deception of Zeus in the fourteenth book of the *Iliad* and Demodokos' lay of Ares and Aphrodite in the eighth book of the *Odyssey*.

These Egyptian elements can be added to the other foreign elements which have been detected in our Homer, Phoenician including Ugaritic, Hittite including Hurrian, and behind these Babylonian and Sumerian. In the case of Egypt it is difficult to see how the borrowing could be late. For the others late borrowing is

[1] G. Maspero, *Les Contes populaires de L'Égypte ancienne*, 84 ff. cf. Germain, *op cit.*, 299 ff.; Stella, *op. cit.*, 138 ff.

[2] See Germain, *op. cit.*, 395 f.; Stella, *op. cit.*, 137 f.; *Od.* 4, 385, 561 f.

[3] Cf. above p. 65.

[4] E.g. Re and Isis (*NET*, 12), Horus and Seth (*NET*, 14), Bata and Anubis (*NET*, 23).

possible, but the way in which these elements are used suggests early borrowing. They are deeply embedded in the fabric of the poems; they have been much transmuted and their parts transposed; some of them have been judged to go a long way back in the Greek tradition by scholars who made no suggestion that they were borrowed. The comparatively recent discovery and decipherment particularly of Hittite and Ugaritic texts have shown us what literature was current in this common Eastern Mediterranean civilization of the second millennium and that much, though enriched and transposed, was inherited through Babylon from the older literature of the Sumerians. Sumerian themes were developed in turn by Babylonian, Hurrian, and so by Hittite and Phoenician poets, who could pass them on both through Crete and Cyprus and direct to Mycenaean Greece. Our Homer preserves memories of Egyptians, Hittites, and Phoenicians of this period as well as of Mycenaeans; and therefore if stories were borrowed in the Mycenaean age, they would have survived in poetry like the historical memories, but in the intervening five hundred years or more would have been expanded and mingled with each other in the same sort of way, as for instance the Sumerian poems in their passage through Babylonian and Hurrian to Hittite. This is in fact what we find – transmuted Creation epic, transmuted Gilgamesh, or Athena and Zeus suddenly acting out of character as if they were Anat and Baal.

How much the manner of second-millennium poetry was also transmuted before our Homer is a question which must be reserved for later discussion. We have however established that Homer preserves much of this manner in his noun-epithet formulae, typical scenes, formulae for opening and closing of speeches, refrain lines, etc. They might, of course, be regarded as borrowings as much as the Gilgamesh story and the Creation myth, but it seems to me wise to draw an essential distinction between matter and manner, even if we suspect that elements of manner may have been borrowed with matter. Whatever the Greeks were before they became part of this Eastern Mediterranean civilization, wherever they came from, however they lived, whatever they sang, from the time of the shaft-graves they had courts which were comparable to the courts of the Hittites and the court of Ugarit. From this moment, as I have tried to show, the manner of poetry was an expression of their way of living, of this courtly, military, theocratic society. In many essentials, and probably in all those elements which affected the manner of poetry, there must have been little change between the Sumerians and the Mycenaeans: gods, Kings, and men had their titles; hymns had their refrains; sacrifices, military and other operations were prescribed in a set form of words, which was then used as their adequate description, and the manner of description in essential terms was transferred to other subjects which did not depend on orders; correspondence had its set forms, which were largely adopted as the set forms of speech in poetry. The manner was also peculiarly adapted to the needs of recording in a difficult script and reciting from a difficult script. Whether Mycenaean poetry was recorded we cannot yet say, and we cannot even be certain that the long tablet in Cypro-Minoan contains poetry; but the possibility is there. If the Mycenaeans like their contemporaries had a taste for medium-scale epic – the Gilgamesh epic has been assessed at 1,400 lines and *Baal* at 5,000[1] – they may have needed reciters as well as poets. Some of the subjects of Mycenaean poetry and something of its manner have been suggested by our discussion of Eastern poetry; more detail can be added by a further consideration of the tablets, of archaeology, and of Homer.

[1] Albright, *A.J.A.*, 54 (1950), 164.

4

MYCENAEAN POETRY

We have had already glimpses of Mycenaean poetry from several angles. From the records Mycenaean society appears as a particular variant of Eastern Aegean society, of which clear traces can be seen in the Homeric epic, and these memories must have been handed down in poetry, since this kind of society did not survive the second millennium. Mycenaean art not only shows singers of various different kinds in action but also represents stories which can be identified with Greek stories, and were therefore presumably handed down in poetry to the classical age. Eastern poetry of the second millennium is surprisingly like Homeric poetry in manner and matter: the manner is much more suited to an age of great courts than to an age of small cities, and seems therefore to be a survival in Homer; some of the matter is so deeply embedded in our Homer that it is difficult to believe it was recently borrowed.

To make this picture more precise and detailed (and at the same time to confirm the suggestions already made) we must look again at the tablets, at the archaeological remains, and at Homer. Miss Lorimer in her great book[1] has given a full account of the archaeological remains and related them to Homer; her work will save much discussion of detail here. Something however can be added from later excavations, and we now have the invaluable evidence of the tablets for institutions and language. The general principle must be that elements of Mycenaean civilization in Homer (whether detected by comparing his text with the tablets or with archaeological remains) can only be accepted as evidence of Mycenaean poetry when we have reason to suppose that these elements did not survive the Mycenaean age.

Sometimes Mycenaean memories survive with their terminology demonstrably unchanged; sometimes we cannot say whether the

---

[1] *Homer and the Monuments* (=*HM*), 1950.

terminology has changed or not; often we can say for certain that a
modern passage nevertheless contains Mycenaean elements. This
third type of survival has an interest of its own: where a Mycenaean
memory is enshrined in a Mycenaean formula, we cannot be
certain that its context is also ancient, but a Mycenaean memory in
modern dress has probably only survived as an element in its
context. To give a simple example, the 'silver-studded sword' is
certainly Mycenaean and seems not to have survived into the third
Mycenaean period;[1] the words for 'silver' and 'sword' are certainly found on the tablets and probably also a form of the word
for 'stud';[2] the formula 'silver-studded sword' has therefore survived unchanged from at least the fifteenth century; it is a tiny
piece of Mycenaean poetry, but it fills the end of a line so conveniently that its presence tells us nothing about the date of its
context. The other extreme may be illustrated by Hektor's withdrawal from the battle in the sixth book of the *Iliad*[3] 'the black
hide beat upon his neck and ankles'; only the early Mycenaean
body-shield could do this, and the line is unique, so that it seems
to be a memory of an incident connected with Hektor; a later poet,
who did not visualize the scene, added the next line 'the rim
which ran round the outside of the bossed shield'. We shall have
to keep these extremes in mind as we consider the various kinds
of evidence at our disposal: metre, language, style, subject-matter.
If it is then possible to associate Mycenaean characteristics and
stories with particular heroes and gods, we can consider further
their relation to the names in the tablets, to the known Mycenaean
sites, and to the history of the second millennium. We may then
be able to form some picture of Mycenaean poets in Mycenaean
palaces.

The metre of contemporary Eastern epic seems to have been
measured by stress rather than quantity, and there is no reason to
suppose that the hexameter itself, let alone the elaborate rules
observed by Homer, are a legacy from the Mycenaean age. But
the headings of three tablets[4] containing orders can be scanned in
double short rhythm, two as paroemiacs (a very ancient Greek
metre as the fact that it was used for proverbs shows) and one as a
pendant hemiepes; as more is learnt of Mycenaean Greek, more
examples may be found, and metrical beginnings to operation

[1] *HM*, 273. [2] *Docs.* 347. [3] *Il.* 6, 117f.
[4] KN Og 0467; PY An 1, 35.

92

orders may prove to have been the rule. At least these certain
examples show how easily Mycenaean Greek with its uncontracted
vowels could be adapted to double short rhythm whether
anapaestic or dactylic.

The tablets give valuable evidence of the grammatical forms
and language of the Mycenaean age. The most interesting of the
grammatical forms are the genitives in -*oio*, -*ao*, -*aon*, the ending
-*phi* as an instrumental, sociative, and locative case in the plural,
the use of the dative-locative case with the prepositions ἐκ and ἀπό,
the writing of the digamma, and the avoidance of vowel contractions. Often Homer keeps to Mycenaean practice in these
respects, and this adherence proves that the tradition behind his
poetry leads back to the Mycenaean age; where Mycenaean practice
is extended, modified, or disregarded, we can be certain that we are
dealing with post-Mycenaean phraseology, and this will help us
to distinguish the usage of post-Mycenaean poets. The converse
that a Mycenaean form indicates a Mycenaean word or phrase is
not always true; the genitives and the ending in -*phi*[1] (which was
later extended from the plural to the singular) were often metrically convenient and easy to forge. Often however the combination
of a Mycenaean form with Mycenaean subject-matter points to a
surviving fragment of Mycenaean poetry.

A similar restriction must be applied to vocabulary. Mycenaean
words which survived in ordinary use are of no interest to us,
since we cannot tell when they came into poetry; thus to know,
as we now do, that the Greek word for gold was borrowed from
the East in the Mycenaean period does not help us, because gold
continued to be called *chrysos*. The tablets show that much of the
terminology for textiles and agriculture remained unchanged; but
they also give the words for certain luxury articles and weapons,
and for certain forms of military and social organization which
we have no reason to suppose survived the Mycenaean age; where
these recur in Homer, it is justifiable to speak of survivals from
Mycenaean poetry. These will be considered later in connexion
with formulae and subject-matter. Before the tablets had been
deciphered, a group of words common to Homer, and to either
the Arcadian or the Cypriote dialects or both were regarded as
good evidence for Mycenaean poetic vocabulary, but few of them
tell us much about early poetry except *wanax*, which is now

[1] On -*phi* see now Lejeune, *B.S.L.*, 52 (1956), 187.

attested on the tablets.[1] To be safe, we must know not only that a word is Mycenaean but that what it describes went out of use after the Mycenaean age.

A major study of Homeric language was published a couple of years before the tablets were deciphered, Manu Leumann's *Homerische Wörter*. A number of strange Homeric usages are there explained as misunderstandings by later poets of the work of earlier poets. These misunderstandings are of various kinds, and it is now possible to date some of them. To start with a simple instance,[2] the later developments of γλαῦκος 'grey-blue etc.', βλοσυρός 'fierce etc.' are developments from old cult expressions γλαυκῶπις Ἀθήνη, Γόργω βλοσυρῶπις – 'owl-faced' and 'vulture-faced' (to which Leumann adds βοῶπις πότνια Ἥρη 'cow-faced'). Now that we know that the Mycenaeans spoke Greek we can associate the first two words with the bird appearances of Mycenaean goddesses of which we have spoken. The masculine form of -opis is -ops and recurs in several Mycenaean names like Aithiops; and Glaukos, which Leumann regards as a shortened form derived from *Glaukopis*, already appears as a name in Pylos. We are therefore justified in regarding these 'old cult expressions' as reaching our Homer from Mycenaean poetry.

Two phrases can be dated by military practice. In strangely archaic lines[3] Hektor says: ' I can wield to the right, I can wield to the left my dry cow. That for me is shield warfare.' Leumann rightly says that Hektor emphasizes his technique of mobile defence against Ajax' more static method with his body-shield, and regards this as the original use of the formula 'shield warfare', from which he traces several later passages. Hektor is here giving the new tactics of the hand-grip shield, which had been introduced at least by the time of the Warrior vase[4] (fig. 7). Such a statement is likely to come when the tactics were new; this with the strangely archaic βῶν and ταλάϝρινον seems to fix the passage as Mycenaean rather than later. Leumann also traces the later sense of κορύσσειν 'stir up' from the original κεκορυθμένος αἴθοπι χαλκῷ, 'helmeted with bright bronze'. This is originally a longer expression which is a metrically convenient variant for the short κορυθαίολος

[1] Cf. particularly C. M. Bowra, *C.Q.*, 20 (1926), 166f.; *J.H.S.*, 54 (1934), 54f.; M. Leumann, *Homerische Wörter*, 262ff.; P. Chantraine, *R.P.*, 26 (1953), 60; C. J. Ruijgh, *L'Élément Achéen dans la langue épique*.

[2] Leumann, *op. cit.*, 141f.   [3] *Il.* 7, 238f.; Leumann, 196f.

[4] Cf. above p. 38, n. 3; Lorimer, *HM*, 186.

῞Εκτωρ 'bright helmeted Hektor'; yet another metrical variant is χαλκοκορυστής, 'bronze helmeted'. Bronze helmets are Mycenaean and not likely to have been common again until late in the eighth century; κόρυς is the word for helmet on the tablets, and αἴολος occurs in Knossos as the name of an ox. 'Bright helmeted Hektor' can therefore safely be accepted as a fragment of Mycenaean poetry. We shall return later to the general question of Mycenaean military terms and the possibility of associating them with particular heroes.

Many of the misunderstandings which Leumann has detected are due to faulty division of words. It is worth considering whether any sort of chronology can be established for these faulty divisions and whether they tell us anything about the history of poetry. Where Leumann has been able to establish a considerable chain of descendants, the earliest and correct use cannot be very modern. Thus he believes[1] that on an original ταλάφρων 'courageous' was formed ἀταλάφρων 'cowardly', which is applied to the child Astyanax. It came to mean not so much 'cowardly' as 'childish' and on it was moulded ἀταλαφρονέων in this sense. This was then divided as ἀταλὰ φρονέων, and in this form is used of the girls and boys carrying the grapes on the shield of Achilles, dancing as they go. By this time ἀταλός had become a word on its own ('tender' or 'skittish'), and on it were formed the verbs ἀτάλλειν 'gambol' and ἀτιτάλλειν 'bring up', which both occur in our *Iliad*. Leumann believes that the inscription on the Attic Geometric jug[2] from the Dipylon cemetery, which should probably be dated soon after 750, ἀταλώτατα παίζει 'sports most skittishly' is directly inspired by the use of the word in the Homeric shield of Achilles. I see no need for that, and doubt whether the *Iliad* was known in Attica so early. I prefer to suppose that ἀταλός had already reached the stage of meaning 'skittish' before the Ionian migration, since in any case some time must be allowed for the two verbs to develop from it before the date of our *Iliad*. Another long series leads from δηιοτῆτος to ἕκητι.[3] Δηιοτῆτος 'hostility' was falsely divided as

---

[1] Leumann, 139f. on *Il*. 6, 400; 18, 567–72. Cf. however Ruijgh, *op. cit.*, 109.

[2] Athens, N. M. 192: Furtwängler *A.M.*, 6 (1881), 106, pl. 3. Full references are given in *B.S.A.*, 50 (1955), 39.

[3] Leumann, 127f.

δὴ ἰοτῆτος 'then from ill will'; the new word was declined to produce a dative ἰοτῆτι and the meaning changed from 'ill will' to 'will'; on the analogy of this the contrasting ἀέκητι 'against the will' was formed, and finally on this again ἕκητι 'in accordance with the will'. Clearly this took some time; yet one point suggests that this false division was not made before the hexameter was well developed. Hermann Fränkel's[1] work on the Homeric hexameter seems to show that the rules for coincidence of word endings and metrical pauses grew stricter. If the false division took place in a line like *Iliad* 12, 248: εἰ δέ σν δηιοτῆτος, the singer broke his line at the popular place after the first syllable of the second foot instead of at the equally popular place at the end of the first foot. It may be that these pauses were already established as desirable a century or so before our *Iliad*. The influence of a popular metrical pause may have assisted another wrong division: our manuscripts give in the ninth book of the *Iliad* (64) (πολέμον) ἐπιδημίον ὀκρυόεντος. Elsewhere in the *Iliad* κρυόεις 'bloody' is used of fight and battle, and Hesiod uses it of war (πόλεμος). The strange form ὀκρυόεις is used again of Helen in the sixth book of the *Iliad* (344) and later in poetry dependent on Homer. In the pre-migration period the Mycenaean genitive ἐπιδημίοιο had changed to ἐπιδημίοο, and thus ἐπιδημίοο κρυόεντος became a good verse end. In the post-migration period the genitive contracted to ἐπιδημίον; this change coupled with the desire for the popular break after the fourth foot, led swiftly to the new form ἐπιδημίον ὀκρυόεντος and established ὀκρυόεις as a poetic word well before the time of our *Iliad*, where it is misappropriated to Helen. Another kind of wrong division (if a failure to divide can be so called) may be earlier than the last example. Leumann quotes several instances where a new compound word has been made by combining a preposition used as an adverb with the word after it. Greek prepositions were in origin adverbs. On the Mycenaean tablets *paro* and *meta* are already used as prepositions, but *hypo* is still used as an adverb and *epi* (*o-pi*) apparently as both adverb and preposition; compound verbs and adjectives were already freely formed. It is interesting that one of the lines which Leumann[2] regards as a starting-point for a new word of this kind occurs in a Mycenaean context. Aeneas and Pandaros are setting out on Aeneas' chariot; Aeneas urges that they should attack

---

[1] *Wege und Formen*, 117f. [2] *Il.* 5, 220; Leumann, 206; *Docs.* 90, 411.

Diomede 'with horses and chariot' (the plural sociative in *-phi* is Mycenaean), and 'make trial, going in opposition (ἀντί), of his strength' (βίην). But in our manuscripts ἀντιβίην appears as a single word, and it must be so taken (with the sense of 'violently') in several passages; from this was formed a new adjective ἀντίβιος, and from this again an adjective ἐναντίβιος. All this development had taken place by the time of our *Iliad*.

The starting-points of the various Leumann series which we have examined can be arranged in a rough chronological order: *Mycenaean*, owl-faced Athena etc., bright-helmed Hektor, shield warfare; *Pre-migration*, ἀντὶ βίην, ἀταλαφρονέοντες, probably also δηιοτῆτος; *Post-migration*, ὀκρυόεις. The reason for establishing this sequence at some length is first to provide further evidence that Homer belongs to a poetic tradition going back to the Mycenaean age. Secondly, a new point has hereby become clear. What we have called 'wrong division' occurs already in the pre-migration period. It cannot therefore be due to miscopying texts written in alphabetic script without word division, since the alphabetic script was surely not introduced so early (and some of the earliest alphabetic inscriptions have word dividers). Similarly, wrong division of this kind could not be caused by copying Mycenaean texts, by reciting from Mycenaean texts, or by dictating to Mycenaean scribes, because Mycenaean scribes in the vast majority of cases used word dividers. It must therefore be due to mishearing; a young oral poet misinterprets an older poet's rendering. This seems to me the clearest evidence that we have, other than analogy, for a purely oral tradition in post-Mycenaean poetry.

Our study of Mycenaean poetry (to which we can now return) has already taken us beyond the single word to the formula: silver-studded sword, owl-faced Athena, bright-helmed Hektor. Before going further we may ask whether the tablets themselves show any formulae which may have been taken over into contemporary poetry. Some of these have been noted above in the discussion of Eastern poetry. The refrain technique – the repetition of lines to mark corresponding stages in the narrative – was there traced to refrains in cult songs. Cult songs have been lost; in their place we have to be satisfied with the ritual text from Pylos[1] in which offerings are brought to different divinities at different shrines. We can imagine that, in a society accustomed to

---

[1] Tn 316; cf. above p. 73.

orders and reports in this form, poets would naturally use refrains and typical scenes.

The series of six tablets[1] giving orders for coastal defence has also been mentioned. They give us first the official titles of the nobles of Pylos, secondly a military formula, and thirdly the form of a military operation order. Each section ends 'and with them the Count MN'. It is significant that the formulae which Homer uses for Nestor touch these titles at three points. The Counts of Pylos are called either by proper name and family name (e.g. Alektryon the Eteoklean)[2] or proper name and ethnic (e.g. Kaesamenos the Ampukan). The second type is rare in Homer and I only remember, besides 'Gerenian Knight Nestor', 'Eurybates the Ithacan' and 'Argive Helen'. The first type is commoner: Nestor (and Antilochos) the Neleian, Ajax (and Teucer) the Telamonian. Sthenelos the Kapaneian son, Philoktetes the Poiantian son, and Tityos the Gaieian son are made on the same model, and we may compare Homer's 'Aigialeia, wise Adrastine' (herself paralleled by Marpessa Euenine) with the tablets' Di-ko-na-ro the Adrastan. The much commoner form of patronymic in -ides or -ades is not found on the tablets, but is certainly pre-migration in date. The adjectival and ethnic forms are therefore clear cases of Mycenaean titles taken over into poetry. But Count itself may also have left a legacy in poetry. The interpretation of the Mycenaean word e-qe-ta as ἐπέτης is undoubted, and it means companion or Count. Homer has a strange word *hippota* which is only used as a title, notably with Peleus, Nestor, Tydeus, and Oineus. To him writing when cavalry was just beginning to become important in Ionia it meant knight, but in Mycenaean times it must have meant horse owner in the sense of chariot owner, and have had the form *i-qo-ta*, which is a telescoped form of *i-qo-po-ta*.[3] I suggest that, as the Counts were the élite of the chariotry, their title e-qe-ta became transformed into *hippota*, and was handed down in this guise, so that 'Gerenian Knight Nestor' is in fact 'Gerenian Count Nestor'.

When Ventris knew only one of the coastal defence tablets and had not yet established that the middle third person singular of the verb in Mycenaean was -toi and not -tai, he took e-qe-ta as

---

[1] PY An 657, etc., *Docs.* 188 f.; cf. above pp. 21, 73.

[2] Compare the Homeric βίη 'Ετεοκληείη, etc.

[3] Schwyzer, *Gr. Gr.*, I, 499, n. 6.

a verb (ἕπεται instead of the noun ἐπέτης) and compared the Homeric line 'and with them followed (εἶπετ') swift-footed Achilles'.[1] There is however still no reason why 'and with them followed' should not be a very old military formula. But the formulation of the coastal defence tablets opens a much bigger question than that. Whether we accept Palmer's interpretation of o-ka as 'command' (in which case the Homeric ὄρχαμε λαῶν 'commander of troops' is likely to be a Mycenaean survival) or Mühlestein's as 'ship', we have an operation order, of which a heading and ten sections in common form survive: 'Command (or ship) of X at Y', then names of chariot owners, then numbers of infantrymen, 'and with them Count MN'. If we then turn to the Catalogue of Ships in the second book of the *Iliad*, we find that although there are many variations for special reasons, some later accretions, some adaptation of phrasing for metrical reasons, the common form which underlies all the sections is 'All that dwelt in Y, Z, etc., them led A, and with him followed *n* ships.' We can easily imagine that for a major expedition Mycenae would receive from Pylos a tablet (or papyrus) consolidating detailed information, such as is given by the coastal defence tablets, in the form: 'From Pylos, etc. etc. So many charioteers, so many foot soldiers, and with them the Count Nestor the Neleian, and with them follow ninety ships.' With the coastal defence tablets before us and the roughly contemporary naval tablet from Ugarit (noted above) it is difficult to deny that the Catalogue of Ships may go back to an actual operation order, which was absorbed into Mycenaean poetry.

One other rather curious stylistic analogy exists between the tablets and Homer. A typical chariot tablet from Knossos[2] reads '2 chariots inlaid with ivory, assembled, crimson, fitted with bridles with leather cheekstraps, horn bits'. Ventris compared the syntax to an auctioneer's catalogue, but it appears occasionally in Homer:[3] the slaves prepare for Nausikaa a 'wagon, high, well-wheeled, fitted with a basket', and Kalypso gave Odysseus an 'axe, big, fitted to the hands, of bronze, sharpened on both sides, but in it a handle, very fine, of olive wood, fitting well'. This is a

---

[1] *Il.* 18, 234.

[2] KN Sd 0401, *Docs.* no. 266, cf. the furniture tablets, *Docs.* nos. 243 ff.

[3] *Od.* 6, 69; 5, 234, cf. 10, 314 Circe's chair; *Il.* 13, 611 Peisander's mace; 16, 131 greaves.

way of describing which proceeds from the whole object to its
parts, adding the parts on in a string of words in apposition. It is
an efficient style but unpoetical, and I think it may have entered
Mycenaean poetry from the tablets, and survives in descriptions,
which did their job efficiently but did not particularly interest the
poet. He is much more interested in Penelope's couch than in
Circe's chair, and there he has partly expanded, partly woven the
Mycenaean description into the narrative.[1]

In the first chapter I sketched the outlines of Mycenaean society
as we can reconstruct it from the tablets and from parallels in
contemporary Near Eastern societies. The divine or near divine
King lived in his palace surrounded by beautiful objects and served
by a multitude of slaves. He had his counts, and there was a wider
circle of nobility owning land from the King, which was worked
by their tenants; some of them formed the chariotry, and some
were mayors of towns and villages, responsible for the craftsmen
and land workers of their districts. After death the King lived on
in a royal tomb. All grades of society were held together by the
services which they paid directly or indirectly to the palace: this
is the element which justifies the use of the word 'feudal' to
describe the system. With the destruction of the great palaces the
whole system vanished and was only known to Homer through
its survival in poetry. This general picture is true of the whole
Mycenaean period, but some Mycenaean weapons and some pieces
of armour can be dated early or late. Chariot fighting, bronze
helmets, and thrusting-spears belong to the whole period and
do not survive after it; silver-studded rapiers, body-shields, and
boar's tusk helmets are early, but body-shields and boar's tusk
helmets survived, I believe, in art to characterize gods and past
heroes. In the late Mycenaean period the body-shield was replaced
by the single-grip shield, by the metal corselet or armoured shirt,
and by greaves. The single-grip shield alone survived through the
pre-migration period to Homer's own time; metal helmet,
corselet, and greaves disappeared before leather helmet, jerkin,
and leggings, single thrusting-spear before twin throwing-spears,
bronze sword before iron sword. Whether archers also survived
seems extremely doubtful; we have already noted their prominence in Mycenaean art. Mycenaean objects and institutions in
Homer are evidence of Mycenaean poetry. Where his terminology

[1] *Od.* 19, 55 f.; cf. below p. 111.

coincides with the tablets, we have not only the subjects but also the language of Mycenaean poetry. As we examine these survivals, we must consider how far they can be associated with particular heroes, and how far they are fossilized survivals, retained or introduced where the poet found them metrically convenient.

I start with weapons and fighting where there is some possibility of distinguishing between early and late Mycenaean. The 'silver-studded sword', as we have seen, is a formula which tells us nothing about its possessors. The 'slender edged sword' is a similar fossil describing the early rapier. The boar's tusk helmet occurs only once but is very carefully described;[1] it has a pedigree and is finally lent by Meriones to Odysseus; this, however much remodelled, is a very old description of a royal gift, owned, interestingly enough, by the Cretan Meriones. The body-shield is worn by Hektor when he goes back to Troy, as we have noted;[2] there it is brought up to date by an encircling rim. In another place[3] he is described as edging forward under the shield, which sounds like body-shield tactics; and a little later[4] his opponent Periphetes of Mycenae trips over the edge of his shield, which 'stretched to his feet'. Hektor seems therefore to go back to the early Mycenaean period. The same is true of Ajax. Unlike the 'silver-studded sword', the 'shield like a tower' is never given to any hero but Ajax, and he has it three times.[5] In one passage his companions were ready 'to take his shield when weariness and sweat assailed his knees';[6] this implies the body-shield, and Miss Lorimer points out that when Hektor's spear is diverted by the crossing of two straps on Ajax' chest, one from his shield, one from his sword, Ajax must be wearing the body-shield because it alone is slung from the left shoulder.[7] Besides the Cretan Meriones with his early boar's tusk helmet, perhaps we may also claim the Cretan son of Kastor (the name is found on the Knossos tablets) as early Mycenaean because of his body-shield; at any rate when he tricks Thoas out of his cloak, he is only wearing shield and loincloth, and the shields cover the party's shoulders as they sleep.[8] The body-shield had an adjective, 'man protecting', ἀμφιβροτήν,

---

[1] *Il.* 10, 261; Lorimer, *HM*, 212; cf. above p. 27.   [2] *Il.* 6, 117.
[3] *Il.* 13, 806, cf. 16, 609 (Meriones); 13, 158 (Deiphobos).
[4] *Il.* 15, 645.   [5] *Il.* 7, 219; 11, 485; 17, 128. Lorimer, *HM*, 181 f.
[6] *Il.* 13, 710   [7] *Il.* 14, 403, cf. 16, 106.   [8] *Od.* 14, 482.

but this survives as a metrically convenient fossil and tells us nothing of its users.

Ajax and Hektor were however brought up to date later and given hand-grip shields. Hektor's statement of the new tactics should, as we have seen, be soon after the change and therefore late Mycenaean rather than pre-migration. For Ajax' shield with a boss on the middle and for the warriors who hold their shields away from them to parry blows we cannot name a date.[1] The pointed boss of this shield could be used offensively and so this shield also had its adjective, 'violent', θοῦρις. With the small, hand-grip shield corselets and greaves were necessary, and corselets and greaves of metal seem not to have survived the Mycenaean age. Bronze greaves are not important, although we can now say that they were known in the Mycenaean age, and so may have given rise to the formal epithet 'well-greaved' and the line in arming scenes about 'fair greaves fitted with silver ankle clasps'.[2] Corselets of three types gave rise to three stock phrases: 'bronze-shirted', 'daedal corselet', 'plate of the corselet', χαλκοχίτωνες, θώρηκος πολυδαιδάλου (the use of this formula in the genitive cannot be earlier than the pre-migration period, because the -oio genitive is impossible in verse, but the nominative could be Mycenaean), θώρηκος γύαλον. All three types can be found on the tablets. The first is the armoured shirt: a Knossos tablet,[3] headed 'fine linen', includes 'shirt, 1 kg. of bronze . . . shirt adornments (e-pi-ki-to-ni-ja), 1 kg. of bronze'. I take the bronze to be made into disks for sewing on the shirts, and the wearer could then be called 'bronze-shirted'. The second is the band corselet. The word, thorex, is found on the Pylos tablets, and both at Pylos and at Knossos an ideogram is used for corselet which shows horizontal bands.[4] This looks very like the Eastern corselet which Miss Lorimer adduced for the special corselet with its 'paths' of kyanos, gold, and tin, presented to Agamemnon by Kinyras of Cyprus. The word 'paths' is similarly used of ivory bands on a chariot at Knossos.[5] Kyanos here also points towards the Mycenaean age, when it was used for inlay in precious furniture. Such

[1] Il. 7, 267; 13, 163; 20, 163, 261.
[2] H. W. Catling, Op. Ath., 2 (1955), 21 f.; B.C.H., 78 (1954), 125 (Patras).
[3] KN J 693. Cf. however Docs. 320.
[4] Discussion and tablets, Docs. 375 f.
[5] Il. 11, 19 f.; Dussaud, A.S., 6 (1956), 63; Docs. no. 276; Lorimer, HM, 197, 208.

a many-coloured corselet is the model for the stock phrase 'daedal corselet'. Achilles' 'variegated starry corselet' may have been of the same type.[1] The Knossos tablets also have a second corselet ideogram without bands but surcharged *qe*; the full word *qe-ro₂* occurs alongside a bronze object, which looks like a corselet, and in conjunction with helmet adornments and helmets.[2] I think it is probable that this second type of corselet is the lobster corselet and that the word *qe-ro₂* developed into γύαλον of the stock phrase. Homer preserves the memory of two special corselets of this type: one belongs to Meges of Doulichion, given to him by his father Phyleus, who had received it as a present from Euphetes of Ephyra,[3] the other to Asteropaios, the ambidextrous spearman who was killed by Achilles.[4] Agamemnon, Achilles, Meges, and Asteropaios can be added as late Mycenaean warriors to the earlier Ajax and Hektor.

'Bright-helmed Hektor' has been noted above as a Mycenaean formula for a Mycenaean hero. No other metal helmet is individual, but a number of phrases connected with helmets may be traditional. Metal helmets are now well attested for the Mycenaean age, and the Mycenaean word κόρυς is the commonest Homeric word for helmet.[5] Chariot fighting is attested by the monuments from the shaft-graves to the latest frescoes; we have also noted a Mycenaean formula 'with horses and chariots'. The Knossos tablets record over 400 chariots in various states of assembly and over 500 pairs of wheels,[6] and the Pylos tablets over 160 pairs of wheels. The terminology of chariots has changed before Homer, and the chariot which Homer knows himself is the light racing chariot. But the decorated chariots of Mycenaean times – we can add to the Knossos chariot inlaid with ivory wheels from Pylos with ivory rims and others bound with silver and bound with bronze[7] – are remembered in the metal adornments which decorate the chariots of Agamemnon, Achilles, Rhesos, and Diomede.[8] The epithet *hippiocharmes* (chariot-fighter), which is applied to Troilos in the *Iliad* and to Amythaon (a name found on the Pylos tablets) in the *Odyssey*, has been recognized as derived from the Mycenaean word for chariot.[9] Nestor, instructing his chariots to

---

[1] *Il.* 16, 130.   [2] *Docs.* 380.   [3] *Il.* 15, 529.   [4] *Il.* 23, 560.
[5] See discussion *Docs.* 376f.; D. H. F. Gray, *CQ*, 41 (1947), 114f.
[6] *Docs.* 365, 371.   [7] *Docs.* 374f.   [8] *Il.* 4, 226; 10, 322, 438; 23, 503.
[9] *Od.* 11, 259; Mühlestein, *Mus. Helv.*, 12 (1955), 123.

keep their line as they advance, says that 'so the men of old used to sack cities and forts', and his own youthful battle against the Epeians was a chariot battle.[1] Agamemnon also is thinking of chariot fighting when he tells his men to whet their spears, prepare their shields, feed their horses, and look to their chariots.[2] Hektor prides himself on his grim deeds with spear and horsemanship, and more than once orders a chariot charge against the Greeks.[3] Although the chariot is normally used for transporting heroes from place to place, Homer also remembers Mycenaean chariot fighting, and the weapon is the thrusting-spear.

The thrusting spear is also used in many battles fought on foot. Plenty of traditional formulae are used in these battles, and both the noun ἔγχος and the adjective χαλκήρης are found on the Knossos tablets. The line used in arming scenes 'he took the valiant spear which fitted in his hands' has the Mycenaean word for spear and the Mycenaean plural locative -phi for 'in his hands'.[4] Two heroes have special spears: Achilles and Hektor. Achilles has an ashen spear, which the Centaur Cheiron gave Peleus from the peak of Pelion; Hektor has an eleven-cubit spear with a golden collar, for which the only evidence quoted by Miss Lorimer is a sixteenth-century example from Egypt inlaid with a Minoan design.[5]

The last Mycenaean weapon which need be mentioned is the bow. Both in Knossos and Pylos tablets record large quantities of arrows; a list from Pylos gives five bowmakers and Toxotas (archer) is a name in Knossos. We have also seen that the archer is represented in Mycenaean siege scenes.[6] Arrowheads have recently been found in quantity in a royal tomb at Pylos of the early Mycenaean period, as well as at Knossos, but according to Miss Lorimer[7] the pre-migration period is 'an all but total blank'; she then adduces Attic Geometric vases of the eighth century, but these, as we shall find, are evidence for pre-migration poetry, not for post-migration fighting. So in fact archery seems to have been far more important in Mycenaean times than later; and the great archers of Homer are likely to be Mycenaean heroes, remembered in poetry. They are Herakles, Eurytos, Iphitos, Odysseus,

[1] *Il.* 4, 300f.; 11, 742f. [2] *Il.* 2, 382f.
[3] *Il.* 11, 502; cf. 289; 15, 346; 16, 833.
[4] *Il.* 3, 338, remodelled for two throwing-spears in 16, 139.
[5] *Il.* 16, 140f.; 6, 319; *HM*, 260.
[6] Cf. above pp. 21, 58; PY An 207; KN X 7624; *Docs.* 302, 357, 361.
[7] *HM*, 280; Marinatos, *das Altertum*, 1 (1955), 140f.

Meriones, Teucer, Philoktetes, Pandaros, and Paris. There are two famous bows:[1] Odysseus' bow, which was a present from Iphitos, son of Eurytos, and the bow of Pandaros. Pandaros' arrowhead is of iron and the axes which are used for the archery contest in the *Odyssey* are of iron;[2] but the latter are certainly precious iron[3] since they come from the king's treasury, and the former is probably the same. Here again is a Mycenaean echo.

War service is part of feudal service, but special services may raise a great warrior near the status of the King. Our Homer knows the story of the oath sworn by Helen's suitors to avenge any attempt to remove her from her husband. This story however both presupposes her removal by Paris, and can only have been invented when feudal allegiance to Agamemnon no longer seemed a satisfactory reason for the assembling of the Greek army. Nevertheless the terms in which the heroes speak of their engagement are equally applicable to feudal service: 'exacting payment for Menelaos and you',[4] 'the undertaking which I made'.[5] Homer remembers two individual cases from the Peloponnese: Euchenor of Corinth went to Troy to avoid 'the painful fine of the Achaeans' and Echepolos of Sikyon gave Agamemnon a mare 'that he might not go with him to windy Troy'.[6] The relation between Agamemnon and the Kings is repeated between the individual Kings and their nobles and even between these nobles and their dependents. Thus Achilles can demand the military service of one of the seven sons of the Myrmidon Polyktor.[7] One of the words on the Knossos tablets for feudal dues is *opa*. In the *Iliad* it is used once of Phoinix and five times of the Cretans.[8] The Cretan Meriones, the owner of the boar's tusk helmet and regularly described as 'the equal of the murderous Enyalios' (the Cretan war god attested on the tablets), is the *opawon* of Idomeneus and himself has Koiranos as his *opawon* and charioteer. Phoinix is described as the *opawon* of Peleus, who had made him King of the Dolopes and given him many soldiers to pay *opa* to him.

For special services the great warrior like the King may be 'honoured as a god'. Sometimes he is given a *temenos* like the

---

[1] *Od.* 21, 11; *Il.* 4, 105 f.   [2] *Il.* 4, 123; *Od.* 21, 81.
[3] Cf. D. F. H. Gray, *J.H.S.*, 74 (1954), 1 f.
[4] *Il.* 1, 159, cf. *Od.* 14, 70.   [5] *Il.* 2, 286, cf. 4, 267.
[6] *Il.* 13, 669; 23, 297.   [7] *Il.* 24, 396 f.
[8] Cf. above p. 14; Meriones: *Il.* 7, 165; 17, 610. Phoinix: *Il.* 23, 360; 9, 483 (cf. *C. & M.*, 17 (1956), 156).

Commander of the Army in Pylos, whose name we unfortunately do not know.[1] The *temenos* is special land, otherwise only owned by gods and Kings, and implies divine status. Among those who possess or are promised a *temenos* in Homer, Bellerophon, Meleager, Glaukos, and Aeneas have received it or hope to receive it for military services.[2] Meleager, like Hektor whose military services also bring him divine honours,[3] is the son of the King, and the son of the King may often have been the Commander of the Army. But Bellerophon is a brilliant outsider, and it is as brilliant outsiders that Menelaos and Agamemnon hope to settle Odysseus and Achilles in their respective kingdoms.[4] The gift of a city or cities, as we have seen, corresponds to Eastern practice in the second millennium. The seven cities offered to Achilles by Agamemnon are inhabited by men rich in flocks and herds, who will honour Achilles with gifts as if he were a god and 'beneath his sceptre pay their shining dues'. The word for 'dues', *themis*, is only used here in this sense but is found with the same meaning on Knossos tablets; 'shining' suggests that olive-oil was one of the dues as at Knossos.[5] The passage has preserved a very clear Mycenaean memory.

The two other definable classes who are honoured as a god in Homer are priests and Kings. On a Knossos tablet[6] the priestess of the Winds is recorded with the Diktaian Zeus, the Daidaleion, Teiresias, and All the Gods as receiving an allotment of oil, and on a Pylos tablet[7] Drimios, priest of Zeus, is recorded with Zeus and Hera as receiving a gold bowl at the shrine of Zeus. So in the *Iliad* Dolopion, the priest of Skamander, and Onetor, the priest of Idaean Zeus, were both 'honoured as a god', and it may be relevant to note that in the *Odyssey* Maron, priest of Apollo, dwelt in the wooded grove of Apollo.[8] Both at Knossos and at Pylos the tablets just quoted give evidence for a number of shrines at a number of different places, which were at least able to house offerings, and the title 'key-bearer' itself implies a shrine; it occurs several times at Pylos, and is in Homer's mind when he speaks of Theano opening the doors of Athena's temple at Troy.[9] Chadwick[10]

---

[1] Cf. above p. 11.

[2] *Il.* 6, 194; 9, 578; 12, 310; 20, 184.

[3] E.g. *Il.* 22, 394, 433.

[4] *Od.* 4, 174; *Il.* 9, 149 ff.

[5] Cf. *C. & M.*, 17 (1956), 155; KN, As 821, Fh 339.

[6] KN Fp series; *Docs.* 303 f.

[7] PY Tn 316; *Docs.* 284 f.

[8] *Il.* 5, 78; 16, 605; *Od.* 9, 198.

[9] *Il.* 6, 298.

[10] *Docs.* 358.

has suggested that the *ka-ko na-wi-jo* of a Pylos tablet is not
'bronze for ships' but 'bronze from temples', and if this is right,
each of the sixteen communities of Pylos had its temple. It seems
clear that the Mycenaean age had both shrines in the palace and
shrines outside the palace. After the Mycenaean age the great
palaces no longer existed and the divinity no longer dwelt with the
ruler, who was for this reason also no longer divine. Thus while
we can only sometimes say that a temple mentioned in Homer is
not Mycenaean, we can be certain, as Nilsson saw long ago, that
when Athena enters the house of Erechtheus she is behaving as a
Mycenaean goddess would.[1] Pfeiffer[2] has recently argued that the
golden lamp, with which Athena lights Odysseus and Telemachos
while they remove their arms, has nothing to do with ordinary
lamps, but is the lamp which Athena, and only Athena among the
Olympians, traditionally has, and that it was kept in the Mycenaean
palace of Athens. The golden lamp of the Erechtheum can be
accepted as a Mycenaean memory, but our Homer remembered it
here only because he was used to portable lamps; we have enough
evidence to show that the Greeks never forgot the use of portable
lamps between the Mycenaean age and their common appearance
in the seventh century.[3]

The palace of Erechtheus with its golden lamp is a special case
of the relationship between a Mycenaean divinity and a Mycenaean
ruler, whose own divinity or near divinity is attested by the words
wanax and *temenos*. The word *wanax* and its derivatives are common enough in Homer, and sometimes they mean little more than
noble. Generally however he applies them to rulers who would
have been Kings in the Mycenaean age, and two uses are interesting here. Agamemnon is 'King of men'; the title is not unique
but is given also to Augeas, Anchises, Aeneas, Euphetes, Eumelos;
they only have it once each but Agamemnon has it continually;
it is his label and he is 'King of men' just as Achilles is 'fleet-
footed' and Hektor 'bright-helmed'. It is therefore fair to regard
this as a title remembered from Mycenaean poetry and particularly
connected with Agamemnon. The second use concerns Alkinoos;

[1] *Od.* 7, 81; Nilsson, *MMR.* 488; *Homer and Mycenae*, 212.

[2] *S.I.F.C.*, 27/8 (1956), 426 on *Od.* 19, 34.

[3] Mycenaean and Sub-Mycenaean: Persson, *New Tombs at Dendra*, 108.
Protogeometric: Desborough, *B.S.A.*, 51 (1956), 130. Geometric: E. Gjerstad,
Op. Arch., 4, 19; S. Benton, *B.S.A.*, 48 (1953), 329.

wherever Phaeacia is to be located in space, there is no doubt that he is a Mycenaean King. 'He was King over all the Phaeacians', and 'twelve noble kings (*basilewes*) are rulers in the land, and I am the thirteenth'.[1] This relationship between the King and his kings can be paralleled in Mycenaean Pylos as we have seen.[2] Alkinoos also has a wife whom 'the populace address like a god when they see her' (the title *wanassa* seems to have been known in Pylos), and 'he tipples like an immortal on his throne', which reminds us of the royal thrones at Knossos and Pylos (fig. 8); his *temenos* is close to, if not actually in, the 'lovely grove of Athena'.[3]

The phrases 'like a god', 'like an immortal' are proved to be pre-migration by the maintenance of the digamma, and pre-migration in these instances presumably means Mycenaean. There is no reason why the other phrases for god-like should not have been made at the same time, but our Homer sometimes suppresses the digamma and admits contracted terminations in oblique cases. More particularly Homer has a group of phrases connected with Zeus and a group of phrases connected with Ares. Besides 'Zeus born, Zeus nurtured, dear to Zeus' (noted above)[4] there is 'equal to Zeus in council' and the simple δῖος, which is translated 'godly' but meant originally 'belonging to Zeus'.[5] Two special passages[6] must be mentioned: Tyro bore Pelias and Neleus to Poseidon, and 'they both became strong servants of great Zeus', one of them became king of Iolkos and the other of Pylos. Here a 'servant of Zeus' is probably a ruler. The other passage is the description of Minos as 'familiar friend of great Zeus'. Taken with the description of Minos 'bright son of Zeus, giving rulings (*themis*) to the dead',[7] this phrase remembers the Cretan King receiving his law code from Zeus, like Hammurabi, and dispensing justice to his people. The phrases connected with Ares overlap part of the series connected with Zeus. We find 'dear to Ares', 'belonging to Ares', 'servant of Ares', 'companion of Ares' (the exact relationship expressed by *ozos* is not clear). 'Equal to Ares', we have noticed, has a doublet 'equal to Enyalios', which is the unique description of the Cretan Meriones. 'Dear to Ares' is given once to Meleager but is used particularly of Menelaos, and he appears also with the short form 'belonging to Ares'. If the King's affinity is to Zeus,

---

[1] *Od.* 7, 10; 8, 390.   [2] pp. 15 f.   [3] *Od.* 7, 71; 6, 309; 6, 293.
[4] p. 11.   [5] Cf. perhaps *diwija* in PY An 607.   [6] *Od.* 11, 255; 19, 179.
[7] *Od.* 11, 568; cf. above p. 25.

the Commander of the Army's affinity is to Ares, and I think we may suppose that, just as Meleager and Meriones were the Commanders of the Kings Oineus and Idomeneus, so King Agamemnon's Commander was once Menelaos. The simple adjective, which I have translated 'belonging to' and the phrase 'servant of' Zeus or Ares, may perhaps originally have implied something like apprenticeship: thus we find in Pylos 'smiths belonging to Potnia', in Hesiod the carpenter is called 'slave of Athena', and in Homer the smith is 'taught by Hephaistos and Athena';[1] we find in Pylos a slave of Artemis, and in Homer 'a good hunter, for Artemis herself taught him'.[2] But this relationship, however much transmuted, survives into classical times in the relationship of craftsmen to their gods.

The picture on the Hagia Triada sarcophagus (fig. 6) suggests that the King was honoured as a god after his death as in his life, and the magnificent burials of the shaft-graves and beehive tombs would naturally be interpreted to mean that he lived on in his tomb. One of the men buried in the shaft-graves showed signs of embalming.[3] Memories of this certainly survive in the anointing of Hektor with rose-oil to preserve his flesh and in the pouring of nectar and ambrosia into Patroklos' nostrils for the same purpose; they can only have survived in poetry.[4] Funeral games must originally have been held to please the man who lived on in the tomb, but the custom survived probably unbroken into classical times. Similarly the jars of honey and fat put on Patroklos' pyre[5] and many of the other offerings belong to inhumation customs, but such offerings can go on when the reason for them is forgotten. Even the invocation of Teiresias (although he was perhaps given divine honours in Knossos) need not be Mycenaean, since the rite could be continued elsewhere, and in fact we know that a Teiresias was buried by the immigrants when they arrived in Asia Minor.[6] So we are left with a few phrases which go back to the period of inhumation, and the knowledge that, while the burial

[1] PY Jn 310 etc.; Hesiod, *Op.* 430; *Od.* 6, 233.

[2] PY Es 650/5; *Il.* 5, 51.

[3] Persson, *RGPT.* 16, fig. 2. Cf. also below p. 115.

[4] *Il.* 23, 186; 19, 38.

[5] *Il.* 23, 170. For amphorae of honey cf. KN Gg 10 etc., *Docs.* 309f.

[6] *Od.* 11, 25; Proclus' summary of *Nostoi*; Mylonas (*A.J.A.*, 52 (1948), 75) compares the very special rites performed in the tombs of absent warriors at Dendra.

customs may seem to imply one kind of belief about the state of the dead, quite inconsistent beliefs can coexist with them: the man may be buried with rites that imply that he lives on in his tomb, but some may believe that he has gone to a blissful existence in Elysium, and others may hold that he has a shadowy existence in a dark, dank underworld. Nor can cremation among the Hittites or in Troy VI or isolated early cremations in Knossos, Leukas, Pylos, Argos, Rhodes, and Attica[1] be used as evidence that Homer's cremations derive from Mycenaean poetry; the dominant Mycenaean rite was inhumation, and it took a general change of custom to bring cremation into poetry.

The King lived in his palace surrounded by beautiful objects and served by his slaves. That the women slaves of Odysseus or Alkinoos should prepare the wool and spin it, grind the corn, get the meals ready, or that the old Eurykleia should teach the younger women,[2] is not unexpected since the women always did such work, but Homer has given a number of fifty both for Ithaca and Scheria, which must have been far in excess of any household since the Mycenaean period. The Mycenaean reality[3] was larger still; figures cannot be calculated for Knossos, but I reckon for Pylos 669 women, 392 girls, 281 boys (and in addition 272 men and boys described as belonging to the women). In Knossos we find that some of the women are under instruction. Their skills, where they can be identified, are in the production of textiles and food. Many of the women at Pylos are labelled by foreign ethnics: they come from Knidos, Miletos, Lemnos, etc. One tablet calls them 'captives',[4] the same root is used in an adjective, noun, and verb in the *Iliad* and the *Odyssey* to describe the capture of captive women who served the heroes. Homer also names the East Aegean, Lesbos, Skyros, Tenedos, Lyrnessos, as their homes, places which were raided by Achilles in the early stages of the Trojan war.[5]

One function of the women on the Pylos tablets is to be 'bath-pourers':[6] the word is used of an attendant and as an adjective for a

[1] Add to Lorimer, *HM*, 104f. the evidence for Knossos, Pylos, Attica in *J.H.S.*, 76 (1956), Suppl. 7, 16, 32.

[2] Cf. *Od.* 7, 103ff.; 18, 315; 20, 105; 22, 422.

[3] Cf. *Docs.* 155f.; Bennett in *Études Mycéniennes*, 121. Cf. above p. 17.

[4] PY Ad 686, *Docs.* no. 16, cf. *Il.* 20, 193; *Od.* 1, 398; 3, 106.

[5] *Il.* 9, 660; 11, 624; 20, 191.

[6] PY Ab 553, *Docs.* 160; *Od.* 20, 297 (slave); *Il.* 18, 346 (tripod).

tripod in Homer, and both in the *Iliad* and the *Odyssey* the heroes
are bathed by women slaves and then anointed with oil. This
luxurious bathing is a Mycenaean memory, and possibly a very old
memory as Homer does not use for bath the Greek word *lewotreios*,
which is found on the tablets, but the pre-Greek word *asaminthos*,
which originally meant a bathing place on the sea-shore.[1] It is
inevitable to compare the 'two silver *asaminthoi*, two tripods, and
ten talents of gold' given to Menelaos in Egypt with the Pylos
tablet[2] recording three baths (*lewotreioi*), three water pots, three
phialai, and other vessels (fig. 1). The bathing scenes in Homer
take place in the palaces of Pylos, Sparta, Ithaca, Scheria, and
Troy.[3] In Pylos Blegen found a clay bath-tub with a drain built
into a room which was next to a store of olive-oil, so that anointing could immediately follow bathing as in Homer.[4]

Of the beautiful objects in Mycenaean palaces of which the
memory was handed down, however distorted, in poetry, we have
mentioned the inlaid dagger blades, Penelope's couch, and the
golden dogs which guarded the palace of Alkinoos.[5] The technique of metal inlay was a distant memory when the iron worker
Hephaistos applied it to Achilles' shield, and another such
memory may survive in the group of lion and dappled fawn on
Odysseus' brooch,[6] which sounds much more like a piece of
Mycenaean inlay than a geometric bronze group; the double-shank
pin itself may well belong to Homer's own time[7] and is no less
unsuitable than Achilles' shield to carry such decoration. Penelope's couch is also a memory since Homer preserves no detail of
its decoration, as he might have done if he had seen the Mycenaean
throne with ivory decoration (fig. 2) which survived till near his
own time at Delos. The word *dinotos* etc. in the sense of 'engraved'
is used of Paris' bed, the sword-sheath which Euryalos gives to
Odysseus, and Penelope's couch, made by the artist Ikmalios,[8]
who seems to have a Mycenaean-speaking name. Two forms of
the same word appear on the tablets in the sense of 'engraved',
but later the word appears to mean 'with concentric circles'.[9]
Penelope's couch was decorated with engraved ivory and silver.

[1] Cf. Deroy, *Glotta*, 35 (1956), 171.   [2] PY Tn 996, *Docs.* 338.
[3] *Od.* 3, 464; 4, 48; 8, 454; 17, 86; *Il.* 22, 444.
[4] *J.H.S.*, 76 (1956), Suppl. 16.   [5] Cf. above pp. 28, 27, 32.
[6] *Od.* 19, 226.   [7] Cf. Jacobsthal, *Greek pins*, 140.
[8] *Il.* 3, 391; *Od.* 8, 404; 19, 55. See *Docs.* 332f. On Ikmalios cf. Ruijgh,
op. cit., 136.   [9] *Il.* 13, 406.

Ivory (and very probably silver) is well attested on the furniture of the tablets. Therefore the 'silver-studded throne' of Hephaistos[1] may well be a Mycenaean formula, and not, as it is tempting to think at first sight, a Homeric forgery on 'silver-studded sword'. Yet another memory of Mycenaean furniture is contained in Nestor's *kyanos*-footed (or panelled?) table, on which the 'dove cup' is put.[2] Nestor's cup is clearly a memory; he brought it from home and no one else could lift it; it was not a cup but a soup tureen and had a false bottom like many household pots found in Crete. This use of *depas* (found again when Circe makes her brew)[3] corresponds with its use on tablets both from Knossos and Pylos, and one in the Pylos list, like Nestor's, is a big one with 'four ears'. The gold cup from the shaft-graves, however, is according to Marinatos not a dove cup but a falcon cup, used by the king for libations, like the special cup which Achilles had brought from home for libations to Zeus.[4] The Pylos tablet which records the silver baths also lists three *phialai* which are shown by the ideogram to be large pans with a handle at each side. *Phiale* in classical times is a saucer used for libations and the word seems to have been already so used in Homer's lifetime, but in the funeral games of Patroklos the fifth prize for the chariot race is a 'two-handled *phiale* which has never been put on the fire',[5] and this must be a Mycenaean cooking pot.

Blegen[6] found not only the bath of Nestor's palace at Pylos but also a waiting-room with a white stuccoed bench, which he compares to the 'dressed stones, white, shining with ointment, before the lofty doors', where Nestor went and sat in the morning to give his family their orders for the day. 'Dressed stones' are also mentioned as the material of the house of Circe and of the house of Priam;[7] Circe's house[8] had a Mycenaean flat roof off which Elpenor fell, and the wall built to defend the Greek ships had a stepped base, which seems to be unknown in the Aegean but to be

---

[1] *Il.* 18, 389, cf. *Od.* 7, 162.

[2] *Il.* 11, 628 ff., cf. PY Ta 642 etc. For the 'dove cup' cf. PY Ta 641 with M. Ventris, *Archaeology*, 1954, 15 f.; S. Marinatos, *Festschrift B. Schweitzer*, 11 f. For the brew cf. Delatte, *Cycéon*, 711 f. For *depas* cf. Collinge, *B.I.C.S.*, 4 (1957), 55 f. See fig. 1a.

[3] *Od.* 10, 316. [4] *Il.* 16, 226–7, cf. above, p. 33.

[5] *Il.* 23, 270; cf. H. Luschey, *die Phiale*, 12.

[6] *J.H.S.*, 76 (1956), Suppl. 15; *Od.* 3, 406 f.

[7] *Od.* 10, 210; *Il.* 6, 242. [8] *Od.* 10, 554; *HM*, 418.

an accurate memory of the wall of Troy VI.[1] The general plan of Homeric palaces, the courtyard with porch and colonnade, the large *megaron* with porch, central hearth, and columns, the many small rooms, correspond to Mycenaean palaces and differ completely in scale from early Greek houses, although they are *megara*. Some features of Odysseus' house in the *Odyssey*, its side doors, passages, and stairs, can only be Mycenaean. The evidence has been recently reviewed by Miss Gray:[2] she suggests that knowledge of the proper sort of house for the heroes of legend to live in was preserved in the vocabulary of oral poetry and in the stories continually retold by the poets; in particular, a special feature of Odysseus' house,[3] a small door opening out of the back of the *megaron* into a corridor which leads both to storechambers and to a door opening into the porch of the *megaron*, may be an individual Mycenaean reminiscence like the description of the boar's tusk helmet or of Hektor with his body-shield bumping against his neck and ankles.

From the traditional formulae which for one reason or another have been connected with the Mycenaean age two kinds of information can be derived. First, they show that Mycenaean poets operated with formulae and therefore that the comparisons drawn in the last chapter between the manner of Homer and the manner of Eastern poetry are valid for the Mycenaean poetry, from which Homer is descended, as well as for Homer himself. Secondly, they show in general the subjects of Mycenaean poetry. We can now say that Mycenaean poets sang in double short rhythm, using formulae, refrains, and typical scenes, of their kings in peace and war, of their houses, furniture, and beautiful objects, and of their fighting and their armour. We have to consider next what individual incidents and descriptions tell us about particular heroes, whether in fact we are in a position, if we use all our resources, to say anything about the characters and plots of Mycenaean poetry.

Within the Mycenaean period itself, as we have said, we can distinguish early and late. The most important early object is the body-shield, and the fact that the Greek chariotry of Knossos in the period immediately before its fall were equipped with corselets proves that it had gone out of use by the second half of the

---

[1] *Il.* 12, 258; 16, 702; Lorimer, *HM*, 433.
[2] *C.Q.*, 49 (1955), 1f.   [3] *Od.* 22, 126f.

fifteenth century, although its memory was preserved in art, cult, and literature. Body-shield stories cannot have originated after the fifteenth century, and must be at least 200 years older than the Trojan war, if we accept the modern high chronology for the sack of Troy VII A.[1] This sack of Troy took place less than fifty years before the sack of Pylos and the destruction of the houses outside the citadel at Mycenae. Therefore all Mycenaean weapons and armour except body-shields, boar's tusk helmets, and silver-studded rapiers would have been used in it. On the other hand men in authority named on the tablets from Pylos and Mycenae can hardly have been born before the sack of Troy, and whether any Trojan names from an early poem on the sack of Troy could have been given to men recorded on the tablets is therefore extremely doubtful. It is quite certain that men with Trojan names on the Knossos tablets can have nothing to do with the historical sack of Troy VII A. Yet on my reckoning nine men bearing the names of Trojan heroes appear on the Knossos tablets, six such names appear both on the Knossos tablets and on the Pylos tablets, six further Trojan names appear on the Pylos tablets and two more on the tablets from Mycenae; one name is common to Knossos, Pylos, and Mycenae. These names are a warning against too ready belief in the historicity of epic poetry.

The Trojan names on the tablets form about a quarter of the total of mythological names on the tablets, and the mythological names in their turn form about a quarter of the total names for which a reasonable Greek form has been found.[2] Of course names are even more difficult to fix than vocabulary words, since their meaning cannot be regulated by the context. But for the longer names alternatives are few or non-existent, and for many of the shorter names the renderings that have been given are compelling. Mere figures mean nothing and no two investigators would arrive at the same answer, and I only mention figures to give some sort of general idea of the numbers involved. On my count rather over 110 of the 400 or so Greek names in Linear B are common to Knossos and Pylos, and 14 are shared by Mycenae with some other site. On our evidence it is fair to say that the stock of names is not very large and shows a considerable overlap between

[1] Cf. G. R. Huxley, *B.I.C.S.*, 3 (1956), 24. On relation of Pylos to Troy, cf. Blegen, *A.J.A.*, 61 (1957), 133.
[2] On the personal names see *Docs.* 92 f.

fifteenth-century Knossos and thirteenth-century Pylos, Mycenae, and Thebes. What we should like to know, of course, is whether men were named, as now and as often in classical Greece, after the heroes of an existing mythology. That we cannot say, but in some favourable cases it will be possible to suggest that this was the case. The minimum gain which can be derived from the names on the tablets is the assurance that in a story which on other grounds we believe to be Mycenaean this or that name is in fact a Mycenaean name. Coincidences with the tablets are therefore worth noting as we review the Mycenaean heroes.

Four heroes go back to poetry of the early Mycenaean period: Ajax, Hektor, Meriones, and Cretan Kastor (or rather his son). Ajax is dated by his body-shield, and although much of his fighting has been modernized, the shield is always remembered and to some extent gives him his character as the stubborn defender. The name occurs on a Knossos tablet, and his patronymic 'Telamonian' is in the Mycenaean adjectival form. His brother, Telamonian Teucer, as a great archer, is also Mycenaean. Between them they kill two Trojans with tablet names, Pyrasos and Ophelestas, and a third Simoeisios, whose father's name, Anthemos, occurs at Knossos. The original opposition between Ajax and Hektor may well be Mycenaean. Hektor himself had a body-shield and fought with Periphetes of Mycenae, who tripped over his body-shield. Periphetes' father Kopreus has a name recorded both at Knossos and Pylos, and Hektor's name, like that of Priam and Tros, can be found at Pylos. The original Hektor was brought up to date with a hand-grip shield. He gets his traditional epithet from a Mycenaean bronze helmet, he is a chariot fighter with a special heavy spear, he is the near divine commander of his father's army, and after his death there is a clear reference to embalming. His wife Andromache warns him that the enemy may climb the citadel, and her father after his death was wept by the nymphs.[1] Nothing so far puts Hektor on the eastern side of the Aegean, and the body-shield battles suggest that he started on the mainland of Greece.

The problem has, of course, long been recognized, and many solutions have been propounded. Now the wealth of Trojan names on the tablets joins the other evidence to show that the story of the siege of a town by the sea, defended by extremely

[1] Cf. above pp. 36, 58.

interesting people, grew up on the mainland of Greece. The Mycenaeans may have had a trading post in Troy VII A, as at Ugarit and elsewhere, but that is no reason for supposing that they borrowed the whole of Trojan local history instead of merely borrowing interesting stories and retelling them of their own gods and heroes. Homer's knowledge of Trojan heroes is so complete and consistent that I see only two possibilities: either Troy VII A was a Greek-speaking kingdom and a member of the circle of Mycenaean kingdoms like Knossos and Pylos, or the story of the siege of a town by the sea was elaborated for centuries in the Mycenaean circle, and then given a new setting in the East when Troy VII A was attacked. At present the latter seems the likelier solution.

Besides Hektor's Mycenaean armour and Priam's Mycenaean palace, we have already noticed the special bow and iron-tipped arrows belonging to Pandaros, who seems to have moved down from the chariotry to the archers.[1] His name also is found at Knossos. Antenor's name is found both on the Knossos and the Pylos tablets, where he is a mayor (*basileus*). It is a strange coincidence that in Homer Antenor has a son Laodokos and in Pylos a Laodokos holds land at *Pa-ki-ja-ne*, where Antenor is mayor.[2] The other Laodokos in Homer actually comes from Pylos; he is the charioteer of Nestor's son, Antilochos. It is tempting to suppose that the Antenor story was already formed; another son of Antenor, Pedaios, was killed by Meges, the owner of the Mycenaean lobster corselet, and his name is found at Knossos.[3] Homer knows eleven sons of Antenor, who are interesting for one thing or another, and his wife Theano was priestess of Athena at Troy. It was also Antenor who wanted to give Helen back to the Greeks, so that he had an essential part in the siege story.

Aeneas has no such essential connexion with the siege story but is certainly Mycenaean; he is the son of the goddess Aphrodite and is twice saved in battle by a god, by Apollo in the fifth book and by Poseidon in the twentieth; his name is found on a tablet from Mycenae. Phegeus' name is also known from Mycenae. In Homer[4] he and his brother, Idaios (a name known at Knossos and Pylos), are the sons of Dares, priest of Hephaistos; when Phegeus

---

[1] *Il.* 5, 194; cf. above pp. 12, 15.
[2] *Il.* 4, 87; PY Ea 802; Fn 50/3; Vn 130/7; *Il.* 17, 699.
[3] *Il.* 5, 69.   [4] *Il.* 5, 10f.

is killed by Diomede, Idaios is saved by Hephaistos, who covers him with darkness. Yet another of Homer's interesting Trojans has a name known at Knossos, Pedasos;[1] his mother was the spring nymph Abarbaree and his father the eldest son of Laomedon.

All these Mycenaean elements may have been included in the siege story before it was attached to Troy. When it was attached to Troy, Eastern elements were added – the knowledge of how the walls were built and other topographical details. The Mycenaeans already knew of the Hittites, and probably also of dealings friendly and unfriendly between the Trojans and the Hittites; these bits of history were added to the siege story. In particular the essentially historical story of Bellerophon could be added and Bellerophon's descendants made Priam's allies. The Bellerophon story itself goes back, as we have seen,[2] to the fourteenth century, so that the Iobates who appears on the Knossos tablets is earlier than the historical event, and presumably the Lycian king was given a Greek name. Later tradition connected Sarpedon, who was the son of Bellerophon's daughter Laodameia and Zeus, with Crete, and this story may also have some historical foundation.[3] Both Bellerophon and Sarpedon are thoroughly Mycenaean: in both stories the relation between divine King and divine Commander and the reserve land allotted to them is Mycenaean; moreover Zeus makes special arrangements for Sarpedon's burial, when he is killed; the final battle has been completely modernized, but the prelude in which the trace-horse is hit and cut away by a rapier is certainly Mycenaean.[4] Glaukos on the Pylos tablets may recall the Glaukos of the story, but other heroes also had this name.

The final pair of body-shield warriors are Cretan, Meriones and the son of Kastor. Odysseus' story about the son of Kastor makes him, as we have seen, a body-shield warrior in a night ambush, and when this is over he goes on to Egypt where he is accepted by Pharaoh, as presumably was the 'Captain of the Blacks' on the Knossos fresco if his troops are Ethiopians. Odysseus' story may derive from an early Cretan poem; the name Kastor is found on the Knossos tablets and so is Aithon, the name which Odysseus adopts for his Cretan tale to Penelope.[5] Meriones besides his body-shield has the early boar's tusk helmet. He is also an archer,

---

[1] *Il.* 6, 21.   [2] Cf. above p. 25.   [3] Cf. Marinatos, *R.A.*, 34 (1949), 5 f.
[4] *Il.* 16, 431 f., 467 f., cf. Leumann, *op. cit.*, 22 f.   [5] *Od.* 19, 183.

and is regularly described as 'equal to Enyalios' (the Cretan war god) and the liegeman (*opawon*) of Idomeneus. His own liegeman comes from Lyktos;[1] Lyktos is known from the tablets, like other places in Crete remembered by Homer – Knossos, Phaistos, Kydonia, Amnisos with its cave of Eileithyia, and perhaps Miletos and Gortyn.[2] Meriones is the Commander, and Idomeneus, son of Deukalion, the King. The feminine name Idomeneia and the name Deukalion are found on the Pylos tablets. It is tempting to argue that Cretan stories were already known in Pylos. If so, the Pylian Kokalos may be named after the Sicilian King with whom Daidalos took refuge. Daidalos already had a shrine in fifteenth-century Knossos, and the Lady of the Labyrinth was worshipped there, so that there is every reason to believe that these stories were already known.[3] The *Odyssey*[4] preserves a version of the Ariadne story in which Theseus stole the bride of Dionysos, the god of ecstatic dances, and she was subsequently killed by Artemis. Again the names on the tablets add to the artistic evidence that these stories were already known in Mycenaean times: men at Knossos bore the names of Seilenos, Iakchos, and possibly Pentheus; in Pylos a man was called Theseus, and Dionysos and Artemis were worshipped. To these memories of Mycenaean Crete can be added Minos as the 'familiar friend of Zeus', dispensing justice, and Rhadamanthys in Elysium.[5]

Although he has no body-shield to date him early in the period, Nestor, King of sandy Pylos, has Mycenaean titles; he remembers massed chariot fighting; he has a Mycenaean 'cup' and table; and his palace has been found with its bath and white seats. His elaborate sacrifice to Athena is occasioned by a Mycenaean bird epiphany.[6] His campaign against the Epeians[7] has been accepted as preserving a piece of Mycenaean history: in it he fights from a chariot, and his opponents the twins Aktorione Molione, whom elsewhere he met in a chariot race, are saved by Poseidon (they are in any case pre-migration, as their story came down in varying form to Homer, Hesiod, and Attic Geometric artists). In his other campaign, against the Arcadians, he slew Ereuthalion, who was

---

[1] *Il.* 17, 622.   [2] *Il.* 2, 645 f.; *Od.* 19, 175 f.
[3] Cf. above p. 50.   [4] *Od.* 11, 322.
[5] *Od.* 19, 178; 11, 568; 4, 564. The reference in 7, 323 is not clear to me.
[6] *Od.* 3, 372 ff.
[7] *Il.* 11, 670 ff.; Bölte, *Rh. Mus.*, 83 (1934), 345; Huxley, *B.I.C.S.*, 3 (1956), 21.

armed with a special iron mace, not a normal weapon but a piece of Mycenaean precious iron.[1] The tablets preserve a number of place-names which agree with Nestor's kingdom as defined by the Catalogue and by the description of his campaigns:[2] Pylos, Aipu, Kyparisseeis, Amphigeneia, Helos, and Pheia. Nestor is already probably a character in poetry by the time of our tablets. In the last days of Pylos men were called after him (in the long form Nestianor), his father Neleus (in the Mycenaean form Neelawos)[3] and his father-in-law Klymenos: Neleus' wife Chloris came from Orchomenos and the names of Iasos and Minyas from her pedigree occur on the tablets. Neleus himself was the son of Poseidon and Tyro; Tyro was the wife of Kretheus and bore him Aison, Pheres, and Amythaon, to whom Homer gives the Mycenaean adjective, *hippiocharmes*.[4] Kretheus, Aisonios, and Amythaon are found on the tablets as names of men. On the tablet with the ritual offerings[5] Iphimedeia shares a shrine with the dove goddess and Diwija. Iphimedeia was the wife of Aloeus, she was raped by Poseidon and bore Otos and Ephialtes, who threatened to climb heaven.[6] Aloeus and Ephialtes are the names of men on the tablets. Thus the names on the tablets suggest that the Catalogue of Heroines in the *Odyssey* has preserved a good deal of Pylian mythology. The discovery of the palace at Pylos gives this an historical setting, and now the discovery of a Mycenaean palace at Iolkos suggests that the tradition that Neleus migrated from Iolkos to Pylos may also have a historical foundation.

Achilles' name is found both at Knossos and at Pylos, but otherwise the Myrmidons are only represented by the name Epeigeus at Pylos. As Achilles is essentially a fighter, he is presumably 'swift-footed' in battle rather than on the track; he represents the mobility of the hand-grip shield as against the static warfare of the body-shield. He also had a metal corselet, a special spear, and a decorated chariot, all of which should be Mycenaean. His father is a Count and has established Phoenix as a 'feudal' lord in his territory, just as Agamemnon hopes to establish Achilles by the gift of his daughter and seven cities. Achilles' mother is the goddess Thetis, and the relationship between Zeus, Thetis, Achilles, and Patroklos is so like the relationship between Shamash, Ninsun,

[1] *Il.* 7, 141.
[2] *Il.* 2, 591 f.; 7, 135.
[3] Cf. L. R. Palmer, *Eranos*, 54 (1956), 8 f.
[4] Cf. above p. 103.
[5] PY Tn 316, *Docs.* no. 172.
[6] *Od.* 11, 305; cf. *Il.* 5, 385.

Gilgamesh, and Enkidu in the Gilgamesh story that it is difficult
to avoid the conclusion that the Achilles story was adapted to the
Gilgamesh story at a very early date. Achilles' fight with the river
in which he is aided by Hephaistos belongs to the same world
where gods and humans mix on equal terms. But Achilles also
operates on a purely factual historical level. Besides his actual
fighting during the later books of the *Iliad* Achilles is noted as a
sea-raider, who has carried off captive women and other booty
from various places in the Eastern Aegean, which lay within the
area of Trojan influence: 'Twelve cities I sacked by sea, and eleven
by land in the rich country of Troy.'[1] This is presumably a real
memory of Mycenaean raiding, to which the nationality of the
captives recorded on the Pylos tablets bears witness. Two interesting pieces of loot from Achilles' operations are remembered.
One is the 'lovely inlaid lyre with a silver bridge', which he took
when he destroyed the city of Eetion (Andromache's father).[2]
The other is the silver mixing bowl made by the Sidonians which
Patroklos received as a price for Priam's son Lykaon.[3] This is a
famous piece, like the pedigree bowl which Menelaos was given
by the King of Sidon. It was a gift from the Phoenicians to
Thoas, son of Jason and Hypsipyle, who ruled Lemnos with his
brother Euneos; Euneos gave it to Patroklos in return for
Lykaon, whom Achilles had captured and sent to Lemnos; Eetion
of Imbros ransomed Lykaon and sent him to Arisbe, from where
he got home. This is a fascinating glimpse of Bronze Age raiding
and the machinery set up to get the best advantage out of it.

Menelaos is in some ways the least clear cut and satisfactory of
the major heroes, and shows signs of having been pieced together
from different Bronze Age traditions. If, as I have suggested, in
one tradition 'Menelaos dear to Ares' was the Commander of
King Agamemnon's army, by the time of Homer he has lost his
position to the younger and more brilliant Achilles. If he was the
hero of a version of the siege story, which was adapted to the
Ugaritic story of Keret, a version in which he pined for his lost
wife, then besieged the town to get her back and succeeded in this
after a preliminary embassy had failed, his leading part in the
expedition was diminished when the story, perhaps because it had
to be adapted to the actual siege of Troy VII A, was changed and
the expedition became Panhellenic. Menelaos in the *Odyssey*, with

[1] *Il.* 9, 328.   [2] *Il.* 9, 186.   [3] *Il.* 23, 741 (cf. *Od.* 4, 615); 21, 35 ff.

his splendid palace filled with riches secured in his eastern wanderings including gifts from the King of Sidon and from Egyptian Thebes, with his stories of Egyptian Proteus and the promise of an Egyptian paradise, has convincing Mycenaean traits, and his herald, Eleoneus, has a Mycenaean name, but this seems to be yet another tradition which has been associated with the name of Menelaos.

Once Agamemnon was thought of as the leader of a Panhellenic expedition against Troy, his figure tended to be modernized and made more splendid.[1] His title *wanax* is however certainly Mycenaean; so is his breastplate and his decorated chariot and his chariot fighting. His ancestral sceptre[2] made by Hephaistos and given by Zeus to Hermes and by Hermes to Pelops, is a pedigree Mycenaean object like the boar's tusk helmet. Düring[3] pointed out fifteen years ago that the names of his three daughters, Chrysothemis, Laodike, and Iphianassa 'serve to characterize Agamemnon as King, endowed with divine as well as human power, ruling his subjects with might'; now that *themis* is established as a Mycenaean word for feudal due, perhaps Chrysothemis should be understood as an allusion to dues paid in gold; thus Mycenae got the adjective 'golden', and the formula[4] must be a Bronze Age survival, since Mycenae never recovered its wealth after the sack. Whether the gruesome stories told of Agamemnon and his ancestors were already current in Mycenaean times we cannot know; it is worth noting that the names of Tantalos, Thyestes, and Orestes, as well as a derivative from Atreus, have been recognized on the Pylos tablets, and the description of the singer[5] in whose care Agamemnon left his wife seems to fit the Mycenaean rather than the later world. There are three possible connexions with history in the story of the house of Atreus. It was long ago conjectured that Myrtilos, the charioteer of Oinomaos, derived his name from the Hittite King, Myrsilis, and now Myrtilis occurs as a feminine name on a Pylos tablet. Barnett[6] has recently suggested that Myrtilos may have been a Hittite expert sent to teach the Greeks the art of the chariot. He also suggests that the Attarissyas with a hundred chariots who caused much

[1] Cf. Jachmann, *Maia*, 1955, 245 f. (much exaggerated).
[2] *Il.* 2, 101 f.   [3] *Il.* 9, 145; I. Düring, *Eranos*, 41 (1943), 94.
[4] *Il.* 7, 180 etc.   [5] *Od.* 3, 267.
[6] *The Aegean and the Near East*, 215. Cf. in general, Gurney, *Hittites*, 38, 51; Huxley, *B.I.C.S.*, 3 (1956), 24 f.

trouble to the Hittites in the latter part of the thirteenth century was the son of Atreus himself, Agamemnon. Whether the identification is accepted or not, these Hittite documents seem to be evidence for large-scale Mycenaean activity in Asia Minor in the late thirteenth century. This large-scale overseas expedition, however connected with the sack of Troy VII A, implies a unified command and a muster list. In Mycenaean terms unified command is expressed as the feudal allegiance of the other Greek kings to Agamemnon.[1] The muster list survives in the Catalogue of Ships in the second book of the *Iliad*, which we have seen to be Mycenaean in its basic form and has seemed to many scholars to be Mycenaean also in its basic content. Huxley[2] has recently argued for a date in the L.H. III B period soon after the middle of the thirteenth century, and the coincidences of place-names with the Pylos and Knossos tablets have been noted above. The muster took place at Aulis, where a Mycenaean cemetery has recently been discovered, and the first town mentioned, Hyrie, has yielded a Mycenaean stele decorated with ships.[3] Thus a historical king of Mycenae, who reigned in the thirteenth century and led a large expedition to Asia Minor, contributed largely to the Homeric Agamemnon, and his exploit must have come into poetry before the end of the Mycenaean age.

In the Boeotian section of the Catalogue Thebes is omitted, and this is again consistent with the archaeological evidence for a sack before the III B period. Elsewhere in Homer[4] the earlier wealth of Thebes is remembered; troubles following the death of Oedipus led to the unsuccessful attack of the Seven from the Peloponnese; and later their sons were successful. This sack of Thebes is put before the Trojan war, but scarcely half a century before as the archaeological evidence requires; such shortening of the time sequence is not unexpected in a poem which focuses everything on to the Trojan war. The Theban story is only incidental to the *Iliad* and the *Odyssey*, but the allusions show that poet and audience know much more than they state explicitly. If a late Mycenaean artist had painted Eriphyle watching the Seven setting out for Thebes, his picture would have resembled the Warrior vase. Mycenaean names in the story are Amphiaraos

[1] Cf. above p. 105.   [2] Cf. above p. 114. *B.I.C.S.*, 3 (1956), 21.
[3] *J.H.S.*, 76 (1956), Suppl. 18; Blegen, *Hesperia*, Suppl. 8 (1949), 39 ff.
[4] *Il.* 9, 381; 4, 375 etc.; 23, 677.

(Knossos), Adrastos, Eteokles, Polyphontes, and Astyoche (Pylos, the last occurs in the masculine form Wastyochos). The occurrence of Amphiaraos at Knossos may mean nothing; on the other hand Amphiaraos' peculiar relation to Zeus and his final translation might well be a very old story. Adrastos and Eteokles are both patronymics of Counts at Pylos, and it is possible that the names had come into these families from poetry during the hundred and fifty or more years between the sack of Thebes and the sack of Pylos; one of the sons of Eteokles in Pylos was called Alektryon, the name of a man who seems to be a Boeotian in the *Iliad*.[1] The adjectival form of the patronymic Eteokles survives in the Homeric formula: βίη ʼΕτεοκληείη. Of the heroes connected by Homer with the Theban story Sthenelos has the Mycenaean adjectival form of the patronymic, Tydeus is a Count, Diomede has a decorated chariot and a lobster corselet made by Hephaistos. Diomede also routs first Aphrodite and then Ares in battles which belong to an age when divine Kings could meet and rout divinities.

Odysseus in the *Iliad* hardly concerns us; he has his considerable place in the action, and he shares with Menelaos the unsuccessful embassy when he was entertained by Antenor, but all that we can say for certain is that at some time and place an important warrior in the siege story was given the characteristics of the resourceful hero of the *Odyssey*. The Odysseus of the *Odyssey* is Mycenaean: he is a divine King who has a *temenos* and a palace with a large number of foreign slaves; his wife has a Mycenaean couch and he has a Mycenaean brooch; he is an archer and precious iron is part of his treasure; his triumph with the bow over his rivals may have been borrowed from a Hittite story; his wanderings are adapted from the Gilgamesh epic and in these wanderings he reaches Phaeacia, which is a Mycenaean fairyland. His attack on the Kikones is of a piece with Achilles' sea-raids at the beginning of the Trojan war.[2] He and his associates are armed and fight against the suitors with single spear and shield.[3] The boar hunt could be a Mycenaean memory, as boar-hunters are illustrated in Mycenaean art.[4]

Two names in Ithaca are interesting: Aigyptios and Neritos. Aigyptios is the old hero who opens the meeting of the assembly in the *Odyssey*;[5] his name occurs on a Knossos tablet at a time

---

[1] *Il.* 17, 602.　　　　[2] *Od.* 9, 39f.　　　　[3] *Od.* 16, 295; 22, 292–3.
[4] *Od.* 19, 392. Cf. above p. 57.　　　　[5] *Od.* 2, 15.

when it was natural for a Mycenaean to be named after the Nile; whether the name survived in poetry or in a succession of descendants we cannot say; only family or poetic tradition could account for a man being called Aigyptios between the fall of Mycenae and the late seventh century, when Egypt was again known to the Greeks. The fountain outside the town of Ithaca was made by Ithakos, Neritos, and Polyktor;[1] Leumann regards Neritos as derived from a misunderstanding of an old formula 'countless forest' which lies behind Homer and Hesiod. Now however the Pylos tablets record a sheep owner called Neritos, and there is no reason why we should not accept all the Homeric uses of Neritos as Mycenaean names, whether the man was called after the mountain or the mountain after the man. Hesiod's 'countless forest' is then either a misunderstanding of a proper name or an entirely new formation. Unfortunately the establishment of Neritos as a good Mycenaean name does not help the difficult geographical problem of Ithaca's location. At least we know that both Leukas and Thiaki had Mycenaean settlements, and Miss Lorimer's solution that a migration took the name of Ithaca from Leukas to Thiaki at the end of the Mycenaean age may well be the right solution. Then Odysseus' description of his home to Alkinoos, the ambush laid by the suitors and Telemachos' escape may all be survivals from Mycenaean poetry in spite of the geographical confusion.[2]

Homer only gives us hints that Mycenaean Athens had the place in Mycenaean poetry which the considerable Mycenaean remains in Attica suggest. The hints are however enough: Theseus and Ariadne, Athena's residence in the house of Erechtheus, Athena's golden lamp. The story of the Minotaur, of the bull of Marathon, and of the Centaurs are all likely to be Mycenaean, as we have seen.[3] The name of Peirithoos is found at Knossos and the name of Theseus at Pylos; the aged Nestor recalls that in his youth he was summoned from distant Pylos to fight with them against the Centaurs.[4] We have seen also that the story of Demeter and Kore may well have been represented on Mycenaean frescoes. Demeter was worshipped at Pylos and the

---

[1] *Od.* 17, 207; cf. 9, 22; 13, 351; *Il.* 2, 632; Hesiod, *Op.* 506; Leumann, *op. cit.*, 243 f., 331.

[2] *Od.* 9, 21 f; 4, 845; 15, 29; 299. Lorimer, *HM*, 494 f., on the theories of Dörpfeld and others.   [3] Cf. above p. 56.   [4] *Il.* 1, 263 f.

King was 'initiated' there. The later sanctuary at Eleusis was built over the Mycenaean palace, in which was found a thirteenth-century jar with a Linear B inscription including a place-name and a personal name both known from Knossos.[1] It is possible therefore that the name of Keleus both at Knossos and Pylos derives from Keleos, King of Eleusis, with whom Demeter took refuge. A minor Attic hero, whose name appears on the Knossos tablets, is Pandion.[2]

Of all Greek heroes Herakles has the most intimate and continuous connexion with the gods, although again in our Homer he is only on the fringe of the story. We have noted already that the name of Kopreus, the herald of Eurystheus, is known both at Knossos and Pylos, and that the story of Herakles and the Cretan bull may well derive from Minoan practice. The Pylos tablets have the names of Erythras and Eueres, two sons of Herakles. Nestor dates Herakles' raid on Pylos in his own childhood,[3] and Kopreus' son, as we have seen, fought with a body-shield. So also Herakles destroyed an earlier Troy, Laomedon's Troy. The building of this Troy by Apollo and Poseidon, Herakles' battle with the monster, Laomedon's refusal to give him the horses which he had himself received from Zeus as a payment for Ganymede, Herakles' wanderings caused by Hera on the way home, all these recall Eastern epic and therefore may well be Mycenaean.[4] Herakles, the Mycenaean archer,[5] used his skill against two gods, Hades and Hera: he shot Hades in Pylos, and Hades went for healing to the god Paieon, who is also called in to heal the wounded Ares and in the *Odyssey* is known as the father of Egyptian medicine:[6] he appears with Athena, Poseidon, and Enyalios as a god on a Knossos tablet. Leumann[7] has suggested a very ingenious origin for the strange formula 'dark-clouded blood': 'dark-clouded' is a much more suitable epithet for Zeus than for blood; some poet therefore must have wrongly combined 'Zeus dark-clouded, blood' so as to get 'Zeus, dark-clouded blood'; a speaker who addressed Zeus about blood is likely to be a god wounded by a mortal; the attack of Herakles on Hera gives just such a situation,

---

[1] Cf. Rubensohn, *J.d.I.*, 70 (1955), 1f.; Mylonas, *A.E.*, 1936, 61.
[2] Cf. *Il.* 12, 372.   [3] *Il.* 11, 690.
[4] *Il.* 21, 441; 20, 145; 5, 640; 266; 14, 299; 15, 18.
[5] Cf. *Od.* 8, 224; 21, 14.
[6] *Il.* 5, 392f.; 395f.; 5, 900; *Od.* 4, 232.   [7] *Op. cit.*, 202f.

and Leumann finds here the subject of the earlier poem. I think we may add that the false combination cannot have been very recent when our Homer wrote; a recent poet would hardly have overlooked the popular bucolic caesura, which the correct interpretation of Leumann's supposed line would give: Ζεῦ πάτερ, ἀργικέραυνε, κελαινεφές. Thus from this side, too, an early date is indicated for the Herakles story. Homer has a single brief reference to Herakles' labours, but it is very tempting to suppose that they represent conquests performed for the King of Mycenae, as Persson suggested;[1] the animals represent the surrounding cities by the same sort of symbolism as has been observed on the stele (fig. 4) from the shaft-graves.[2]

Herakles is perhaps the best known of the children of mixed parentage, one divine and one human, but there are many others – we have noticed Achilles, Neleus, Aeneas, Ephialtes. Such stories are likely to have been invented in the days when kings were divine (the Europa story is attested in Mycenaean art), and our Homer sometimes only remembers them in catalogue form.[3] The fact that Ephialtes is the name of a man in Pylos, while the mother Iphimedeia, as well as the father Poseidon, is worshipped there as a god, encourages us to believe that the giant Ephialtes and his exploits against the gods were already mythical in Mycenaean Pylos. This is slight evidence that the various struggles between the younger and older gods had already been adapted from Eastern poetry in Mycenaean times. I need not repeat here the instances already given in the last chapter.[4] We saw there that besides the Creation myth in its various forms, other Ugaritic epics and Egyptian stories influenced the Greek picture of the gods. The Ugaritic epics in particular give parallels for the cruelty of the gods, to each other and to men, which sometimes shocks us in Homer. The division of heaven, darkness, and the sea between Zeus, Hades, Poseidon is a very much softened version of the struggle between Baal and Yamm and between Baal and Mut;[5] but when Zeus or Hera hurls Hephaistos out of heaven, the Eastern violence is clear. When Hera hurled Hephaistos out of heaven,[6] Thetis received him. This Thetis is not one of the fifty

---

[1] *Il.* 8, 362f. Persson, *Dragma*, 394.   [2] Cf. above p. 32.
[3] *Il.* 14, 317f.; *Od.* 5, 118f.; 11, 235f. (cf. above 49).
[4] Cf. above p. 84.   [5] *Il.* 15, 187f., cf. above p. 85.
[6] *Il.* 1, 590f.; 18, 395.

daughters of Nereus but the sea goddess herself, and when she brings Briareon to Olympos to save Zeus from the other gods,[1] she has something of the Akkadian Tiamat (female salt water), who raised monsters to help the older gods against Marduk. The story of Hephaistos and Thetis has a parallel in the story of Thetis saving Dionysos; the two strands are woven together in the marriage of Peleus and Thetis, when Dionysos gave Thetis a golden amphora made by Hephaistos, a golden amphora to be used to house the bones of Achilles and Patroklos.[2] The last episode cannot however be Mycenaean since it implies cremation, and therefore the elaboration of the marriage story, which is itself, as noted in the last chapter, not unlike the Ugaritic wedding of Keret, may well be later than the marriage story itself. The elaboration raises a more general question, which must soon be faced. For the moment we may be content to have established a possible development of mythology: the local Mycenaean pair of mortal Peleus and immortal Thetis have a brilliant son, Achilles; his story is then adapted to the Gilgamesh epic, and Thetis becomes a goddess who can influence Zeus; she then develops further into the sea goddess who helped Zeus and saved other gods, and the marriage of Peleus and Thetis became a great occasion attended by the gods. The further elaboration of this story would seem to lead beyond the Mycenaean age.

So far we have only spoken of the gods in relation to mortals and each other. For the gods performing each their own particular functions our best guide is works of art, supported (where possible) by the names on the tablets:[3] the aspects of the gods identified there and surviving in Homer were presumably also described in Mycenaean poetry. Such are the armed Athena, Zeus and his scales, Hermes or Apollo singing to his lyre, Poseidon driving his chariot over the sea. In discussing representations of gods, objects from all over the Mycenaean world were used, and the close likeness of their themes is strong evidence for a common Mycenaean theology, which would be reflected in poetry about the gods. The sceptic may however say that gods are never named in Mycenaean art, and therefore identical gods doing the same thing may yet have had different names in the different places from which the

---

[1] *Il.* 1, 396.
[2] *Il.* 6, 130; 23, 92; *Od.* 24, 74. On the marriage see Lesky, *S.I.F.C.*, 27–29 (1956), 216f.   [3] Cf. above pp. 43 ff.

representations come. In some cases this is no doubt true; in particular there were many mistresses and probably more than one master of animals. On the other hand the tablets show that Zeus and Poseidon were worshipped both at Knossos in the fifteenth century and at Pylos in the thirteenth; no stress therefore can be placed on the fact that Athena, Enyalios, Paieon, Eileithyia are only found at Knossos, and Hera, Hermes, Artemis, Dionysos, Demeter only at Pylos. The religious tablets are far too few to make this division significant, and we are fully justified in using works of art as evidence for a common theology.

This brings us to the more general question of the centres and production of Mycenaean poetry. How far is it possible to argue from community in religion, language, writing, and art to community in heroic poetry? The common aspects of the gods (I do not mean to suggest for a moment that there were not many and great local differences) mean that there were common elements in cult songs at different places, not only common epithets but also common stories told about particular gods and the relation of the gods to each other. The epithets would be transferred from cult songs to heroic poetry and so give us 'owl-faced Athena', 'lady Athena' and 'cow-faced lady Hera'. I see no difficulty in believing that 'vulture-faced Gorgon' was another of the same kind, since we know of a Gorgon-headed Artemis in Rhodes in the late seventh century. Homer's description of the strong, swift Ate followed by the wrinkled, squinting, lame Prayers[1] is undoubtedly modelled on a chorus of ugly women dancing round an uglier leader, and this may well go back to masked choruses in honour of a 'vulture-faced Gorgon', and the bird-headed demoness with wings on a fourth-century Etruscan jug gives a good idea of such a monster.[2] We have the evidence in art for Mycenaean choruses and for dances of men and women, which must have been accompanied by song. Probably many more epithets of the gods than we can prove go back to this Mycenaean religious poetry: 'cloud-gathering Zeus' has a close Ugaritic parallel in 'cloud compelling Baal'. On all analogy of later hymns cult songs should also contain stories about the gods, and we have seen reason to trace many back to the Mycenaean age; so we should expect that when the Creation myth was taken over it became a cult song of

---

[1] *Il.* 9, 502, cf. *Greek Theatre Production*, 156.

[2] Beazley, *E.V.P.*, 218; Trendall, *Vasi dipinti del Vaticano*, pl. 67e, 274.

Zeus. These cult songs are the kind of poetry which would surely have been recorded in writing, if any poetry was recorded in writing; and it is difficult to see any reason why they should not have been recorded.

The further and much more important question is how what we have called heroic poetry was performed. On the Hagia Triada sarcophagus (fig. 6) the lyre-player and the flautist play while the sacrificial victim is being slain and the libations are poured. Song must have accompanied their playing, and the song may have celebrated the exploits of the dead king who stands by the door of his tomb. Although the evidence for a cult of the dead in the Mycenaean age is extremely slight (but perhaps the 'thrice-hero' and 'lord of the house' to whom gold cups are brought on a Pylos tablet should now be added),[1] the magnificent burials imply that the great dead were remembered, and it would be very natural that their exploits should be sung on their anniversaries. This would mean a local poetry in each of the great Mycenaean centres celebrating their great dead, and such poetry would very naturally contain the elements which strike us as a curious blend of myth and fact: for instance the adaptation of the Gilgamesh story to the sea-raider Achilles. This local poetry would however tend to be conservative and patriotic: the characteristics and exploits of the local hero would be preserved, and in any exploits which he shared with other Mycenaeans his part would be emphasized. Here again, if such poetry was performed at an annual festival, it might well be recorded.

But we have also to reckon with a third kind of poetry, which may have been more international. The divine singer seated on a rock playing his lyre, who is represented on the fresco from Pylos (fig. 9), is the god of solo singers, and proves that there were solo singers as well as choruses in the Mycenaean age. When the embassy came to Achilles, they found him playing a decorated lyre, which he had taken from the city of Eetion, Andromache's father, and singing the 'fames of men'.[2] The 'fames of men' is κλέα ἀνδρῶν; it may not be irrelevant to note that -klewes is

---

[1] Tn 316, Docs. no. 172, cf. in general Karo, Schacht-Gräber, 333; Nilsson, MMR, 584f.; Mylonas, A.J.A., 52 (1948), 78; Robinson Studies, 1, 64ff., particularly 100f.; Sp. Marinatos, das Altertum, 1 (1955), 148; K. Kerenyi, Saeculum, 7 (1956), 388. Cf. above pp. 53, 109f.

[2] Il. 9, 186f. Cf. above p. 120.

found as the last element of five Mycenaean names;[1] 'fame' in the sense of 'record of great deeds' would seem therefore to be Mycenaean. The pedigree lyre, on the analogy of other pedigree objects, should also be Mycenaean; and the beehive tomb of Menidi in Attica yielded besides plates of a boar's tusk helmet fragments of the finely carved frames of two lyres.[2] Was this the tomb of another warrior poet like Achilles? It is unlikely that all Mycenaean warriors were poets, and the figure of a Mycenaean court poet may well be preserved in the singer with whom Agamemnon left Klytemnestra when he went to Troy, and who had to be removed before Aigisthos could have his way.[3] I quote him rather than Demodokos at Alkinoos' court or Phemios at Odysseus' court, because he is a person of much greater importance, and the more detailed picture of Demodokos may contain later elements. If we content ourselves for the moment with Achilles singing the 'fames of men', with the warrior poet of the Menidi tomb, and with Agamemnon's singer, we have nevertheless in them evidence for poetry about heroes sung at a court by singers, who were familiar with the workings of the court and, in the case of Achilles and the Menidi poet, with contemporary warfare. It is such poetry sung at the court for the court which we should expect to reflect the court style, the correct description of the King or warrior, the scenes described in fixed terminology, and the fulfilment of orders in the words in which they were prescribed. Such poetry also would tend to be brought up to date: when body-shields went out, the heroes would fight with handgrip shields and other such changes would appear at any rate in the important parts of the story. A new historical event in which the King took part would be told in the terms of an old story, retaining much of the old story to fill out the parts for which the King had nothing convincing to tell; it is in this kind of way, I think, that the new story of the siege of Troy absorbed many of the characters from the much older siege of a town by the sea. A really important event like the siege of Troy tended also to attract into its own orbit heroes whose past exploits were now outshone but who were too important to lose, like Ajax and Hektor.

This court poetry was also international in various senses. Some of the events which it described like the attack on Thebes or the siege of Troy were international events. The Kings travelled

---

[1] *Docs.* 95.   [2] Lorimer, *HM*, 456.   [3] *Od.* 3, 367f.

to each other's courts in peace and fought with or against each other in war. The picture of Odysseus sending Demodokos a cut off the joint and asking for the song of the Trojan horse is entirely convincing;[1] the court singer must be ready with a song, which will please the stranger because it recalls his experience. He may know the story because the King has brought it home from his travels, or he may even have travelled himself. The evidence of Mycenaean art certainly suggests that famous artists travelled, and there is no reason why famous singers also (as distinct from warrior poets) should not have travelled. In the *Odyssey*[2] the list of *demioergoi* consists of prophets, doctors, carpenters (artists like Ikmalios?), singers, and heralds: they are all stated to be strangers whom one would or would not wish to summon from elsewhere. The case for this being Mycenaean rests on the interpretation of *demioergoi*; the word is only used in these two passages, and it is arguable that it does not yet mean craftsman but has its earlier meaning of 'worker of the public land', in the special sense that the visiting expert was maintained at the public expense; by Homer's time the 'feudal' system, by which craftsmen were 'workers of the public land', had vanished, and *demioergos* survived with two quite distinct meanings: 'craftsman' and 'magistrate'.[3] If this is so, the *Odyssey* retains a memory of the singer, as well as the artist, as a visiting expert. We may then add famous singers to the warrior poet and the King as travellers, who provided international communications at the highest level within the Mycenaean world and between the Mycenaean world and its outposts in the Eastern Aegean. Only such high-level international communication can explain the borrowing of stories from outside the Mycenaean world and the uniformity of religion and fresco themes within it, however different within the main framework local interpretation of the borrowed stories may have been. The uniformity of writing and language in the Linear B inscriptions known to us from Knossos, Pylos, Mycenae, Tiryns, and Thebes must not be overstressed, as it may show the uniformity of scribal language rather than uniformity of court language. Yet as long as no evidence is forthcoming either for organization or for training of scribes, uniformity of court language and therefore of poetic

---

[1] *Od.* 8, 474f. [2] *Od.* 17, 382; 19, 135.

[3] Cf. above p. 13; Chantraine, *Mélanges Diès*, 41f.; Gordon in *The Aegean and the Near East*, 140; Murakawa, *Historia*, 6 (1957), 385f.

language, which has been shown to depend on court language, seems the simpler explanation.

We may suppose then that the great singers of the Mycenaean courts had first- or second-hand knowledge of the whole Mycenaean world and to a lesser degree of the outside world which impinged on it. They sang primarily for the entertainment of their own courts, but when guests arrived or when they themselves travelled they needed a wider range of song than local exploits. Was this poetry improvised like the poetry of Demodokos or not? If it was improvised, how do we account for the accurate preservation of the Catalogue of Ships? And if it was recited, how could the poet fit it to the particular occasion, to the mood of the King at the moment, or to the arrival of an unexpected stranger? This is perhaps an unreal dilemma. We need not suppose that in the Mycenaean age the Catalogue of Ships was known anywhere except at Mycenae. There it may have been versified at a very early stage for recitation on solemn occasions, which celebrated the King who had led a combined expedition to the East. It belonged therefore to our second class of Mycenaean poetry, the local celebration of the great dead, which, as we have said, may well have been recorded. In another way also the dilemma is unreal. The places at which international court poetry was sung were local courts; the warrior poet would know the local poetry celebrating the great dead, and the famous singer would have himself composed some of it; both could draw on it as they wished for the songs which they sang at banquets to entertain their King and his visitors from abroad. These songs however were improvised for the particular occasion, and embodied the contemporary knowledge which the warrior poet or the famous singer had gained on his travels. For this kind of Mycenaean poetry the description of Demokodos and Phemios[1] is as true as it is for later poetry. Odysseus says that Demodokos sings 'as one who himself was present or has heard from another', and Phemios claims that he is self-taught and god has made all sorts of songs to grow in his mind; the word for song means path, and the path is composed of the formulae, which enable the poet to find his way through his material. Phemios is the oral poet who knows all the

---

[1] *Od.* 8, 488; 22, 347. On the method of singing, the pauses, and the discussions of the songs in the *Odyssey* see H. Fränkel, *Dichtung und Philosophie des frühen Griechentums*, 15; he also gives modern parallels.

stories and has his mind full of formulae; these make it possible for him to improvise the required story in the most suitable way for the audience of the moment. This kind of poetry is fluid in a sense in which the other two are not; it changes as new events occur and horizons widen or contract; but in time no doubt it influenced the older and more fixed poetry which celebrated the dead Kings, and brought this also up to date. The improvising poets do not (at least at this stage) invent the formulae, but the formulae come from the Court style; they are extremely useful for the improvisation of the court poet and very welcome to his court audience, but their origin lies, as we have seen, in titles of gods and men, in royal correspondence and operation orders, and in the refrains of cult hymns. They characterize all court poetry, whether recorded or not, but they are particularly helpful to the poet when he improvises.

Thus, I think, we may suppose that there were three main kinds of poetry at every Mycenaean palace: cult songs, songs about the great Kings of the past sung on their anniversaries, and songs sung at banquets, which dealt with the international present but laid a strong emphasis on the exploits of the present local King. All were in the Court style and the terminology overlapped, particularly between the second and third class, and especially when the song sung at the banquet was also about the Kings of the past. The first two kinds were local and tended to remain fixed, because they were sung on solemn occasions; they may have been recorded. The third kind was always improvised for the particular occasion, and showed such knowledge of the wider world as the poet could display for the particular audience.

If this picture is generally true, there follows an important negative conclusion, which will have to be tested in later chapters. None of these poems is likely to have been very long. There is no reason to suppose that even the festival poems exceeded the length of 5,000 lines assumed for the *Baal* of Ugarit, and this length itself would require a complete eight-hour day to recite; for an improvised poem of the same length the time required would be longer and probably at least five sessions of two hours each would be needed.[1] Therefore a Mycenaean Wanderings of 'Odysseus' (rather over 2,000 lines) is perfectly possible, but the

[1] Cf. H. T. Wade-Gery, *The Poet of the Iliad*, 69. Details of modern performers of improvised poetry are given by Lord, *A.J.A.*, 52 (1948), 42.

Odyssey at its present length is out of scale; this does not in the least suggest that a Return of 'Odysseus' and a Travels of 'Telemachos' may not also have been performed at the Mycenaean court of Leukas or Thiaki, but they would be performed separately from the Wanderings. Similarly the *Iliad* is out of scale; but each Mycenaean court would have its own siege story with considerable detail of defenders and attackers and its own tales of the prowess of its own Kings; when the siege story was retold as the story of the Panhellenic attack on Troy, the local King and even his ancestors would still play the leading part and the rest would be included only as necessary background, but the singers knew enough of the prowess of other Kings to be able to enlarge parts of the background, when necessary, to entertain a particular guest. If caution may be forgotten for a moment and the personal names on the tablets called in evidence here, they attest the width of knowledge which the poets possessed: the names at Pylos belong not only to the mythology of Pylos but also to the mythology of Argos, Mycenae, Crete, Athens, and Troy (or rather wherever the defenders of the siege story were at home). Therefore, while really long poems with highly complicated plots are unlikely, any one Mycenaean court knew a good deal about the poetry of the neighbours. We shall have to consider how many different lines of descent can be traced from the Mycenaean palaces whose stories we know to our Homer in Ionia; but even if some of the lines were broken or diverted in the dark ages, any line of tradition leading down from one of the great palaces is likely to have preserved far more than its own local stories, and to have carried with its own stories the salient characteristics of other heroes and the outline of their doings.

If this picture of Mycenaean poetry is not wholly misleading (and details will certainly need altering and even outlines redrawing as new evidence is discovered), Mycenaean poetry was composed in Court style about the gods, kings and nobles, present and past, of the Mycenaean palaces, their behaviour in peace and at war, their friends and their enemies, their weapons and their possessions. Court style means essentially the use of formulae, and formulae, though deriving from the terminology of military and theocratic courts, were of the greatest help to improvising poets, as well as to poets dictating to scribes writing a difficult script. Cult songs and songs about the great dead preserved the past, and are likely to have changed slowly, particularly if they were recorded, as contemporary Eastern poetry was. The great dead were gods in their lifetime and lived on in their tombs; because they were divine, their stories were a mixture of myth and fact; because they were potent, they were brought into stories with a much later historical setting. The songs improvised at banquets were sung by men who themselves took part in great events or knew those who were taking part in great events, by men who travelled and learnt not only the stories of other courts but also stories from outside the Mycenaean world. Their songs were the international and contemporary element in Mycenaean poetry, which was no doubt in time reflected back into the songs about past heroes and the songs about the gods. In Eastern poetry we have to assume the existence of such a changing element to account for the alterations which can be observed in the Gilgamesh story and the Creation myth as they pass through the centuries and across frontiers. In the Mycenaean world we have the evidence of the solo singer of the Pylos fresco, the warrior poet of Menidi, and Achilles with his pedigree lyre, singing the fames of men. This kind of poetry derives from a court, but could survive when the court disappeared.

5

THE COLLAPSE OF MYCENAEAN CIVILIZATION AND THE IONIAN MIGRATION

ycenae fell according to the most recent dating about
1100 B.C., and our *Iliad* and *Odyssey* were probably
written in Ionia during the eighth century. The intervening period is the dark age of Greek history. Towards the end
of that period, say for the last century or a little more, the conditions were maturing which made the *Iliad* and the *Odyssey* possible:
a new certainty of life in Asia Minor and some degree of affluence,
changes in the language which made it yet more adaptable to epic
verse, a new style in art with something of the complexity of
large-scale epic, and the introduction of alphabetic writing. For
the present, however, we have to study the dark years between
roughly 1100 B.C. and 900 B.C. to see by what routes memories of
the Mycenaean age passed to Ionia, and what changes occurred
in the subject-matter and form of poetry and art during these two
centuries.

The Mycenaean age was a time of great palaces linked in a
common system with each other and more loosely with the Near
East and Egypt, great palaces enjoying art and poetry, which were
international in the senses described in the preceding chapters.
These great palaces were with perhaps the single exception of
Athens destroyed. Their Eastern counterparts, the Hittite capital
and Ugarit, had also been destroyed before the end of the
thirteenth century, and Egypt met two great attacks late in the
thirteenth century and early in the twelfth. Thus the international
civilization of the Mycenaean world was shattered on both sides
of the Aegean. Communications between the Greeks and the Near
East and Egypt were broken for a very long time, and the Greek
world became isolated, poor, and fragmentary. The causes of this
wide breakdown of civilization do not concern us, and the discussions about the Dorian invasion and the identification of the

Peoples of the Sea can be left firmly on one side. The facts of impoverishment and isolation are clear. The great palaces fell, and the people who interest us most are the people whose wanderings led them in time to Ionia. With the great palaces the whole theocratic feudal system collapsed, and in the dark period and for long afterwards Greek communities were much more isolated, and therefore became much more individual than before. But memory did not survive only in the minds of the wanderers; some must have survived in the descendants of the Mycenaeans in Greece itself and some perhaps in the Mycenaean colonies overseas.

Of the great Mycenaean palaces Pylos and Iolkos were burnt about 1200 B.C. and at about the same time the houses outside the citadel of Mycenae were destroyed, although the citadel itself survived about a century longer. Thebes had already been destroyed before the Trojan war, if the evidence quoted in the last chapter is to be trusted. Tiryns, Argos, and Sparta, all lost their glory or were actually sacked towards the end of the twelfth century. In some places, however, we have evidence of a continuous tradition from Mycenaean to classical times. Thus in Pylos itself not very far from Nestor's palace a beehive tomb at Tragana was apparently used again and again for new burials in Sub-Mycenaean and Protogeometric times,[1] from the eleventh to the tenth century, and this presumably shows that survivors lived on in the neighbourhood (as also in Asine, which, it will be remembered, was part of Nestor's kingdom) but not that their memories could have reached the outside world. Other Mycenaean tombs[2] near Nestor's palace were not reused after the Mycenaean period but were evidently discovered in the eighth century, and their occupants were then worshipped as heroes. In Mycenae itself some graves[3] of the Protogeometric and Geometric period help to fill the gap between the latest Mycenaean and the late eighth century, and provide just enough evidence for continual habitation. Not far below the palace a precinct, which went back to the eighth century, was found, in which Agamemnon was worshipped as a hero; J. M. Cook[4] has argued that here too the

[1] Wade-Gery, *A.J.A.*, 52 (1948), 115f.; Desborough, *Protogeometric Pottery* (quoted hereafter as Desborough), 281.

[2] Marinatos, *das Altertum*, 1 (1955), 140ff.

[3] Desborough, *B.S.A.*, 49 (1954), 258f.

[4] *B.S.A.*, 48 (1953), 31f.; *Geras A. Keramopoullou*, 112f.

cult was instituted as a result of the diffusion of the Homeric poems. He quotes further instances of new eighth-century hero cults from Sparta (Menelaos), Mycenae (Tomb of Klytemnestra), Argos, Athens, Kephallenia; and to these must be added Marinatos' graves in Pylos and the tombs of the Hyperborean maidens at Delos.[1] Thus beside the evidence for shadowy survival we have evidence for a revival of interest in the great past in the eighth century, but we may consider whether this is not too early for the Homeric poems to have reached the mainland. Perhaps the same conclusion is suggested by the evidence from Ithaca.[2] Here too occupation was continuous from Mycenaean to classical times, although the royal palace may have been abandoned at the end of the Mycenaean period. But some time after 1000 B.C. and before 800 B.C. a series of important dedications started: bronze tripod cauldrons were dedicated in the cave at Polis, and later dedications there were certainly made to Odysseus. It seems therefore that games in honour of Odysseus were held in Ithaca at least from the ninth century. By the middle of the eighth century Ithaca had come under Corinthian domination, and before the end it was receiving imports from Ionia.[3] These sites give evidence for a shadowy survival through the dark period and a new interest in the great Mycenaean heroes after it is over. This new interest was felt not only by the survivors but also by the new Dorian nobles, and showed itself in such different ways as the Corinthian claim to Bellerophon, the 'tragic' choruses in honour of Adrastos at Sikyon, and the forged dedications which Herodotus saw at Thebes.[4] The revival implies some new impulse which the shadowy survival could not itself provide. Nothing suggests that honours were continuously paid to the Mycenaean dead or that songs continued to be sung at their festivals. The revival emphasized the distance between their past splendour and the little men of today.

Another class of places which may be mentioned in passing, because they do not greatly concern us, are the places where there may have been continuity of divine worship. They do not greatly

[1] Cf. Mylonas, *Robinson Studies*, I, 102 f.

[2] S. Benton, *B.S.A.*, 35 (1935), 52 ff.; 39 (1939), 8; 44 (1949), 311.

[3] M. Robertson, *B.S.A.*, 43 (1948), 97, 122; S. Benton, *B.S.A.*, 48 (1953), 259, 335.

[4] Corinth, cf. T. J. Dunbabin, *J.H.S.*, 68 (1948), 59. Sikyon, Hdt. 5, 67. Thebes, Hdt. 5, 59.

concern us, because the stories which survived there are more likely to have been divine legends embodied in hymns than the heroic legends in which we are primarily interested. In many places a later Greek temple was built on a site in which Mycenaean remains were found, but it is not always possible to show from the continuity of the remains that continuous worship was paid there. Such continuity is however certain in the cave of Eileithyia at Amnisos, the temple of Apollo at Delphi, the temple of Aphaia at Aegina, the temple of Artemis at Delos (the ivory throne of the latter (fig. 2) is now believed to have been on view until it was put into the foundation deposit of the new Artemision in the eighth century), and the hall of initiation at Eleusis.[1] In all of these (and probably many other places) the old cults went on and new arrivals did not greatly change them, but the legends which thus survived were divine legends rather than heroic legends, and even where the later temple was built on the palace of the Mycenaean King he would be remembered for his association with the goddess rather than for his connexions with other Kings.[2]

Eleusis brings us into the neighbourhood of Athens, and in Mycenaean times Eleusis was probably already part of the Athenian Kingdom.[3] Athens is the one place which had a continuous importance from Mycenaean to classical times. Very recently it has been claimed that Iolkos in Thessaly, the city of Pelias from which the Argonauts sailed, had an unbroken history from 2300 to 700 B.C., and that the inhabitants maintained a high standard of civilization throughout this period.[4] If this claim proves true and if a route from here to Ionia can be shown, there is a real possibility of a continuous and firm tradition from the Mycenaean age having been thus handed down. At present we only know that this palace also was destroyed by fire about 1200 and was not inhabited in the Protogeometric period. It is curious that Iolkos is linked with Pylos by the tradition that Neleus and Pelias were

[1] Nilsson, *MMR*, 457f. For Delos ivories cf. above p. 27. For Eleusis see Mylonas, *The Hymn to Demeter and her Sanctuary at Eleusis* (1942); Rubensohn, *J.d.I.*, 70 (1955), 29f.

[2] The heroes and heroines discussed by Pfister (*Würzburger Jahrbücher*, 3 (1948), 147f.) are perhaps similar special cases of Mycenaean heroes or heroines who achieved a particular kind of divine status in cult.

[3] Cf. Huxley, *B.I.C.S.*, 3 (1956), 22.

[4] *The Times*, 10, xii, 56. See now *To Ergon*, 1956, 43f.

brothers, and there is little doubt that Iolkos belonged to the international Mycenaean community in the Mycenaean period, as is shown by its imported pottery.[1]

Of Athens we know much more. We have already seen evidence of Athenian legends in Mycenaean art and Athenian names on Mycenaean tablets. We have noticed that Athena was behaving as a Mycenaean goddess when she entered the house of Erechtheus.[2] The evidence of pottery[3] for continuity through the dark period is clear: late Mycenaean changed to Sub-Mycenaean late in the twelfth century, Sub-Mycenaean to Protogeometric early in the eleventh century, Protogeometric to Geometric at the beginning of the ninth century. This sequence is important because it not only shows continuity but with Protogeometric the first beginning of a new style, which flowers in the glorious late Geometric of the eighth century, but also looks forward to classical Greek art. At the same time as the new style in art iron was introduced for spearheads, swords, and knives, and cremation had already become the normal rite for burial, both points of chronological importance for the *Iliad* and the *Odyssey*. Cremation was used sporadically in the Mycenaean period, as has been seen,[4] but in Attica from the beginning of the eleventh century to the end of the ninth it is practically universal and must be due to some special compulsion. The great amount of Protogeometric pottery found in Athens means a rise in population, and this again suggests that Athens received refugees; Miss Lorimer[5] lays special stress on the Geometric Cremation Cemetery at Kolophon and suggests that the refugees took the custom on to Ionia; we can then suppose that in Attica itself the major pressure was over by the end of the ninth century, when the inhabitants returned to their habit of inhumation. The parts of Boeotia near Attica and Eretria in Euboea may have caught the custom of cremation from Attica, and the Eretrians probably passed it on to Ischia in the West. The fact that the burials in Ischia take the same form as those in Kolophon suggests a common Athenian origin. But,

[1] Cf. Lorimer, *HM*, 460.   [2] Cf. above p. 107.

[3] Cf. Desborough, particularly 290f., where he suggests that his dates may have to be raised fifty years. This raising accords with the evidence given by Albright and Hanfmann in *The Aegean and the Near East*, 163, 165 ff.

[4] Cf. above p. 110.

[5] *HM*, 106; Desborough, 306. On Ischia see G. Buchner, *RM*, 60/61 (1953–4), 37f.

whereas the Dorian mainland remained unaffected, the inhabitants of the Dorian islands, Thera, Kimolos, and parts of the Dodecanese cremated, perhaps because they too were refugees; they had lost their graves on the mainland and in the early stages they had not yet decided that they were going to stay in their new home. In Athens itself the evidence of the Mycenaean buildings seems to suggest that the city was twice unsuccessfully attacked, once in the late thirteenth century and again at the beginning of the eleventh century.[1] The former attack would roughly coincide with the sack of Pylos and the latter with the sack of Mycenae. This later attack on Athens may have been the one successfully resisted by the refugee king, Kodros, and this success may have opened the door to a flood of refugees. The evidence for this attack is in fact the abandonment of the Acropolis as an inhabited fortress and the spread of the dwellings and cemeteries over a wider area. Notably the Kerameikos begins its life as a cemetery in the Sub-Mycenaean period.

The Greek tradition that refugees from Pylos passed through Athens on their way to Ionia is, therefore, likely to be true, but an exact equation of the historical events with the traditional genealogy is difficult. Let us suppose then that Pylos fell about 1200, that Athens expanded considerably after an unsuccessful attack about 1100, that the pressure of refugees made cremation necessary at about the same time, and that the major pressure was over before 800. The new Protogeometric style, which looks forward to the future, started well before 1050; about 1000, pottery in the late Protogeometric style was being made and for the next sixty years or so was exported all over the Greek world. In particular, late Protogeometric Attic pottery was found in quantity in Smyrna and yielded about 850 to a local Geometric style.[2] This would suggest that refugees passed on to Ionia between 1050 and 850.

Before considering the evidence from Asia Minor the mainland tradition must be discussed. According to Pausanias the descendants of Nestor expelled from Messenia were Alkmaion his great-grandson, Peisistratos his grandson, the sons of Paion (his grandson), and with them Kodros' father, Melanthos, who was the great-great-grandson of Nestor's brother, Periklymenos.

[1] Broneer, *A.J.A.*, 52 (1948), 111; *Antiquity*, 1956, 9.
[2] J. M. Cook, *J.H.S.*, 72 (1952), 104; Desborough, 314.

Presumably Nestor was considerably younger than his brother Periklymenos, and the elder Peisistratos considerably younger than the other sons of Nestor. If we suppose that this Peisistratos was born shortly before the Trojan war, the younger Peisistratos, his son, would be born twenty to thirty years after the Trojan war and the expulsion have taken place about sixty years after the Trojan war. Melanthos belongs to the same generation as the younger Peisistratos, and his son Kodros should have been born, therefore, about sixty-five years after the Trojan war. Kodros' sons, who led the migration to Ionia, should, therefore, have been born about a century after the Trojan war. The traditional date of the Trojan war is impossible on the archaeological evidence.[1] With the new high date for the sack of Troy we get: 1230, sack of Troy; 1170, expulsion from Messenia (after sack of Pylos); 1165, birth of Kodros; 1100, Kodros' defence of Athens and death. We may add here two names from the Pylos tablets which connect with the genealogical line: Periklymenos, Boros, Penthilos, Andropompos, Melanthos, Kodros, Neileus. That Neileus may be a later shortened form of Neelawos has already been mentioned. Kodros' own name is the name of a smith in Pylos. Ventris[2] suggested that the last King of Pylos was Echelaon and noted the similarity with Echelaos son of Penthilos, the descendant of Orestes who colonized Lesbos. It is curious to find Penthilos also among the Pylian ancestors of Kodros. Is it possible that Echelaon belonged to the same family as Penthilos and that some marriage connexion brought the two names across into the family tree of Mycenae?

The story of the refugees from Pylos is also connected with constitutional changes in Athens, which interest us because, however difficult they may be to establish in detail, they certainly mark the end of the divinity of the King. Aristotle[3] notes succinctly the stages: (1) the King ruled alone, (2) the polemarch was associated with him, (3) the archonship was instituted in the time of Medon or of his successor, Akastos, when the sons of Kodros gave up the kingship in return for the archonship, (4) the archons were elected for ten years, (5) the archons were elected annually.

[1] On the traditional chronologies see Jacoby, *Klio*, 1902, 406f.

[2] *Docs.* 137.

[3] *Ath. Pol.*, 3, cf. Cadoux, *J.H.S.*, 68 (1948), 70f., particularly 88f.; Jacoby, *F.H.G.*, IIIb, no. 323a, F 23 and commentary.

The second stage is essentially the situation we know from Homer and the Mycenaean tablets, when the King has a Commander of his army (*Wanax* and *Lawagetas*). The third stage is dated to the time of the Ionian migration by Pausanias: it arose from the quarrel between the sons of Kodros, Medon and Neileus, as to which should succeed him, and the unsuccessful Neileus migrated. The fourth stage was dated by ancient authorities in 753/2 and the fifth in 683/2. The fourth stage belongs to the period of alphabetic literacy and I see no reason to doubt its details. Nor do I see any reason why the names of earlier kings should not have been remembered, together with a memory of the change from Kingship to kingship.

The third stage is the important one: not only has the new magistrate no pretence to divinity, but at the same time the King has become a priest instead of a King. The new magistrate is called the archon, and it seems highly probable that the King becomes *basileus* instead of *wanax* at the same time; at least the title *wanax* leaves no trace later. Thus even in Athens, the city least affected by the Dorian invasion, the divine King did not long survive the Mycenaean age. With this change, which is in essentials a change from monarchy to aristocracy, even if the archonship remained the preserve of a single family until the middle of the eighth century, the palace became the temple of Athena (and we have seen that there is some archaeological evidence that this happened about 1100). This is the situation assumed in Homer[1] when he describes how Athena nursed Erechtheus and 'set him in her rich temple; there the sons of the Athenians placate him with bulls and rams on his anniversary'. Erechtheus was a Mycenaean King, and the Mycenaean Athena 'entered the strong house of Erechtheus'.[2] When he died, his worship was continued at his tomb. But with the passing of the Mycenaean King the story was remodelled so that Athena took the baby to her temple. It is, of course, possible that the King of Athens lost his divinity before the new division of functions, and it would be natural to suppose that this happened when the refugee kings supplanted their predecessors; but of this we have no evidence. We can only say for certain that he must have lost his divinity with the division of functions, and tradition connects this with the sons of Kodros

[1] *Il.* 2, 547 f., cf. Mylonas, *A.J.A.*, 48 (1952), 77.
[2] *Od.* 7, 81, cf. above p. 107.

and the migration. The new kind of kingship and not the old will then have been taken overseas by the emigrants.

The East was not new ground to the Greeks. In the Mycenaean age they had conquered Troy; they had settlements in Cyprus, Ugarit, and Alalakh, of which we have spoken; there were also Mycenaean settlements at some of the places which later became Greek cities, and others of them got Mycenaean pottery from their neighbours. A brief survey of Asia Minor from North to South will serve various purposes: it will show from where the Greeks crossed the Aegean and what areas the different parties reached, what memories they brought with them and what survivals they may have found, what contact they had with the East, what were the dates of the various settlements and where poetry may have survived or revived.

Troy itself after the catastrophe to Troy VII A was 'still importing some Mycenaean pottery of the so-called Granary style, but the eleventh and tenth centuries represent a long period of slow fusion of an intrusive European element with the surviving Trojan, and Troy does not seem to have been occupied by the Aeolians until after 700 B.C.'[1] The victory over Troy seems to have been a barren victory; some Mycenaeans may have lingered on there and in Aeolis for a time, but there certainly was no continuity of settlement. Lesbos also provides no evidence for a Mycenaean settlement, although Mycenaean pottery had been imported for some time before the Trojan war.[2] Nor is there any reason to suppose that Skepsis under Mount Ida was occupied by a member of the Trojan royal family: it is much more likely that its rulers, whoever they were, owed their name of Aineiadai to the Ionians (and particularly the Milesians), who were interested in keeping them friendly and supported their claim to Troy, which commanded the route to the Black Sea; thus the *Iliad* asserts that Aeneas and his descendants shall reign over the Trojans, and Arktinos of Miletos in his *Sack of Troy* arranged for Aeneas to escape from Troy when Laokoon was devoured by the snakes. The Aeolian *Little Iliad* by Lesches of Mitylene, however, sent Aeneas off to Thessaly with Neoptolemos.[3] This is eight-century

---

[1] Blegen, *B.S.A.*, 37 (1937), 11; Wade-Gery, *Poet of the Iliad*, 79.

[2] Stubbings, *Mycenaean pottery in the Levant*, 22.

[3] *Il.* 20, 307; Arktinos *apud* Proclus; Lesches, fr. 19. Cf. Strabo, 607; Schadewaldt, *Iliasstudien*, 124, n. 2.

manipulation of legend for political ends, and presupposes that Aeneas is already recognized as a figure of importance in the Trojan story. We need not look to Skepsis either for a survival of poetry or for the court where Homer sang.

The Greek occupiers of Lesbos and Aeolis traced their descent back to Agamemnon. Strabo speaks of Locrian settlers in Kyme soon after the Trojan war, followed by a mixed Boeotian and Thessalian migration led by descendants of Agamemnon; one party went by Thrace and the Propontis and reached Lesbos, and the other 'wasted time in Locris' and then settled in Kyme. Strabo evidently supposes that the Aeolian migration started in the generation after the Trojan war but arrived about the same time as the Ionian migration. It is interesting that Penthilos, the son of Orestes, who led the migration from Arcadia to Thrace and to whom the Penthilidai of Lesbos traced their ancestry, and his son Echelaos, who led them across the Hellespont, had names connected with the Pylian pedigree of Kodros.[1] The Aeolian occupation of Lesbos presumably goes back at least to the time of the tenth-century Protogeometric pottery found there,[2] and the Penthilidai were still ruling in the early seventh century, a governing family like the Medontidai earlier in Athens. Doubtless they had their traditional poetry, but the earliest poet known to us, the eighth-century Lesches of Mitylene, who wrote the *Little Iliad*, is stylistically completely under the influence of Homer. Traditional poetry presumably also existed in Aeolis, but there is again nothing to show that it had any effect on Homer (or indeed on Hesiod) and Wade-Gery has suggested that the eighth-century Agamemnon of Kyme, whose daughter married Midas of Phrygia, got his name not from his remote ancestor but from the *Iliad*.[3] Phrygia provided the background to Aeolis and cut the Aeolians off from older Eastern civilizations. The pottery from Larisa in Aeolis appears to give no evidence for contact with the Greek world before the eighth century.[4]

Ionia also was already known to the Mycenaeans. Phokaia and Smyrna were probably not Mycenaean settlements, but Mycenaean vases found their way there.[5] Chios seems to have been occupied

---

[1] Cf. above p. 142. [2] Desborough, 81, 217.
[3] *Op. cit.*, 7. On Phrygia generally, cf. now Dunbabin, *The Greeks and their Eastern neighbours*, 64f. [4] Desborough, 192, 221.
[5] Stubbings, *op. cit.*, 23; J. M. Cook, *J.H.S.*, 72 (1952), 104.

both in Minoan times and Mycenaean times, and this may account for its connexion in tradition with Poseidon and Crete. There is no evidence for continuity between these earlier settlements and the later Greek settlement, but a memory of Chios may have been handed down in Greece.[1] Kolophon has a Mycenaean beehive tomb and legends of early settlers from Crete and Thebes. Here we seem to touch history.[2] Mopsos, whose father was the Cretan Rhakios and his mother Manto the daughter of Teiresias, is known from Hittite records as one of the allies of Attarissiyas of Ahhiyawa and from an inscription of the late eighth century as an ancestor of the then ruler at Karatepe in Cilicia; Greek legend makes him migrate from Kolophon into Cilicia a year before the end of the Trojan war. Again we have no evidence for continuity between the Mycenaean and Greek settlement of Kolophon, but it is reasonable to suppose that the Mycenaeans at home would remember the settlement and hand down the story. Samos and Miletos may have had continuity of settlement. In Samos, besides late Minoan pottery, a Mycenaean chamber tomb has been found, the earliest altar in the shrine of Hera is dated to the Sub-Mycenaean period, and some Protogeometric sherds of Attic type have been excavated.[3] Legend tells us of an early foundation of Ankaios, son of Poseidon and Astypalaia. There may have been a break between Mycenaean and Sub-Mycenaean; if so, at least the resettlement seems to have been very early. The latest report on Miletos states that ceramic evidence proves that the area round the Athena temple was inhabited without interruption from at least about 1500 B.C. to Roman times.[4] Certainly Mycenaean of all periods has been found, and Protogeometric of Attic type in close contact with the most recent Mycenaean stratum; it is not clear from the report whether 'the most recent Mycenaean' means in fact Sub-Mycenaean, which is needed, if continuity is to be shown. Legend tells of an autochthonous Anax with a son Asterios, and then of Miletos of Crete, who settled Cretans with the earlier Carians. Later when the Ionians and others came from Athens they married Carian wives. In the *Iliad*[5]

[1] Cf. 'Archaeology in Greece', 1953–5, in *J.H.S.*, 73 (1953) – 75 (1955).

[2] Stubbings, *op. cit.*, 23; Barnett, *J.H.S.*, 73 (1953), 141 f.; *A.S.*, 3 (1953), 87 f.

[3] Hanfmann, *H.S.C.P.*, 61 (1953), 56; Ohly, *A.M.*, 65 (1940), 82; Desborough, 216.

[4] *A.J.A.*, 60 (1956), 379. Cf. Stubbings, *op. cit.*, 23; Desborough, 221.

[5] *Il.* 2, 867. Cf. Huxley, *B.I.C.S.*, 3 (1956), 24.

Miletos is mentioned in the Trojan catalogue among the 'foreign-tongued Carians', which suggests that at this moment Miletos was not under Greek control but not necessarily that continuity of occupation was broken. If this refers to the time of the Trojan war, a similar change of control may have occurred earlier in the thirteenth century, because Millavanda, which has been plausibly identified with Miletos, is mentioned in Hittite correspondence first as belonging to Ahhiyawa and then as under control of the Hittites.[1] There may then have been continuity of occupation in Miletus from Mycenaean times to classical times, but it seems to have been a tenuous and doubtful continuity, and we need not suppose that the immigrants found any lively memories or any poetic tradition when they came.

Finally before continuing with the story of the Ionian migration we may mention what happened farther South. Rhodes was occupied first by Minoans and then by Mycenaeans, and this occupation seems to have been continuous from the sixteenth century to late in the Mycenaean period.[2] Kos[3] also was an important Mycenaean centre from the fourteenth to the twelfth century, and perhaps we may also accept Knidos on the basis of the Knidian women at Pylos. These early settlements are reflected in legend by the early rulers, Telchines and Heliadai in Rhodes, and by the descendants of Herakles in the Catalogue of Ships.[4] But both in Rhodes and in Kos there seems to be a break between the latest Mycenaean and the earliest Protogeometric, which marks a new beginning.[5]

Mycenaean settlements at Miletos and Samos may have survived, but everywhere else continuity seems to have been broken, even where late Mycenaean pottery shows that after the Trojan war, Mycenaeans were still there or were still in contact with these places. The Mopsos story shows that some Mycenaeans moved farther South, and perhaps the women from Knidos, Miletos, Chios on the Pylos tablets include refugees as well as captives. Two points are clear from this evidence. First, nothing like a Mycenaean kingdom survived in the East, no settlement strong enough to have handed on a poetic tradition which could have influenced the poetic tradition of the immigrants. Secondly,

[1] Gurney, *Hittites*, 48f., 56. [2] Stubbings, *op. cit.*, 8.
[3] Stubbings, *op. cit.*, 21. [4] *Il.* 2, 653; 676, cf. Huxley, *op. cit.*, 23.
[5] Desborough, 222, 232.

knowledge of the good places in Asia Minor would exist on the mainland in Mycenaean times and could be handed down from generation to generation.

The chronology of the Ionian migration itself is extremely difficult to establish nor is it easy to reconcile the archaeological and literary evidence.[1] It seems natural to connect the earlier stages of the movement (but not necessarily its beginning) with the discovery of lateish Protogeometric in Miletos, the Panionion, Samos, Chios, and particularly Smyrna, where a considerable deposit was found, going well back into the tenth century. Smyrna must be considered first. J. M. Cook[2] writes, 'in the early stages the Protogeometric pottery looks like imported ware alongside the local monochrome pottery, but in the ninth-century levels the painted ware becomes dominant; if the pottery can be used as a guide, it would seem that Smyrna had already passed completely into the hands of the Ionians before the end of the ninth century'. Two good pieces of literary evidence pull in different directions. Pasuanias[3] records that in 688 B.C. Onomastos won the boxing match at Olympia 'from Smyrna, which was already then rated among the Ionians'. This means that Smyrna had recently become a member of the Ionian League, a privilege which they only achieved some time after their capture by Kolophonian exiles.[4] Mimnermos,[5] the seventh-century elegiac poet of Kolophon, writes 'We left Pylos, the town of Neleus, and reached lovely Asia by sea. We settled in fair Kolophon, in the strength of our might, leaders in cruelty and crime. We set out again from the river Aleis and by the gods' will captured Aeolian Smyrna.' This is potted poetic history: taken literally it would mean that the Pylians came straight to Kolophon in 1200 B.C. and captured Smyrna shortly afterwards, which would make Smyrna one of the oldest Ionian cities and its exclusion from the League inexplicable. Mimnermos has telescoped, because he is writing about Gyges' attack on Smyrna in the early seventh century; the allusion to Neleus presumably means that the aristocrats in Kolophon traced their descent from Kodros, and it is enough to show that Athens was a stage in the migration. We can assume any interval we like between the arrival in Kolophon

[1] Cf. particularly Roebuck, *C.P.*, 50 (1955), 26f.
[2] *J.H.S.*, 72 (1952), 104.
[3] Pausanias, 5, 8, 7.
[4] Pausanias, 7, 5, 1 with Hdt. 1, 143, 3.
[5] Fr. 12D.

and the capture of Smyrna. We can, therefore, accept the Ionian capture of Smyrna sometime before 800 and its inclusion in the League about 700, when the earliest large temple was built. The quantity of Protogeometric pottery 'in style closely related to Attic' in Aeolian Smyrna shows that contact between Attica and Asia Minor existed, and perhaps implies that the Ionian migration had already occurred or was already in progress, but not necessarily that Kolophon was the intermediary at this stage.

Roebuck has argued that the twelve cities which formed the Ionian League consisted of an original nucleus of Miletos, Myous, Priene, Ephesos, Kolophon, Lebedos, and Teos, all clustering round the Panionion on the Mykale peninsula, and later additions Chios, Phokaia, Klazomenai, Erythrai, Samos (Smyrna, as we have seen, was added after the number of twelve had been reached and so was a sort of supplementary member). He supposes that 'the growth probably occurred during the ninth century, and the original nucleus of the League would have been in existence in the tenth century'. Let us look at such evidence as we have.[1] Neileus, the son of Kodros, founded Miletos with a mixed crowd of Athenians, Ionians, Boeotians, and others. As we have seen, he may have found Mycenaean survivors there, but according to the tradition the immigrants killed the men and married Carian wives; nevertheless Pausanias records that the shrine and oracle of Apollo at Didyma went back beyond the Ionian migration, and this may indicate the survival of a Mycenaean cult. Neileus' tomb was shown in Miletos. The Panionion altar of Poseidon on Mykale was attributed to him, and sherds which may be Protogeometric have been found in the neighbourhood.[2] Near Mykale also was 'a sanctuary of Eleusinian Demeter established by Philistos, son of Pasikles, who accompanied Neileus'.[3] Hekataios of Miletos, who was born about 560, traced his descent from a god in the sixteenth generation; Wade-Gery[4] has compared this pedigree with the fully preserved pedigree of Heropythos of Chios, who traced his descent back to Kyprios; Kyprios was presumably the first man of the family to die in Chios, and the family traced their descent to the first immigrant, just as the reigning family of Miletos traced their descent back to Neileus;

---

[1] Hdt. 1, 145 f.; Pausanias, 7, 2 f.; Strabo, 14, 3 f. Other evidence is quoted as relevant.   [2] Desborough, 221.   [3] Hdt. 9, 97.
[4] *The Poet of the Iliad*, 8, 67, 88. Hdt. 2, 143.

fifteen names are mentioned including Heropythos and Kyprios, so that, if we call Kyprios' father a god, the pedigree is exactly the same length as that of Hekataios. Wade-Gery puts Heropythos' death about 450, and then Kyprios should have been born about 970. On the same reckoning of three generations to a century the immigrant ancestor of Hekataios should have been born about 1030 and have reached Miletos at the end of the eleventh century. This is a date to be considered with the other evidence.

The founder of Myous is variously given as Kydrelos, bastard son of Kodros, and Kyaretos, son of Kodros, and we have nothing further to go on. Priene was also a mixed foundation; Aipytos, son of Neileus came first, and later Philotas from Thebes; but the settlement by Aipytos was not a generation later than Miletos, since Androklos, another son of Kodros, was killed defending Priene against the Carians. Neileus must have been old enough to have a grown-up son at the time of the migration, and his son founded Priene on the peninsula, at the seaward end of which Neileus set his altar to Poseidon. Ephesos was founded by Androklos, son of Kodros, who expelled the Lydians and the Leleges; Pausanias again notes the existence of a pre-migration shrine; the priests of Artemis came to terms with the invaders. This Artemis[1] seems to have been the Hittite mother of the gods, who sent her bee to wake the vegetation god Telepinus; the bee is well known in the cult of Artemis at Ephesos, but the story does not seem to have entered Greek mythology, although the cult was already there when the Ionians reached Ephesos. Conditions for borrowing would seem to be ideal but the Greeks did not borrow the story; this suggests that they were less receptive to Eastern stories now than during the Mycenaean age.[2] Androklos attacked Samos apparently with success, but it was recaptured after ten years; he was killed, as we have seen, defending Priene from the Carians. Pausanias was shown his tomb and there is no reason to doubt the correctness of his information, although the statue of an armed man which stood on it must have been a later addition.

Kolophon had a considerable Mycenaean history but then a break; the ancient oracle at Klaros, however, survived. The attack on Smyrna was probably before 800, as we have seen, and there is no earlier Greek material from Kolophon itself. The

[1] Cf. Barnett, *J.H.S.*, 68 (1948), 21. [2] Cf. above pp. 82 ff.

foundation is assigned to three different sons of Kodros, Andraimon, Promethos, and Damasichthon. Promethos was buried in Kolophon. Andraimon, whom Strabo calls Andropompos (the name of his great-grandfather), founded Lebedos and was buried between Kolophon and Lebedos. The remaining city belonging to the nucleus is Teos, which was again a mixed settlement from Orchomenos, old Ionia, Attica, and Boeotia. The Ionian wave led by Nauklos, son of Kodros, would seem to be earlier than the Athenian wave led by Poikes, 'fourth descendant of Melanthos', who should be a generation later, although not much need be made of this. A Hellenistic inscription preserves what seems to be a list of the original holders of large estates (*pyrgoi*) in Teos.[1] Of the twenty-six names preserved the following are interesting: Alkimos is a son of Nestor in the *Iliad*; Alxenor is a Mycenaean name in Pylos and Knossos; Hekadios can be compared with Wekadios in Knossos; Kizon, Kothos, Malios, Merades can be found on the Knossos tablets; Poikes is the founder from Athens; Sthenelos is a son of Kapaneus in the *Iliad*; Philaios is known from Pylos, from the Athenian family, and from the Heropythos pedigree in Chios; Kopreus occurs on the Pylos and Knossos tablets and in the *Iliad*. These names of the earliest settlers are evidence of their mixed derivation, of their Mycenaean origin, and of the basic rightness of the tradition.

Five cities were added to the nucleus. Klazomenai and Phokaia were new settlements; Klazomenai was a secondary settlement from Kolophon; Phokaia was a mixed settlement with Athenian leaders, which later accepted Kodrid kings from Erythrai and Teos in order to join the League; there is no archaeological evidence earlier than the eighth century. Erythrai was said to be originally Cretan, then mixed Cretan, Lycian, Carian, and Pamphylian. Later Knopos (or Kleopos), bastard son of Kodros, collected men from all the cities in Ionia to dwell with them. Knopos, according to Hippias of Erythrai,[2] was killed by usurpers, who obtained forces from Amphiklos and Polyteknos, tyrants of Chios. This again gives a possibility of dating, because Amphiklos of Chios is a known figure. There is no archaeological evidence in Chios for continuity between Mycenaean and Protogeometric times, but according to Pausanias, quoting the fifth-century Ion of Chios, Amphiklos from Euboea took over from

[1] D. W. S. Hunt, *J.H.S.*, 67 (1947), 70.   [2] Ath. 259a.

the Cretans (Strabo mentions a Thessalian element in the mixed mass); Hektor, king of Chios, in the fourth generation from Amphiklos fought with the Abantes and Carians in the island; the Chians then were admitted to the Ionian League and Hektor was given a tripod as a prize for valour by the League. We have seen that the Heropythos pedigree puts the first settlement of Chios into the late tenth century, the time of the small amount of Protogeometric pottery found there.[1] This then will be the time of Amphiklos and his negotiations with the murderers of Knopos. A date in the tenth century for the murder of Knopos agrees with a date in the eleventh century for the foundation of Miletos and Ephesos, if the reliable point in the Erythrai story is the description of Knopos collecting men from all the cities in Ionia and *not* his parentage (and he is only claimed as a bastard son of Kodros). Erythrai may not have been admitted to the League until after the restoration of Knopos' brother Hippotes, perhaps in the early ninth century.

The settlement of Chios can, therefore, be dated in the tenth century, and Hektor, who brought it into the League, will belong to the ninth century; this date again is possible for an alphabetic inscription on the tripod, which seems the likely source of Ion's information about Hektor. Samos, the remaining late-comer into the League, was, as we have already noted, captured for a period by Androklos of Ephesos. This was in the time of Leogoros, the son of Prokles of Epidauros, the leader of the Ionians and Epidaurians who were driven out by the Argives. The settlement was, therefore, a generation earlier, and it might be possible to connect Prokles' settlement with the first altar, with which Sub-Mycenaean remains are said to have been found. The temple of Hera[2] was apparently built in the ninth century at the time of the second altar, and the board-like statue, which was clothed with real drapery, belonged to this temple. The second temple was built early in the seventh century, and this must have housed the 'human-shaped' statue associated with Prokles, who must, therefore, if the name is right, be a descendant of our Prokles. If this difficulty can be thus removed, the archaeological evidence is consistent with a first settlement in the early eleventh century and great activity in the ninth, which might be the time when Samos joined the Ionian League.

[1] Desborough, 217.   [2] Cf. Ohly, *A.M.*, 68 (1953), 25 f.

The problem which remains is to reconcile the chronology which arises from the evidence of Ionian tradition, genealogy, and archaeology with the mainland chronology of the Pylian kings. Of course, the genealogies of the Neleids may be fictitious,[1] but their Mycenaean echoes and the long pedigrees of Hekataios and Heropythos incline me to accept them if possible. Hekataios' ancestor takes us back into the eleventh century for the foundation of Miletos, and he may not have been one of the earliest immigrants. Neileus seems to have been a man of some age when he founded Miletos, since Priene was founded by his son; the foundation of the Panionion on Mount Mykale by Neileus and of Priene by his son must have been part of the same conception as the foundation of Miletos. Neileus' brother Androklos was probably younger since he was killed some time later defending Priene, but he cannot have been born later than 1100 when Kodros died. Provisionally then we may put Neileus' birth about 1125, Androklos' birth shortly before 1100, and the beginning of the migration about 1060. This gives us the following provisional chronology:

1230   Sack of Troy.
1200   Sack of Pylos.
1170   Expulsion from Messenia. Melanthos' arrival in Athens.
1100   Sack of Mycenae. Kodros' defence of Athens and death. Birth of Androklos. Settlement of SAMOS.
1075   Beginning of Protogeometric. Institution of life archonship.
1060   Ionian migration. MILETUS, etc. Attack on SAMOS.
1000   Late Protogeometric. Settlement of ERYTHRAI. Settlement of CHIOS by Amphiklos.
900   Beginning of Pure Geometric.
900/800 Ionian capture of SMYRNA. Settlement of KLAZOMENAI, PHOKAIA. Widening of the League. Return to inhumation in Athens.

The migration was a long and difficult process lasting in all some three centuries. The new foundations in the ninth century and the considerable amounts of Geometric pottery suggest that the volume increased in the later stages, and the return to inhumation in Athens means that Athens, which in the next century

[1] Cf. Momigliano, *S.I.F.C.*, 10 (1933), 259.

took no part in colonization, had provided a large number of the migrants. Down to that stage, however, the immigrants came from many different parts of Greece, as the traditions about Samos, Miletos, Teos, Erythrai, and Chios show, and in the case of Teos this can be checked by the list of nobles owning estates (*pyrgoi*). In that list about a quarter of the names seem to be Eastern, and they must have been local inhabitants who were persuaded into the settlement. The same thing probably happened elsewhere, sometimes successfully and sometimes unsuccessfully; Hektor of Chios at quite a late stage fought the Carians in Chios. Earlier Miletos, Ephesos, and Samos were founded by expelling the inhabitants, and Androklos of Ephesos was killed defending Priene against the Carians. It is unlikely that this was an isolated case, and where an existing Eastern shrine, like that of the goddess at Ephesos, was preserved, its mythology might have no influence on the Greeks. Probably fruitful contact with the East did not revive until the eighth century. Ionian cups of the late ninth century have been found at Tarsos, and may be connected with the tradition that cities in Cilicia were founded from Rhodes and Samos, but this is unlikely to have been a fruitful contact in our sense. Al Mina, the port of the ancient city of Alalakh, was a much more likely place for cultural contacts, but the earliest East Greek pottery found there cannot be put before the first half of the eighth century.[1]

In the period with which we are concerned the immigrants were a mixed body living in a country whose inhabitants were largely hostile and, when they were not, had little to offer. The situation of these immigrants is essentially different from that of the Mycenaean settlements in the second millennium, which were in direct contact with the civilization of the East. The new immigrants had come to a hostile country where they knew that their ancestors had been and had fought a mighty war. Their singers were largely dependent on memory, the memory which their different strains had of their Mycenaean past. They did not sing of the present, or we should know more about this period. They sang of their common Mycenaean past. This was a unifying factor in their present existence, however much city squabbled

---

[1] Hanfmann in *The Aegean and the Near East*, 165 ff; Robertson, *J.H.S.*, 60 (1940) 2 f.; Dunbabin, *op. cit.*, 28, suggests that it may have been an Ionian foundation.

with city, Miletos with Samos or Chios with Erythrai. Among the various strains the dominant one was the Pylian-Attic strain which had led the expedition, and very early Neileus expressed this by founding the altar to Poseidon on Mykale. The god himself is the god of Pylos and of Athens; but here he had the title Helikonios, and therefore, even if he came immediately from Athens, he came ultimately from Mount Helikon in Boeotia – again a testimony to the mixed nature of the migration. The festival was the common festival of the original seven towns, and later included five further towns. There is no evidence that it had any political function until the time of Kroisos. Its name, the Panionia, emphasized the new unity and not the original differences of the participants. Such a festival, as Wade-Gery[1] says, would be a perfect occasion for an *Iliad*, but that came later. We must for the moment be content with the knowledge that the festival was instituted very early and that it had its full complement of members by the end of the ninth century, but that poverty and disturbed conditions must have militated against any considerable development earlier than this.

The pedigrees of Hekataios of Miletos and Heropythos of Chios show that pride in ancestry was an early characteristic of this society, and Teos preserved the names of the original owners of its large estates. Should we be right in supposing that these cities were aristocracies and not 'feudal' monarchies with a divine or near divine King? This would mean that the division between the new poets and their Mycenaean stories was not only one of time and place but also one of political organization and outlook. The signs to be expected are first the degrading of the King to king or priest or official, and corresponding to this the increased importance of the independent shrine (replacing the palace shrine), secondly the increased importance of the aristocracy and their houses and an emphasis on human genealogy instead of divine ancestry, thirdly, with the development of political institutions, the development of a new type of city surrounded by walls and centred on the Agora instead of the Acropolis. In Athens itself the degrading of the King had begun, as we have seen, at the end of the twelfth century and was probably complete by the time of the migration; the new Agora was apparently much later, in the time of Solon, but there are traces of an earlier Agora

---

[1] *Op. cit.*, 3 f.; cf. also Roebuck, *op. cit.*

nearer the Acropolis. In Ionia we hear of several kings, but they are always called *basileus* and not *wanax*, and *basileus* in Mycenaean times is a noble, the mayor of a village, not the semi-divine King of a considerable territory. In fact, with the destruction of the Mycenaean palaces the top of the Mycenaean social structure was knocked off. Miletos preserved a dim memory of the past in the name of Anax as the original ruler. The kings of the migration called themselves Neileids after the first immigrant Neileus. They were a ruling family like the Medontids at Athens and did not outlast the eighth century. In Ephesos and Erythrai the ruling family called themselves Basileidai, thus proving that their first king was called *basileus* and not *wanax*; in Ephesos the family were still ruling in the seventh century, and in Roman times still had certain privileges and religious duties, including the priesthood of Eleusinian Demeter. Our period shows the rule of a single family; one of them is a hereditary *basileus*, the human ruler of a limited territory and not, like the Mycenaean *wanax*, essentially different from other settlers, who also had their great houses, their pride, and their pedigrees. His rule was not unchallenged as the various stories of exile and revolution show. The development to oligarchy within the family or to include other families cannot be traced in detail: Aristotle, for instance, speaks of the ancient *oligarchy* of the Basileidai at Ephesos.

One sign of this new aristocracy is the form of their names. The families call themselves 'sons of' their original ancestor, and the name ends in *-dai*. We have noticed Neileidai in Miletos, Basileidai in Ephesos and Erythrai, Medontidai (and there are many others) in Athens. The ruling family of eighth-century Corinth were called Bakchiadai, the rulers of seventh-century Lesbos Penthilidai, the rulers of sixth-century Thessaly Aleuadai and Skopadai. There is no sign of this form of patronymic on the Mycenaean tablets, on which the family name is in adjectival form; but it is very common in Homer, and the earliest such patronymics were probably made from the adjective of the ancestral name: thus Peleus makes an adjective Pelewios, and this makes a patronymic Pelewiades. We shall be able to show some linguistic evidence that these formations in Homer can be dated to our period. Outside Homer, apart from the probability that this convenient way of referring to aristocratic families and giving telescoped pedigrees of individuals in them was made early, positive evidence is given by the pedigree of Heropythos: one of his ancestors, who was born about 780, was called Hekaides, and earlier in the pedigree comes Hekaos, the grandson of the original Kyprios and born about 910. Hekaides' name evidently means 'descendant of Hekaos', and this eighth-century use is evidently an extension of an earlier strict use meaning 'son of H'. Probably by the eighth century the suffix -*dai* had come to be used very generally to denote connexion with a family, and thus even occurs in place-names (e.g. the Attic *demes*).

The nobles who settled in Teos had, as we have seen, each their *pyrgos*, probably a fortified house round which the houses of the smaller folk were grouped. Some idea of this sort of site can be formed from the recent excavations at Emporio in Chios,[1] which revealed a walled *acropolis* containing a noble house and a temple of Athena with offerings dating back to the beginning of the eighth century, the time of king Hektor. Traces of some fifty houses were found grouped round the *acropolis*. Down by the harbour traces of another sanctuary site were found which had been flourishing since 800 B.C. Thus Hektor's Chios seems to have consisted of a number of separate settlements grouped round the fortified houses of his nobles. About 200 years later an inscription[2] shows that Chios had a developed constitution with a Council, which because it is called 'Popular' perhaps implies the existence of another 'Aristocratic' Council, and with an official called *demarchos*, who is named side by side with the 'kings'. The plural 'kings' shows that the kingship was by then a magistracy. But we cannot tell when in the 200 years between king Hektor and the inscription these changes occurred, nor have we, as far as I know, any early evidence for a walled city with an *agora* as its centre. But Homer knew it. Scheria[3] was founded as a *polis*: Nausithoos drove a wall round the city and built houses and made temples of the gods and divided the fields; it had an *agora* on either side of the lovely Poseideion. Illogically, the Mycenaean palace of Alkinoos is superimposed on this modern Ionian plan.

In Scheria, as in eighth-century Chios, the temples of the gods are separate entities in the town plan, and in Samos the first temple

---

[1] J. Boardman, *J.H.S.*, 75 (1955), Suppl. 45; 76 (1956), 35.
[2] Tod, *G.H.I.*, i, no. 1; Ehrenberg, *J.H.S.*, 57 (1937), 152; Jeffery, *B.S.A.*, 51 (1956), 161.   [3] *Od.* 6, 9; 266.

of Hera is dated to the late ninth century. In Ephesos and elsewhere, as we have seen, the immigrants respected an existing shrine, and where such shrines survived, they suggested the need of worthy dwellings for the gods. Although the remains in Ionia only take us back to the late ninth century for the beginning of the classical temple, separate shrines for some gods were already known in the Mycenaean age, but the essential change from the palace shrine to the independent temple came with the destruction of the Mycenaean palaces and the degrading of the *wanax* to *basileus*. In Athens this seems to have happened before the migration began.

This long change of social structure, which put the Mycenaean Kings ever further into the golden past, has taken us down to Homer's own time and even beyond. It seemed better to try and give a continuous picture, since for many elements we only have a bottom date so that we cannot say precisely when they were introduced.

6

POETRY BETWEEN THE FALL
OF MYCENAE AND THE TIME
OF HOMER

We have now to consider what we can say of poetry during the early period of this development between say 1100 and 900 B.C., when the migrations were occurring with all the misery and cruelty so brilliantly portrayed by Gilbert Murray in the *Rise of the Greek Epic*,[1] when the aristocrats were becoming self-conscious, when a League of Ionian cities was forming round the altar on Mykale, but before the League was complete, before the political change had fully developed, before enough prosperity had returned or enough self-confidence to honour the Mycenaean heroes with hero cults and games and to name kings after Hektor, Agamemnon, or Aeneas. Memory of stories connected with the gods probably survived where cult places were continuously tended. The second kind of Mycenaean poetry, the songs sung in honour of dead kings at their anniversaries, may have survived at Athens, where Homer knows of the cult of Erechtheus. Whether Iolkos will prove to be another such centre, where above all Argonaut poetry would be preserved, is still uncertain. The kind of Mycenaean poetry that could travel was the third kind, the poetry improvised for special occasions by warrior singers and court singers. The Ionian migration was a mixed migration and each element would bring its own poetry about its own heroes, but this kind of Mycenaean poetry was international in the sense that it had to be intelligible to visitors from other centres and it had to include the deeds of heroes in other centres. Because the new cities were mixed, the great international undertakings of the Mycenaeans are likely to have been particularly popular with audiences. But in these Ionian settlements one strain was dominant, the Pylian-Attic. The majority of the settlements started from Attica; the new inspiration

[1] 71f.

in Protogeometric pottery, which spread over the whole Greek world, was Attic; the later immigrants down to the end of our period came largely from Attica; the League, into which the outliers, Samos, Chios, and Smyrna, were brought, was the Panionian League founded by the Pylian-Attic Neileus. In due course this strain became an Ionian strain independent and going its own ways, but that had hardly happened by 900 B.C. So I believe that for these two centuries, the role of Athens, the unsacked city, to which the refugees came and from which the immigrants went, may have been as important in literature as it was in art.

The chief argument against this view is the theory that the Ionian epic is little more than a transliteration of an earlier Aeolic epic. The evidence for this theory must be briefly examined, but at first sight it now seems unattractive. If the tradition of their descent from Agamemnon is true, the immigrants to Aeolis and Lesbos started out from Mycenae, which on the evidence of the tablets had a dialect scarcely distinguishable from Pylian. By the tenth century both Lesbos and Smyrna were in contact with Attica, and by the end of the ninth, Smyrna was Ionian. In the late eighth century the Cyclic poet Lesches of Mitylene wrote a dialect identical with Homer's. There seems little time or occasion for an Aeolic epic to develop to such proportions that it can be regarded as a necessary stage between Mycenaean poetry and Ionic epic; that in Aeolis also the old stories continued to be sung is, of course, probable. We may consider whether Björck's[1] diametrically opposed solution is acceptable. His detailed examination of the use of 'impure alpha' in the dialogue of tragedy led him to formulate the general rule: 'high poetry in Greek may exhibit freely chosen linguistic elements, which cannot be accounted for either by the dialect of the poet or of his public or by the history of the metre. If this is applied to Homer, the possibility arises that the Ionians used certain Aeolic forms, which had no parallels in their own Ionic, without there having been an Aeolic poetry.' This view implies that so far from recomposing an Aeolic epic into Ionic the Ionian poets borrowed certain forms from spoken Aeolic.

We can now, I think, put the problem in a rather different historical setting. First, if, as I have argued, the third kind of

[1] *Das Alpha impurum*, 220.

Mycenaean poetry, which alone concerns us, was international poetry, its language may well have already borrowed words and forms from all the component dialects of the Mycenaean palaces; the tablets from Pylos, Knossos, and Mycenae are strikingly alike in dialect,[1] but the style of documents may be more conservative than poetry and their vocabulary, particularly in verbal forms, is limited. Secondly, the mixed character of Ionian settlements would have tended to preserve and even to extend the mixed character of poetic dialect. Thirdly, from the eighth century at least the spoken and written dialects were diverging fast from the dialect of epic poetry, which largely preserved its ancient manner, just as in the eighth century local Geometric styles are clearly distinguishable. Thus Lesches of Mitylene, as we have seen, shows no trace of Aeolic in the fragments of the *Little Iliad*; both Eumelos of Corinth and Hesiod of Ascra cheerfully suppress the digamma when it suits them, although the digamma is written in our earliest Corinthian and Boeotian inscriptions; they adopted even modern Attic-Ionic licenses as being in the epic manner, although the forms conflicted with the local practice in speech and writing. The so-called Aeolic features[2] of epic dialect must be put in this perspective. Aeolic features which are attested on the Mycenaean tablets will have been in the poetic language from Mycenaean times: these are words compounded with *eri-*, datives of *s*- stems in *-essi* (on which others were modelled), *pt-* for *p-*; as the tablets also use *apu-* for *apo-* such formations as ἄλλυδις, ἄμυδις may possibly also be very early. All these can have passed into Attic-Ionic from Pylos. Once in Pylos *qe-* is written as *pe-* (as *qi-* is occasionally written for *pi-*); a similar very early development of the labio-velar into a labial instead of a dental might account for πέλομαι, πελώριος and Φήρ, but Φήρ is better regarded as the Thessalian name of a Thessalian monster and πελώριος may belong to the same context; whatever is the explanation of πέλομαι, it would seem to be a very early component of epic language (πίσυρες on the other hand, may be a late borrowing for metrical convenience). Risch[3] has argued that,

---

[1] Cf. *Docs.* 75.

[2] On the main features to be considered cf. Cauer, *Grund-fragen*, 148 ff; Meillet, *Aperçue*, 162 ff.; Schwyzer, *Gr. Gram.*, I, 106 ff.; Page, *The Homeric Odyssey*, 160. I am grateful to Dr. O. Szemerenyi for help and suggestions; the errors which remain are mine.

[3] *Mus. Helv.*, 12 (1955) 61 f.; cf. Chadwick, *Greece and Rome*, 3 (1956), 38 f.

where Ionic agrees with Arcadian and Cypriote against Aeolic, these differences go back to the second millennium; the most important of these doublets for Homer are the modal particles ἄν and κε and the infinitive active of the thematic verb in -ναι and -μεν; here the tablets do not show which forms were used in Pylos; but as the forms seem to be indistinguishably mixed in Homer they may well belong to international Mycenaean poetry, and it would be wrong to regard either as intrusive at the expense of the other. Similarly, although here we have no control, what we know as the Aeolic and Ionic forms of the first and second person pronouns in the plural coexist in Homer and may have co-existed from very early times. In the remaining cases Aeolisms can only be dated from their contexts. 'Dark night' and 'white sheep' are such fixed formulae that they should be early; κεκλήγοντες, a perfect participle declined like a present, occurs only in late contexts in the Iliad; the words compounded with ζα- instead of δια- are either extremely rare (ζάκοτος, ζαφλεγής, ἐπιζάφελος)[1] or occur in contexts which for other reasons are likely to be late (ζαχρηής, ἀζηχής, ζαής); ζάθεος and ζατρεφής are blameless otherwise but always occur with a different noun, which suggests a late free method of making formulae. Chadwick suggests also that apocope in prepositions is a relatively late development.[2] Thus when the so-called Aeolisms in Homer are inspected, they can be divided into a class which came into Attic-Ionic from the Mycenaean dialect of Pylos and are, therefore, not Aeolic at all, a second class which is certainly very early and might be due to borrowing by the main dialect of Mycenaean poetry, thirdly, a couple of fixed formulae which are likely to be early, and fourthly, a number of words and forms which seem from context or use to be late borrowings from the dialect of the mixed settlers in Ionia or of their neighbours in Aeolis. Thus the dominant strain of poetic language was already in Mycenaean times a mixed strain; in Attica during our period it became what can be called Attic-Ionic but was still open to loans, particularly from settlers from other areas of Greece and later from neighbours in Asia Minor; after about 900, however, it developed on its own in Ionia and though strongly conservative included some uses

[1] Cf. also βέρεθρον, πολυπάμων, βόλομαι.
[2] Op. cit., 43; on their use in Homer cf. Richardson, Hermathena, 77 (1951), 65 f.

which can be shown to be contemporary Ionic as distinct from contemporary Attic.

There are three main kinds of evidence which can give some idea of poetry in the dark centuries. First, certain linguistic forms, certain changes of custom (cremation and the introduction of iron have already been mentioned), and certain memories can be dated to this period. Secondly, if the general picture that has been drawn is accepted, it follows that where the same stories are told with variations not only in Homer but also in some mainland poem contemporary or nearly contemporary with him, both the Ionian and the mainland version go back to a common mainland source; in many cases this is ultimately Mycenaean poetry, but it may be possible in some cases to detect what has happened to the story in the meantime. Thirdly, certain kinds of poetry, other than narrative poetry and hymns to the gods, are presupposed by the *Iliad* and the *Odyssey*, and it may be possible to suggest that they already existed in the dark period especially if they can also be shown to be behind Hesiod and his contemporaries.

The new type of patronymic in *-des* has already been mentioned. It seems to be post-Mycenaean, but as it frequently preserves the Mycenaean dissyllabic genitive in *-ao* instead of the late genitive form which is scanned monosyllabically, it must have been introduced in our period, and it occurs in conjunction with the *-oo* form of the second declension genitive, which again belongs to our period inasmuch as it is a stage between the long Mycenaean form *-oio* and the later monosyllabic form *-ou*.[1] These are the only two linguistic changes which need be mentioned. The *-oo* genitive is never written in our texts, but must be restored in certain passages to preserve the metre. Three of these tell us something of poetry in this period.[2] The Phocian contingent in the Catalogue of Ships is led by Schedios and Epistrophos, sons of great-hearted Iphitos, son of Naubolos; the line will only scan if the *-oo* genitive is restored: υἶες Ἰφίτοο μεγαθύμοο Ναυβολίδαο. Thus the new genitive is associated with the new patronymic here. This shows that this line is a post-Mycenaean addition to the Catalogue, if we believe that the Catalogue preserves a Mycenaean operation order. The addition is a brief genealogy giving the father and the grandfather of the leaders concerned. Seven other leaders (or pairs

---

[1] Cf. *Eranos*, 54 (1956), 35 f.
[2] *Il.* 2, 518; 21, 104; 9, 64 (cf. above p. 96).

of leaders, are given grandfathers as well as fathers in the Catalogue, and I have noticed three other genealogies of the same length and form in the *Iliad* and seven in the *Odyssey*. Here, I think, we may see a reflection in poetry of the aristocratic families' pride in pedigrees: even unimportant families must have their pedigrees, and the poets invented a convenient short form for expressing them.

Two other interesting phrases demanding the new genitive are 'Ιλίοο προπάροιθεν 'before Troy' and πολέμοι' ἐπιδημίοο κρυοέντος 'bloody war in the land'. The first is a tiny piece of evidence that the Trojan war was a subject of poetry at this time. The second is used by Nestor when he denounces the man who desires civil war. The word *epidemios*, with its suggestion of visiting the land like a plague, is the kind of description to be expected from an age which had seen the destruction of the Mycenaean palaces or remembered them not too distantly. Their destruction is actually foretold in a dialogue[1] between Zeus and Hera, which links them with the Trojan war. Zeus is prepared to let Hera sack Troy, if he may sack her cities; she answers that he may sack 'Argos and Sparta and broad-wayed Mycenae' whenever he grows angry with them. The gods are made responsible, and the sack of Troy and Mycenae alike is attributed to their hatred. This is a historical pointing of the old Eastern story of the hostility of the gods to mankind, and we shall have to consider later whether the interpretation as well as the memory belongs to this period.

One of the results of the sack of the palaces and the flood of refugees into Athens was the adoption of cremation as the normal burial rite. The rite was taken on to Ionia by the migrants, and, therefore, when Homer speaks of cremation he is probably speaking of the rite which he himself knows. To show that cremation was already described in Athenian poetry in our period (and that is the point, if it is accepted that Ionia owed cremation to Athens) it is necessary to establish first that the rite is sometimes felt to need explanation, secondly that the rite is sometimes used for the kind of special occasion for which we believe it was adopted, and thirdly that it has given rise to poetic formulae which are likely to be old. We have discussed already the probability that funeral processions and funeral games were Mycenaean,

[1] *Il.* 4, 31 ff.

164

and I shall argue later that they were remembered in Athenian poetry of this time. They imply that the dead man lives to enjoy his games, and many of the details suggest the same belief. But Patroklos in the *Iliad* and Achilles in the *Odyssey* were cremated. In the *Iliad*[1] before the funeral Patroklos' ghost visits Achilles as he sleeps: 'Bury me as quickly as possible, let me pass the gates of Hades. The souls keep me away. . . . I shall not come back again from Hades, when you have given me my portion of fire.' If the implication of the elaborate funeral rites is that the great man lives on in his tomb and can benefit his descendants, the new rite of cremation has the contrary implication that the dead man must be admitted to Hades and confined there. It may be, as Mylonas has suggested,[2] that with inhumation the dead man was believed to go to Hades when his body had decayed, and that cremation was used sporadically when it was desirable that he should go there quickly (as, for instance, when his body was left on enemy soil and might benefit the enemy or when his tomb was to be used again for a new burial). But the rich tombs and elaborate funerals show that the emphasis was on his continued existence in the tomb, and now the emphasis is switched to his speedy departure to Hades. Patroklos' ghost makes an emphatic statement of the new belief. Another is made by Odysseus' mother,[3] when he, like Achilles, has tried and failed to embrace the shadowy form: 'The sinews no longer hold flesh and bones together but they are overcome by the victorious force of blazing fire, as soon as the breath leaves the white bones and the soul is gone on wings like a dream. But you must seek your way back quickly to the light. Know all these things that you may tell them to your wife later.' The new belief is something of importance which the family should know, and it seems to me that these two programmatic statements are likely in their original form to have been made soon after cremation became universal. There are two cases[4] where the special occasions for which we believe the rite was introduced are found in Homer: Elpenor died in Circe's house and begged Odysseus to burn him with his arms; he must be sent to Hades as quickly as possible because his grave is out of Odysseus' control, as soon as he has left the island. Similarly Achilles burnt the body of Eetion, Andromache's father, with

[1] *Il.* 23, 71 f.   [2] *A.J.A.*, 52 (1948), 69 f.
[3] *Od.* 11, 219.   [4] *Od.* 11, 74; *Il.* 6, 418.

his arms. This is the generosity of an enemy, who again has to leave the grave. Such cases must have been common in the flight before the Dorian invasion and in the migrations. If the point of cremation is to speed the dead to Hades, then not only the formulae 'to give a man his portion of fire, to step on the cruel pyre' but also the formulae 'to pass the gates of Hades', 'to go to Hades', or 'within the house of Hades', or 'to Erebos' are expressions of the new belief, and these were all established by the time our Homer wrote.

The introduction of iron[1] cannot be dated in the poems to our period rather than to the period of Homer himself, since all the swords found in the Protogeometric graves at Athens were iron, and after that iron never went out of use. We can say for certain that useful iron, as distinct from precious iron, must be post-Mycenaean, and this provides some evidence for the retelling of the old stories in modern dress. The metal was difficult to obtain and difficult to work, and therefore is likely to have been used for weapons before it was used for tools and implements. Homer never speaks of an iron sword (and the iron mace and Pandaros' iron arrowhead are probably Mycenaean precious iron), but Miss Lorimer[2] has shown that a number of blows which sever whole limbs can only have been delivered with an iron sword and, therefore, must be additions to Bronze Age fighting. Its metaphorical use for hardness or strength or noise or brightness could be introduced any time after the metal was known; and so could the description of the smith at work; he is described as working iron, even when he is working in quite different materials. The two similes which mention iron tools are likely to be late as we shall see. 'Iron itself draws a man on' is clearly the comment of a man who expects weapons to be made of iron.[3]

The use of the iron sword can only be detected some five times in the *Iliad* and once in the *Odyssey*. A much more obvious change in weapons is the substitution of two throwing-spears for the single thrusting-spear. The change is a change from close-range fighting (where in the old days mobility had been given by chariots) to long-range mobile fighting; the retreat of refugees

---

[1] See Gray, *J.H.S.*, 74 (1954) 1 f., who discusses all the passages.
[2] *HM*, 267, e.g. *Il.* 5, 81; *Od.* 10, 440.
[3] Smith: *Il.* 18, 475; *Od.* 8, 273. Similes: *Il.* 4, 485; *Od.* 9, 391. 'Iron itself': *Od.* 16, 294; 19, 13.

may have occasioned it. Blegen[1] has published a grave from the Agora of about 900 B.C. with two spearheads; otherwise the direct evidence is limited to a single Late Geometric grave in the Dipylon cemetery. The warriors on Attic geometric vases are, however, commonly armed with two spears, and in the battle scenes spears are shown flying through the air. Miss Lorimer[2] concludes: 'That the new is common to Attica and the *Iliad*, which presumably means Ionian, is an interesting point and one which recalls the common attitude of these regions to cremation; it also suggests that the change to the throwing-spear was made in Greece before the Ionian migration.' The important principle enunciated here must be considered later. For the moment let us look at the throwing-spear in Homer. Two[3] of the standard lines from the arming scenes describing the warrior taking his spear also occur in a slightly altered form in which he takes two spears: 'he took his valiant spear which fitted in his hands' is put into the plural with 'shafts' instead of 'spear'; the other needed a little more alteration, and 'two shafts tipped with bronze' took the place of 'spear shod with sharp bronze'. Neither these altered lines nor the repeated line 'he spoke and whirling his long shaft hurled it' nor the formulae 'brandishing sharp shafts', 'hit with his shaft', 'hurled his shaft', etc. can be dated; they must be post-Mycenaean, because the throwing-spear is post-Mycenaean; on the other hand they have none of the linguistic marks of lateness, and they are so well established that they must have been part of poetic language long before our Homer. Evidently when the new tactics and equipment came in, the poets brought the old stories up to date because the audience liked to think of the heroes of the past as equipped and fighting in their own way. Agamemnon may have started with a body-shield, then he was given a Mycenaean corselet and a hand-grip shield, and now he takes two throwing-spears when he arms for his battles in the eleventh book of the *Iliad*, but in most of the ensuing fights he still uses the thrusting-spear alone. The stories were only partially brought up to date and sometimes not very successfully. Paris has two spears at the beginning of the third book of the *Iliad*,[4] and before his duel with Menelaos they cast lots to see which of

[1] *Hesperia*, 21 (1952), 134.   [2] *HM*, 258.
[3] Compare *Il*. 3, 338 with 16, 139; 15, 482 with 11, 43.
[4] *Il*. 3, 18; 317; 338; 346; 355; 361.

the pair shall throw first, but Paris then arms himself with a single thrusting-spear, then they both throw unsuccessfully and finally Menelaos draws his sword. Paris arms for close combat and the fight ends in close combat with the sword, but it has been remodelled into a duel with throwing-spears. The final fight between Achilles and Hektor[1] is close combat; Hektor is attacking with his sword when Achilles drives the spear into his throat; but the fight has been modernized with a preliminary duel for throwing-spears. Both heroes have famous Mycenaean thrusting-spears, which are remembered, and they cannot, therefore, be armed with two throwing-spears. Achilles used his spear in the final fight, and therefore, when he misses in the preliminary duel Athena gives it back to him; Hektor used his sword at the end, and therefore, when he has thrown his spear and asks for another Deiphobos is too far away to give it him. A few fights, like the last fight of Sarpedon and Achilles' fights with Aeneas and Agenor, only have the throwing-spear, and these must be post-Mycenaean.[2] In the *Odyssey*[3] the battle with the suitors is a throwing-spear battle, and Telemachos fetches each of the four attackers two spears; but Melanthios only fetches the suitors one spear each, and at the end Odysseus and Telemachos are thrusting with their spears. We cannot say at what date individual stories were remodelled, and some of these instances may be the work of our Homer; the evidence that some of the remodelling was early lies in the well-established formulae, which show no marks of late language, and the agreement of the scenes with the scenes on Attic geometric vases.

Miss Lorimer's principle that what is common to Attic geometric vases and Homer is likely to have an origin in Greece before the Ionian migration can be applied further. The figure scenes of Attic geometric pottery[4] are illustrations of contemporary Attic poetry, and where likenesses to Homer can be seen we must suppose a common original in pre-migration poetry. Two assumptions are made here; the first is that these scenes are earlier than any probable knowledge of our Homer in Attica, and the

[1] *Il.* 22, 306f.; 273f.; 289f. Cf. below p. 217.

[2] *Il.* 16, 462; 20, 259; 21, 581f.

[3] *Od.* 22, 110; 144; 292f.

[4] Cf. *B.S.A.*, 50 (1955), 39f. for a full discussion and detailed references for the vases.

second that the figure scenes on Attic geometric vases are taken from myth rather than from contemporary life. The absolute dating of Attic geometric vases is difficult, and the period of time needed for the development of the figure style has been variously estimated from a maximum of a century to a minimum of twenty-five years; but I think there would be general agreement that the monumental amphorae and kraters (figs. 21–2), which provide some of the most interesting parallels, should not be dated after 750 B.C.; thus they antedate the *Iliad* and the *Odyssey* or at least Athenian knowledge of the poems. The late Geometric figure vases, which precede Proto-Attic, probably belong to the last quarter of the eighth century but do not overlap into the seventh. It is, of course, possible that in the late eighth century with the development of festivals communication of poetry between the East and the West was quicker and earlier than we imagine; even so the unbroken thread of mainland tradition in Attica must have had some strength and persistence. The argument that the figure scenes of Attic Geometric pottery are based on poetry rather than contemporary life rests on three propositions: first, that some scenes, for instance a man fighting a lion, must be mythical; secondly, that the representation of scenes from everyday secular life is unlikely at so early a date in the history of classical Greek art; thirdly, that the artist often shows that he wants the scene to be interpreted as mythical by giving his warriors a kind of shield which recalled the Mycenaean body-shield but had no counterpart in real life.

If Geometric figure painting lasts roughly from 760 to 700, Athenian soldiers of the earlier part of this period used the round hand-grip shield with a pointed boss of the kind found in Athenian cemeteries (the successor of the Mycenaean hand-grip shield), and in the later part wore the round hoplite shield slung on the left arm, which is in fact worn by files of men on some Attic geometric vases of about the last third of the century.[1] There is no room between these two for the extraordinary and impractical Dipylon (or Boeotian) shield, which is, however, perfectly explicable as a conscious reminiscence of the body-shield of the Shaft-Grave period. A few Mycenaean precious objects which showed the body-shield may have survived; among

[1] See S. Benton, *B.S.A.*, 48 (1953), 340. E.g. Athens, Benaki Museum, 559: *B.S.A.*, 42 (1947), 150, pl. 19.

the Mycenaean ivories[1] which were buried in the foundation
deposit of the new Artemision at Delos towards the end of the
eighth century, and therefore were presumably visible in the
sanctuary up to that date, was a warrior with a body-shield (fig. 2).
The shape could also have been transmitted as an ornament in
textiles, or in other precious objects of which we have some
evidence.[2] It is even possible that such shields were made for
ritual or ceremonial purposes throughout the intervening period,
but of this we have no evidence, unless the small clay model of a
Dipylon shield in the British Museum[3] is to be explained as a
dedication after such a parade; but it may rather be a dedication
by someone who wanted to allude to the heroic past like his
contemporary in Ischia,[4] who remembered Nestor's beverage in
the eleventh book of the *Iliad* when he wrote a Homeric couplet
about a love potion. When the Dipylon shield appears in heroic
scenes on seventh-century Proto-Corinthian and later vases,
Miss Lorimer calls it 'a deliberate piece of romantic archaizing',
'deliberately introduced to mark the scene as heroic'. I believe
this description is equally true of its appearance on Attic geometric
vases of the eighth century. The artist knows that the heroes of
the past had shields like this, but he has no notion how big they
really were (they never come below the knee) and he has no
notion of how men fought with them (allusions to body-shield
fighting are rare enough in our *Iliad*); he introduced them to show
that the scene he was painting had some connexion with the
heroic past. Thus these Attic paintings are yet another sign of the
revival of interest in the heroic past, like the hero cults, the tripods
in Ithaca, and the new large-scale epic poetry. Several vases[5] show
a pair of Dipylon shields suspended over something which looks
like an altar and between two or more seated men with rattles;
the natural interpretation is that this is a ceremony conducted at
the tomb or shrine of a hero.

For the moment these vases interest us because they may provide evidence for poetry before the completion of the Ionian migration. In their battle scenes spears fly through the air 'yearning

---

[1] See above p. 27, n.5.
[2] See R. Higgins, *B.I.C.S.*, 4 (1957), 33 on the so-called Boeotian shield.
[3] Lorimer, *HM*, 156, pl. 7, 2–4.
[4] Buchner and Russo, *Rendiconti Lincei*, 1955, 215; Page, *C.R.*, 6 (1956), 95 f.
[5] *B.S.A.*, 50 (1955), 42, n. 30; J. M. Cook, *B.C.H.*, 70 (1946), 99, fig. 1.

to taste flesh'.[1] The manner of fighting is Homeric: we see sword fights and spear fights, and archers like Teucer, Paris, and Pandaros in the *Iliad*. The absence of evidence for archery in Geometric Greece suggests that these archers are figures in poetry. A single example, a jug in Copenhagen[2] from the Dipylon cemetery in Athens, will show a good many of the elements of this fighting (fig. 20). A ship, on which are a steersman and two warriors with Dipylon shields, one with throwing-spear, the other with sword and a bow, a pair like Ajax and Teucer, is attacked from both ends. From the right come a man with a throwing-spear and a man with spear and sword; then a defender in a Dipylon shield falls with four spears (or arrows?) in his shield and one in his forehead – Agamemnon slew Oileus with a spear in the forehead, 'nor did the bronze helmet ward off the shaft'; finally an attacking archer. From the left comes first an attacker, who holds his small shield 'out from him', like Deiphobos in his fight with Meriones; then an attacking warrior with a Dipylon shield 'collapses backwards as he falls' like Peisander; then two figures who cannot be clearly made out; then an attacker in a Dipylon shield, carrying two throwing-spears; and finally a man falling forward with a spear through his middle – Hypsenor was hit 'in the liver beneath his heart and straightway his knees were loosed beneath him'. Other combat postures known in Homer (the grip on the helmet, a man 'struggling round the weapon', a man clutching the ground with his hand, a man falling 'like a diver') can be quoted from other vases, but these will be enough to show that the tradition of fighting is the same.

Opinion has varied whether the battles on and round ships represent the battle for the ships described in the *Iliad* or raids such as Achilles' raid on Lyrnessos and Odysseus' raid on the Kikones, and the first landing at Troy with the death of Protesilaos has also been suggested for one vase. Sometimes[3] the ship is departing, with men lying transfixed under bow or stern and

[1] *Il.* 21, 168 etc. For the battle scenes cf. Lorimer, *HM*, 239, 300 etc.; Schadewaldt, *Von Homers Welt u. Werk*, 115 f.; Chamoux, *R.A.*, 23 (1945), 87 f.

[2] Copenhagen N. M., 1628. *B.S.A.*, 50 (1955), 44, n. 45, fig. 2. Ref.: Ajax and Teucer, *Il.* 12, 400; Oileus, *Il.* 11, 95; Deiphobos, *Il.* 13, 162 (cf. above p. 102); Peisander, *Il.* 13, 618; Hypsenor, *Il.* 13, 411.

[3] References: *B.S.A.*, 50 (1955), 44, n. 44; Dunbabin, *op. cit.*, 21, while doubtful about mythological interpretation, notes the irrelevance of these scenes to contemporary Athens.

corpses on deck. Geometric conventions are difficult to interpret, and it is possible that the corpses are really on land and that the rowers are only there to show that the ship *can* move; here an unsuccessful raid, like Odysseus' raid on the Kikones, is certainly a possible interpretation. In other pictures,[1] as on the jug in Copenhagen (fig. 20), the ship is stationary and presumably beached as in the *Iliad*; the battle may take place along the whole length of the ship, at bow or stern, or both, and on shore beside the ship, and the dead are 'fallen in the dust in front of the black ship'.[2] It is difficult to see what great battle for ships would be a favourite subject for poetry except the original landing and the battle for the ships in the Trojan war, and we know that the Trojan war was already the subject of poetry.

Many of these vases show a funeral (figs. 21–3), and warriors with Dipylon shields often participate in these funerals.[3] Their presence raises the question whether the funeral scenes are also heroic rather than contemporary. A glance at later pictures of funerals shows that these funerals are conceived on a much grander scale than their successors, and we have noted that grand funerals and funeral games were Mycenaean and that the rite of cremation was a later insertion. A comparison of the funerals on the vases with the great funerals in Homer suggests that they have a common ancestry, and that the Attic vases represent funerals of the great heroes rather than contemporary funerals. The funerals of Patroklos, Hektor, and Achilles follow the same general pattern. The dead man is put on a bier;[4] this appears on all the vases. At some stage he is anointed and dressed;[5] on the vases the corpse is sometimes clothed and sometimes naked; this depends on whether the painter feels that he should show both legs or not; but above the body normally hangs an enormous shroud woven in a chess-board pattern (Penelope's famous weaving was a great shroud for Laertes, and Achilles was buried in the raiment of the gods).

The dead man is mourned by people of different sorts: Patroklos and Achilles are mourned by their fellow soldiers, and similarly among the mourners on the vases besides the fairly rare Dipylon warriors, of whom we have already spoken, men frequently appear

[1] References: *loc. cit.*, n. 45. [2] *Il.* 15, 423.
[3] References: *loc. cit.*, n. 35–38. [4] *Il.* 18, 233; 24, 720; *Od.* 24, 43.
[5] *Il.* 18, 351: 24, 587; *Od.* 24, 67.

wearing helmet and sword or sword alone. There is a chorus of women mourners who may stand or kneel or sit.[1] Their lamentation is led either by members of the family (Achilles and Briseis for Patroklos, Thetis for Achilles, Andromache, Hekabe, and Helen for Hektor) or by professional singers, seated men for Hektor and the Muses for Achilles.[2] On the early vases it is often difficult to distinguish between male and female; the later vases show unarmed male choruses as well as female choruses, and some of the early choruses are certainly female. The kneeling mourners seem to be female, as no division can be seen between their legs (fig. 21). The sex of the seated mourners is also difficult to distinguish; it is tempting to suppose that the eight seated mourners on an early krater in the Louvre[3] are male professionals like those at Hektor's funeral and that the women standing on a dais on two vases[4] are female professionals like the Muses. The members of the family can be seen in the figures giving the dead man a wreath or a spray, or touching the shroud or the bier, or standing or sitting close to the body, sometimes actually on the bier; sometimes a woman holds a child on her knee,[5] like Tekmessa with Eurysakes by the body of Ajax in Sophocles' play, a scene which surely goes back to an epic original.

Two vases[6] (fig. 22) show the bier mounted on a wagon for the *ekphora*, and it is worth remembering that Hektor's body was placed on its bier and the bier was then placed on Priam's mule cart. The body is followed by men in chariots and men on foot,[7] and they drive and march round the burning pyre. This chariot drive is represented on many vases (fig. 22), and sometimes Dipylon warriors on foot are interspersed among the drivers. Sometimes the artist seems to be doubtful whether he is representing the chariot drive or the chariot race in the ensuing games: one vase[8] has a tripod cauldron, the prize for the race, inserted among the chariots.

The funeral games again raise the question whether the painter

[1] *Od.* 24, 58; *Il.* 18, 30; 19, 280.   [2] *Il.* 24, 720; *Od.* 24, 60.
[3] Louvre A 517: *Enc. Phot.* II, 258–9; *CV*, III, Hb, pl. 1–2.
[4] Brussels A 1506; Oxford 1916. 55. Both illustrated *A.M.* 53 (1928), Beilage 8.
[5] Athens, N. M. unnumbered: Kunze, *Festschr. B. Schweitzer*, 52, pl. 5–6.
[6] Athens, N. M. 803, 990: Lorimer, *HM*, 156, fig. 11; *Il.* 24, 589.
[7] *Il.* 23, 129; *Od.* 24, 68.
[8] New York, 14, 130.14: *A.J.A.*, 19 (1915), pl. 17, 20, 23.

is not often thinking of poetic accounts rather than or as well as actual games. Homer speaks of games 'at the funeral of heroes when a king has died', and Hesiod won his tripod at the funeral games of 'warlike Amphidamas', which had been advertised long before.[1] But these seem to be rare and great occasions which would hardly occur so often in Athens as the vases imply. Certainly the vases agree very well with Homer's account of the funeral games of Patroklos. The events there are first the chariot race with an 'eared tripod' (like those on the vases) for first prize. The chariots have two horses as in most of the races on the vases; but four-horse chariots and three-horse chariots (fig. 23) occur both on the vases and in Homer.[2] The second event, boxing, is illustrated on the kantharos (fig. 24) in Copenhagen;[3] the third, wrestling, on an open krater in Athens,[4] which also shows two boxers and a cauldron on a stand (drawn in section). The fourth event is the footrace, for which the prize is a silver mixing bowl made by the Sidonians; a krater in Athens[5] shows the footrace and a most elaborate griffin-handled krater (drawn in section) standing on an ornamented stand; the painter evidently knew such Oriental works in Athens and drew from his knowledge, but the coincidence with the *Iliad* is still remarkable. The same vase, besides showing a chariot race with four-horse chariots, illustrates also the fifth contest, the fight of men in armour, which also appears on the Copenhagen kantharos (fig. 24).

The identification of mythical scenes in Geometric vase-painting is notoriously difficult because inscriptions are not used and the style precludes individualization. Nevertheless, identification is sometimes possible, and in one of the funeral scenes we can say what funeral the painter had in mind. On a krater in New York[6] three of the drivers in the chariot frieze are double figures, whom Hampe identified as the Aktorione-Molione, the twins who defeated Nestor 'by their number' at the funeral games of

[1] *Il.* 24, 87; Hesiod, *Op.* 654.

[2] Four-horse: Athens, N. M. 810, *K.i.B.* 112, 8, 13. *Il.* 11, 699; cf. *Od.* 13, 81. Three-horse: Agora P 4990, *Hesp.*, Suppl. ii, 55. *Od.* 4, 590.

[3] Copenhagen, N. M. 727: *CV*, pl. 73, 5; 74, 2–6; *B.S.A.*, 50 (1955), 40, n. 19.

[4] Athens, N. M.: *A.M.*, 17 (1892), 226, fig. 10.

[5] Athens, N. M. 810: cf. above p. 120, n. 3.

[6] New York, 14, 130.15: *A.J.A.*, 19 (1915), pl. 21–23; Hampe, *Sagenbilder*, 47; Cook, `B.S.A.*, 35 (1935), 206; *Il.* 23, 630ff.

Amarynkeus, king of Bouprasion. The triplication of the twins is not necessarily fatal to the interpretation; the painter may repeat a composition which pleases him without saying thereby that its members are plural instead of single; the trick could easily be caught from the contemporary makers of gold bands, who used stamps. The twins are found again on a jug (fig. 25) from the Agora;[1] the two ends of the two crests of the helmets are connected and a square shield covers the two bodies, and they are attacked by two men, each with spear and sword; Hampe identified this scene with Nestor's attack on them in the battle with the Epeians, when they were saved by their father Poseidon. The story naturally interested the Athenians because of their connexion with Nestor, and a slight difference is visible between the mainland and the Ionian version: on the vases they are Siamese twins and according to Hesiod[2] (and later Ibykos) they were Siamese twins, but Homer never mentions this either where he gives each a son or in the two passages in which they come into conflict with Nestor. Homer suppresses the monstrosity, but the story itself must go back to pre-migration times.

Centaurs also must be mythical and were already represented in Mycenaean art, and we have seen reason to suppose that the battle between Theseus and Peirithoos and the Centaurs is a very early story.[3] It has been recognized on a Geometric neckamphora in Copenhagen (fig. 26).[4] Eleven Centaurs march round the body of the vase, and two more are seen on the back of the neck; on the front of the neck a Centaur holding a branch in each hand approaches a man wearing a *petasos* and also holding a branch in each hand. He is a traveller and they are not fighting. The branches are not weapons but the kind of branches carried by dancers or suppliants. The meeting is peaceful, and we should not think of a battle but perhaps of Peleus and Cheiron, another story which is likely to be old and is known both by Homer and by Hesiod.

Herakles also can be identified. The evidence for his being a Mycenaean hero has already been quoted. On an Attic jug now in Copenhagen[5] Brommer identified a man throttling the last of

[1] Agora P 4885. *B.S.A.*, 50 (1955) 41, n. 21.; *Il.* 11, 707ff.

[2] Hesiod, fr. 13 (9 Loeb); Ibykos, fr. 2 D.; *Il.* 2, 621 (if it should be so interpreted).   [3] Cf. above p. 124.

[4] Copenhagen, N. M. 7029. Add to bibliography in *B.S.A.*, 50 (1955), 49, n. 87, Dugas, *R.E.G.*, 56 (1943), 5.

[5] Copenhagen, Ny Carlsberg, 3153, *B.S.A.*, *loc. cit.*, 40 for references.

a row of birds as Herakles and the Stymphalian birds (fig. 27). A similar scene occurs on an early seventh-century Boeotian bronze fibula, which also shows a man fighting a lion. Another extremely similar Boeotian fibula shows a man slaying a hydra with a crab in attendance. As the last can only be Herakles and the hydra, they can all be accepted as pictures of Herakles. Then we can also identify a man fighting a lion on Attic geometric vases as Herakles. This scene recurs again on a Geometric fragment from Chios; so that the story evidently goes back to pre-migration poetry. I should like to hazard an interpretation of a much discussed Attic geometric scene: on the kantharos in Copenhagen (fig. 24) a man is held in the jaws of two lions. The pair of lions may be merely due to desire for symmetrical grouping. Commentators assume that the man is being eaten, but there was a version of the story of Herakles and the sea monster in which Herakles put on something made for him by Athena and called 'a surrounding wall'; thus equipped he entered and destroyed the monster. Homer will have nothing to do with this miraculous covering, and his 'surrounding wall' is a fort built to protect Herakles when the monster comes out of the sea.[1] Again the Ionian and mainland versions have diverged.

A more difficult problem is set by the shipwreck on the neck of an Attic jug (fig. 28) in Munich.[2] The ship has capsized and a warrior rides the keel; nine other warriors are in the water among the fish. Hampe identified it with Odysseus' shipwreck. H. Fränkel in reviewing Hampe's publication says that 'it represents soldiers (or pirates) whose ship has capsized with the result that they certainly, probably, or perhaps drown'. The first question is whether the artist wanted to suggest survival for one man or two. There is no doubt about the keel rider. Fränkel thinks that the man to his right intends to lie along the keel and grasp it (like Odysseus when his raft was shipwrecked). I think, with Hampe, that the keel rider who is centred under the lip of the jug is the only survivor, and that the man to the right is already overboard like the rest of the crew. Odysseus' escape, therefore, remains a possibility. A vase of approximately the same date from Ischia[3]

[1] Beazley, *Etruscan Vase-painting*, 124. *Il.* 20, 145.

[2] Munich, 8696: Hampe, *Gleichnisse*, 27, pl. 7–11; H. Fränkel, *Gnomon*, 28 (1956), 570. *Od.* 12, 405f. (=5, 130).

[3] Buchner, *R.M.*, 60/61 (1953–4), 39f., pl. 14, cf. *Od.* 3, 132; 24, 291.

shows a shipwreck from which none survived, as the crew are being eaten by fish. The two together suggest that Returns of Heroes ending in a shipwreck were early a theme of mainland poetry.

The difficulty of interpreting these Geometric pictures is illustrated by the well-known bowl[1] with a warrior mounting a ship, clasping by the wrist a woman who holds a wreath. Paris and Helen, Theseus and Ariadne, Jason and Medea, Hektor and Andromache have been suggested. But Kirk's argument that gripping by the wrist is a sign of salutation rather than abduction is impressive. The scene is heroic because of the Dipylon shield on the stern of the ship. It might be Odysseus' departure as described by Penelope: 'when he left his native land and went, he took my right arm by the wrist and said'. But we have no certain clue.

In spite of all their uncertainties these pictures give us some idea of the themes of Attic heroic poetry about the middle of the eighth century. Where the events (as distinct from the names of the actors) are close to scenes in Homer, we must suppose that similar scenes were described in pre-migration poetry. Where we can add names,[2] as for the Aktorione-Molione and for Herakles, perhaps also for Peleus meeting Cheiron and Odysseus on the keel, we can say further that the stories go back to pre-migration poetry, and we have seen also that some of the battles on ships may well belong to the Trojan war, which language too shows to have been a subject of pre-migration poetry. For the Aktorione-Molione it could also be shown that the mainland version of Hesiod and the Attic vases had diverged from the Ionian version of Homer, and a possibility of a similar divergence was noted in the story of Herakles and the sea monster. The agreement between eighth-century vases and Hesiod over the Siamese twins is a small piece of evidence for the rightness of Miss Lorimer's view[3] that Hesiod acquired his poetic education in Athens: he 'was probably born and certainly brought up in Boeotia. His education included the composition and recitation of hexameters; if he went

---

[1] British Museum, 1899, 2–19.1: Fränkel, *loc. cit.*; Kirk, *B.S.A.*, 44 (1949), 114, 149f. *Od.* 18, 257.

[2] Other possible identifications: Achilles and Troilos, J. M. Cook, *B.S.A.*, 46 (1951), 46. Odysseus and Circe, Weickert, *R.M.*, 60–61 (1953–4), 56.

[3] *HM*, 461.

abroad to acquire it, he can only have gone to Attica, since he assures us that he did not cross the sea.' The assumption, which in this chapter I have tried to make plausible, is that Homer and Hesiod inherited a common poetic tradition, which had only finally diverged into an Ionian and mainland stream in the ninth century. It seems the most satisfactory way of explaining the Hesiodic passages in Homer and the Homeric passages in Hesiod, and the only way of reconciling such divergent views as the following: Leumann 'So much seems to me absolutely certain, that Hesiod knew and used definite parts of our *Iliad*', and Page, 'The Boeotian poets, of whom the most famous was Hesiod, lived and worked remote from the stream of the Homeric epic.'[1] It would take too much space to follow out all the cross connexions between Homer and Hesiod, and I confine myself to three instances, which are particularly relevant to my theme: the Catalogue of Heroines, the Bellerophon story, and the Suitors of Helen.[2]

We have seen that the Catalogue of Heroines in the *Odyssey*[2] preserves among the names from the pedigrees of Pylos and Iolkos some which recur on the Mycenaean tablets. It should, therefore, be old. Hesiod preserves much the same information in the Catalogue of Women, and it has been argued by Page and others that the passage in the *Odyssey* was composed in close imitation of a poem from the school of Hesiod. I believe that a common ancestor in pre-migration poetry is a more likely solution. Two particular heroines may be mentioned here, Tyro and Chloris. The Tyro passage in Hesiod appears to have had three lines which were identical with lines in the *Odyssey*, and one of them should be latish as it contains the verb ἀτιτάλλω, which was only formed after ἀταλός was created by false division.[3] A late common ancestor is as good an explanation as borrowing here. The Chloris passage is more complicated. In the *Odyssey* she married Neleus and had three sons, Nestor, Chromios, and Periklymenos, and a daughter Pero, who married Bias after his brother Melampous had captured the oxen of Iphikles for Neleus. The Pero story is partly told in the Catalogue of Heroines and

---

[1] *Hom. Wörter*, 330; *Homeric Odyssey*, 36.

[2] *Od.* 11, 235f. Tyro: 235–9; Hesiod, fr. 130; *P. Tebt.* 271; Merkelbach, *Archiv für Papyrusforschung*, 16 (1956), 30, C. Chloris: *Od.* 11, 281f.; 15, 225f.; *Il.* 11, 692; Hesiod, *P.S.I.*, 1301; Merkelbach, D.; fr. 14–15; Cf. Heubeck, *Odysseedichter*, 215, n. 4.   [3] Cf. above p. 95.

partly in the account of Theoklymenos, who was descended from Melampous. Bias is named in neither passage of the *Odyssey* but is named by Hesiod, who knows that Periklymenos was shot by Herakles when he had changed himself into a bird and that Nestor alone of the twelve sons of Neleus was saved. This (without the picturesque detail) is the version given by Nestor as the background to his story about the battle with Epeians in the *Iliad*. Momigliano[1] suggested that the twelve sons of Neleus in the *Iliad* are a reflection of the twelve cities of the Ionian League, whereas the trio of the *Odyssey* comes from the earlier mainland version. The reverse suggestion that an original twelve, which survived in Nestor's tale and in the mainland version of Hesiod, was reduced to three named sons in the Ionian *Odyssey* is less attractive but not impossible. Whichever is true, the *Odyssey* account of Chloris cannot have been borrowed from Hesiod; a common pre-migration ancestor must be assumed, from which the mainland or the Ionian version diverged. If Momigliano's suggestion is right, we should have to assume that the mainland version (presumably in Athens) was still fluid at the time of the completion of the League, in the late ninth century. This again is possible, since we had some reason to suppose a late common ancestor for the Tyro passages.

The Bellerophon story,[2] which seems to reflect historical events of the Mycenaean age, also has divergent mainland and Ionian versions. In Hesiod his father is Poseidon, and in Homer Glaukos. Hesiod omits the story of Proitos' wife and all the labours except the Chimaira. Hesiod's Bellerophon, however, has Pegasos, whereas Homer's Bellerophon 'trusts to the portents of heaven'. It is impossible to tell whether Homer knew of Pegasos and left him out as an undesirable marvel, like the 'surrounding wall' in the Hesione story, or whether Pegasos was added to the story on the mainland. Hesiod's Chimaira has three heads; but Homer's Chimaira is less clearly defined, so that an Athenian vase-painter in the late seventh century, when the *Iliad* was known in Attica, could represent her with three bodies.[3] The Chimaira with three

---

[1] *S.I.F.C.*, 10 (1933), 278.

[2] *Il.* 6, 152f. cf. above p. 25; Hesiod, fr. 7b and 245 (fr. 7 Loeb, Merkelbach, B.); *Theog.* 319f.; Dunbabin, *Robinson Studies*, II, 1179.

[3] Athens, Kerameikos, Inv. 154; Kübler, *Altattische malerei*, 24, 74; Beazley, *A.B.V.*, 3/3.

heads (as well as Pegasos) is found very early on Corinthian vases, and Dunbabin has suggested that Bellerophon was annexed by Corinth in the eighth century and that the Corinthian poet Eumelos was responsible. Here again we may see the late interest in celebrating Mycenaean heroes.

The 'Suitors of Helen' was also part of Hesiod's Catalogue of Women.[1] Each suitor is separately described, and the sections are roughly parallel in beginning and ending and in phrasing. When they were assembled Tyndareos made them swear that if anyone removed Helen, they would all take vengeance on him, an oath which presupposes the existence of the story of Paris and Helen. Achilles, we are told, was not among the suitors because he was only a boy. Helen married Menelaos and bore Hermione, but Zeus proposed to destroy mankind so that goddesses should not marry mortals any more. This must have led up to the rape of Helen and the Trojan war, which are foreshadowed both by the oath and by the inclusion of Achilles as a non-suitor. The story has connexions both with the Catalogue of Ships in the *Iliad* and with the *Cypria*. In our *Iliad* the Catalogue of Ships belongs to the tenth year of the war, but the careful exclusion of Philoktetes and Protesilaos[2] has convinced many that our Homer remodelled an earlier list giving the muster at Aulis at the beginning of the Trojan war. Originally, as we have seen, this was a Mycenaean muster list. In the pre-migration period it was not only embellished with genealogies but also changed from a list of vassals of Agamemnon to a list of suitors of Helen. The old reason for the muster was no longer satisfactory in a disunited world invaded by Dorians, and a new one was found. It must have been now that a genius converted the version of the old siege story which made it a war for a woman (the version borrowed from the Ugaritic *Keret*) into a war to recover Helen from Troy. The muster of vassals became the muster of her suitors who were sworn to revenge. One minor divergence between the Hesiodic suitors and the Homeric list is just the kind of divergence that we have learnt to expect: Podarkes is the brother of Protesilaos in Homer, but in Hesiod they have different fathers.

The *Cypria* began with the old Eastern theme of the gods' desire to destroy mankind. We have noticed already that this was

---

[1] Fr. 94–6; fr. 68 Loeb; Merkelbach, G. H.
[2] *Il.* 2, 698, 718. Cf. Wade-Gery. *op. cit.*, 49 f.

probably a very early borrowing and affected the *Iliad* in various ways.[1] In the *Cypria* Earth complained to Zeus about the weight of overpopulation and the lawlessness of mankind; Zeus first made the Theban war and then proposed to use thunderbolts and storms, but was persuaded instead to marry Thetis to Peleus so that she should become the mother of Achilles and the Trojan war should ensue. There followed the marriage of Peleus and Thetis (which, we have seen, was elaborated in the post-Mycenaean period).[2] At the marriage the three goddesses quarrelled, and this led to the judgement of Paris and the Trojan war. The story in the *Cypria*, which is also presupposed by our *Iliad*, is basically the same as the story in Hesiod but shows considerable disagreement in detail. In the *Works and Days*[3] the 'divine race of heroes who are called demigods' was destroyed at Thebes and Troy. They are called 'demigods',which suggests that Hesiod here had in mind the version of his Suitors of Helen; there Zeus proposed to destroy mankind 'to make an end of the lives of demigods that goddesses should not mate with mortals'. The continuation in Hesiod's version is extremely obscure; but Zeus certainly made a storm, and the earlier mention of Achilles and of the Suitors' oath must have led up to an account of the Trojan war, however brief. Zeus' motive here is different – not pity for Earth but the desire to stop mixed marriages – and the timing is quite different: the storm here takes place after the marriage of Helen instead of being planned before the marriage of Peleus and Thetis. The idea, which is common to both, that the gods destroy mankind by natural catastrophe and by war was early borrowed from the East. The application of this idea to the Trojan war must date from the time when it had become obvious that the Trojan war, though successful, was the beginning of the end for the Mycenaean age; the destruction of Pylos already showed this, but with the destruction of Mycenae the conclusion was inescapable that the age of heroes was over, and the old Eastern story, which was already in the poets' repertoire, was applied to the new events: Zeus' plan was to use the Trojan war to destroy the race of heroes, and this idea is developed rather differently in the mainland version and the Ionian version. The destruction of the mainland cities is a kind of epilogue, which by the time of the *Iliad*, and

---

[1] *Cypria*, fr. I (Allen). Cf. above p. 86.
[2] Cf. above p. 127.   [3] *Op.* 156f.

probably long before, was seen as a bargain between Zeus and Hera.[1]

Much of what has been said in the preceding pages may seem unnecessary to those who accept the view that Greek mythology was formed in the Mycenaean age. But the long period between the end of the Mycenaean age and our Homer is obscure, and it seemed desirable to see what light can be thrown on poetry in the intervening period. Certain positive conclusions emerge apart from the evidence for the existence of particular stories in this period. Neither the poems nor the stories which they contain were so far away from everyday life that they were not brought up to date. Poetic language was probably already in Mycenaean times a mixed language, and during the dark period it both received new words and absorbed new forms alongside the old. The stories were altered to admit the throwing-spear in combat and cremation in funerals, but again the old was preserved alongside the new. Such poetry had two faces, one turned towards the past, which was irrevocably gone with all its riches and its complexity, the other towards the audience in the present. The old stories in much of their old setting were kept alive because they were brought up to date in certain ways like military tactics and burial rites, which immediately concerned the hearers, and because the language was also brought up to date so that it remained not hopelessly far removed from contemporary speech.

The audience were primarily the survivors of the Mycenaean age and their descendants, both those who remained in Greece and those who emigrated, and the places where the poets sang must have been the nobles' houses. I hesitate to speak with Page[2] of a court, because the word 'court' suggests to me something on the Mycenaean scale, and that scale did not survive the sack of the Mycenaean palaces; but I do not deny, of course, that, where there was a king or a ruling family, he or they were likely to have had better houses and more poetry than the normal run of nobles. This poetry is the descendant of the third kind of Mycenaean poetry, the poetry improvised for special occasions by warrior singers and court singers. The picture of Demodokos at the court of Alkinoos is in essentials true of the poet in the smaller royal or noble house of Ionia as well as of the poet at the Mycenaean

---

[1] *Il.* 4, 31 ff. cf. above p. 164.   [2] *Homeric Odyssey*, 145 f.

court.[1] Both sang, both improvised in formulaic diction to suit
the particular occasion, both, therefore, were poets of short,
sung poetry, not long spoken poetry. The major differences, if
the picture which I have tried to draw of both ages is at all like
the truth, were two: the Mycenaean poet had at his back, as it
were, the poetry about the local Kings, which was possibly
recorded, and the poetry that he improvised at the court was
partly about the past and partly about the present, and partly an
interweaving of the present and the past, the historical and the
mythical. The poet of the dark ages probably had no records but
only his memory, and the poetry that he improvised was always
about the past, and a past which, however long some of its
memories may have been, was compressed for the purposes of
poetry into a comparatively small number of generations from
rather before the Theban war to a little after the Trojan war.

There is one other difference which must be discussed for a
moment. The use of formulae by the Mycenaean poet was a
reflection of the style of the King's court. This was its origin, but
it also proved extremely useful for improvising in poetry. The
use of formulae by the poet of the dark centuries was a continuation of the same tradition when court language no longer existed.
It survived because it was useful to the poet; its ability to absorb
new forms and new words kept it from becoming too far divorced
from contemporary language, and no doubt its archaisms and
its formality had a nostalgic charm. But it was already a poetic
language in a different sense from the language of Mycenaean
poetry. We have been accustomed since the epoch-making work
of Milman Parry to regard this language as the language of oral
poetry, of poetry always improvised for each particular occasion
so that the story could be adapted in length and detail to the
desires of the particular audience. In the case of Mycenaean poetry
we had to admit that we could find no reason why it should not
have been recorded; script, papyrus, the Eastern examples were
all there, but the Eastern examples showed that recording in a
difficult script and reciting from a difficult script required the
same poetic style as improvisation. For the dark ages the majority
of scholars assert the absence of writing between roughly 1100
and 850, and only a few like Wace[2] have urged that the Greeks
were far too intelligent to have forgotten the use of writing once

[1] Cf. above pp. 132f.   [2] In *Docs.* xxviii.

they knew it. Against the preservation of writing we can urge the collapse of the Mycenaean palaces with their complicated accounting, the collapse of the system which held them and the outside world together, and the absence of papyrus from the Greek world. For the preservation of writing we can urge the analogy of Cyprus[1] and the existence of skins: Herodotos[2] says that the Ionians have long called papyri skins, because, when they had no papyri, they used to use skins, and the Cypriote word for schoolmaster meant 'skin-smearer'. The problem cannot be solved on the evidence at present available, but the possibility that compressed information, such as is contained in catalogues and genealogies, was recorded cannot be denied. The analogy of Eastern poetry shows that recording in a difficult script made no difference to the technique of poetry, and positive evidence for Greek oral composition in the dark ages is given by the long Leumann series based on wrong division, some of which must be dated in this period.

One further general conclusion may be drawn from our survey. In spite of the freedom of improvisation certain forms of poetry had been established long before the time of our *Iliad*. By this I mean partly the formation of narrative and partly the invention of schemes for grouping material. The clearest case of the formation of narrative is the case which we have just examined. The convergent (and divergent) testimony of the *Iliad*, the *Cypria*, and Hesiod suggests very strongly that between the fall of the Mycenaean palaces and the end of the Ionian migration the Trojan war story had been remade into a story of the expedition by Helen's suitors to recover her, and that the story of the gods' desire to destroy mankind had become the story of the wedding of Peleus and Thetis followed by the judgement of Paris as a prelude to the Trojan war. The tracing of the stories of epic through their earlier stages is a treacherous path which I do not intend to tread further; this case seems to me fairly safe, because at one end we have the Mycenaean characteristics of the heroes concerned and the actual occasion of the Trojan war and at the other the convergence and divergence of mainland and Ionian versions. The oath of the Suitors (and, therefore, the wedding of Helen and, therefore, the rape of Helen) only came into

[1] Cf. the evidence given by V. and J. Karageorghis, *A.J.A.*, 60 (1956), 351.
[2] Hdt. 5, 58. Cf. Lorimer, *HM*, 526, n. 2.

the story when the old feudal compulsion to join Agamemnon no longer made sense, and the view of the Trojan war as a method adopted by the gods to bring the age of heroes to an end only arose when the Mycenaean palaces had fallen. They must have been poets of genius who had these superb ideas for organizing the traditional material.

I can think of no better name than the principle of coagulation for the common element uniting various different forms of poetry which I believe to be pre-Homeric and probably to have originated in the dark period. All these forms are catalogues of one kind or another. They consist of summary information about a number of individuals which can be produced in various forms. The evidence that the principle was invented on the mainland in the pre-migration period is first the coincidences and divergences between the Homeric and Hesiodic accounts of the suitors of Helen and of the Pylian heroines, secondly the fact that the Homeric 'Suitors of Helen' is itself an embroidery of a much simpler list of contingents which was ultimately based on a Mycenaean operation order, and that a post-Mycenaean but pre-migration date is given for some of the embroidery by the conjunction of the new forms of patronymic with the *-oo* genitive. In these instances we can see how the same coagulated information can be used for different forms of poetry. Beside the minimal genealogies of the Suitors of Helen in the Homeric Catalogue of Ships we can put the longer genealogy of Aeneas in Homer, which also has its Hesiodic parallel;[1] these genealogies, I suspect, reflect the pride of the aristocracies, who are coming to power in the cities. The genealogy is one poetic form. Another is shared by Hesiod's Suitors of Helen and Homer's Pylian heroines; the Catalogue is divided into sections, which have a common introductory formula: 'and from X. there wooed' or 'and Chloris I saw whom once'. The origin of the form lies in the prescriptions of ritual discussed above,[2] but here it has become a convenient poetic form for organizing masses of parallel material. Two other instances of essentially the same form occur in the *Iliad* but are probably much older than the *Iliad* itself as forms. One is the consolation poem,[3] of which the keyword is 'endured'. Three sections are given in Dione's consolation to Aphrodite – Ares,

[1] *Il.* 20, 215 f.; *Ox. Pap.* 1359; Merkelbach M. 3.
[2] Cf. p. 73.   [3] *Il.* 5, 382; 18, 117; 24, 602.

185

Hera, Hades – and when Achilles quotes the death of Herakles to his mother and the endurance of Niobe to Priam, Homer evidently has the same or similar consolation poems in mind. The other may be termed 'the mutability of human fortunes' and may in origin also be a song of consolation, but in the *Iliad*[1] Homer has torn it to pieces and expanded the sections for his own purposes; yet it is still possible to see behind Diomede's account of Lycurgus, Glaukos' account of Bellerophon, and Achilles' account of Peleus a shorter poem in which the three heroes were listed probably with others as instances of prosperity which turned into adversity. The Bellerophon story is linked to the Lycurgus story by the line 'but when he *too* became hateful to all the gods'. The Bellerophon story starts 'on him the gods bestowed beauty and lovely courage', and the Peleus story starts 'So also the gods gave Peleus glorious gifts'; Peleus' transition to adversity comes in much the same form: 'but on him *too* the god laid evil'. All these various poems are instances of what I have termed the principle of coagulation, the listing of parallel instances in parallel form. The simplest and most artless opening formula is the Hesiodic 'and such as', and the minimum use of the principle is the list of names, like the list of Nereids in the *Iliad*.[2] Such lists are almost a mnemonic, and it may well be that such a principle is specially suitable for oral poetry, although it must also be granted that it is specially suitable for the recording of much information neatly and succinctly.

However that may be, two inventions seem to have been made in the dark period. One is particular, a new shape for the Trojan war story, which we may generalize as the principle of narrative composition on a large scale. The other is general, the principle of coagulation, the principle of preserving a lot of information by assembling a number of parallel instances in a variety of common forms. These inventions must almost have been made in Athens, because they descended both in the mainland and in the Ionian streams, and it is just this power of composition and organization which is the new element in Athenian art in the dark period.

[1] *Il.* 6, 130; 156f. especially 200; 24, 534; cf. Lorimer, *HM*, 471.
[2] *Il.* 18, 39f.

7

PROTOGEOMETRIC
AND GEOMETRIC ART

The history of Greek poetry before Homer is at best a
reconstruction from various pieces of evidence; the
literature itself is lost. For art we are in a better position,
since, besides other isolated survivals, we have a continuous
series of decorated pottery bridging the period between the full
glory of the Mycenaean palaces and the new flowering of Greek
archaic art in the seventh century, and pottery is in no sense a
minor art. Even the less attractive products of the Minoan and
Mycenaean potter were evidently highly prized, since they not
only travelled to distant places but were preserved there long
after their date of fabrication.[1] The same was true of Attic Protogeometric pottery which, as we have seen, rapidly spread over
the Greek world and beyond, and very early also the new ceramic
products of Ionia are found far away from their place of manufacture. Pottery in Athens was a major art now as later; but for us
its contribution is even more important now than later, because
for the dark centuries no literature survives and we have not
even records, as we have for the Mycenaean age. Yet Attic pottery
faithfully preserves the memory of a spiritual revolution, a new
pride in craftsmanship, a new feeling, therefore, for the function
of the vase and its parts, a new organization of its decoration in
ever more complicated systems, and in the eighth century the
reintroduction of figure decoration with entirely new principles
of stylization.

Two main subjects claim our attention, because both of them
may tell us something about the poet as well as about the artist.
The first is the composition of abstract designs into a rhythmical
decoration related to the shape of the vase. The history of composition can be traced from the late Mycenaean period through Sub-
Mycenaean and Protogeometric to Geometric. The vase-painter

[1] Cf. above p. 30.

187

combines his non-representational patterns like a musician into ever more complicated systems, and the most elaborate of those systems devised about the middle of the eighth century are large-scale symphonies, which can be profitably compared with large-scale epic poetry. Representations of animals and men are rare between the Mycenaean period and the eighth century. But before the middle of the eighth century considerable figure compositions have been given the most important places on the vase; from that time onwards abstract patterning becomes less interesting and careful, and its organization into systems is abandoned as figure scenes occupy more and more of the available space. The subjects of these figure scenes were discussed in the last chapter; but they are also statements by the artist about the external world, different both from the earlier Minoan-Mycenaean statements and the later Greek archaic statements, of which the beginnings can be seen towards the end of the eighth century. To try and expound the artist's statement and to compare it with the poet's statement is our second main subject.

We need not be too precise about chronology. We can accept the transition from Mycenaean to Sub-Mycenaean about or rather before 1100 and from Sub-Mycenaean to Protogeometric rather before 1050; then late Protogeometric belongs to the tenth century and yields to Geometric about 900; within Geometric we need to distinguish first, Pure Geometric, then the Elaborate style of the middle decades of the eighth century, roughly 760 to 730, into which figure decoration is introduced, and thirdly the Late style, which is dominated by figure decoration and is itself gradually transformed into the archaic style, known rather confusingly as Proto-Attic. The finer details of this chronology do not concern us. The difficult question of the chronological relationship between Protogeometric pottery and the Ionian migration has already been discussed; the fact that the wide distribution of late Protogeometric is connected with the migration is clear.[1] Similarly the other important fact, that the earlier large-scale figure compositions are earlier than any possible date for the knowledge of our Homer in Attica, seems to me equally clear.[2] The archaeological material is well organized. The Mycenaean pottery of Attica has been studied by Stubbings;[3] the

[1] Cf. above pp. 140ff., 153.　　　　　　　　[2] Cf. above pp. 168f.

[3] B.S.A., 42 (1947), 1f. (referred to in following notes as Stubbings).

excavations of the great cemetery of the Kerameikos have yielded a wealth of pottery from the Sub-Mycenaean, Protogeometric, and Geometric periods, which has been published with full commentary and many parallels by Kraiker and Kübler;[1] Protogeometric has also been specially studied by Desborough,[2] and Geometric by Kahane, Young, J. M. Cook, and Kunze.[3]

For Athens then the material is plentiful and easy to consult. Very broadly the change between Mycenaean and Geometric may be described as a change from flowing shapes with naturalistic decoration to precisely articulated shapes decorated with rhythmically organized abstract decoration. This is, however, only a very imprecise statement since Mycenaean natural forms had become desiccated and fragmentated long before the end of the Mycenaean period, and a new figure style and the beginnings of naturalistic ornament had been introduced before the end of the Geometric period. But there is an essential and revolutionary difference between a formalism which consists of the repetition of desiccated fragments of natural history and a formalism which consists of the organization of abstract patterns into a rhythmical design. It is this change which constitutes the beginning of classical Greek art.

Mycenaean jars are of various types. The great amphora of the 'Palace Style' with handles on the shoulder continues into the last Mycenaean period with a narrower higher neck, banded decoration, and formal patterns between the handles on the shoulder. Only one late example is reported from Attica[4] and none from the Sub-Mycenaean period. It is possible, however, that a memory survived, since amphorae with shoulder handles are found again in the Protogeometric period. A very fine example from the Kerameikos[5] may be mentioned here because it shows how far the Athenian potter had advanced by the late Protogeometric period. The shape is compact and solid; the flaring neck picks up the curve of the squat egg-shaped body, and is

---

[1] *Kerameikos, Ergebnisse der Ausgrabungen*, i, iv, v (referred to in following notes as K.).

[2] *Protogeometric Pottery* (referred to in following notes as Desborough).

[3] Kahane, *A.J.A.*, 44 (1940), 481; Young, *Hesperia*, Suppl. ii; J. M. Cook, *B.S.A.*, 35 (1934–5), 166f., 202f.; *B.S.A.*, 42 (1947), 139f.; Kunze, *A.E.*, 1953–4, 162f.; *Festschr. B. Schweitzer*, 48. Cf. also Dunbabin, *J.H.S.*, 68 (1948), 68. [4] Stubbings, 44, fig. 19a.

[5] *K.* iv, pl. 12, Inv. 2131; Desborough, pl. 6; Lane, *Greek Pottery*, pl. 4.

crowned by the sloping lid, which finds a re-echo in the short reverse curve of the knob. The vase is black except for a band of triangles on the lid, the shoulder band, and a narrower band immediately below the shoulder, which echoes the triangles on the lid by diamonds filled alternately with hatching and chess-board. The shoulder band itself is a frieze: central is a panel of chess-board, flanked by a narrow light on dark ribbon; on either side is a hatched panel, itself flanked on either side by a dark on light zigzag: the whole may be expressed, a-B-a, c-D-c, a-B-a. Thus there are two principles of decoration: first, the vertical decoration which emphasizes the shape – the sequence of black belly, light diamond band and light shoulder band, black neck, black lid punctuated by light triangle band – and secondly the purely decorative frieze of the horizontal shoulder band with its symmetrical patterns. The further elaboration of these two principles will be seen in the succeeding Geometric period.

A quite uninteresting small type of Mycenaean jar[1] with handles very low on the shoulders and the minimum of formal decoration in the shoulder zone was still made in the Sub-Mycenaean period, when it was still quite undistinguished and ornamented often with a wavy line between the handles. But in the Protogeometric period the shape became interesting and important. This Protogeometric belly-handled amphora was used chiefly for female cremations. The earliest example,[2] just after the Sub-Mycenaean period, has still the Mycenaean shape and the Mycenaean wavy lines between the handles, but the shape has been made light and precise, and the new compass-drawn concentric circles decorate the shoulder. Later the neck becomes taller and the body more egg-shaped. I mention a single example[3] of the late tenth century (fig. 29): the shape has been developed out of all recognition, and the neck's inward curve beautifully echoes the curve of the body. The whole vase is black except for the band between the handles. This band is decorated with a symmetrical pattern consisting of a central hatched panel flanked on either side by a single row of diamonds and outside these again concentric circles: A-b-C-b-A.

Two other closely related types of Mycenaean jar[4] are amphorae

---

[1] Stubbings, 44, fig. 19d. [2] K. 1, pl. 54, Inv. 563; Desborough, pl. 4.
[3] K. 1, pl. 56, Inv. 576, neg. 3424; Buschor, *Gr. V.*, pl. 6.
[4] Stubbings, 44, fig. 19e 1 and 2.

in the sense of the word found on the Mycenaean tablets, vases with two handles stretching upwards from the shoulder and joining the neck. They differ from each other in that the handles of the first run right up to the lip, whereas the handles of the second return to the neck below the lip. The first does not continue after the Protogeometric period, but one example[1] is interesting as the low neck is decorated with two horses in separate panels, one of the very rare instances of figure drawing in the Protogeometric period. The second is the normal cinerary urn for men. The Mycenaean example[2] from the latest years at Mycenae has a black lip, a squat body with a broad band on the shoulder and at the widest part of the body and two narrower bands below: a small scroll decorates the shoulder, and a formal flower hangs below the handles. In the Sub-Mycenaean period[3] the lip is thicker and the neck more clearly marked off from the body. The body at its greatest width is decorated with three broad bands bounded above and below by three narrow bands. A flower hangs from the neck on to the shoulder between the handles. In the Protogeometric period[4] the neck becomes taller and wider in proportion to the body and the body becomes higher and more egg-shaped. The shoulder zone is decorated with concentric circles or semi-circles; the outside ones echo the handles; the central one, for which sometimes a vertical ornament – double zigzags, hatched panel, or hatched diamonds – is substituted, picks up the neck. The neck is often black; the body below the handle zone may be black with narrow reserved lines about two-thirds of the way down or may have a broad black band below the handle zone and again above the foot – the two techniques of light on dark and dark on light already described.

Among the many Protogeometric vases of other shapes it is perhaps only necessary to mention a single vase (fig. 30), a mixing bowl.[5] The shape is a continuation of the late Mycenaean shape well known from the Warrior vase (fig. 7).[6] The technique is light on dark. The handle zone is decorated with vertical bands which run as follows: double zigzag, concentric semi-circles, two double zigzags about black band, light on dark ribbon, diamonds,

---

[1] *K.* IV, pl. 8, Inv. 911; Desborough, pl. 6.
[2] Wace, *Archaeologia*, 82 (1932), pl. 12, n. 5.   [3] Desborough, pl. 2.
[4] Desborough, pl. 3.   [5] Munich, 6157: Desborough, pl. 12.
[6] Cf. above p. 38.

hatched panel, chess-board panel, hatched panel, two double zigzags about black band, diamonds, light on dark ribbon, concentric semi-circles, double zigzag. The patterns, therefore, run a.b.2a.c.d.E.F.E.2a.d.c.b.a. One cannot help feeling that the symmetry got out of hand, and that after the second hatched panel (E) the painter put in his two double zigzags (2a) where he should have painted diamonds and ribbon (d.c.).

Already in this period a revolution has been effected both in shapes and in decoration. The flowing lines of Mycenaean shapes have given place to a clear division between the separate parts of the vase. This means often that the proportions are altered: the neck becomes taller and narrower, the body more spherical or ovoid, the foot is reduced to a wide but shallow and secure base. This clear articulation of parts may be altered in detail but remains a characteristic of Attic pottery until late in the seventh century and recurs again in the middle of the sixth. The elements of decoration have changed. Men and animals have vanished, except for the very rare horses. Ornament formed by the drying up of natural forms, flowers or creatures, has given place to the abstract forms which give the new style its name of Proto-geometric, concentric circles drawn with the compass, zigzags, diamonds and the like. In applying this decoration the artist has to consider two questions, first its organization within a single horizontal band (and here his answer is either a continuous frieze formed by the repetition of like elements or a symmetrical arrangement of up to five different elements about a centre), secondly the relation of the pattern bands to the shape of the vase. Handle zone, shoulder, and zone of greatest diameter remained the favourite places for applying pattern bands. The new high necks presented new possibilities for an echo of body decoration. The fat bellies are less suitable for closely set horizontal lines and bands than the slimmer lower parts of Mycenaean amphorae and kraters, and the earlier Protogeometric artists used horizontal bands and lines sparingly to mark off the bodies into well-defined areas such as shoulder, area of greatest diameter, tapering lower part. Later potters covered more and more of the vase with black glaze so that sometimes only the handle zone was reserved and carried patterns giving a new but very effective contrast between light and dark.

At the beginning of the Geometric period, the end of the tenth century and the beginning of the ninth, vase-painters seem to have been fascinated with the beauty of black glaze, which shows off the shape of the vase, and decoration was restricted to a minimum – a reserved and decorated band on the neck and just below the shoulder and little more. But from about the middle of the ninth century, pattern bands invaded the black more and more, until by the middle of the eighth century the vases were covered with pattern bands in the most complicated syntax ever devised by Greek potters. After that figure scenes were so much more important than pattern bands that the patterns became uninteresting or even careless. In the ninth century the syntax was still fairly simple and sometimes extremely attractive. I choose one example of each of the three surviving amphora shapes and a krater. The amphora with handles rising from the shoulder to join the neck below the rim was the shape with the greatest future and became in due time the ordinary neck amphora of archaic and classical Athens. A good ninth-century example (fig. 31) from the Kerameikos[1] has two main decorated areas – on the neck between the handles, and below the shoulder round the area of greatest diameter – and a subsidiary band lower down the body; the rest of the vase is black. The proportions of black to decoration are roughly 6 to $6\frac{1}{2}$, reading downwards from the rim: neck, 1 black, 3 decorated; body, 2 black, 3 decorated, 1 black, $\frac{1}{2}$ decorated, 2 black. The neck decoration is symmetrical vertically about the large maeander in the middle: double dogtooth, zigzag, maeander, zigzag, double dogtooth. The main body decoration runs: single dogtooth, double dogtooth, large maeander, double dogtooth, single dogtooth. But the lower single dogtooth, instead of turning downwards to balance its upper counterpart, turns upwards and so pulls up over the area of intervening black the single dogtooth which forms the lower subsidiary band. The symmetry is broken in order that three bands of dogtooth on the body may point upwards to the neck.

The belly-handled amphora does not last much beyond the middle of the eighth century when, however, some glorious examples were produced. A ninth-century pot (fig. 32) of this shape[2] is slimmer, narrower-necked, and sharper-footed than its Protogeometric ancestor (fig. 29). Decoration has invaded the

[1] Kerameikos, Inv. 2140, *K.* v, pl. 28, neg. 4331.
[2] Kerameikos, Inv. 2146, *K.* v, pl. 46, neg. 4288.

neck and shoulder as well as the band between the handles, and a band is reserved low on the body. The bands of black and decoration or reserve rate roughly 5½ to 5: neck, 1½ black, ½ decoration, 1 black; body, 1½ decoration, 1 black, 3 decoration, 1 black, 1 black. The neck is decorated with a single battlement pattern. The shoulder has bands of single dogtooth, hatched diamonds, double dogtooth. The handle zone has bands of single dogtooth above and below. All three bands of single dogtooth point upwards and so pull the eye upwards as on the neck amphora just described. As on the Protogeometric belly-handled amphora, the handles are echoed in the decoration of the handle zone by concentric circles and the neck by an elaborate central panel; here, however, the broad central panel is itself echoed on each side by a narrow panel between the concentric circles and the handles, thus giving an a.b.3a.b.a scheme between the handles. The individual vertical patterns in the panels recur but not symmetrically.

An eighth-century shoulder-handled amphora (fig. 33) in Copenhagen[1] shows many of the same traits: slimmer body, narrower and higher neck, and four bands of single dogtooth all leading the eye upwards from different levels on neck and body. Here the lines which mark the greatest width of the vase divide the vase into a decorated half and a black half. The black half is, however, punctuated by four groups of thin reserved lines, and its black bands are echoed in the upper half by a narrower black band at the base of the neck. The proportion of black to decoration is much the same as on the earlier vases, but they are not so much interwoven as before. The decorated bands make three systems. The neck has single dogtooth, single zigzag, quadruple zigzag, single zigzag, single dogtooth: this is the largest system. Between the handles a large maeander is framed between single zigzags above and below and narrow panels of zigzags to left and right. Below the shoulder a band consisting of groups of vertical lines alternating with quartered squares is set between two bands of single dogtooth. This vase shows first a balance between decoration and black, secondly grouping of decoration in three symmetrical systems, thirdly the break of symmetry by the universal and intended upward pull of the single dogtooths, the lower two of which on neck and body should point downwards to make the symmetry perfect.

[1] N. M. 6683: *CV*, pl. 69, 7.

The Geometric krater has again a high foot like the earlier form of Mycenaean krater instead of the squat solid form of the Warrior vase (fig. 7), which continued into Protogeometric times (fig. 30). A fine ninth-century krater[1] (fig. 34) has the main decoration in the handle zone so that the handle zone contrasts with the four black bands of the lower body. The foot is divided into an upper-channelled stem and a lower black foot, but the lowest and widest part of the foot has an upward-pointing single dogtooth, which leads the eye up to the band of upward-pointing dogtooth immediately below the handle zone. The handle zone itself is much damaged, but the scheme seems to have been a central horizontal panel flanked by two vertical panels, and on the extreme outside a half panel containing a horse facing inwards (underneath the horse the half panel is black). The whole arrangement gives a slight thrust inwards and upwards: the horses are over a black half panel and face inwards; the vertical panel consists of diamonds, single zigzag, large maeander, single zigzag, so that the maeander is inward of its centre; the horizontal panel consists of triple zigzag, large maeander, quadruple zigzag, single zigzag, so that the large maeander is above its centre. The symmetry of the whole band may be represented as a.b.c.*d*.c.*D*.c. *d*.c.b.a.

In all the Geometric vases so far described the decorated (or reserved) bands constitute a light area contrasting with the broad bands of black glaze, which may amount to as much as half the total height of the vase. In the middle decades of the eighth century the broad black bands (but not the fine lines) vanish entirely or are restricted to the area immediately above the foot and are replaced by bands of pattern or figures, which are divided from each other by fine horizontal lines usually in threes. The whole vase or at least the whole of the decorated area is a pinkish-brown field to be covered by rhythmical bands of pattern or figures in golden-brown to black. It is impossible to examine many of these extremely complicated decorations, and I propose to take first three examples which probably come from a single workshop,[2] then a few contemporary vases in which the figure decoration is much more prominent, and finally two late neck

[1] Kerameikos, 290, *K.* v, pl. 20, neg. 4373, 4374. For the horse see fig. 38.
[2] Cf. Nottbohm, *J.d.I.*, 58 (1943), 1. Note however the reservations of Kunze, *Festschr. B. Schweitzer*, 58.

amphorae from the last quarter of the century. The actual repertoire of patterns (apart from figure scenes, bird or animal friezes) is not large – chess-board, diamonds, leaves, maeanders, quartered squares, dots, dogtooth (now generally either in outline or with hatched interior instead of solid), zigzag, and short wavy vertical lines. What is new is the use of complicated variants of some of these patterns to fill much wider bands. One of the most remarkable, if not the most remarkable of all Greek vases, is the belly-handled amphora[1] from the Dipylon cemetery (fig. 21), which is just under five feet high. The neck is higher, fatter, and straighter, and the body much longer below the handles than are the earlier examples of this shape (figs. 29, 32). The bottom of the body is broken but it is probable that it was black with groups of fine reserved lines. The three lowest zones of decoration on the body, diamonds, dots, and dogtooth, repeat in the same order the decoration of the rim, its supporting moulding, and the top-most zone of the neck. Ten more zones of diamonds separate the pattern bands of neck and body and hold the whole vase together by their reiteration. A wider band, consisting of diamonds between upward- and downward-pointing dogtooth, decorates the top of the shoulder and is repeated under the figure scene between the handles, at the same time picking up the diamonds and dogtooth at the top of the neck and at the bottom of the decorated area of the body. The other repeated element in the decoration is the maeander, which is found in four forms – simple battlements, key pattern, elaborate key pattern, and super-elaborate key pattern. Superelaborate key pattern decorates the main zone of the neck, with key pattern and grazing deer above it and key pattern and reclining deer below it; the symmetry is broken so that the two animal friezes may lead the eye downwards to the funeral scene between the handles. Elaborate key pattern is used for the horizontal bands above and below the handle zone and for vertical strips on either side of the figure scene. Thus it forms an outside frame to the figure scene and ties it to the superelaborate key pattern on the neck. Within this outer frame-work a band of key pattern above the figure scene (corresponding with the diamond and double dogtooth below) echoes the key pattern on the neck and is itself echoed by the key pattern below the lower elaborate key pattern and re-echoed by the simple

[1] Athens N. M. 804. References are given *B.S.A.*, 50 (1955), 46, n. 58.

battlements yet lower; a band of leaves divides this lowest variation of the maeander from the bottom diamond, dot, dogtooth
bands. As on the neck, the bands above and below the main
decoration repeat in direct and not in reverse order, so as to give
an upward movement towards the neck. In earlier Geometric
vases this upward movement was secured by making all the
dogtooth ornament point upwards; here, however, the symmetrical order of the bands is changed to secure the same effect.
Reduced to its simplest terms, the decoration of this great surface
consists of three interlaced systems: (1) diamonds, dogtooth, and
dots, (2) maeander with three variations, (3) figures, animals, and
leaves; the funeral scene forms the most important decoration of
the body and the superelaborate key pattern the most important
decoration of the neck. Each system consists of elements of
different size and importance, and it is their interweaving which
gives the whole design its peculiar perfection.

Two other vases, which may come from the same workshop,
are a long-necked jug in Copenhagen[1] about 3 feet high (fig. 35)
and a pitcher in Athens[2] about 2 feet 8 inches high (fig. 36). Both
have a superelaborate key pattern for the main zone of the neck,
a superelaborate diamond pattern for the main zone of the body,
and an elaborate key pattern framed by metopes on the shoulder.
On the Copenhagen jug the decoration again consists of three
main systems. The superelaborate diamonds of the main body
zone are picked up by simple diamonds once above and twice
below. The superelaborate key pattern on the neck is picked up
on the body by the elaborate key pattern on the shoulder (flanked
by triglyph, swastika, triglyph, on either side), then by the key
pattern immediately below, then by the battlement pattern below
the main zone. On the neck the key pattern and battlement pattern
are repeated above and below the superelaborate key pattern, but
between the key pattern and the superelaborate key pattern a
zone of wavy vertical lines and a zone of double battlements are
interposed. The zone of wavy lines is repeated below the lowest
band of diamonds on the body and below it again is a zone of dots
and then black bands and fine lines. The shape of the whole vase
is picked up by the long-necked bird which forms the knob of the

[1] Copenhagen N. M. 4705: *CV*, pl. 71, 5.
[2] Athens N. M., 226: Wide, *J.d.I.*, 14 (1899), 205, fig. 71; Pfuhl, *M.U.Z.*,
fig. 11; Cook, *B.S.A.*, 42 (1947), 154. Stockholm N. M., 1704, is close.

lid and testifies that, however abstract and formal the Geometric artists' designs may be, the world of living creatures may always invade it.

The lid of the pitcher in Athens can be lifted by a tiny pitcher, which is decorated with quadruple zigzag on the neck and double dogtooth and horizontal bands on the body. Both the patterns and the horizontal bands are echoed on the pitcher itself. The superelaborate diamonds of the main body zone are picked up by the simple diamonds, which divide the wider pattern bands of body and neck (as on the two preceding vases), but they also have three further echoes. First they recur in the diamond square which forms one of the two metopes on each side of the shoulder band. Secondly, their zigzag outline echoes the quadruple zigzags on the neck of the little pitcher, the triple zigzags of the lowest band of the neck and the zigzags of the triglyphs of the shoulder, and is echoed by the single zigzag which forms the lowest zone but one of the body decoration (the lowest zone above the final bands is dots as on the other two vases). Thirdly, this main zone as a whole is a thick dark zigzag on a light ground and so repeats in reverse the light zigzag on a dark ground formed by the inward-turning dogtooth on the body of the little pitcher. Finally, the superelaborate key pattern of the neck echoes a simple key pattern above it and is echoed by the elaborate key pattern which forms a panel between the metopes and triglyphs of the shoulder band.

On the great amphora from the Dipylon cemetery (fig. 21) the animal bands take up no more space than the narrower pattern bands, and the funeral scene is no wider than the superelaborate key pattern on the neck. Thus no damage is done to the complicated rhythmical system of patterns. On smaller vases figure scenes take up proportionately more space; thus the three jugs[1] with the naval battle, the shipwreck, and the Siamese twins are under ten inches high. The jug with the naval battle (fig. 20) has three figure scenes on neck, shoulder, and body separated by horizontal lines; only the lip is decorated by dots. The shipwreck is on the neck of the jug in Munich (fig. 28); the shoulder has hare and hounds and the body a band of birds, but there is room above and below these for zigzags, which pick up the hatching on the lip. Zigzags occur again below the neck scene and above and below

[1] Cf. above pp. 171, 174, 176.

the Siamese twins on the Agora jug (fig. 25); here the shoulder
has a simple key pattern and the lip dots. Even the much larger
kraters are far less adventurously decorated than the great
amphora with the funeral scene. One in Athens[1] with a funeral
scene (fig. 22), in which the dead man on his bier is being transported on a cart, may be compared with the late ninth-century
krater (fig. 34) from the Kerameikos.[2] The bowl and the foot are
much taller, so that the whole vase is four feet high. The balance
of the black and decoration remains the same and the foot is decorated with dogtooth as before; this is picked up above by zigzags
below the two bands with figure scenes. The upper part of the
foot is decorated with a key pattern echoing the elaborate key
pattern of the lip, which is framed above and below by dots. The
lowest band of decoration is wavy vertical lines. The patterns of
this early vase are competent and careful and the echoes from
neck to foot and foot to body are well conceived, but the painter's
real interest is in his two figure scenes.

This shift of interest is even clearer in the considerable number
of neck amphorae made in the last quarter of the century. J. M.
Cook[3] explains why they were substituted for pitchers 'as the
principal vase in later Late Geometric graves. The neck amphora
with its narrower neck offered a more level field below the
shoulder, and so it returned to favour as the vehicle of the new
representational movement.' Let us look at two examples with
interesting pictures, where nevertheless the artist still has some
interest in pattern. One is the amphora with a funeral scene
(fig. 23) from the Agora[4] and the other the amphora with Centaurs
(fig. 26) in Copenhagen;[5] both are between a foot and eighteen
inches high, and have the new proportions of high wide neck and
small slim body, which form a complete contrast to the small
slim neck and large ovoid body of the ninth-century amphora
(fig. 31) from the Kerameikos.[6] Both have figure scenes for the
main decoration of neck and body, and both have snakes in relief
on lip, handles, and shoulder. The Copenhagen amphora has
triple diamonds on the neck above the junction of the handles
and triple zigzags above and below the picture; on the body
zigzags, diamonds, and zigzags separate the shoulder from the

[1] N. M. 990, cf. above p. 173.   [2] Kerameikos 290, cf. above p. 195.
[3] B.S.A., 42 (1947), 151 ff.   [4] Cf. above p. 174, n. 2.
[5] Cf. above p. 175.   [6] Kerameikos 2140. Cf. above p. 193.

main scene, and double zigzags and diamonds separate the main scene from the bands of the lower part of the body. The Agora amphora has a subsidiary figure band of male and female mourners above the funeral scene on the neck, and below it diamonds with curves above and below their points (this is the beginning of the curvilinear ornament which is largely substituted for rectilinear ornament in the next generation, the beginning of Proto-Attic). The body has battlement pattern and triple chess-board between the shoulder and the main scene, and zigzag and wavy verticals between the main scene and the horizontal bands; the chess-board picks up the chess-board pattern of the shroud over the corpse on the neck. Apart from the narrow horizontal lines dividing the bands, the chess-board is the only pattern link between neck and body. The tradition of interesting pattern lasts into this generation, but the future lies with what Cook calls the new representational movement.

The summit, therefore, of Geometric decoration was reached in the great vases of the middle decades of the eighth century (figs. 21-2, 35-6). The movement started in the Sub-Mycenaean period, and in the Protogeometric period the new principles of clearly defined shapes, clearly organized decoration, and of symmetrical balance within horizontal bands were established. The taller Geometric shapes suggested decoration by a vertical system of bands, which were at first symmetrically disposed about the areas of most interest, except that the symmetry was broken by the direction of the dogtooth bands, which bound the whole vase together. In the middle decades of the eighth century the whole vase became the field for decoration and was covered by interwoven systems of bands, each system having its most complicated and interesting member at a position of major importance on the lip, neck, or body of the vase. Before proceeding to discuss the new principles of figure decoration, we may ask what sort of demands the people who enjoyed this revolution in the highly prized art of the potter are likely to have made of their poets. Myres'[1] detailed comparison of Geometric composition with the composition of the *Iliad* and the *Odyssey* will be noted later; his general statement should be quoted here: the 'pattern' of the *Iliad* and the *Odyssey* 'profoundly separates the literary

---

[1] *Who were the Greeks?*, 498f., 511f.; *J.H.S.*, 52 (1932), 264f.; *B.S.A.*, 45 (1950), 252f.; *J.H.S.*, 72 (1952), 1f.; *J.H.S.*, 74 (1954), 121f.

background of both poems from anything Minoan, and relates it to the artistic background of the Geometric art of the centuries from the tenth to the eighth'. In this form the statement seems to me true and extremely important. On its application two reservations may be made at the outset. All Myres' examples are metope friezes of eighth-century vases; he, therefore, hardly considers any kind of composition except symmetrical balance within a horizontal band of decoration, whereas the new and exciting element in mid-eighth-century vase-painting, as we have seen, is the complicated rhythmical balance of the pattern bands themselves. Secondly, complicated symmetrical balance within a single band goes back, as we have seen, into the tenth century. This principle of composition, therefore, goes back into the pre-migration period, and here we may reasonably see a new will to organize material parallel to that which we have had reason to attribute to pre-migration poets.

If we ask what we should expect a mid-eighth-century audience, which enjoyed the great vases of the middle decades, to ask of its poets, the answer would be first poems on a grand scale with a wealth of detail, secondly that the shape of these poems should be intelligible – that the great occasions should produce great scenes clearly marked as such and the lesser occasions should be graded so that they lead up to or away from the great occasions in an orderly but not necessarily straightforward progression, thirdly that the number of themes should be limited so that the relevance of one occasion to another should be clear, and fourthly that similar elements should be similar even if they are on a different scale – that one scene of sacrifice should resemble another whether it is told in two lines or twenty and that a hero should be similarly described whether his description fills one foot or three and a half. These compositional questions will be considered in the next chapter, when we have added the further questions which are prompted by Geometric figure-drawing.

To the most superficial observer the difference between Minoan/Mycenaean and Geometric scenes is startling. It must, of course, be remembered that colour adds a great deal to the charm and the realism of frescoes and dagger blades, and we must start by forgetting colour. We must then forget trees, plants, and flowers, and a great deal of marine and animal life. We must also forget the flowing curves which give Minoan and Mycenaean animals their appearance of volume without the aid of perspective or shading. These two elements, colour and flowing outline, divert the modern spectator's attention from the conventions of this art. Yet if we look at the Hagia Triada sarcophagus[1] (fig. 6) again, we see that all heads and legs are profile, but eyes are frontal in the profile heads; the door of the tomb has been twisted to face us, although the dead King is surely standing in his doorway; and at the other end the woman pours libations into a bowl which stands between two pillars, but pillar, bowl, and pillar are put in line. Thus the artist has combined two distinct methods: where there can be no mistake, he records directly what he sees; but he uses also conventional forms where they are needed to make his meaning clear. The Warrior vase[2] (fig. 7) shows the same conventions of frontal eye in profile head, profile legs, and figures strung out in column, since, even if the defenders marched off in single file, the attackers surely attacked in line and not in column. But the painter, although he has no colour, has done the maximum with outline, thick paint, diluted paint, added white to render the visual impression: the defenders are not particularly good-looking, but they are all different, and the details of helmets, shields, armoured shirts, and leggings are rendered with great care. We should like to know how they and the attackers carried their shields, but here the artist's respect for visual impression has prevented him from telling us. In the large frescoes, where the area to be decorated is much higher, the artist may use the extra height to show what is going on in the background: on the wall of the Megaron at Mycenae[3] a chariot horse can still be seen above the warrior, who is hurled off the wall, while the palace ladies look on; a chariot battle is evidently going on outside the besieged town, and the space above the palace is used to show it.

Mycenaean art included, therefore, a large conventional element in spite of its convincing naturalism. This conventional element should rather be called a narrative or explanatory element. It is conventional in two senses: it conflicts with the visual impression, and it is repeated regardless of individual differences. It is narrative and explanatory in the sense that it tells the spectator more than the visual impression can. This narrative or conventional element has increased enormously in Geometric art. Colour and outline have been abandoned for pure silhouette.

[1] Cf. above p. 35, n. 1.   [2] Cf. above p. 38, n. 3.   [3] Cf. above p. 59, n. 2.

Geometric painters of the middle decades of the eighth century used outline or reserve very little, just enough to show that the long journey from pure, abstract silhouette (as seen in the rare early Geometric and Protogeometric horses (fig. 38)) to realism had begun, a journey which took the classical inventors and exploiters of perspective and shading into territories undreamed of by Mycenaean or Minoan or any other artists of the second millennium. In the earliest Geometric figure scenes the human figure consists of a head with clearly marked chin, thin neck, triangular body, thin legs and arms. Sex is not always shown: on the great amphora in Athens (fig. 21) the two figures on the extreme left are certainly men because they have swords, and the kneeling figures under the bier and the little figure to the right of the bier are probably women because they have skirts. On the great krater in Athens (fig. 22) the breasts of the female mourners are shown, and the heads of the figures, including the dead man, have a reserved eye. On the late vases (fig. 23) women may have hatched skirts and long hair, but outline for faces did not become established until the seventh century. One of the earliest files of individual soldiers is on the late Benaki amphora,[1] but they are differentiated by the charges on their new hoplite shields and not by their faces like the uniformly equipped soldiers of the Warrior vase.

These men, who look like sculptors' armatures, may be identical and their postures may be repeated from vase to vase so that they can be described, as we have seen, in Homeric formulae; but we are seldom in doubt what they are doing, if we listen to the painter sympathetically. We ask in vain how the soldiers of the Warrior vase hold their shields, but we have no doubt that on the Copenhagen jug (fig. 20) the man approaching the ship is 'holding his shield far away from him' by its single grip while his right hand draws his sword, or that Nestor on the Agora oenochoe (fig. 25) is using his sword against the Aktorione-Molione. Nestor's shield does not matter because he is fighting offensively, and so it is omitted; he is given a throwing-spear in his other hand, because the sword battle had been preceded by a spear battle. But in fact the whole scene is an interpolation into the series of three chariots celebrating the funeral of Amarynkeus, King of Bouprasion; the painter adds to the story of the funeral, in which

[1] Cf. above p. 169, n. 1.

the twins won the chariot race against Nestor, the other story that Nestor would have killed them in battle if Poseidon had not rescued them.

Compared with this commentary on the visual scene the conventional views and the narrative perspective of the Mycenaean painter seem mild, and the Geometric painter used this principle of commentary as his normal method of representation. Thus in funerals the shrouds in which the dead bodies are wrapped are obviously noteworthy; the Geometric painter draws them as an enormous chess-board pattern above the corpse; on the great amphora in Athens (fig. 21) the shroud is cut out round the corpse. More than that, the dead man on the great krater in Athens (fig. 22) is drawn so that both arms, both legs, triangular torso, and profile head are seen; in fact he is a standing man who has been revolved through ninety degrees and inserted in the space left between the bottom of the shroud and the top of the bier; the painter feels the need to say that he had two arms, two legs, and a manly chest. On the same vase the chariot drive is also represented. The late Mycenaean picture of the chariot of Poseidon (fig. 14)[1] has the occupants convincingly standing in the chariot, their legs concealed by the sides of the chariot; the artist knows that from the side he can only see one wheel and one horse, and he is content to render this impression: he tells a little more than he could see, if, as seems probable, he has shown rather more of the front of the chariot than could be seen and so has pushed the side-pieces farther over the wheel than they actually went. The Geometric artist is not content with the visual impression: he says unmistakably that there are two horses each with four legs and that the chariot has two wheels. He says in addition that the chariot has a floor (the hatching here represents the thongs), a solid front and an open rail on each side, and in order to say this clearly the floor is tipped up towards the spectator and the rails are put at the front and back. All Geometric pictures of chariots show at least one of these distortions, and the realism of Mycenaean chariot scenes is not regained until the seventh century. So too, if the prize for the race is a tripod cauldron or a cauldron,[2] it may be drawn in section with a vertical line or lines rising out of it to show that it can be used for boiling but is at the moment, as Homer would say, a 'fireless cauldron'.

[1] Cf. above p. 48, n. 2.   [2] E.g. Athens, N. M. 810, above p. 174.

The same sort of conventions, as we have seen, govern the Geometric pictures of ships. Therefore, although the ship on the Copenhagen jug (fig. 20) has steersman and oars, there is no reason to suppose that it is recently arrived or soon to depart, and although it is attacked from the bow and stern, it is much more likely that the painter means us to think of two or more ships drawn up stern first and attacked from the land. Two considerations are dominant: what space is available and what the painter wishes to say. On the Munich jug (fig. 28) he wished to say that a ship full of soldiers capsized and one was saved by riding on the keel, and the convenient space was the neck of the jug. The centre is the inverted ship with its keel rider. The men are shown to be soldiers by their crests and breastplates (this is the significance of the hatching); the whole area is shown to be sea by the 'cannibal fish'. The men must neither stand upright nor lie down; their chaotic postures show that they are out of their natural element: they clutch vainly at the ship or at each other. The picture is perfectly convincing but is in no sense a realistic representation of space. So too the great funeral scenes tell the story from when the dead man is anointed, dressed, and laid on the bier; he is lamented by his kinsfolk, by professional singers, and by a chorus; then the men in armour take him out for burial. All this is shown in a single pictorial field on the great krater from Athens (fig. 22), and Hampe[1] is right in saying that the two men with swords at the left end of the main zone of the great amphora from Athens (fig. 21) arrive at the end of the lamentations to take the dead man out for burial.

Attic Geometric art should not be called primitive, although it has not the kind of photographic realism which literary scholars appear to demand in painting. It is a highly sophisticated art with its own conventions, which serve its own purposes. As with the shapes and the ornamentation, a revolution separates it from late Mycenaean painting. In this revolution figures were reduced to their minimum silhouettes, and out of these minimum silhouettes the new art was built up. The silhouettes could be given a number of postures: they could stand, march, row, drive, fight, die, lament, or whatever else was required of them. But always their essential structure must be clear, and this is one of the legacies which remains in archaic and classical art, when the schematic

[1] *Gleichnisse Homers*, 24.

silhouettes have filled out and have been individualized by inner markings: a late Mycenaean clothed figure is a voluminous dress with a head on the top and feet at the bottom, but from the Geometric period onwards a Greek artist never forgets the structure of the underlying body. The silhouettes were put together into a number of scenes, and here two principles are clear. The first is that unique actions or unique persons are hardly ever represented, and for this reason it is extremely difficult to name the precise mythological scene which the painter had in mind. The second is that the painter always wants to tell more than could be seen at any one moment from any one place. The ship is fully equipped for movement even if it has been beached for years; the chariot must show both its wheels, its rails, front, and floor, and the man all the parts of his body; if the Siamese twins took part in a chariot race with Nestor they also fought with him, and this too should be recorded.

The recognition of these principles makes it possible to convert them into literary terms, as we have already done with the principles of decoration. First we should expect those who enjoyed the figure scenes of Geometric pottery to ask for typical rather than unique scenes and that such scenes should be expressed in typical language rather than individual language. Secondly, we should expect that such poets would tell us more than is strictly relevant for the scene in hand. In three different ways Homeric epic conforms to this demand. It has often been pointed out that standing epithets are used when they are irrelevant: Achilles is swift-footed when he is sitting talking to Priam; in the same way the Geometric painter paints the dead man so that all the parts of his body are visible. Swiftness is an essential part of Achilles, a distinguishing characteristic, which must not be forgotten when he is not displaying it; nor must it be forgotten that the dead man was a hero and a great fighter in his life; that is why he was given such a costly funeral. Secondly, the loving care which the very economical Geometric painter spends over chairs, couches, cauldrons, ships, and chariots is matched by Homeric descriptions of works of ordinary craftsmanship, some of which, as we have seen, are very old in form or matter or both, but must owe their place in our Homer to contemporary love of craftsmanship. Thirdly, on the vases one story leads to another; Amarynkeus' funeral might have been complete in itself, but the presence of

Nestor and the Siamese twins suggested his battle with them; so also in the poems cross-references to other stories – the Theban heroes or Meleager or the interesting minor Trojans – are taken up and exploited. Within the single scene this means, as we have seen, a certain disregard of spatial relationships. The parts are given their known value even when this conflicts with their seen relationship to the whole. The result is a paratactic aggregate and not a hypotactic system, and in detail this love of parataxis is what distinguishes Homeric sentence construction from the fully developed periodic style of fifth-century prose.

Many of the characteristics which have been described are, as we have seen, much older than the eighth century, and we only see them in Homer and in Geometric figure scenes in their latest development. What is new in the vases of the middle decades is the grand scale of the whole decoration, the intelligible shape of the whole composition as an interweaving of a finite number of themes, of which each is repeated on a different scale but with like elements; to this may be added an overall unity of style, which avoids violent contrasts within the figure scenes themselves or between the figure scenes and the pattern bands. This unity between the pattern bands and the figure scenes is achieved partly by the reduction of all the figures to armatures so that a figure scene as well as a pattern band is built up of a number of like elements, partly by the filling ornament, which minimizes the contrast between the figures and their background, partly by the composition of the figure scenes, which are either friezes like the pattern bands or symmetrically composed about a centre like the metope and triglyph bands, and partly by the interweaving of pattern bands and figured bands over the surface of the vase. These superb great rhythmical compositions are unique; they were produced by a few great artists in a comparatively short space of time. They show the magnificent application of principles and technique which had been achieved by generations of craftsmen since the fall of the Mycenaean palaces. And they gave their successors principles which were never quite forgotten and could be applied later in new forms. But long before the end of the eighth century the artists had started in a new direction – towards contrasts and individualization and smaller scenes with larger figures. So too in literature the seventh century belonged to Archilochos, not to Homer.

8

HOMER AND HIS IMMEDIATE
PREDECESSORS

I. LATE ELEMENTS IN THE *ILIAD* AND THE *ODYSSEY*

The Ionian migration was a long process, but the great majority of migrants seem to have passed through Attica before the end of the ninth century, and by this time also the full membership of the Ionian League was established. During this long period the Mycenaean stories had been told and retold; in the process they had been in some respects brought up to date, and the poets had devised new formulae alongside the old formulae; they had also devised certain forms of poetry, in which the new desire for definition and organization, which distinguishes post-Mycenaean from Mycenaean pottery, can be appreciated. The memory of the Mycenaean past was kept alive through the dark period by these poets, but in the ninth and still more in the eighth century the Greeks showed themselves aware of their past in other ways too – hero cults, games, dedications, royal names, and political manipulation of legend; and this awareness belonged to the Greeks as a whole whether they claimed Mycenaean ancestors or not. However much its members might quarrel with each other, the Greek world had settled down into something like its classical shape and felt itself Greek, and because Greek possessed of a common glorious past in which it was important to every member to have a share. Moreover, a certain amount of prosperity had been achieved so that celebration could be on a more generous scale than before: one sign of this is the magnificence of Attic Geometric pottery in the eighth century. But the further the *polis* developed towards its classical form, the greater the difference between the heroic and the contemporary world[1] and, therefore, the greater the difficulty of bringing the old stories up to date.

When I speak of Homer and his immediate predecessors, I

[1] Cf. Snell, *Entdeckung des Geistes*[3], 207.

mean not only the period in which the *Iliad* and the *Odyssey* were themselves produced but the preceding century or so. The lower limit is the date of the latest integral elements in the *Iliad* and the *Odyssey*. The upper limit cannot be precisely defined, but I use the period to include the linguistic phenomena which Risch[1] dates after 900 and subject-matter which is likely to be late, notably references to hoplite armour and *polis* organization: roughly the upper limit may be taken as coinciding with the entry of Chios into the Ionian League. The examination of the late elements in the Homeric poems has two objects. It will establish a probable date for the *Iliad* and the *Odyssey*. Secondly, it may tell us something about the poets of this period. We can ask whether they made new formulae embodying modern linguistic usages with the same freedom as their predecessors. If they did, their technique had not essentially changed. We can ask whether the new linguistic elements are evenly distributed or occur in clusters; if they occur in clusters, they will show something of the technique of the latest poets, how they retold the old stories. We can ask similarly where late subject-matter occurs, whether the poets of this period brought their stories up to date as freely as earlier poets or whether they emphasized the difference between the heroic past and the present. If we can define the technique of the later poets, we shall be in a better position to examine the *Iliad* and the *Odyssey* as complete works of art, to ask under what conditions they were produced, and whether they are the work of a single poet or not.

The most important conclusion of Risch's linguistic study for our purposes is that the normal vowel contractions and the loss of digamma belong to the period after 900. Among the vowel contractions are the new genitives of the *a* stems and *o* stems, case-endings which have interested us already.[2] The forms which in Mycenaean were disyllabic (*-ao, -aon, -oio*) are written in Homer texts *-εω* (more rarely *-ω*), *-έων* (more rarely *-ῶν*), *-ου*, when they are scanned as monosyllables. In Attica[3] in the middle of the eighth century the genitive plural of the *a* stems was written -ON; it was written and scanned monosyllabically; the same inscription also shows that the digamma was neither written nor scanned in Athens at this time. In the inscription of the third quarter of the

---

[1] Risch, *Mus. Helv.*, 12 (1955), 61 ff.; cf. *Eranos*, 54 (1956), 34 f.

[2] Cf. above pp. 93, 163.

[3] The Dipylon jug cf. above p. 95, n. 2.

eighth century from Ischia[1] the -*ou* genitive is written -*o* not only where it must be scanned -*ou* but in two other positions where in Homer we should be tempted to substitute -*oo* and -*oio*. Moreover, ἵμερος αἱρήσει presupposes the Homeric formula ἵμερος αἱρεῖ, which involves vowel contraction. A seventh-century inscription from Delos[2] on a dedication by a Naxian writes the *a* stem genitives -ηο and -ηον, the *o* stem genitive -*o*, and an *s* stem genitive -εος, but scans them all monosyllabically. The chief interest of these inscriptions is to show how the earliest text of Homer is likely to have been written, but they also confirm the evidence of our late texts of Hesiod, the Cyclic poets, and the earliest elegiac poetry as to poetic usage from the middle of the eighth to the middle of the seventh century. Where do the *Iliad* and the *Odyssey* come in this series?

In all that follows I treat as late: vowel contractions which cannot be resolved, the short genitives of -*a* and -*o* stems where the earlier forms cannot be substituted for them, synizesis and similar phenomena which seem to belong to the same feeling that produced contraction, and disregard of digamma. These have been-given an approximate absolute date by Risch – after 900. With some hesitation I have included the uses of -*phi* as a singular case-ending, since they can only have been introduced by poets who had long lost the memory of the Mycenaean restriction of -*phi* to plural locatives and instrumentals. I have excluded all words or forms which cannot be thus absolutely dated. Many words and forms are regarded as late by the philologists, but late in this sense means relatively late and not absolutely late, and some of these relatively late words and forms have been shown in fact to be Mycenaean. Shipp's admirable work,[3] which was written before the Mycenaean tablets were deciphered, has shown that these words and forms, like the absolutely late forms, are commoner in similes, comments, and digressions than elsewhere in the *Iliad*. I have excluded them from my count because, although many of them may well be absolutely late, we have no means of determining this; they cannot date their contexts, although it may be argued that the contexts can be used to date them.

If the absolutely late forms are counted, the average for the

---

[1] Cf. above p. 170.   [2] Nikandra, *I.G.*, xii, 5, 42.
[3] *Studies in the Language of Homer*, Cambridge, 1953.

Iliad is 11 per 100 lines and for the *Odyssey* 13 per 100 lines. The inscribed epigrams which I have quoted are too short for reliable statistics, but it may be noted that the single line from Athens shows 2 late forms, the two lines from Ischia 1 certainly (if we exclude the 2 -*o* stem genitives for which earlier forms could be substituted), and the three lines from Delos 5. The elegiac poet Kallinos of Ephesos, writing about the middle of the seventh century, has 9 late forms in 20 lines,[1] an average of 45 per 100 lines, although only two of the words in these twenty lines are not found in Homer. Statistically, however, Hesiod's *Works and Days* with over seven hundred lines gives a sounder comparison, and here the average is 30 late forms per 100 lines. On this evidence the *Iliad* and *Odyssey* would naturally be dated well back into the eighth century, even if due allowance is made for greater conservatism in poems which drew so largely on tradition. Such a date is consistent with the free quotation, borrowing, or allusion in the mid-seventh-century poets, Kallinos and Archilochos, and the illustration of Homer on seventh-century vases. In the seventh century outline drawing and the occasional addition of inscriptions makes the identification of mythological scenes certain, but leaves the question open whether the painting is dependent on local poetry or Homer. Two pieces of evidence, however, suggest strongly that the *Iliad* and *Odyssey* were known abroad by the middle of the seventh century. The first is the Attic vase already quoted[2] which shows the Chimaira as described in the sixth book of the *Iliad* at a time when a different version was current in Corinth. The second is the existence of nearly contemporary pictures of Odysseus and Polyphemos on Attic vases found in Eleusis and Aegina, on a locally made vase in Argos, and on a vase of possibly Etruscan style in the West;[3] this surely implies the circulation of a famous version of the story, which must be the ninth book of the *Odyssey*.

If the evidence of language, quotation, and illustration combine to put our *Iliad* and *Odyssey* back into the eighth century, the question arises what date is demanded by the subject-matter.

---

[1] Fr. 1 Diehl. [2] Cf. above p. 179, n. 3.

[3] Eleusis: Mylonas, *Praktika*, 30 (1955), 29. Aegina: J. M. Cook, *B.S.A.*, 35 (1935), pl. 53. Argos: Courbin, *B.C.H.*, 79 (1955), 1. Caere: Buschor, *Gr. V.*, fig. 53; Pfuhl, *M.U.Z.*, fig. 65; Rumpf, *M.U.Z.*, pl. 6, 1; Schweitzer, *R.M.*, 60–61 (1953–4), 78f.

Seventh-century or later elements in the subject-matter of the Homeric poems have often been discussed, and the general tendency over the last quarter of a century has been to eliminate more and more of them. A recent list[1] gives as Post-Geometric 'the lamp of Athena, the brooch of Odysseus, the procession to offer a robe to a seated statue of Athena, any references to the hoplite equipment and tactics which revolutionized Greek warfare about 700 B.C., the gorgoneion on the shield of Agamemnon'. The lamp of Athena and the brooch of Odysseus have been already shown to be old.[2] The offering of the robe to Athena in the sixth book of the *Iliad* is late linguistically, and this aspect will be considered later, but there is nothing late in the subject-matter. Processions to seated goddesses were already subjects of Mycenaean art, and the priestess and the keybearer of the dove goddess at Pylos received 'pieces of cloth', when the goddess received animals.[3] In Athens the procession which brought a peplos to Athena was undoubtedly very old, much older than Geometric vases which illustrate it; the poets could have taken its memory to Ionia, and in Samos the ninth-century statue of Hera was clothed on festal occasions with real drapery.[4] Why this particular rite was introduced at this place in the *Iliad* is another question, for the moment it is enough to have shown that nothing in the subject-matter need be dated after the eighth century.

That Agamemnon[5] should go out to his one individual series of fights in great glory is obviously right. His breastplate is a Mycenaean pedigree piece,[6] but his two spears belong to a later period, although when he fights he chiefly uses a single thrusting-spear. Naturally his shield must be worthy of him: it is 'man-protecting' like a body-shield, 'violent' like a hand-grip shield with a sharp projecting boss. Then two lines describe a central boss of *kyanos* and round them twenty bosses of tin; the Mycenaean *kyanos* is already unsuitable, but central boss and surrounding minor bosses are a possible decoration for a hand-grip shield, and

---

[1] Gray in *Fifty Years of Classical Scholarship*, 29 f.

[2] Cf. above pp. 107, 111.　　　　　[3] Cf. above pp. 54 f. and PY Un 1189.

[4] On the rite cf. C. J. Herington, *Athena Parthenos and Athena Polias*, 32. On the vases cf. *B.S.A.*, 50 (1955), 48. On Hera cf. Ohly, *A.M.*, 68 (1953), 40.

[5] *Il.* 11, 15 ff. cf. above p. 121; Lorimer, *HM*, 185, 189 f.

[6] The snakes and the rainbow may be modern symbolism, as H. Fränkel thinks, *Dichtung etc.*, 56.

this is reasonable poetic elaboration. But then we find 'on it (the shield, not the boss) was set a vulture-faced Gorgon with grim look and about it Fear and Terror'. This is a new picture, and the poet must have in mind something like the bronze votive shields in the Idaean cave (fig. 37), which have been dated in the eighth century.[1] Miss Lorimer rightly says that the earliest surviving Gorgoneion shield charge cannot be dated before the middle of the seventh century; but this is not necessarily the earliest that was made, as a Gorgon head of the type which later became traditional is found in terracotta[2] at Tiryns in the late eighth century; nor is it clear that Homer was thinking of the traditional Gorgon's head here; if Leumann's[3] interpretation of βλοσυρῶπις as 'vulture-headed' is right and if the meaning was still alive, then Homer was thinking of a bird head and his Fear and Terror may also be animals or monsters. This kind of elaborate shield decoration is unlikely before the eighth century, but there is no need to bring it any later. Evidently the arming of Agamemnon was already a great moment in Mycenaean poetry; it was brought up to date piecemeal – he kept his Mycenaean breastplate but his spears and shield were modernized; then an eighth-century poet heard of the new splendid shields and added this on to the top of Agamemnon's existing shield, thus piling up his magnificence. The Gorgon's head without the qualification 'vulture-headed' occurs in two linguistically late passages, but they are sufficiently protected by the Tiryns Gorgon.[4]

The new shields with decorated bronze faces must have given Homer the idea for the shield of Achilles, the description of which shows a high proportion of late linguistic forms. He knew from traditional poetry that the Mycenaeans had objects decorated in different-coloured metals like the dagger blades from the shaft-graves. He did not know how they were made; as Miss Gray has shown, his Hephaistos made preparations as if he were going to work iron and wrongly included tin and *kyanos* (itself a good

---

[1] *K.i.B.* 101; Lamb, *Gk. Bronzes*, 55; Kunze, *Kretische Bronze Reliefs* (chronology, 247f.); Benton, *B.S.A.*, 39 (1939), 52f.; Hencken, *A.J.A.*, 54 (1950), 295; Amandry, *B.C.H.*, 1944, 45 (Delphi); Dunbabin, *The Greeks and their Eastern neighbours*, 40. The example illustrated is Kunze, no. 1.

[2] Nauplion Museum: Hampe, *Frühe griechische Sagenbilder*, 63, pl. 42.

[3] Cf. above p. 94.

[4] *Il.* 5, 741; *Od.* 11, 635; cf. also *Il.* 8, 349 which implies the traditional type.

Mycenaean decorative material for furniture) in the ingredients. Actual memories of the scenes on works like the silver siege vase (fig. 5), the lion hunt dagger blade (fig. 3), or the Harvester vase (fig. 16), may have survived in poetry.[1] Homer also probably knew contemporary Phoenician bronze or silver bowls decorated with battles and sieges and lion hunts, which drew on an ancient Oriental tradition and one of which had reached Athens soon after the middle of the ninth century.[2] But to decorate a shield so elaborately would hardly have occurred to him before the time of elaborate shield decoration. The new shields fired his imagination, and he decided to give Achilles a superb shield embodying old memories and new experience. Its description marks the centre of the pause between the fighting over the body of Patroklos and Achilles' re-entry into battle. Detailed reconstruction of the shield is impossible, but Homer conceived the scenes as a picture of life on earth, surrounded by Ocean (the rim of the shield) and surmounted by the heavenly bodies (on the central boss). On the boss Hephaistos '*wrought*' the heavenly bodies; in the zone surrounding the boss he '*made*' the city at peace and the city at war; in the next zone, he '*put*' ploughland, cornland, and vineyard; in the next zone he '*made*' cows attacked by lions and herds of sheep, and '*painted*' the dance (with its reminiscence of Daidalos and Ariadne); on the rim he *put* Ocean. Homer thought of a boss, three zones, and a rim; and this corresponds nearly enough to the five layers of metal which he gives the shield in a later book.[3] He divided the description into sections by changing the verbs; the Underworld scenes of the *Odyssey* are articulated in the same way, as we shall see.

Hoplite equipment and tactics need no longer be dated as late as 700. Miss Gray, in fact, notes that a bronze breastplate was recently found with Late Geometric pottery in Argos,[4] and hoplite shields already appear on Attic vases before the last quarter of the eighth century.[5] Apart from its large blazon the distinctive characteristic of the hoplite shield is that it is fixed in position by a band on the arm. The hoplite shield, therefore,

---

[1] Cf. above p. 93.
[2] Cf. *K.i.B.*, 104–5; Kübler, *K.* v, 162; *Robinson Studies*, ii, 25.
[3] *Il.* 20, 268; cf. the five *ptyches*, 18, 481.
[4] *J.H.S.*, 74 (1954), pl. 8.
[5] Cf. above p. 169 and *B.S.A.*, 50 (1955), 41 f.

implies hoplite tactics, men in line protecting each other, wearing bronze breastplates, and fighting with the thrusting-spear. They are essentially a solid line not mobile units like their predecessors with the hand-grip shield and the throwing-spear. We do not know when the new equipment and tactics were introduced in Ionia. Herodotus[1] thought that blazons and armbands were invented by the Carians, and if there is any truth in this the Ionians would presumably have been the first Greeks to borrow them and would have passed them on to the mainland. Two other pieces of evidence, mentioned by Miss Lorimer,[2] seem at first sight to conflict with each other. Before 663, Psammetichos, king of Egypt was using Ionian and Carian mercenaries described as 'bronze-men', who must be hoplites. But Kallinos 'forecasting or commenting on the events of 652 or thereabouts, exhorts his compatriots to resistance with the throwing-spear and with no other weapon'. I am not certain that this interpretation of Kallinos is justified. The poem has three references to spears. 'The sound of throwing-spears' certainly refers to the enemy, presumably the Kimmerians. 'Holding up his spear and packing his brave heart beneath his shield' certainly refers to Kallinos' fellow citizens and sounds like a hoplite advancing. The third reference 'and let him throw his spear for the last time, as he dies' is unclear because the preceding line (or lines) is lost; it is arguable that it is an imprecation on the enemy rather than an exhortation to a friend, as it is modelled on the Homeric line 'may this man shoot for the last time', which is Eurymachos' imprecation on Odysseus. Kallinos may, therefore, be rousing Ephesian hoplites against Kimmerian spear-throwers. This interpretation is further supported by a silver statuette of a hoplite from Chios, which Miss Gray dates in the first half of the seventh century.[3] We need not, therefore, suppose that the cities in Ionia were any later than the Athenians in adopting hoplite equipment and tactics, which would give a date about the middle of the eighth century.

A date in the third quarter of the eighth century is possible for the *Iliad* and the *Odyssey* on these grounds, and the arguments from language, quotation, and illustration forbid a later date. A small confirmatory point noted by Scott may be mentioned

[1] Hdt. i, 171, 4.
[2] *B.S.A.*, 42 (1947), 120, quoting Hdt. ii, 152 and Kallinos fr. 1 D.
[3] *J.H.S.*, 74 (1954), 4; *B.S.A.*, 42 (1947), 88, fig. 5.

here: in both poems loincloths are worn for athletic contests;[1] this custom was abandoned at the Olympic games in 720; the new nudity was already reflected in Hesiod's account of Hippomenes and Atalanta, and it is unlikely that the Homeric athletes would not have followed the fashion; this was the kind of change in which the aristocratic world was interested, as is shown by the introduction of the four-horse chariot into the Mycenaean story of Nestor's war in Elis.[2] These lines are linguistically late and evidently an eighth-century addition to the old story, which otherwise preserves the traditional style. Although according to Pausanias the chariot race was not introduced in Olympia until 696, four-horse chariots are represented on Attic Geometric vases soon after the middle of the eighth century. The other two four-horse chariots in Homer[3] are also recent additions. Hektor in a moment of glory, when he hopes to capture two very remarkable pieces of armour which are never mentioned elsewhere, Nestor's all-golden shield and Diomede's corselet made by Hephaistos, urges on his four horses, who have been given wheat and wine by Andromache; this is a flight of fancy at a great moment, and the two horses are increased to four because this is the number in the latest racing chariots. (It may be noted that the succeeding duals are permissible because the four horses have been carefully paired.) Essentially the technique here is the same as in the arming of Agamemnon. The *Odyssey* chariot is in a simile; the bounding and the speed of the four horses illustrate the movement of the Phaeacian ship which will at last bring Odysseus home; the poet uses a striking innovation of his own day for his comparison.

So far the late elements, which establish the date of the *Iliad* and the *Odyssey* in the third quarter of the eighth century, can be explained as the high-lighting of traditional stories by occasional modern references. Does this also hold for the hoplite passages? The *Odyssey* has none.[4] In the *Iliad* references to individual warriors must be separated from references to masses. The individuals are

[1] *Il.* 23, 683; *Od.* 24, 89; Thuc. 1, 6, on which see Hammond, *B.S.A.*, 49 (1954), 97; Hesiod, *Catalogue*, fr. 22 Rz, 14 Loeb. Cf. Scott, *Unity of Homer*, 9.

[2] *Il.* 11, 699ff. cf. Lorimer, *HM*, 328.

[3] *Il.* 8, 185; cf. Gray, *J.H.S.*, 74 (1954), 8; *Od.* 13, 81.

[4] Wade-Gery, *Poet of the Iliad*, 62 quotes *Od.* 9, 39, where however there are throwing-spears; 14, 257 = 17, 426, where 'the blaze of bronze' comes from the Egyptians, *not* the Greeks, cf. above p. 65.

more difficult to detect than the masses, because they fight duels and the essentially hoplite line of battle cannot appear. Of their equipment metal helmet, corselet, and greaves and the single thrusting-spear are as likely to be Mycenaean tradition as hoplite innovation, and where helmet or corselet have any sort of pedigree or special description they are certainly Mycenaean. But there is a possible clue to retouching. The hoplite, however humble, shone from head to foot – helmet, corselet, shield, greaves. The Mycenaean warrior might have helmet and corselet, but his shield was not bronze and his leggings were commonly of leather. In the intervening period bronze helmets and breastplates vanished; although the boss of the hand-grip shield was bronze, the bronze shield face was not introduced until the eighth century. Therefore a Mycenaean hero may shine; but if he 'shine all over', like Hektor[1] at the beginning of his great drive to the ships, this may be retouching by a poet who knew hoplites. When at the end of this drive Hektor crossed the wall, 'he shone with grim bronze, in which he had clothed his body, and had two spears in his hand', and this again may be retouching since the two spears are an anachronism with either a Mycenaean or a hoplite corselet. Miss Gray, in her excellent treatment of metal in Homer, also sees a Geometric corselet when Hektor is killed: the poet says that only his throat was exposed, the rest of his body was covered by the bronze arms which he had taken from Patroklos. The Mycenaean Hektor may have been so killed, but the first line has two late marks (-ou genitive and synizesis) and, as Shipp notes, the poet has broken up an old formula ('fair arms') because he wants to add his prefabricated line[2] about the armour taken from Patroklos; the audience must be warned of the provocation to Achilles and reminded of the fateful moment in the seventeenth book when Hektor put this armour on and Zeus prophesied his death. After his prophecy Zeus 'fits' the arms to Hektor's body and grim Enyalios Ares enters him; he appears to his Trojans 'shining in all the armour' of Achilles, and after exhorting them leads a charge. Miss Gray has noted the suitability of the word 'fitted' for a Geometric corselet. This is the only place in the Homeric poems where the Mycenaean god Enyalios is reduced

[1] Il. 11, 65; 12, 463; 22, 322. Cf. Gray, J.H.S., 74 (1954), 9; Shipp, Studies in the Language of Homer, 130.
[2] Il. 17, 187; cf. Schadewaldt, Iliasstudien, 104 ff.

in status to an epithet or title of Ares. The charge of the Trojans 'with their weight, holding up their spears' (the phrase echoed by Kallinos) sounds like a hoplite charge. Thus all the passages where Hektor may be suspected of wearing modern armour, like the passage where he drives four horses, come at important places in the poem, and we can see a late poet emphasizing these moments and thereby connecting them with each other; in particular the passage where Zeus prophesies Hektor's death in the seventeenth book looks forward to the event in the twenty-second book, and when it occurs the poet looks back to Hektor's assumption of Patroklos' armour. The combination of late subject-matter and late language have shown us also a late piece of composition or at least a late pointing of the story.

Mass glare is a safer guide to hoplites than individual glare. When the Greeks are mustered before the poet invokes the Muses for the Catalogue of Ships, 'the all-shining gleam of wondrous bronze, as they came, rose through the sky to heaven',[1] like a disastrous forest fire on the top of a mountain, which can be seen from far away. This simile is not demonstrably modern, but there is no reason to suppose that it does not come from the poet's own experience. The following simile – they gradually pour noisily from the ships and huts to the plain like birds noisily moving across the Asian pasture-land about the streams of Kaystrios – is modern in language and localized near Ephesos, a new image appealing to the experience of the audience. Then the simile of flies about a milk pail again appeals to common experience: so also the marshalling of the host by their leaders, who are compared to goatherds sorting their flocks. Among them is Agamemnon 'in eyes and head like Zeus, in waist like Ares, in chest like Poseidon'. The memory of some Oriental comparison lies behind this and it glorifies the king at the moment when his forces are going to be recorded. Finally he is compared to a great bull among the cows, in a modern simile drawn from common experience. The whole passage is a magnificent piece of modern embroidery designed to show the brilliance, noise, energy, and discipline of the army and the greatness of its leader before the poet gives his remodelled version of the list of Helen's Suitors, which was itself the embellishment of the old Mycenaean operation order.

[1] *Il.* 2, 457 f.; cf. Bowra, *Tradition and Design*, 124.

In the fourth book, after the truce has been broken by Pandaros, Agamemnon inspects his leaders and exhorts them to fight. When he came to the Ajaxes, they were arming and a cloud of foot-soldiers followed them, like a black cloud driven over the sea by the West Wind with a promise of storms, which makes the goatherd drive his flocks into a cave:[1] 'so with the Ajaxes . . . moved close-pressed, blue-black phalanxes, bristling with shields and spears'. The bristling shields and spears, the dark gleam, the close array show that the poet is thinking of hoplites. He describes them as 'like *kyanos*', that is dark gleaming blue instead of brightly shining, to get the comparison with the cloud 'blacker than pitch', and the description is apt if the sun is behind them. Thus the simile is beautifully attuned to illustrate the compression, colour, speed, and power of the hoplite line and the need to take protective action. Simile and description bring the heroic story into the experience of the eighth-century audience.[2] When Agamemnon's inspection is over,[3] the poet again glances at contemporary hoplites before he passes to the traditional in-dividual combats. A linguistically late simile again compares the orderly, relentless advance of the Greek phalanxes to the sea and the West Wind: here a great wave comes in from the sea and roars up the shore. 'About them all the bright armour shone, in which their ranks were clad.' Then the Trojans bleating like sheep in all their different languages, then the gods stirring up the battle, and then the clash of shields and spears of 'bronze-corseleted men'. This adjective only recurs when the same lines are repeated to mark the beginning of the next day,[4] and clearly the verses refer to the clash of two lines of hoplites. The general battle concludes with another linguistically late simile: the roar and labour of battle is compared with the mingling of two mountain torrents heard from afar by a shepherd. Fränkel suggests that the shepherd is added because the poet felt that the din was only real if someone was there to hear it, but I think it is likely also that he meant his audience to remember the goatherd of the earlier simile when the foot-soldiers with the Ajaxes appeared as hoplites; that, therefore, the last simile marks the end of the hoplite battle by recalling the first intimation of it.

[1] *Il.* 4, 274.   [2] Cf. *Il.* 7, 61, with H. Fränkel, *Hom. Gleichn.*, 30.
[3] *Il.* 4, 422–56; cf. Bowra, *Tradition and Design*, 125.
[4] *Il.* 8, 60–65.

The hoplite passages[1] show that the last poet or poets brought the fighting up to date like all the poets before them. But the procedure is different. This is retouching rather than remodelling. The hoplite passages are few in number and they are self-contained; therefore they hardly affect the traditional duels. Hektor is the only great hero who at certain moments is retouched as a hoplite, and this has a clear compositional purpose: he so appears at the beginning of his drive to the ships, at the moment when he crosses the Achaean wall, when he puts on Patroklos' arms, and when he dies (even if, as is likely, in the Mycenaean duel he also died from a spear thrust in the throat). The purpose of the mass hoplite passages is not essentially different from the similes which go with all except two of them: the scale, importance and horror of the Trojan war at important moments is either stated in terms of modern experience or compared to modern experience. Two of these passages, the mustering of the army before the Catalogue of Ships and the preparations and battle after the Pandaros episode, also show how the poet of the *Iliad* composed considerable scenes with systems of related or echoing similes, a technique of composition which will be discussed later.

In the hoplite passages there is some justification for supposing that we can see the work of the last poet. A good many other passages either imply that their composer was Ionian or that he lived in the advanced Iron Age or are marked as late by late linguistic forms. Here we can at least detect the immediate ancestors of the last poet, if not the last poet himself. They may be divided into two main classes, according as they refer to modern geography or to modern civilization. They serve the general purpose of making the poems alive and vivid; many of them occur in similes or comments rather than in the narrative itself, and many of them are late linguistically. Hera's journey to Ida and Poseidon's journey from Samothrace to Troy were composed by someone who could envisage the prominent geographical points.[2] The proposed homeward journey time of Achilles and the actual journey time and homeward route of Nestor[3] would make sense to a contemporary, but the traditional returns of heroes may have included some details of this kind. A storm in the Ikarian sea, the violence of the wind from Thrace,

---

[1] Cf. also *Il.* 13, 130f., 339f.; 16, 212f.; 19, 359f.
[2] *Il.* 14, 225f.; 13, 12f.   [3] *Il.* 9, 363; *Od.* 3, 168.

the struggles of a victim being sacrificed to Poseidon Helikonios
at the Panionion, the new technique of dyeing ivory employed
by Eastern women (like the birds in the Asian meadow discussed
above) are all modern Ionian experience embodied in similes.[1]
When Achilles' voice rings out from the beleaguered Greek camp
like a trumpet in a besieged town, there may be a reference to
a recent piece of Ionian history, the capture of Erythrai; and the
late passage in which Ino rises from the waves to give her wimple
to Odysseus may be a reference to a contemporary religious
custom at Samothrace.[2] Farther afield still the palm tree at Delos,
to which Odysseus compares Nausikaa, and the wealth of the
temple at Delphi, which Achilles says is not worth as much as his
life, were present knowledge to the poets and their audiences.[3]
The geography of Ithaca is confused, as we have seen;[4] the island
sometimes seems to be Leukas and sometimes Thiaki, and even
the story of the ambush for Telemachos refers sometimes to one
and sometimes to the other island; this confusion seems to be
very old, and none of the information about Thiaki is so detailed
that it must be regarded as modern. The poet knows little about
the West except that Phoenician traders might land in Ithaca,
iron from Corcyra might be exchanged for copper in South Italy,
slaves could be bought or sold in Sicily;[5] this scanty knowledge
fits a time when colonization was only just beginning, and when
an East Greek cup was imported into Ischia in the third quarter
of the eighth century its owner could already inscribe it with
verses in the latest Homeric manner.

The temples of Apollo and Athena at Troy are modern
fictions invented for particular scenes of the *Iliad*[6] and modelled
on known temples in Ionia and Greece. Alkinoos of Phaeacia
has a Mycenaean palace, but his town has the walls, temples,
agora, dockyards of a modern Ionian town and a site remarkably
like Smyrna.[7] Here the modern plan provides a plausible introduction to the Mycenaean fairyland into which the poet is going

---

[1] *Il.* 2, 145 (cf. Hampe, *Gleichnisse Homers*, 7); 9, 4 (linguistically late); 20,
404; 4, 141 (cf. Wade-Gery, *op. cit.*, 2f.).

[2] *Il.* 18, 219 (cf. Wade-Gery, *loc. cit.*); *Od.* 5, 346 (cf. Germain, *Genèse de
l'Odyssée*, 288).   [3] *Od.* 6, 162; *Il.* 9, 404.   [4] Cf. above p. 124.

[5] *Od.* 13, 272; 1, 184; 24, 211; 20, 383. Cf. Dunbabin, *The Western Greeks*,
1f.; Ischia, cf. above p. 170.

[6] *Il.* 5, 446 (7, 83 may be earlier); 6, 88.

[7] Cf. above p. 157. *Od.* 6, 9; 262f.; 7, 44; 8, 5 (the first is linguistically late).

to bring his listener. Elsewhere the modern city and its life is used partly, as here, directly to make the heroic world come alive, partly as contrast, and partly to illustrate certain features of heroic actions. Fighting must be mainly heroic, as we have seen, but there is no reason why Andromache, Penelope, and Calypso should not wear Ionian dress, and Helen have a modern wheeled basket, why Hephaistos should not be equipped as an iron worker and make modern wheeled tripods, or Bellerophon carry a modern folded tablet,[1] they are more realistic and intelligible if they do. The peaceful city and the agricultural scenes on the shield of Achilles are contrasted with the grim fighting before and after. The city is a modern city with streets of houses (as also in two late similes), and an *agora*, in which a trial is taking place: trials in the *agora* are also found in two similes.[2] The simile of the unjust judgements in the *agora* which cause divine displeasure and ruin can be paired with the late simile of the just king who causes prosperity, and the picture of the arbitrator leaving the *agora* parallels the simile of the two men quarrelling about the boundary of a common field, which occurs in a late context. In the city at peace the words *laos* and *demos* are used interchangeably in the meaning of citizens, as in the long fragment of Kallinos already mentioned; the old military meaning of *laos* has evidently been forgotten, and the new sense is found in many passages of the *Iliad* and the *Odyssey* including the simile of the 'people' stretching the bull's hide so that the grease sinks in.[3]

The agricultural scenes on the shield including the attack of the lions on the cows are paralleled in the late similes of winnowing, reaping, irrigation, tree-growing,[4] and of the many long lion similes at least eight are late linguistically;[5] we must suppose that the lion was a present danger to Ionian farmers, even if the poet records its roaring only once. Part of modern life also is the activity of craftsmen. We have noticed that Hephaistos behaves like an iron worker, and that in a simile a Maeonian or Carian woman stains ivory. The poor woman weighing out her wool, and the drilling of the ship's timber (to illustrate the piercing of

[1] Dress: *Il.* 22, 469 (late); *Od.* 1, 334; 5, 230 (late). Helen: *Od.* 4, 131 (late). Hephaistos: *Il.* 18, 372 ff., 468 ff. Bellerophon: *Il.* 6, 169.

[2] *Il.* 18, 496 cf. Streets: *Il.* 17, 737; 20, 252 (Gray, *C.Q.*, 49 (1955), 9). *Agora*: *Il.* 16, 387; *Od.* 12, 439. Cf. *Od.* 19, 109; *Il.* 12, 421.

[3] *Il.* 17, 389. [4] *Il.* 5, 499; 11, 67; 21, 257; 17, 53.

[5] *Il.* 5, 136; 11, 113; 12, 41 f.; 12, 293; 16, 487; 16, 756; 17, 61; 18, 318.

the Cyclops' eye), are linguistically late;[1] and the simile of gilding silver used twice in the *Odyssey*,[2] when Odysseus is beautified by Athena to win first Nausikaa and then Penelope, is taken from a modern technique. But the craft similes which cannot be dated by language or at all closely by subject-matter cannot be dissociated from these: the high-pitched roof beams, the woodcutters, the shipwright cutting down a tree, the chariot-maker cutting down a tree, the shipwright with his plumb-line, the hull or the mast of a cargo ship as a measure of size, or the tempering of the blade of an axe.[3] These are all apt illustrations because they are drawn from the experience of the audience. Finally, a few similes seem to draw on poetic experience rather than actual experience:[4] the king whose just conduct is matched by agricultural prosperity is an old theme, the exiled murderer arriving at a rich man's house has epic parallels, the nightingale is bewailing Itylos. These are similes in form but in subject they are mythological precedents, like the story of Meleager in Phoinix' speech to Achilles.

Thus the modern world of Ionia is used partly to bring the old stories up to date, partly to contrast with the heroic world, and partly to illustrate aspects of the heroic world.

2. FUNCTION AND DISTRIBUTION OF SIMILES

Illustration is the function of the similes. It is easy to say (and has been said) that the similes must be late or else they would not perform their function. But, as we have seen,[5] some similes are certainly and some very probably Mycenaean, and these were handed down with the traditional stories, sometimes connected with particular heroes. In the first place a distinction must be drawn between similes and short comparisons. All the similes which seem to be old either because of their subject-matter or because of their language (postponed ὡς with digamma) are in origin short comparisons, although they were often expanded

[1] *Il.* 12, 432; *Od.* 9, 384.

[2] *Od.* 6, 232 = 23, 159; Gray, *J.H.S.*, 74 (1954), 4.

[3] *Il.* 23, 712; 16, 633; 13, 389 = 16, 483; 4, 483; 15, 410; *Od.* 5, 249; 9, 321; 9, 391. On these and on the similes revealing Ionian geography, see Platt, *Journal of Philology*, 24 (1896), 28 ff.

[4] *Od.* 19, 109; *Il.* 24, 480; *Od.* 19, 518. Cf. also *Il.* 2, 781; 13, 298.

[5] Cf. above p. 82.

later. As far as I can see, the similes which are found in Eastern poetry of the second millennium are all short comparisons. Four chief types may be noted, all of which can be found in Homer. The kind of comparison which hovers between comparison and identity we have seen in talking of Mycenaean divine epiphanies, and similarly in Hittite 'He fled, Anus: (like) a bird he moved in the sky.'[1] The single-term short comparison may be exemplified from the Sumerian Gilgamesh poem: 'like a bull he stood on the great earth'.[2] A double-term comparison from the Akkadian Gilgamesh has already been quoted: 'like a lioness deprived of her whelps',[3] and a double-term comparison is found on the stele (fig. 4) from the shaft-graves at Mycenae where the lion killing the deer is put beneath the warrior killing his foe.[4] The fourth type is the induction comparison, where a number of short comparisons illustrate the same point; in Ugaritic 'like the heart of a cow for her calf, like the heart of a ewe for her lamb, So's the heart of Anath for Baal',[5] or in Homer 'like an oak or a poplar or a tall pine'. Comparisons of these kinds were handed down in traditional poetry and new ones were made. Lion comparisons in mainland poetry can only have been traditional since Greece had no lions; yet it is very tempting to suppose that, when an eighth-century artist in bronze relief showed two warriors (perhaps Apollo and Herakles) fighting for a tripod and below them two lions fighting, he was saying that the warriors fought like lions, and that the various Geometric pictures of lions, lion and deer, hounds and hare (figs. 20, 28) are reflections of contemporary poetic comparisons.[6] But nothing in them suggests that mainland poetry went beyond the kinds of comparison which are found in Eastern poetry of the second millennium, and many very old comparisons still performed their illustrative function perfectly well: it was not necessary to know lions to be aware of their strength in relation to deer or their dislike of losing their cubs.

But the Homeric long simile has a much more complicated function than these short comparisons. The comparison[7] of

---

[1] *NET*, 120, 23.   [2] *NET*, 49, 88.   [3] *NET*, 88, 19.
[4] Cf. above p. 32.   [5] *NET*, 140, ii, 6.
[6] Cf. Ohly, *Gr. Goldbleche*, 76 ff.; Hampe, *Gleichnisse*, 30 ff. Cf. the shoulder friezes of the jugs in Munich and Copenhagen.
[7] *Il.* 18, 318; cf. p. 82 above.

Achilles mourning for Patroklos to a lion mourning for its cubs may well have come straight down from Mycenaean times when it was borrowed from the Gilgamesh epic, but in the *Iliad* the short two-term comparison (lion: Achilles=cubs: Patroklos) has been expanded, as the late language shows, into a four-line simile. The cubs have been stolen by a hunter. The lion comes back and grieves. Then it tracks the hunter through many thickets, for it is possessed by violent wrath. This must reflect Ionian experience like the other late similes in which the lion attacks herds and farms (several of them also are expansions from the old short comparison 'like a lion').[1] The new addition to the old comparison is the hunter, and the lion's anger is thereby turned into action against the hunter. Thus the simile not only illustrates Achilles' grief but also the long-drawn-out action in which this grief will issue, and in the speech which follows Achilles says that he will not bury Patroklos until he has brought back Hektor's arms and head. Illustration is an adequate term to describe the original double comparison in the Gilgamesh epic; but here, what is in origin an illustration of grief, has been developed into a kind of working model of the situation, which tells the audience not only what Achilles felt about Patroklos but what he feels about Hektor and how he will act towards Hektor. This complicated function has been fully recognized in many admirable discussions of the Homeric simile:[2] besides its primary function of illustrating appearance, sound, space, time, quantity, physical or mental situation, the long simile may also provide a whole picture to explain a whole event. Here one more example may be given: at an important moment in the fighting for the wall 'the Trojans could not put the Achaeans to flight but they held on, just as a careful craftswoman holds the scales; she holds the balance and makes the wool equal in either pan as she draws the balance up, that she may win a poor pittance for her children. Even so their battle was strained equally.'[3] Homer wants to bring home this moment of crisis in the long-ago battle of the Trojan war. The Greeks were just holding a Trojan break-through, which would

---

[1] E.g. *Il.* 5, 136; 20, 165. Contrast Dunbabin, *The Greeks and their Eastern Neighbours*, 46.

[2] E.g. Fränkel, *Hom. Gleichnisse*; Bowra, *Tradition and Design*, 114; Severyns, *Homère, III*, 153f.; Shipp, *Studies in the Language of Homer*, 81f.; M. Coffey, *A.J.P.*, 78 (1957), 113.

[3] *Il.* 12, 432. Cf. also above p. 219 on 4, 274.

carry the Trojans to the Greek ships and both save Troy and prevent the Greeks returning home. The two battle lines are taut and straining, just as the two strings holding the scale pans are taut and straining, but they quiver this way and that, just as the two pans quiver when the woman adds a little more wool; the military operation is desperately important, just as the woman's weighing is desperately important because it is her only means of getting food for her children. Again a working model, proved late by language and clearly derived from contemporary life, is provided to illustrate the ancient situation, but here we may reasonably see a forerunner of the working models provided a century and a half later by Thales and his successors to explain the unknown workings of the universe. In the developed Homeric simile lies the germ of Ionian philosophy and science.[1]

In the preceding paragraphs subject-matter and language have been the criteria for dating similes. Those already quoted give a good idea of the subjects of later similes. The other linguistically late similes have subjects which are in themselves undatable: natural phenomena such as waves, storms, mountain torrents, stars, living things such as birds, animals, insects, fish, perennial human activities such as hunting, and a few comparisons of men to individual gods or goddesses, which are modern adaptations of very old themes.[2] An important point which emerges from this examination is that there is no exact correlation between late subject-matter and late language. In the *Iliad* the similes with the coloured ivory, the poplar felled by iron, the high-pitched roof, the Icarian sea, the sacrifice to Poseidon Helikonios all have late subject-matter but no late linguistic forms; in the *Odyssey* the palm tree at Delos, the gilding of silver, the tempering of iron, the cargo ship, and the market place are modern elements in similes which are linguistically blameless. Rather under a third of the long similes of the *Iliad* show absolutely late linguistic forms, and the proportion for the *Odyssey* is considerably lower. We need not be surprised by this. A poet who works so much with traditional diction and traditional formulae does not necessarily betray his modernity within the short compass of a simile. The fact that he often does not will help us when we come to consider other kinds of recent material; if linguistic usage establishes that for instance

[1] Cf. Snell, *Entdeckung des Geistes*[3], 284.
[2] *Il.* 7, 208; *Od.* 4, 14; 19, 54. Cf. above p. 108.

some transition passages are late, a transition passage which shows no late usages need not be regarded as traditional just because it has no marks of late language. As far as the long similes are concerned, a sufficient number of them is dated late by language and subject-matter to establish the lateness of the whole class, when we remember also the argument that the long Homeric simile (as distinct from the short comparison) does not seem to have any ancestors in earlier poetry.

The long similes then are modern, and the distribution of similes, ancient, expanded, and new, must be the work of the last poet. Can we see any principles governing this distribution? Can we discover why he makes a working model for this situation and not for that? Besides the obvious use to mark an important occasion,[1] we have noticed the use of similes as an element in the composition of longer scenes. When the army is mustered before the Catalogue of Ships, no less than six similes indicate its qualities and the greatness of its leader. After Pandaros has broken the truce Agamemnon calls on his leaders to fight and inspects them before the general battle starts.[2] The inspection falls naturally into sections as Agamemnon visits in turn Idomeneus, the Ajaxes, Nestor, Odysseus, and Diomede, and these sections of increasing length are held together by refrain lines as Agamemnon goes from group to group. Before going to the individuals he first encourages the energetic and rebukes the idle. The idle are 'bemused like fawns', who 'have no vigour in their hearts', and are thus tied by contrast to the first of the individuals, Idomeneus, who is 'like a boar in vigour'[3] – both are old short comparisons, but the first has been expanded into a simile to contrast with the second. The hoplites with the Ajaxes are like a threatening dark cloud driven over the sea by the West Wind, perceived by a goatherd.[4] After the inspection is over, the Greeks advance like a wave driven by the West Wind (no simile intervenes between these two);[5] the Trojans are like bleating sheep. The general battle concludes thirty lines later with the simile of the converging torrents heard from afar by the shepherd, who is included to remind us of the goatherd in the prelude to this action.

The general action is thus rounded off and individual actions follow. The first victim falls like a tower; the combatants leap on

[1] Cf. above p. 224.   [2] *Il.* 4, 223.   [3] *Il.* 4, 243, 253.
[4] *Il.* 4, 275.   [5] *Il.* 4, 422, 433, 452.

227

each other like wolves; Simoeisios falls like a poplar. All three are old short comparisons, but Simoeisios is interesting to the poet because he is the son of a river, and therefore the poplar becomes a special poplar sought out by a chariot-maker for his wheels. Simoeisios belongs to the class of interesting minor Trojans, no less than five of whom have their death marked by a simile.[1] There is no further simile until Diomede enters the battle seventy lines later. Bowra[2] sees the similes in the fifth book as marking the beginning, internal transitions, and end of Diomede's individual battle. When Diomede enters the battle, fire blazes from his head and shoulders like an autumn star.[3] This is a brilliant beginning. Supernatural fire is otherwise reserved for Achilles when he stands by the ditch.[4] The autumn star is later used for Achilles when Priam sees him before the last battle with Hektor.[5] After this brilliant opening a string of individual battles follows which ends with the comparison of Diomede to a torrent sweeping away bridges.[6] The picture sums up the preceding eighty lines of fighting. It recalls the comparison of the meeting of the two armies to the meeting of two mountain torrents, and is echoed three times later, always with a different adaptation. Then a new action starts: Diomede is wounded by Pandaros and retires from the battle: but Athena gives him new strength, like a lion which has been hit by a shepherd as he leaps the fence; he avoids open places but finally leaps out again.[7] So Diomede rejoins the battle and kills three pairs of Trojans; his fourth pair are sons of Priam, and again he is like a lion leaping on a herd.[8]

Again a new action starts. Aeneas and Pandaros plan and attack. Diomede kills Pandaros, and Aeneas (like a lion) bestrides his body. Diomede attacks. Aphrodite tries to save Aeneas but is wounded by Diomede. Apollo rescues Aeneas and Aphrodite takes refuge in heaven. Diomede (like a god) attacks Apollo. Apollo sends Ares to urge on the Trojans. Sarpedon chides Hektor because the sons and sons-in-law of Priam are cowering (like hounds round a lion). Hektor exhorts the Trojans to stand; the Trojans wheel their chariots to attack and the dust whitens

---

[1] *Il.* 4, 482 (poplar); 8, 306 (poppy); 11, 114 (lion and deer); 17, 53 (olive tree).   [2] *Tradition and Design*, 123f.   [3] *Il.* 5, 5.
[4] *Il.* 18, 205.   [5] *Il.* 22, 26. Cf. Hektor in 11, 62.
[6] *Il.* 5, 87. Cf. 4, 452; 11, 492; 13, 137; 17, 747.
[7] *Il.* 5, 136.   [8] *Il.* 5, 161.

the Greeks as the heaps of chaff grow white with winnowing.[1] This is the first long simile (as distinct from short comparisons) for over three hundred lines and shows that the poet is returning to normal fighting after Diomede's excursion against the gods. Ares urges on the Trojans; Aeneas reappears among his people. The Greeks hold their ground, like dark clouds stationary on the tops of the mountains while the winds sleep,[2] another weather simile like those of the earlier general battle. The fighting goes on: Agamemnon kills a companion of Aeneas and Aeneas kills two interesting Greeks, who are compared to two marauding lions;[3] they fall like pines. The battle goes on, and then Hektor comes into the fray with Ares and Enyo. Diomede decides on discretion, like a weak man who decides that he cannot cross a torrent in flood.[4] This simile contrasts with the earlier comparison of Diomede to a destructive torrent. Rather more than a hundred lines later the action changes: Hera and Athena drive out in their battle wagon. Three similes[5] close together mark their arrival among the Greeks. Their horses leap as far as a man can see who looks from a peak across the sea. When they get off their chariots they walk like trembling doves. They come to the Greeks round Diomede, who are like hungry lions or boars. The first of these similes enhances the glory of the goddesses; the second seems wholly inappropriate and must be a survival of the Mycenaean bird epiphany; the third shows that the Greeks are going to take the initiative again. Athena encourages Diomede and drives his chariot against Ares, whom he wounds. Ares shouts like nine or ten thousand warriors, and shoots up to heaven like a storm cloud suddenly gathering in the heat.[6] The shout of Poseidon is similarly described when much later he encourages Agamemnon; this is probably an old Eastern description of the voice of god. The dark storm cloud is as appropriate to Ares, the god of war, as to the Greek army, for which it was used before; but here it is used in a new way because Ares goes up to heaven and the removal of the cloud is a relief to mankind: similarly the Greek relief after the first attack of Patroklos is compared to the removal of a cloud, revealing all the mountains and the sky. The attack on

---

[1] *Il.* 5, 499.   [2] *Il.* 5, 522.   [3] *Il.* 5, 554.
[4] *Il.* 5, 597, cf. 87.
[5] *Il.* 5, 770, 778, 782. On 778 cf. Nilsson, *MMR*, 492.
[6] *Il.* 5, 860 (cf. 14, 148), cf. above p. 75; 5, 864, cf. 16, 297.

Ares is parallel to Diomede's earlier attack on Aphrodite; Ares, like Aphrodite, is received with some scorn in heaven but is doctored by Paieon so that his wound dries up like milk curdled by verjuice.[1] This last simile is illustrative like the comparison of Menelaos' wound to stained ivory; it rounds off the scene of Ares in heaven. The major action ends with the return of Athena and Hera to Olympos, and the battle then goes on without the gods.

The whole sequence which we have examined occupies rather over 1,200 lines from the beginning of the inspection to the return of the goddesses to heaven. This can be represented in a table in which the lines are numbered continuously so as to show the relation of the similes to the story. In this table short comparisons are placed in brackets, the similes are classed, where suitable, as beginning, end, or middle according as they mark the beginning or end of a section or are used as a transition. The subject-matter of the similes is given a letter where it recurs either within this length of narrative or has an obvious outside reference (and the same letters are used below for the similes in the other books).

Lines	Subject	Similes
1–198	Inspection.	20: fawns contrasted with 30: boar. 52: prospective simile: A. cloud, B. West Wind, C. shepherd.
199–233	General battle.	199: beginning simile: B. West Wind, D. wave. 210: sheep contrasted with (silence). 229: end simile: E. torrents, C. goatherd.
234–264	Individual fights.	239 (tower), 248 (waves), 259: end simile: F. poplar.
265–320	Individual fights.	
321–403	Diomede's battles.	326: beginning simile: G. fire like autumn star. 398: end simile: E. torrent.
405–475	Diomede wounded and fights again.	447: middle simile: H. lion. 472: end simile: H. lion.
477–551	Aeneas and Pandaros.	
552–585	Sthenelos and Diomede.	610 (lion).
622	Aphrodite and Diomede.	
674	Aphrodite in heaven.	
722	Apollo and Diomede.	749 (daimon).
765	Apollo and Ares.	770 (daimon) echoing 749.
782–807	Sarpedon and Hektor.	787 (hounds and lion).

[1] Il. 5, 902, cf. 4, 141.

Lines	Subject	Similes
808–837	Trojan attack and Aeneas.	810: beginning simile: winnowers. 835: end simile: A. cloud.
838–872	Individual fights.	865: end simile, H. lions.
873–900	Individual fights.	
901–936	Hektor's battles.	903: (*Ares and Enyo*) contrasted with E. torrent.
937–967	Tlepolemos and Sarpedon.	
968–1021	Individual fights.	
1022–1090	Hera and Athena prepare.	1081: end simile: watcher on peak, (L. doves).
1091–1146	Athena and Diomede.	1093: beginning simile: H. lions or boars.
1147–1174	Diomede and Ares.	1171: end simile: shout.
1175–1217	Ares in heaven.	1175: beginning simile: A. cloud. 1213: end simile: verjuice.
1218–1220	Hera and Athena return.	

Key: A. Cloud, B. Wind, C. Herdsman, D. Sea, E. River, F. Tree, G. Light, fire, etc., H. Lion or boar, L. Birds.

Considerable stretches have no simile at all or only short comparisons, notably the long stretch from where Aeneas enters the battle to where Apollo stirs up Ares. Contrasts may be shown either by contrasted similes or by a single simile contrasted with a straight statement: the Greeks are silent but the Trojans bleat like sheep. Beginnings and ends of sections of action are often marked by similes, but beginning and end similes of an individual section are not in this stretch of narrative related to each other: it would be fanciful to suggest that the storm over the sea at the beginning of the general battle is the same storm which swells the mountain torrents at the end. The cross-references between similes in this stretch are across sections rather than within sections.

The rest of the *Iliad* shows the same technique of contrasts and cross-references, and occasionally a use of massed similes, which does not occur in the stretch examined but which we noticed in the great muster of Greek troops before the Catalogue. The use of two similes close together to point a contrast need scarcely be further illustrated, but a very good example links the ninth book to the eighth:[1] the Trojans have been in the main victorious, and their watch-fires burn like stars round the moon on a fine night,

[1] *Il.* 8, 555; 9, 4 cf. 3, 23, 33; 12, 447, 451, etc.

which makes the shepherd rejoice. The Achaeans have been in flight, and their leaders are racked with worry like a sea beaten into waves by the North and West Wind. Here the contrast extends beyond the emotions of the two parties to the similes themselves: the fair land-weather of the one is contrasted with the foul sea-weather of the other. In the earlier simile (G.C.) the camp-fires are directly compared with the stars, and then a further comparison arises between the joy of the shepherd and the joy of Hektor, which has been expressed in his preceding speech. Fränkel recalls that the chiefs in the *Iliad* are habitually called 'shepherd of the army', and therefore the shepherd here is to be equated with Hektor. It will be remembered that in the mustering of the Greek army the leaders are like goatherds easily sorting out their flocks; so also in other similes[1] the herdsman who perceives the storm or fails to prevent the lion's ravages is not simply a picturesque addition to the simile but adds a further point of correspondence: the event has a relevance for some responsible person. The contrasted comparison of the Greek leaders to foul weather at sea belongs to one of the sets (B.D.) of which two examples occurred in the fourth book. There bad weather was compared with the movement of lines of battle. Here the Greeks have indeed suffered bad weather of this kind, and this bad weather is transferred into the souls of their leaders. In the same way the misery which shakes Agamemnon after the Embassy is like the lightning which heralds a storm, and Nestor's indecision after the collapse of the Wall is like a sullen and brooding sea.[2]

The great battle scenes in the middle and later books of the *Iliad* show both how similes echo each other and how they are massed to mark particular occasions. Here I am only concerned with similes used in these two ways and shall not mention any others. In the eleventh book,[3] when Agamemnon has been wounded, an action starts which ends with the retreat of Ajax. Hektor enters the battle, calling upon his troops like a hunter urging his hounds on a wild boar or lion (H.). Then he rushes into the fray like a fierce wind stirring the sea (B.D.), after he has killed a number of named Greeks he falls on the multitude, again like a storm at sea with clouds and waves driven by the West

---

[1] *Il*. 2, 474; cf. also 4, 275; 15, 630, etc.   [2] *Il*. 10, 5; 14, 16.
[3] *Il*. 11, 292; 297, 305; 324, 414, 474, 548, 558.

Wind (B.D.): here a short section is opened and closed by two echoing similes, a device which is not found in the narrative of the fourth and fifth books. Then Odysseus and Diomede enter the battle like two boars falling on hounds (H.). Diomede is wounded and Odysseus is left alone. The Trojans surround him like hounds and hunters surrounding a boar (H.). He kills many of them but is wounded, and Ajax with Menelaos comes to his aid. The Trojans are like jackals round a stag which has been wounded by a hunter; the jackals scatter when a lion appears (H.). Menelaos takes Odysseus out of the battle. Ajax fights on like a torrent sweeping trees away (E.). Hektor and Paris wound Machaon in another part of the field, and Nestor takes Machaon away; Hektor moves over towards Ajax. Zeus makes Ajax retreat, and he goes like a lion driven out by dogs and men from a steading which it has attacked at night (H.). Five of these similes refer to big beasts. The comparison of warriors to lions or boars is probably old; it belongs to the induction type. When Hektor enters the battle, it is developed into a long simile which is echoed first by two boar similes and then by two lion similes; the boars are hunted by huntsmen and hounds; the lion's victim in the first lion simile has been wounded by a hunter and is being devoured by jackals, another kind of dog; in the second lion simile the lion is a marauder but he also is chased away by men and dogs. This series of five similes are composed as variations on a single theme: wild beasts against dogs and men. The story then goes on with a unique simile for Ajax' retreat: the donkey which goes into the cornfield regardless of the boys driving it.[1]

Further instances of this technique of cross-reference could be given from the intervening books, but I propose rather to examine Achilles' return to the fighting and his final duel with Hektor. The removal of Patroklos' body is embroidered with massed similes[2] (like the muster of the Achaeans before the Catalogue). The Trojans are like dogs attacking a wounded boar (H.), the war is as fierce as fire burning down a city (G.), the pair carrying the body are like mules carrying a beam up a rocky path (unique), the Ajaxes hold the Trojan advance like a wooded headland diverting the onrush of a torrent (E.), the other Greeks

---

[1] Sheppard (*Pattern of the Iliad*, 104), who has many interesting comments on simile patterns, finds here an echo of the reapers in the cornfield, *Il.* 11, 67.

[2] *Il.* 17, 725 ff.

scatter before Aeneas and Hektor like small birds scattering before a hawk (L.). All these except the mules are variations on known themes. When Achilles appears at the ditch,[1] as we have already seen, he flames like a beacon which may bring help to a besieged island (G.), and shouts with the voice of a trumpet blowing the alarm in a besieged town. The besieged town and island recall the flaming city of the earlier simile; the beacon above the sea looks forward to the light from the fire in the mountain croft telling the toiling sailors that they are nearly home, one of the massed similes[2] describing the brilliance of Achilles when he finally puts on his armour. The burning city, the besieged island, and the besieged town are, if I mistake not, new in the repertoire of similes, and I think they are meant to be remembered as a warning that the war is now coming near Troy again. After the battle with Aeneas and the battle with the river, which is illustrated by a number of unique similes all involving water,[3] Achilles drives the Trojans towards Troy and makes them pain and woe, like the pain and woe of a burning town.[4] Then, after the interposition of Agenor and Apollo, he speeds towards the gates like a prize-winning chariot-horse, a new simile which prepares the audience for the pursuit of Hektor round the walls of Troy; and as he comes Priam sees him shining like a baleful autumn star (G.) (an image used earlier for Diomede at the beginning of his great battles and for Hektor in the eleventh book).[5] Both these images recur later in variations. At the beginning of the pursuit Achilles' armour gleams like blazing fire or the rising sun, and as he delivers his final blow his spear point shines like the evening star.[6] At the end of the first section of the pursuit, before Athena intervenes, Achilles and Hektor are again compared to racing chariot-horses.[7] Finally, the lamentations of the Trojans at Hektor's death are 'just as if the whole of craggy Troy were smouldering from the top':[8] thus the image of the burning town is called up again and here directly applied to Troy, when the danger to Troy is acute and has only been postponed by the necessity of burying Patroklos. The technique is the same as in the earlier passages of the *Iliad* which have been examined: massed similes

[1] *Il.* 18, 206.
[2] *Il.* 19, 366, 374, 381, 398.
[3] *Il.* 21, 12, 22, 257, 282, 346, 362.
[4] *Il.* 21, 522.
[5] *Il.* 22, 22, 26. cf. above p. 228.
[6] *Il.* 22, 135, 317.
[7] *Il.* 22, 162.
[8] *Il.* 22, 410.

underline striking moments, sections of the action are marked off
by similes, and the whole is held together by echoing similes.

All through the *Iliad* similes perform two functions: they illustrate by providing a more or less exact working model of the
original, and they have a compositional function of underlining
a particular event either to show its importance (massed similes)
or to relate it to other events by contrast or by echo. The unique
similes are particularly adapted to the first function, but some of
the more elaborate variations of e.g. the lion similes also fulfil
the same end. The sets are particularly suited to the second function
because they are variations on established themes and are
immediately recognizable as such. The main themes are all
established early in the *Iliad*: the first long lion simile occurs when
Menelaos sees Paris,[1] and most of the other themes have already
been stated in the two assemblies and the muster in the second
book. All are thus in the minds of the audience so that they will
recognize the succeeding variations and appreciate the contrasts
and echoes. It is convenient to talk about themes and variations,
but a more precise account can be suggested. Often it can be
shown that long similes have been expanded from short comparisons and these short comparisons can often be shown to be
old. These inherited short comparisons stood to verbs rather as
standing epithets to nouns: heroes attacked like a lion or boar,
their enemies fled like birds or fawns, footsoldiers surrounded
their leaders like a cloud, the dying warrior fell like a tree, war
raged like fire or storm. These old short comparisons were the
themes which Homer expanded into long similes adapted to the
particular scene that he is describing. But however many variations
he composes they are all variations on a limited number of themes,
and each set of variations has a common origin in a particular
short comparison: all lion similes contain a lion and the vast
majority are applied to heroes in action. Therefore, as each new
lion simile turns up it is recognizable as one of the set. The
recurrence as a variation is much more noticeable than the
repetition of a short comparison, since the simile consists of two
or more lines instead of two words or at most half a line.

A few long similes are repeated exactly:[2] we have noticed that

---

[1] *Il.* 2, 144 (A, B, D), 455 (C, G), 459 (L); 3, 23 (H).

[2] *Il.* 5, 860 = 14, 148; *Od.* 6, 232 = 23, 159; *Il.* 9, 14 = 16, 3; *Il.* 6, 506 = 15,
263; *Il.* 11, 548 = 17, 657; *Il.* 13, 389 = 16, 482.

the voice of Ares is described in the same terms as the voice of Poseidon, and the beautification of Odysseus for Nausikaa is the same as the beautification of Odysseus for Penelope (gilding silver). Agamemnon and Patroklos both weep like fountains of dark water. Paris and Hektor are both compared to a horse galloping over the meadows, when they go out to battle. The remaining two pairs belong to sets of similes: a long lion simile for the unwilling retreat of Ajax is repeated for Menelaos, and the fall of both Asios and Sarpedon is compared to a tree felled by shipwrights. One other repetition, 'like ravenous lions or wild boars, whose strength is not slight',[1] is well applied to the duel of Ajax and Hektor but much less suitably to the Greeks round Diomede, and here the poet may be using a traditional short comparison; but where long similes are repeated neither later interpolation nor traditional inheritance need be invoked in explanation: the poet has chosen to repeat instead of varying. In two cases at least the repetition is extremely effective if the audience remembers the previous occurrence: Agamemnon weeps like a fountain before he makes his unsuccessful appeal to Achilles, and Patroklos also weeps like a fountain before he makes his successful appeal to Achilles. Similarly when Odysseus faces Penelope it is right to recall his earlier approach to Nausikaa. The variations, on the other hand, have all the charm of variations on a known tune, or, in terms of contemporary painting, of the repetition of the same pattern in different forms, which is characteristic of Geometric art. Outside these sets are the considerable number of unique long similes: the woman staining ivory, the woman weighing wool, the verjuice, the sandcastles, the dream race. These are unique pictures drawn from present-day experience to illustrate the particular event.

No distinction has been drawn so far between the *Iliad* and the *Odyssey*. The *Odyssey* has far fewer similes than the *Iliad*, but this difference fades away when it is remembered how much of the *Iliad* and how little of the *Odyssey* is concerned with fighting. The vast majority of the *Iliad* similes are in the accounts of fighting, and in particular the sets of similes in the *Iliad* are derived from short comparisons which described warriors and fighting. This use of similes to provide themes and variations with which to illustrate the fighting is not needed by the poet of the *Odyssey*: he

[1] *Il.* 5, 782 = 7, 256.

is not concerned with the battlefield, and his subject-matter is too varied either to need this kind of decoration or to provide the uniform background for it. The other uses of similes are, however, common to the two poems, and the *Odyssey* shows both old and new uses. Among the very old short comparisons not concerned with fighting are the comparison of gods to birds, men to gods, and perhaps also fine textiles to sun, moon, or stars: all these are found in the *Odyssey* as in the *Iliad*.[1] The old formula 'like a god' is twice expanded in the *Iliad* into a full simile when a hero is compared to Ares;[2] in the *Odyssey* 'like a goddess' is expanded several times into a simile; the fullest is the comparison of Nausikaa, the loved daughter of Arete, outshining her maidens to Artemis hunting with her nymphs to Leto's joy.[3]

This beautiful and elaborate simile is part of a long sequence: and in this sequence the *Odyssey* comes nearest to the compositional use made of similes in the *Iliad*.[4] In his voyage to Phaeacia, Odysseus' raft is first tossed like thistledown in an autumn wind, then Ino appears like a shearwater and gives her 'wimple' to Odysseus before disappearing again like a shearwater, Odysseus is wrecked and the planks are scattered like a heap of chaff: in our terminology this is a variation of the thistledown simile, and both are closely allied to the winnowing simile in the fifth book of the *Iliad*.[5] Odysseus then bestrides his plank like a rider; when he sees land, it is as welcome as the recovery of a sick father to his children; he clings to a rock like a polyp being dragged from its lair, and he finally lies under a heap of leaves like a 'seed of fire' preserved under the ashes in a lonely place.[6] The shipwreck and the escape are made vivid by this series of unique similes. There is no long simile again until the moment before Odysseus wakes, when Nausikaa and her servants are compared to Artemis and her nymphs. In contrast (and the *Odyssey* like the *Iliad* points contrasts by giving each term a simile)[7] Odysseus is like a hungry lion. He compares Nausikaa first to Artemis, picking up the earlier simile, and then to the palm tree on Delos, where Artemis

---

[1] E.g. *Od.* 1, 320 etc.; 2, 5 etc.; 15, 108 etc.   [2] *Il.* 7, 208; 13, 298.

[3] *Od.* 6, 102; cf. 4, 14 (=*Il.* 24, 699) etc.

[4] Cf. however, *Od.* 9, 190–394; 10, 113–24.

[5] *Od.* 5, 328, 337, 353, 368, cf. *Il.* 5, 499.

[6] *Od.* 5, 371, 394, 432, 488.   [7] E.g. *Od.* 22, 299 and 302; 384 and 402.

was born.[1] The similes emphasize the qualities of the two at this meeting, which culminates when Athena beautifies Odysseus like gilded silver.

Two similes in this sequence claim further attention. The hungry lion is a good contrast to the beautiful but possibly dangerous goddess and her nymphs. It belongs to the *Iliad* fighting themes and is, therefore, a good comparison for the hero of the Trojan war because of its reminiscence of the *Iliad*.[2] So Menelaos sees the suitors as deer in a lion's den, and after the fight with the suitors Odysseus is like a lion which has destroyed a bull.[3] It is more difficult to see why Penelope[4] is compared to a lion hemmed in by a crafty circle of men, when she desperately wonders whether Telemachos will escape the ambush of the suitors or not. The simile is more suitable to Telemachos than to her, but should we say that she lives Telemachos' doubts in her imagination? We have in fact noted a similar case in the *Iliad*: just before the Embassy the leaders of the defeated Achaeans are racked with worry like a sea beaten into waves by the wind; foul sea-weather is a common comparison for battle, but here it is compared to the mind of the leaders who relive the battle.

The other simile[5] which needs comment is the comparison of Odysseus' joy at seeing land after the shipwreck of his raft to the joy of children whose father has recovered from a long illness. First, it is the converse of the simile in the *Iliad*, where Achilles mourns for Patroklos like a father mourning for the death of his newly married son. Secondly, the shipwreck and escape is in fact the beginning of the restoration of Odysseus to his family, and there is a clear reference back to this passage and its simile when Penelope has finally recognized Odysseus and he is as welcome to her as land to shipwrecked sailors. A direct reference from a simile to another stage of the main story we have also noticed in the *Iliad*, where the lamentation for Hektor is compared to the burning of Troy and in the earlier simile of the burning town. Thirdly, the subject of the simile is a father and children; here the reference to Odysseus is obvious: he is a father whose coming will be welcome to his family. I think that the poet may want his audience

[1] *Od.* 6, 102, 130, 151, 162.   [2] Cf. particularly *Il.* 12, 299.
[3] *Od.* 4, 335; 22, 402.   [4] *Od.* 4, 791. Cf. *Il.* 9, 4.
[5] *Od.* 5, 394. Cf. *Il.* 23, 222; *Od.* 23, 233, cf. *Il.* 22, 410.

to be constantly reminded of this theme of family relationship.[1] When Telemachos returns from his travels, Eumaios greets him like a father greeting his son who has returned after ten years of travelling. Here we are only a short distance from the recognition scene between Odysseus and Telemachos, after which father and son weep like vultures robbed of their young by hunters: the joy of reunion is as intense and for the moment has the same effect as the pain of bereavement, and we should remember also that Telemachos has just escaped an ambush. Later still Penelope compares her grief for her husband and her hesitations as to her future to the lament of the nightingale, who slew her son 'in folly': the likeness lies partly in the lamentation, partly in the many changes of the bird's song, partly in Penelope's fear that she also may damage her son if she chooses wrong. Possibly we may go even further and suppose that, when Menelaos sees the suitors as young deer left by their mother in the lion's den,[2] here too the role that the suitors' parents are going to play in the last book should be remembered. Odysseus himself was kind as a father; Telemachos finds that Mentes and Menelaos behaved to him like a good father and Antinoos like a bad father; Menelaos speaks of Nestor as kind as a father.[3] So again and again similes and comparisons take their subject-matter from the theme of family relationship, which is essential to Odysseus' story – the good family which is contrasted again and again with the bad family of Agamemnon. This then is a theme which runs right through the *Odyssey* and to which many of the similes are related, although they do not group themselves into sets like the fighting similes of the *Iliad*. Thus in spite of the difference of subject-matter the similes perform essentially the same function in the two poems.

3. TYPICAL SCENES AND SPECIAL NARRATIVES

If it is true that the similes developed from a number of short comparisons, which originally stood to verbs rather as standing epithets stood to nouns, and that the essential development into complicated pictures was the work of the latest poets or poet, then the same development may be visible in other ancient

[1] *Od.* 16, 17; 16, 217; 19, 518.   [2] *Od.* 4, 335.
[3] *Od.* 2, 47; 1, 308; 17, 111, 397; 15, 152.

recurring elements. We have considered the repeated lines in Eastern poetry under various headings – correspondence formulae, operation orders, and refrains[1] – and supposed that similar repetitions were characteristic of Mycenaean poetry. In Homer we still find the repetition of messages and orders in the exact terms in which they are given, the words of answers conforming as far as possible to the words of questions, and the use of refrains to mark off shorter or longer sections of the narrative. If, however, we look at the so-called 'typical scenes', which have been studied in great detail by Arend,[2] we find a procedure which has some analogies to the use of similes. These are visits, meals, going to bed, landing from the sea, arming, and other such actions. Each of them consists of a sequence of operations which is fixed in order and may have remained for centuries unchanged. Thus for each Homer inherits a stock of formulae and complete lines which he can use, and on the whole the repeated lines show very few signs of recent composition. The repeated lines are naturally most frequent when the operations are least individual. Thus in the visits, although the sequence is fixed – the visitor leaves home, arrives, finds the person concerned, is seated, and speaks – the details are extremely varied, and only the visits of Thetis to Achilles show any considerable repetition. The meal scenes, on the other hand, while showing great variation in the earlier part, which includes a prayer to the god concerned, are much more standardized when it comes to the sacrifice of the animal and the preparation and eating of the meal; even in this part the meal which Achilles prepares for the Embassy is highly individual, but in spite of its individuality it has two lines which are repeated in the very short account of the meal given by Achilles to Priam.[3] The lines in which arrangements are made for the guests to go to bed in Achilles' hut, the palace at Sparta, and the palace at Phaeacia are largely the same; one small point betrays the hand of the last poet. The guests sleep outside but the master sleeps 'in the inner part of the lofty house', and this formula shows an -oo genitive, which should be at least pre-migration: but Achilles lives in a hut, and so the formula is altered to 'in the inner part of the well-built hut' with an irreducible -ou genitive.[4] The arming

---

[1] Cf. above pp. 70 ff.　　[2] *Die typischen Scenen bei Homer*, Problemata 7.
[3] *Il.* 9, 216 f. = 24, 625 f. For the standard form cf. particularly *Il.* 2, 421 ff.
[4] *Il.* 24, 675 = 9, 663; contrast *Od.* 4, 304 etc.

of Paris, Agamemnon, Patroklos, and Achilles is told in identical lines, but all except Achilles have unique breastplates; Agamemnon has a special sword, shield, and helmet, Achilles also has a special shield and helmet; Paris takes one spear, Agamemnon and Patroklos take two spears, and Achilles has a special spear. The interest of these typical scenes is that each of them seems to embody a fixed sequence of operations which there is every reason to believe is old and was probably told in identical language whenever it occurred. But Homer preserves the sequence and adapts the language to his needs at the moment without losing the essential rightness of the descriptions which the old poets had made for identical acts.

As with similes, late linguistic forms sometimes mark special adaptations of typical scenes, such as the arrival of Telemachos in Pylos, Nestor's special arrangements for sacrifice after the epiphany of Athena, or the awakening of Odysseus in Ithaca.[1] But again as with similes the new adaptation is not necessarily accompanied by late linguistic forms. Late linguistic forms are a positive indication of the work of a late poet, but often he may not leave this mark. Both poems in their present form are in any case late, what the presence of late forms tells us is that here certainly is either violent adaptation of the old story or new creation. So far we have considered passages containing late subject-matter, similes, and typical scenes, we can now go on to ask what other kinds of passages show clusters of late linguistic forms and therefore tell us something about the methods and the outlook of the last poets. They may conveniently be grouped in four main classes – special narratives, abbreviations of old stories, commentaries (to borrow a useful term from Shipp), and compositional elements, such as preparations for later scenes, transitions, and recapitulations; the consideration of these last will lead us into the question of the unity of the poems as compositions.

Some special narratives may be briefly considered. In the *Odyssey*[2] the delightful scene where Nausikaa tells her maidens to bathe Odysseus, and he then says that he will bathe himself is late. The description of the island which lay off the harbour of the Cyclops' land also shows a high proportion of late forms, and Myres saw here the kind of description which would be given to

[1] *Od.* 3, 29ff.; 430ff.; 13, 190ff. [2] *Od.* 6, 206-24; 9, 116f.

a prospective colonist of the land he was to occupy. In the *Iliad*[1] the death of Sarpedon is linguistically late and includes two late similes. Sarpedon himself may well be a Mycenaean hero; the special arrangements for his burial are surely an old story, and the killing of the trace-horse must come from a time when chariots were important. But the duel with Hektor is fought entirely with the throwing-spear and must, therefore, be post-Mycenaean, and the linguistically late forms date it to the time of the last poets. It seems very likely, therefore, that its present form has been created for its position here as a prelude to the death of Patroklos.

Another instance of late special narrative is the supplication to Athena.[2] As we have seen, the rite is very old, and would have been known not only to Mycenaean poets but also to pre-migration poets in Athens and to post-migration poets in Samos. It is likely that a supplication to a goddess had occurred already in heroic poetry, and Kakridis[3] supposes that in the Meleager story the Calydonians tried to appease the anger of Artemis by such a supplication. Whether our Homer was inspired by the Meleager story or not, the language shows that this scene is his own creation for this place in the *Iliad*. He has invented a temple of Athena in Troy. Theano is made her priestess because she is the wife of Antenor and therefore interesting in herself like her husband and his children. That in one version of the siege story she was already the priestess of the city goddess and prayed the goddess to break the spear of the attacker seems to me highly likely, and this may be the earlier poetic version which inspired Homer rather than the Meleager story. The reason for the invention would seem to be that Homer decided to break the long sequence of battles with a peaceful interlude consisting of Glaukos and Diomede, Hektor and Hekabe, Hektor and Paris, Hektor and Andromache, Paris and Hektor. The supplication not only makes an impressive scene in this sequence, but Helenos' advice to make the supplication also provides the reason for Hektor leaving the battle and returning to Troy, thus setting the whole sequence in motion.

Both the supplication to Athena and the death of Sarpedon are not only special narratives in the sense that in their present form

---

[1] *Il.* 16, 428f., cf. above p. 168.
[2] *Il.* 6, 86f., 269f., 297f. (cf. above p. 212).
[3] *Homeric Researches*, 56f.

they were created for this particular place in the poem, but they may also have older stories behind them and in that sense are abbreviations. What distinguishes those modern additions which I have called abbreviations of old stories is that in them the abbreviation is undoubted, whether they occur in the main story or only on the fringe. Theano is one of a large number of interesting minor Trojans; and, as we have seen,[1] stories about the Trojans were already in existence in Mycenaean times, whatever was then the geographical location of the poetic Troy. In the *Iliad* they mostly appear only to die, and the series of slaughters becomes more interesting because some particular Trojan has an interesting ancestry or interesting previous experience, and his death is often made vivid by a modern simile. The implication is that Homer inherited stories about a great many Trojans, and these were known to his audience; they would pick up a brief reference, which often betrays to us by its language the fact that it is an abbreviation.[2] More such references could be added where the lateness does not reveal itself in the language. These minor Trojans belong to the story in so far as they are killed; Aeneas has a more considerable part to play, but two passages[3] concerning him are linguistically late: Diomede's attack on Aphrodite and Aeneas' own account of his pedigree. The former is an abbreviation of a Mycenaean theme, like many of the other divine scenes;[4] but another late divine scene, Hermes' meeting with Priam when he goes to ransom Hektor's body, is rather a new creation for this particular point in the story and belongs to the 'special narratives'.[5] The genealogy of Aeneas is cast in a form which is probably, as we have seen,[6] not very old; genealogies in general seem to reflect the pride of the new aristocracies, and this genealogy has a modern political reference, if it is taken with Poseidon's prophecy that the descendants of Aeneas shall continue to rule the Trojans and if that is rightly referred to the desire of Miletos for a friendly dynasty in Skepsis.

So far only Trojans have been considered. Late language often

---

[1] Cf. above pp. 114ff.

[2] E.g. *Il.* 4, 482, Simoeisios; 5, 76, Hypsenor; 8, 302, Gorgythion, son of Priam; 11, 122, sons of Antimachos; 13, 171, Imbrios; 16, 604, Onetor; 17, 51, Euphorbos.　　　　　　　　　　[3] *Il.* 5, 335 f.; 20, 200f.

[4] E.g. *Il.* 1, 530f.; 8, 397f.; 5, 871f.; 13, 23f.; *Od.* 5, 59f.; 8, 266f.

[5] *Il.* 24, 352f. (particularly 425f.).

[6] Cf. above pp. 144, 185.

shows where we have an abbreviated account of events which belonged to the story of the Greeks between the beginning of the Trojan war and the return of Odysseus: instances are the original muster of the Achaeans, the portent at Aulis, Achilles' exploits in the early stages of the campaign, Neoptolemos' exploits after Achilles' death, Odysseus' battle with the Kikones and his protection of Maron.[1] Besides the stories of the Trojan war the Laomedon story told by Poseidon, the Herakles story as told by Athena, Zeus, and Agamemnon in the *Iliad* and by the poet in the *Odyssey*, the Theban story as told by Agamemnon and Diomede, the story of Meleager told by Phoinix, the appeal of Elpenor and the appearances of Tyro, Pero, Tantalos, and Sisyphos in the Underworld are all marked as abbreviations by their late language.[2]

In all these cases the form of the story which we have is certainly late. Many other stories in the *Iliad*, notably Nestor's accounts of his past exploits or Achilles' description of Niobe, show no considerable excess of late language, but its absence is no more a reason for excluding them from the class of late abbreviations than is the similar absence of late language from many long similes a reason for dating them early if a good reason can be found for dating them late. Homer drew on an immense range of stories, and his audience knew enough of them to be pleased by shorthand references: no further justification is needed for the stories of Nestor or the allusions to the Theban war. Many of these stories were Mycenaean in origin, and sometimes we have some inkling of the development of the story between Mycenaean times and Homer. A few cases where probable stages can be shown were discussed in the preceding chapter. Here we are more concerned with the use that the late poet makes of traditional material, but sometimes the view taken of the late poet's procedure has also involved a view of the stages through which the story has developed. The procedure is highly conjectural, as is shown by the wildly conflicting results obtained. Here I confine myself to the late passages in Odysseus' visit to the Underworld and the Meleager story in the *Iliad* – because a

[1] *Od.* 24, 115; *Il.* 2, 299; 9, 325; *Od.* 11, 505; 9, 40f.; 9, 197f.
[2] Laomedon: *Il.* 7, 443. Herakles: *Il.* 8, 362; 15, 18; 19, 95; *Od.* 21, 32. Theban story: *Il.* 4, 370; 14, 113. Meleager: *Il.* 9, 529. Underworld: *Od.* 11, 60, 235, 285, 582, 593.

consideration of them shows two different ways in which the poet worked.

In the present form of the visit to the Underworld, Odysseus tells how he went there on Circe's instructions,[1] and before he started the young Elpenor fell off the roof and was killed (but Odysseus did not know this at the time). When he arrives and makes the prescribed sacrifice, Elpenor is the first soul to greet him and appeals in a linguistically late passage for a funeral, which is duly carried out when Odysseus returns to Circe's island. Evidently the story of a man who forgot his way down off a flat Mycenaean roof was remembered, and the three scenes neatly link Odysseus' departure, his arrival in the Underworld, and his return to Circe's island. Odysseus then tells how he refused to talk to his mother until he has talked to Teiresias. Teiresias tells him of his future to the end of his life. Antikleia tells him of his family and of the fate of the dead. Then the heroines come (and Tyro and Pero show clearly the signs of late composition). Now Odysseus breaks off and after a pause is persuaded to resume, the so-called *intermezzo*.[2] Then the heroes of the war come (Agamemnon, Achilles, Ajax, and others with whom his conversation is not reported), and in this passage the description of Neoptolemos' exploits and the Ajax episode are marked as linguistically late. Finally Odysseus sees Minos, the great sinners, and Herakles, and here the descriptions of Tantalos and Sisyphos have late language.

The analysts are undoubtedly right in supposing that the visit to the Underworld combines different stories. Their case has been most recently put with great eloquence by Page,[3] and his summary is worth quoting: 'we have good reason to believe that there was once an independent poem on Odysseus' Visit to the Underworld, wherein the hero met and conversed with Teiresias, with his mother, and with his former comrades-in-arms. This poem was inserted into the *Odyssey*, and more or less adapted to it, especially by means of some modification of the parts of Elpenor and Teiresias; by the assignment of a speech to Circe, giving a motive for the visit; and by the insertion of the Intermezzo. Whether before or after the junction with the *Odyssey*, two extensive episodes were incorporated: the Catalogue of Heroines and the

---

[1] *Od.* 10, 490.   [2] *Od.* 11, 330–79.

[3] *The Homeric Odyssey*, 21 f. Contrast Heubeck, *Odysseedichter*, 33; Gomme, *Greek Attitude to Poetry and History*, 21.

description of the Hades of King Minos.' Common ground here is that the Nekyia (to give it its convenient Greek name) consists of disparate elements, which did not all originally belong to the story of Odysseus. I should deny all Page's strictures on its quality in its present form and argue that the five-part composition is well fitted for its present place in the story. First, three ghosts *came to* Odysseus – Elpenor, Teiresias, Antikleia. Secondly, he *saw* the women. Thirdly, the story is broken by the *intermezzo*. Fourthly, more ghosts *came to* him, his comrades-in-arms, and he speaks to three (Agamemnon, Achilles, Ajax). Fifthly, he *saw* Minos and others. This is a very pretty balancing composition of five scenes: trio of visitors, spectacle of women, *intermezzo*, trio of visitors, spectacle of men. It is the same kind of composition as the shield of Achilles in the *Iliad*[1] with a similar use of keywords (here *came*, *saw*) to mark the different parts. The linguistically late elements are equally distributed between Elpenor's appeal, Odysseus' conversation with his comrades-in-arms, which Page regards as part of his pre-*Odyssey* independent poem, and the vision of the heroines and the vision of the sinners, both of which he regards as incorporated later. First, it should be noted that nothing in these passages looks in any way later than the other passages which we have called abbreviations, and one element in the description of Tantalos and Sisyphos I should like to regard as characteristic of the style of the last poet. This is the use of frequentatives: in the *Odyssey* it is found again in the Neoptolemos passage and outside the Nekyia in the description of Scylla and Charybdis, and in the *Iliad* notably in Ajax's unwilling retreat in the eleventh book.[2] The chief function of the *intermezzo* is to mark the centre of this balancing composition, and, as Miss Lorimer[3] says, 'this courtly interlude must as a whole be the work of our poet'. It also serves to emphasize the new beginning with Agamemnon and Achilles, and this emphasis is useful because those heroes are to be seen again in the second Nekyia in the last book. Thus the Nekyia was carefully composed for its present position as the climax of Odysseus' wanderings: a series of adventures lead up to the Nekyia and a further series of adventures

---

[1] Cf. above pp. 214f. In both a late section of the main composition has a unique verb (*Il.* 18, 590; *Od.* 11, 601) to mark the beginning of a subsection.

[2] *Od.* 11, 505f.; 12, 235; *Il.* 11, 466. Cf. Chantraine, 314f.; Shipp, 38. Cf. below p. 255. [3] *HM*, 521, n. 1.

lead on to Odysseus' arrival at Calypso's island, whence he reached Phaeacia. Germain[1] has rightly seen the central position of the Nekyia in Odysseus' wanderings; the detailed correspondences between his previous and subsequent adventures can be pushed too far but the disobedience of his sailors after the visit to Aiolos and on the island of the Sun is a certain parallel between the earlier and the later series. If the last poet moved the Nekyia from its former position as a last adventure to its present central position, this would account for the obvious signs of adaptation in Circe's speech and Teiresias' speech, which Page rightly stresses. The pre-history of the wanderings is itself immensely complicated, we can at least detect elements from the Gilgamesh epic, elements from the Egyptian story of the shipwrecked man, and elements from a recent poem about the Argonauts, to which Homer refers when he says that only Argo 'known to all' sailed through the clashing rocks.[2]

The different persons who take part in the Nekyia have each a rather different history to account for their presence. Elpenor is a link backward and forward with Odysseus' wanderings. The heroines, as we have seen,[3] are a remodelling of old catalogue poetry, incorporating information about the Mycenaean age of extreme interest to the Ionian descendants of the Mycenaeans. Of the heroes and sinners Minos is certainly old, and the picture of him administering justice describes one function of the Mycenaean king:[4] I see no convincing reason for supposing that the sinners and Herakles are not also old in subject-matter and seemed to the poet too important to be forgotten. Page attributes to his earlier independent poem Teiresias, Odysseus' mother, and his comrades-in-arms. I am convinced that far behind our *Odyssey* lies a Mycenaean borrowing of the Gilgamesh poem, in which the necessary information, supplied in the *Odyssey* by Teiresias, is supplied in the upper world by Utnapishtim, and Enkidu's visit to Hades and his return to enlighten Gilgamesh is a quite different and later episode.[5] At least three stages have intervened between the Mycenaean borrowing of this story and the *Odyssey*. First, the part of Enkidu, who told Gilgamesh about the Underworld, was

---

[1] *Genèse de l'Odyssée*, 333.
[2] *Od.* 12, 70 (cf. 9, 20). Cf. Page, *op. cit.*, 2f.; Reinhardt, *Von Werken und Formen*, 52f.; and above pp. 82ff.   [3] Cf. above pp. 119, 178, 185.
[4] Cf. above p. 25.   [5] Cf. above p. 83.

given to the hero's mother; this version, as Page and others have seen, must have been told to the hero's wife, and I have suggested that the account of the fate of the dead became especially interest-, ing to the Greeks with the general introduction of cremation in the early eleventh century. Secondly, the part originally played by Utnapishtim in the upper world was given to Teiresias, who was placed in Hades. Teiresias himself is a very old figure if he is to be identified, as I think, with the Qerasija of the Knossos tablets, but according to the *Nostoi*[1] he died in Kolophon and was buried there. This probably means that the immigrants had brought an oracle of Teiresias with them, and if it obtained some fame, it would supply a post-migration reason for Teiresias' part in the Nekyia. Thirdly, this story of a hero's wanderings in search of information became the story of Odysseus, and (not necessarily in the same transference) the story of Odysseus' return from Troy, which involved tying the mythical geography at either end to the Mediterranean; only at that stage could Odysseus' former comrades-in-arms enter the story. Teiresias and Antikleia provide different pieces of essential information, to obtain which a hero might wander to Hades or some other distant place. The comrades-in-arms are part of the scenery of Hades like the heroines and the sinners. They are irrelevant to the old story but interesting to the audience when the old story has become Odysseus' return from Troy, and their presence implies that the story of the Trojan war was current pretty much in the shape that we now know it. The Nekyia has, therefore, a long history behind it; its present form is an elaborate composition by the poet of the *Odyssey* to mark the climax of Odysseus' wanderings.

The Meleager story[2] raises quite a different problem. Odysseus and Ajax with their heralds go to persuade Achilles to fight, and Phoinix leads them. Odysseus and Ajax are the official ambassa-dors, and therefore the verbs describing their journey are in the dual, although the whole party consists of five members. As a centre-piece between the first pair of speeches (Odysseus' proposals and Achilles' refusal) and the last pair of speeches (Ajax' acceptance of defeat and Achilles' final refusal) Homer has put a long speech of Phoinix and a short speech of Achilles.[3]

---

[1] Allen, *O.C.T.*, vol. 5, 108. Cf. above p. 109.
[2] *Il.* 9, 524ff. cf. Kakridis, *op. cit.*, 11f.; Heubeck, *Odysseedichter*, 16f., 23f.
[3] Cf. Myres, *J.H.S.*, 74 (1954), 131.

Phoinix first tells his own story as evidence of his loyalty to Achilles, then paints the picture of the Prayers and Infatuation as a deterrent, and finally tells the story of Meleager as an example. The function of the story is quite clear and is explicitly stated by Phoinix. The great men of the past have been open to gifts and persuasion. Meleager withdrew from the battle in anger with his mother, who had cursed him for the death of her brother. The elders and priests of Kalydon offered him gifts. His father, sisters, mother, and friends tried in vain to persuade him to fight. Finally, when the enemy began to set fire to the town, his wife persuaded him, and he saved the town but then it was too late for gifts. 'It would be a bad thing to have to fight when the ships are on fire. Come now and receive their gifts.' The story of Meleager is a large-scale simile. It is a working model of the present situation and of the future course of action which the poet knows: Achilles will defend the ships when they are burning; unlike Meleager, he will receive gifts but he will lose something far more precious, Patroklos. The validity of a simile lies in present experience; the validity of a heroic story lies in the audience's knowledge of it, and this paradeigmatic use of stories is also our evidence for the audience's knowledge. The story, as told, is difficult to understand because everything which is irrelevant to its function is left out; the audience knew that the Kouretes and Kalydonians had quarrelled over the spoils of the boar hunt, that Meleager had then slain his uncle, and that his mother's curse killed him before he could receive the gifts from his grateful fellow citizens; these facts could, therefore, be left out and the poet could concentrate on the essentials of a parallel, which is telling as an appeal from Phoinix to Achilles but even more important as a presentation by Homer to the audience of the real importance of this moment in his story.

The further problem which the Meleager story raises is a problem of extreme difficulty. In its most general form the question may be put thus: can we detect Homer translating the themes of other stories into terms of his own story in the *Iliad*? So far we have been concerned mainly with old stories, some of them very old, which have been brought up to date and fitted together and adapted and coloured to suit their new setting, and we have just examined part of this process in the story of Odysseus. This, however, is a process of gradual accretion; a commanding figure collects stories from many sources through the ages. What we have now to examine is something different, a late poet's use of other material as a model on which to mould or a source from which to embellish his theme. Cauer[1] discusses with approval the suggestion that the whole *Iliad* was modelled on the Meleager story. Kakridis[2] does not go so far as this but finds that various incidents in the sixth book are inspired by the Meleager story, not only the supplication of the goddess, which we have already considered, but also the supposed anger of Paris, the rising scale of womanly affection which surrounds Hektor, and his leave-taking. The theory is extremely ingenious and the case is very well argued, but for me it remains a possibility rather than a probability; the supplication in its simplest form and the farewell of the defending hero must have belonged to many siege stories and may have been very early a part of the Trojan story. Nor can we say that the Meleager story is the model for the wrath of Achilles. Cauer's argument, that Meleager's withdrawal is far better motivated than Achilles' and that, while Meleager naturally stayed at home with his wife, Achilles has no reason for staying in Troy, leaves Briseis out of account; to say that Achilles is in love with Briseis is not modern sentimentality but his own judgement;[3] and Klytemnestra, Hermione, and Deianira would have understood the forces involved. Quarrels are too common in Greek legend in general and Homer[4] in particular for them all to be derived from the Meleager story. Nor was the anger of Meleager introduced into the story by Homer for the para-deigmatic purpose of Phoinix' speech; Kraus[5] has argued that so great an innovation would, in fact, destroy the paradeigmatic value of the story. If this is accepted, we must suppose a fairly recent version of the Meleager story in which the mother's curse was substituted for the magic of the burning torch (we have noticed similar substitutions in Ionian epic)[6] and that in this version the mother changed her mind and begged her son to fight but presumably, however much she wished it, she could not stop the operation of the curse, which killed him.

The supposition that other parts of the Trojan story itself were introduced into the framework of the *Iliad* narrative is rather

[1] *Grundfragen*, 264.   [2] *Homeric Researches*, 43 ff.
[3] *Il.* 9, 341 f.   [4] *Il.* 6, 326; 20, 179; *Od.* 8, 75.
[5] *W.S.*, 63 (1948), 8 f.   [6] Cf. above pp. 175, 176, 179.

different, since Homer may naturally have looked there for material and the audience expected more than the story of Achilles' quarrel with Agamemnon. We have, in fact, seen that the Catalogue of Greeks was modelled on an earlier Catalogue of the Suitors of Helen. Some recent suggestions of the same kind which are certainly possibilities may be briefly mentioned.[1] Our information about the content of the Trojan war story in the eighth century comes almost entirely from summaries and fragments of the Cyclic poets and may, therefore, include their invention as well as traditional material. The new mutiny at the beginning of the second book of the *Iliad* is certainly surprising as it stands, and Homer's object[2] is presumably to show a low point in morale from which he gradually rises to the splendour of the Catalogue; a mutiny is recorded for the period before the quarrel between Agamemnon and Achilles, when the Greeks were starving. It was quelled by Achilles and solved by fetching the daughters of Anios to feed the army; this story Homer may have borrowed.

Thersites is a curious, lonely figure in the *Iliad*; it is true that he has a great part later when he taunts Achilles with the love of Penthesilea, but that story may rather have been further invention on the basis of the *Iliad* than the source for the *Iliad*; if that is so, it is possible that Homer took Thersites from the Aetolian story: there he ran away from the Kalydonian boar and fell or was pushed over a cliff, which accounted for his physical defects.[3] Then Arktinos, the poet of the *Aithiopis*, which included both the Penthesilea story and the Memnon story, found in the quarrel between Thersites and Odysseus in the *Iliad* the inspiration for his quarrel between Thersites and Achilles, just as he elaborated in terms of the Memnon story the incident in the *Iliad* where Diomede saves Nestor, the transport of Sarpedon's body by Sleep and Death, and the weighing of souls.[4] These incidents cause no surprise in the *Iliad* and are part of traditional poetry; only the transport of Sarpedon's body is individual, and Sarpedon was a very special person. Here it seems possible that the *Iliad* provided the material which Arktinos elaborated.

[1] See particularly Pestalozzi, *Die Achilleis als Quelle der Ilias*; Kakridis, *op. cit.*; Schadewaldt, *Von Homers Welt und Werk*, 115 f.; Kullmann, *Mus. Helv.*, 12 (1955), 253. [2] *Il*. 2, 142.

[3] Plaoutine, *R.E.G.*, 1942, 161. [4] *Il*. 8, 80; 16, 666; 22, 208.

On the other hand it is not obvious why Thetis and her Nereids make lamentation before she goes to see Achilles after the death of Patroklos or why when she reaches Achilles she holds his head and laments as if he were dead;[1] Homer undoubtedly wants to emphasize Achilles' utter despair, and the suggestion that he has been inspired here by the traditional lamentation made by Thetis and her Nereids for Achilles himself is likely. Lamentation by Thetis and her Nereids was as much a part of the story of Achilles as removal by Sleep and Death was part of the story of Sarpedon. It is referred to in the *Odyssey*[2] and Arktinos elaborated it in the *Aithiopis*; here Homer draws on a precious bit of tradition about Achilles' death to paint Achilles' misery at the time of Patroklos' death and to show the whole tragedy of Achilles now that he decides on the short life of glory instead of the long life of obscurity. This view of Achilles, expressed in Thetis' heart-breaking adjective *dysaristotokeia*, 'who have born a hero to misery', is not the creation of Arktinos nor of Homer but of the early poet who modelled Achilles and Thetis on Gilgamesh and Ninsun.[3]

The evidence seems to me good that Homer sometimes used traditional stories about other parts of the Trojan war as the model for scenes in the *Iliad*, and such borrowing should be considered as an explanation for the Wall round the Achaean encampment. In our *Iliad* the attack on the Wall is a thrilling episode in the great series of Achaean reverses which lead up to the attack on the ships and the entry of Patroklos into the battle; Schadewaldt[4] and others are entirely justified in regarding the attack on the Wall and, therefore, the building of the Wall as part of the plan of the *Iliad*. But the Achaean Wall is a curiously impermanent piece of Trojan scenery. It is carefully built within the narrative of the *Iliad*, and at the beginning of the Trojan attack we are told that Poseidon and Apollo destroyed it as soon as Troy was sacked.[5] Moreover, when it is built, Poseidon in a speech which is full of modern linguistic characteristics objects that it will be more splendid than the wall of Laomedon's Troy, and Zeus answers that he and Apollo will be able to destroy it when the Achaeans go home. Homer almost tells us that it is his own invention. As the *Iliad* is planned, the capture of Troy falls

[1] *Il.* 18, 35–52, 71.   [2] *Od.* 24, 47.   [3] Cf. above p. 82.
[4] *Iliasstudien*, 67, 124; cf. Lorimer, *HM*, 477.   [5] *Il.* 12, 1 f.; 7, 444.

outside the poem. I suggest that the Trojan storming of the Achaean Wall is a substitute for this and that Homer remodelled it on an earlier story of the siege of Troy. There are two small pieces of evidence. The Wall according to Miss Lorimer's interpretation had a batter like the wall of Troy VI; it may, therefore, really have been in origin the wall of Troy. Secondly, one of the Lycian assailants, when hit by Ajax as he climbs the fortifications, falls off like a diver – a very good description of the falling man in the siege-fresco from Mycenae.[1] In any case one reason for the assault on the Wall is to satisfy the audience's demand for a siege.

A similar explanation might account for the tenth book, the story of Dolon and Rhesos. The book has some strange words and forms, as has often been noted; but these cannot be dated and the late linguistic forms do not exceed the average for the rest of the *Iliad*. The description of the boar's tusk helmet must ultimately be Mycenaean and Rhesos' decorated chariot should be; the lion skin and leopard skin of Agamemnon and Menelaos may also be old.[2] The story of the two scouts who meet the enemy scout and use his information to kill a newly arrived ally may be a good old story and may even have been long connected with Odysseus and Diomede. But the arrival of a new Thracian ally does not naturally belong to the time sequence of the *Iliad*; the forces are fixed in the Catalogue (including the Thracians under Akamas and Peiroos) and are not changed. The arrival of Rhesos would more naturally belong to a later stage of the story like the arrival of Penthesilea and Memnon. The difference between Homer's treatment of the story of Dolon and Rhesos and the Wall story is twofold. The Wall story had to be abbreviated and completely remodelled so as to become the siege of the Greek camp instead of the siege of Troy, but the Dolon and Rhesos story only needed retelling on the same scale; probably, therefore, more alien language survives here than anywhere else in the *Iliad*. Secondly, the Wall story had to be made convincing and, therefore, the Wall is built early in the *Iliad* and alluded to in the intervening books. The Dolon and Rhesos story is an isolated incident needing no preparation and having no consequences. Homer thought it was a good enough story to include in the

---

[1] *Il.* 12, 258, 444; cf. Lorimer, *HM*, 433; *Il.* 12, 385, cf. above p. 59.
[2] *Il.* 10, 261; 438; 23; 29.

Iliad, and it makes a good contrast both to the quiet scene of the Embassy and to the long series of normal daylight battles, which starts on the next day when Agamemnon takes the field.[1]

Poseidon says that the Achaean Wall will be known all over the world and everyone will forget the wall which he and Apollo built for Laomedon. This is the modern paradeigmatic use of an old story like the use of the Meleager story by Phoinix. It is a scale by which to measure Homer's wall, just as the Meleager story is a scale by which to measure Achilles' position. Both are commentaries as well as abbreviations and lead us into the third main class of passages containing late linguistic clusters. Similarly Agamemnon, at his reconciliation with Achilles, comments on his past infatuation by quoting the infatuation of Zeus, when he allowed Hera to deceive him so that Eurystheus was born before Herakles.[2] Both the infatuation of Zeus and the wrath of Meleager are introduced to illustrate the state of mind of particular characters at important moments, the repentance of Agamemnon for his former infatuation and the wrath of Achilles at its most stubborn, a quality summed up by Diomede when the embassy is over as 'fierceness' (*agenorie*), a word to which we shall return.[3] These two commentaries are psychological in the sense that they contain a judgement on an action which is seen as the result of a particular state of mind. After the death of Hektor two passages[4] are marked by a cluster of late forms: the first contains the Achaeans comments on Hektor and Achilles' hesitation whether he should attack Troy before burying Patroklos; the second is Andromache's reception of the news and her comments. The Achaean comments on Hektor may be compared with a number of other appraising comments, which also show late forms – Menelaos' comment on Trojan behaviour or Euryalos' suggestion that Odysseus looks more like a pirate than an athlete.[5] These comments give the atmosphere of a particular moment by showing how it appears to an observer.

---

[1] On the difficulty of separating the Doloneia from our *Iliad* see Lorimer, *HM*, 485; Von der Mühll, *Kritisches Hypomnema*, 182f.; Dornseiff, *Antike und alter Orient*, 146f. [2] *Il.* 19, 78–144.

[3] *Il.* 9, 700. [4] *Il.* 22, 368–90; 447–59.

[5] *Il.* 13, 619–39; *Od.* 8, 145–64. Cf. *Il.* 16, 742f.; *Od.* 2, 326–40; 4, 70–80; 17, 483–7.

The Andromache passage is more interesting. She hears the lamentations and fears that Hektor is dead: 'Achilles will have stopped him from the disastrous fierceness which always possessed him, for he never remained in the body of the army but always ran far ahead, yielding in valour to no one.'[1] This late passage characterizes Hektor or rather states one essential characteristic of Hektor – 'a fierceness', which differs from the 'fierceness' attributed by Diomede to Achilles because it is displayed in action instead of sulking. But the word is the same, and it is probably a modern formation; the type is not uncommon in Homer, formed from the adjective and expressing a mental quality. The only other place where this word is used is the late simile before the attack on the Wall, where Hektor is compared to a boar or lion surrounded by hounds and hunters and 'its fierceness kills it'. In Andromache's comment the fierceness is shown to be habitual by the iterative verbs 'always possessed', 'always ran' (which again are a sign of lateness).[2] In the rest of the *Iliad*[3] the same quality is attributed to Hektor not only in the lion simile but before that in the earlier scene of leave-taking ('your valour will destroy you'), which Andromache remembers here, and earlier still in Paris' comment on Hektor: 'your courage is like an unblunted axe, driven through wood by a man who skilfully cuts a ship's timber, and it increases his force'. Thus this side of Hektor's character can be traced through the *Iliad* and is summed up in the abstract 'fierceness'. A similar abstract, *eneeie*, which is unique, describes Patroklos' 'gentleness'.[4] Menelaos, when the battle is raging over Patroklos' dead body, cries out: 'now remember the gentleness of hapless Patroklos. For he knew how to be kindly to all while he lived.' The adjective 'gentle' is used three times of Patroklos, and Briseis in her lament says that when her home was sacked he did not allow her to weep but promised to make her the bride of Achilles: 'therefore I weep bitterly for your death; for you were always kindly'. The sack of Briseis' home belongs to the pre-history of the *Iliad* and so establishes 'gentleness' as a permanent quality in Patroklos.

---

[1] *Il.* 22, 457; for the use of abstracts in characterization see Coffey, *B.I.C.S.*, 3 (1956), 31 f.

[2] Cf. above p. 246. [3] *Il.* 12, 46; 6, 407; 3, 60.

[4] *Il.* 17, 670; 17, 204; 21, 96; 23, 252; 19, 295 (with iterative). Cf. Gomme, *Greek attitude to poetry and history*, 20.

Other late characterizing comments could be quoted.[1] Enough has been said to establish two distinct but interrelated points of importance. The first is that the consistent and rich characterisation of Homer's heroes is probably his own. No reader of Homer who is undisturbed by the Homeric question and recent Homeric scholarship needs to be told this. But the operations of the analysts and the fact that it has been possible to see his people as puppets of the gods or as free fields entered by possessive and often personified emotions shows the need of establishing this richness and consistency as probably his creation.[2] Very few of the old standing epithets tell us much about character: Achilles is a mobile fighter and Ajax is a solid fighter. It is true that Odysseus is a man of many wiles and Penelope is very wise, but even these are perhaps professional rather than personal characteristics. Homer has added 'gentleness' to Patroklos' valour as a knight and established it as a permanent quality in his character. He has another rare abstract 'courteousness' (*agano-phrosyne*) to describe Hektor and Odysseus.[3] Helen uses it of Hektor and it is established above all by the earlier scene between Hektor and Andromache. Odysseus' mother uses it of Odysseus and it is established by the description of Odysseus as a kindly king. For both it may be called a civilian characteristic in contrast to the military fierceness of Hektor and professional resource of Odysseus.

The second and connected point is that Homer has a new way of stating these facts. He expresses them by abstract nouns. We cannot, I think, prove that these abstracts denoting states of mind (or body) are late, but the two most interesting ones 'fierceness' and 'gentleness' occur in late contexts, and where they are used to sum up Hektor and Patroklos, they are carefully explained – 'for he always etc.' – which looks as if this is a new use. It seems very probable that a considerable number of new abstracts were formed in Homer's own time to express more sophisticated states of mind for which the old abstracts like fear, desire, etc. were no longer sufficient. The same verbs are used with the new abstracts as with the old, but they become weaker

---

[1] E.g. *Il.* 9, 330f., self-characterization of Achilles; 13, 274, Idomeneus on Meriones.

[2] These problems are very well treated by Schwabl in *W.S.*, 67 (1954), 46f.

[3] *Il.* 24, 771; *Od.* 11, 203.

in the process.[1] When Homer says that fear, exhaustion, or desire seizes or holds a man or his limbs, he is stating a physical fact: the man vibrates or becomes still as if he were in the grip of an external physical force. But to say that 'helplessness possessed his soul' or 'fierceness always possessed him' is to use the same terminology for something different; these phrases mean 'he was then helpless' or 'he was always fierce'. The new abstracts are not external forces which can be spoken of as behaving like gods or demons but rather convenient new generalizing labels for talking about particular qualities, and that is their interest. They point the way to ethical philosophy.

We have not yet considered the third passage of late commentary after the death of Hektor, the comment made on the situation by Achilles himself.[2] Achilles first proposes to attack Troy and then changes his mind and says that they will bury Patroklos first. Its compositional function is to prepare for the burial of Patroklos and the funeral games in the next book, but it is also one of a number of speeches or descriptions of decision or indecision which are shown to be late by their language. We have already noted the late simile of the nightingale which Penelope uses to illustrate both her misery and her hesitations: her unhappiness fills the first part of this late speech and her indecision as to whether she should marry or not the second part.[3] Both her misery and her hesitation find expression in other linguistically late passages of the *Odyssey*; her misery particularly in the repeated account of how she grieves more for Telemachos in his danger than for Odysseus and her hesitation when she finally faces Odysseus after the slaying of the suitors. Odysseus also has a moment of indecision in his first night in his own palace, and again the passage is late.[4] Odysseus' demand to his heart to endure now as he endured the Cyclops eating his companions, until his skill led them out of the cave, is flanked by two similes. The first simile, the bitch bestriding her puppies and barking at an unknown man, illustrates his indignation at the women who are going to sleep with the suitors – a fury which he must not turn into immediate action, just as the bitch must wait for the unknown man to disclose his intentions and just as he

---

[1] Cf. *J.W.C.I.*, 17 (1954), 15.   [2] *Il.* 22, 378–90.
[3] *Od.* 19, 509–34. Cf. 4, 706–25, 810–20; 23, 85 f.
[4] *Od.* 20, 1–30.

himself had had to endure in the Cyclops' cave until he thought of a plan. He endures, but he tosses this way and that, as a man turns a haggis this way and that until it is roasted, pondering how he shall deal with the suitors single-handed. We have noticed before that similes illustrating a mental state may have as their subject an event parallel to that which gives rise to the mental state:[1] Penelope, wondering whether Telemachos will escape the ambush, is compared to the lion in a circle of hunters, when the lion is much more like Telemachos himself facing the ambush. Here the transference is rather different. Odysseus' pondering of different plans is really like the revolving of the haggis before the fire; but his mental movement is converted into bodily movement as he tosses this way and that, and the direct comparison is with his body, not with his mind. All these various examples show Homer's interest in psychology and the various means he has discovered to describe mental events.

Several of the other late speeches contain advice or exhortation, not the taking of a decision but the imposition of a decision on others; they, therefore, result in action and so prepare the reader for what is coming in a shorter or a longer stretch of the poem; they can more usefully be considered with other compositional elements. Before passing to the large subject of Homeric composition, we should, however, note that certain lines are repeatedly used in and after speeches of advice and exhortation: 'that I may say what my spirit in my breast bids me say', 'But I will speak as seems to me to be best', 'So speaking he fired the ardour and spirit of each.' All these have late forms and must in their present shape be recent. It is important to establish the fact that the late poets still invented repeated lines and formulae as their ancestors had before them. The evidence is overwhelmingly clear that the late poets not only disregarded the digamma in old formulae when it suited their purpose (e.g. θεὸς δ' ὥς instead of θεὸς ϝώς) and used the new short forms of oblique cases to decline old formulae which could not have been declined before (e.g. ἀρηιφίλου Μενελάου) but also created new formulae in quantity.[2] In fact the technique of poetry remained the same.

[1] Cf. above p. 238 on *Od.* 4, 791; *Il.* 9, 4.

[2] Cf. in general *Eranos*, 54 (1956), 45 f.; and for discussion of a single example, Severyns, *Homère*, II, 86 f.

4. COMPOSITION OF THE *ILIAD* AND THE *ODYSSEY*

We shall have to face this problem. The poet still uses the very old technique of composing with formulae, which is said to belong to oral composition and oral tradition; and yet our *Iliad* and *Odyssey* are of great size and have a unity which it is difficult to associate with oral composition and which is incompatible with the performance of oral poetry. The unity is given by two kinds of compositional elements, which may be termed static and dynamic. The distinction is this: a static element has to be recognized by the audience as a compositional element, but a dynamic element forces itself on the audience's attention. The attentive listener notices that in the Nekyia he is led through the sequence A. three visitors, B. visions, C. *intermezzo* and that this is then repeated in the order A¹. three visitors, B¹. visions. But when Zeus prophesies that Hektor will shortly be killed after putting on the armour of Achilles, the future events, Achilles' return to the battle and the death of Hektor, are forced on the listener's attention and he waits for them in suspense. The same distinction can be observed in Geometric vase-painting; the static elements predominate – the interwoven systems of a finite number of graded pattern bands and the symmetrical balance of the metope friezes – and these elements led Myres to make his detailed comparisons between Homer and Geometric vase-painting. But the dynamic elements are also there: movement in a vertical direction, towards the lid or towards the foot, is given either by turning all the dogtooth ornaments in the same direction or by breaking the symmetry so that elements repeat in the same instead of the reverse order; movement horizontally is given by the direction in which a maeander points or the direction in which human beings or animals move or animals lie. The parallels between Geometric figure scenes and Homeric epic in the treatment of subject-matter have been summarily discussed above.[1] Here the static elements, the interwoven system of a finite number of pattern bands, graded so that the most complicated and interesting member of each set of patterns occurs at a position of major importance on the lip, neck, or body of the vase, may be compared with the various static elements of composition which we have observed in the *Iliad* and the *Odyssey*. The hoplite passages with

[1] pp. 206f.

their associated similes, the massed similes at important moments in both poems, the contrasted similes, the echoing similes belonging to a finite number of easily recognizable sets, the typical scenes of landing, sacrifice, or arming, which all contain common elements, although they may be expanded or contracted for the particular occasion – all these are elements of static pattern which diversify and unify the long story in the same way as the echoing pattern bands diversify and unify the large surface of Geometric vases. As the patterns are graded, though not necessarily in a strict order of size, from a narrow and unimportant beginning up to an important and wide band, so in the *Iliad* and *Odyssey* a briefly told sequence of events will lead up to an event which is given more prominence. A series of uninteresting casualties leads up to the killing of an interesting minor Trojan, whose death is adorned with a simile. Thus when Patroklos enters the battle, a whole sequence of brief combats leads up to the major duel with Sarpedon, and then the tension is lowered again and gradually built up to the new climax of Patroklos' fatal duel with Hektor. Similarly in the *Odyssey*, Odysseus' adventures with the Kikones, his further voyage, his visit to the Lotus eaters are told briefly and lead up to the long account of the Cyclops.

If these elements may be compared to the pattern bands of Geometric vases, the larger static systems in the poems may be compared to the figure and animal scenes, which occupy the most important positions on the vases. Some of these have also been noticed, most strikingly the organization of Odysseus' wanderings about the Nekyia as an elaborate fivefold centre-piece with the two disastrous disobediences of Odysseus' sailors corresponding on either side. Inside the Nekyia itself the conversation between Odysseus and the heroes of the Trojan war picks up Nestor's earlier lamentation over Troy:[1] 'There Ajax lies, man of Ares, and there Achilles, there lies Patroklos, equal to the gods in counsel, and there my own son, both strong and blameless, Antilochos, swift runner and great fighter,' and is itself picked up by the second scene in the Underworld at the beginning of the last book, in which Achilles, Patroklos, Antilochos, Ajax, and Agamemnon appear again. Still more pervasive are the references to the story of Agamemnon, his wife, her lover, and his son (always to be heard as a contrast to the story of Odysseus, his wife,

[1] *Od.* 3, 109; cf. *HM*, 521.

her suitors, and his son), which come not only in the two Underworld scenes but also in the Council of the Gods in the first book,
in Nestor's speeches, and in Menelaos' speeches.[1] The Wanderings
of Odysseus itself is a story of the past and so is an interlude in
the present story of Odysseus – a very magnificent interlude but
still an interlude as the recall to the present in the *intermezzo* at
the centre of the Nekyia shows. Thus a contrast can be seen
between the present story of Odysseus and other actions past
and present.

If we look at the whole *Odyssey* from this point of view and
further distinguish within it the scenes of action and the quiet
scenes, we find the following general scheme. A. Council of the
gods about Odysseus, who is on Calypso's island. Then the long
story of Telemachos' mission, B. Athena's discussion with
Telemachos, the debate in Ithaka, C. the journey and arrival in
Pylos, the scenes with Nestor, C[1]. the journey to Sparta, the
scenes with Menelaos, B[1]. the suitors' plans to ambush Telemachos and Penelope's awareness (books 1–4). In this sequence
the scenes with Nestor balance the scenes with Menelaos, and both
form a quiet patch inside the action. From now on the poet has
three strands of story: C. Telemachos, B. Ithaka, A. Odysseus.
Another council of the gods carries out the intention of the first
to send Hermes to Odysseus on Calypso's island. Now the
Odysseus story goes on with action, raft-building, shipwreck,
and arrival in Phaeacia. The quiet interlude of Nausikaa leads
into further action (books 5–8). Then Odysseus tells the story of
his wanderings (books 9–12). After this long central interlude,
only broken by the central *intermezzo*, the present story of
Odysseus continues: he leaves Phaeacia, arrives in Ithaka and
comes to the swineherd Eumaios (books 13–14). The Eumaios
scenes may be classed as quiet interludes since they consist largely
of story-telling on either side. Then the story breaks off again to
find Telemachos in Sparta and send him home. Only when he has
left Pylos with Theoklymenos and is sailing through the night
safely away from the suitors' ambush does the poet take us back
to the quiet night conversation between Eumaios and Odysseus.
The new day finds Telemachos landing in Ithaka and on his way
to Eumaios (book 15). From this moment the Telemachos story
and the Odysseus story become one. Eumaios is sent to the city.

[1] *Od.* 1, 35, 298; 3, 193, 234, 263, 303; 4, 91, 521; 11, 409; 24, 96, 199.

Father and son recognize each other. The story switches again to Telemachos' ship, which arrives in the city harbour, followed soon after by the ship containing the men who were to ambush him. The suitors plan another ambush but Penelope protests; in the evening Eumaios returns to Odysseus (book 16). From now on there is only the one story, the present story of Odysseus, and the action continues towards the climax through a long series of events – Telemachos' return to Penelope (with his recital of his visit to Nestor and Menelaos), Odysseus abused by Melanthios, Odysseus recognized by the dog Argos, Odysseus maltreated by Antinoos, the quiet scene of Eumaios and Penelope (book 17), Odysseus and Iros, the quiet scene of Penelope among the suitors, Odysseus abused by Melantho (pendant to the Melanthios scene), Odysseus maltreated by Eurymachos (pendant to the Antinoos scene), the suitors go to bed (book 18), the removal of the arms, quiet scene of Odysseus and Penelope, recognition by Eurykleia (the story of the boar hunt is central), Odysseus and Penelope (book 19), Odysseus' bad night, morning in the palace, insulting of Odysseus, vision of Theoklymenos (book 20); then Penelope proposes the ordeal of the bow; Odysseus alone can string it; the suitors are killed (books 21–2). A quiet scene follows the climax of the suitors' slaying, the recognition of Odysseus by Penelope: but the story cannot end here, it can only end with the re-conciliation between Odysseus and the families of the suitors. The souls of the suitors go to Hades; the second Nekyia picks up the first Nekyia and shows once more the contrast between Agamemnon's return and Odysseus' return. It may also recall to the attentive listener another theme of the first Nekyia. Odysseus there asked his mother not only about Telemachos and Penelope, whom he has already rejoined, but also about his father Laertes, whom he now goes to see. Then the beginning of the great pattern is repeated: the Ithacans debate for and against Odysseus as they had debated for and against Telemachos in the second book, the gods take council (as in book 1) to end the strife in reconciliation, the battle begins and is stopped by Athena.

The chief principles that can be observed in large-scale com-position (in so far as it can be isolated from the details) are first the withholding of the main story, secondly the use of free symmetry, particularly between the beginning and the end but also sometimes internally, and sometimes the use of a straight balance between two adjacent parts of the story, and finally the inter-position of quiet scenes among the scenes of action. The same principles of static composition are observable in the *Iliad*. The story of Achilles from his first anger (with Agamemnon) to the renunciation of his second anger (against Hektor) corresponds to the story of Odysseus from his sojourn on Calypso's island to his reconciliation with the families of the suitors. Achilles is withheld till even later in the poem than Odysseus; but he makes a long appearance in the first book for the Quarrel and in the ninth book for the Embassy and short appearances in the eleventh book, when he sends Patroklos to Nestor, and in the sixteenth book, when Patroklos returns and gains his request to lead the Myrmidons into battle. As in the *Odyssey*, Achilles, when he finally takes the field, moves through a series of events up to the climax when he kills Hektor; after that, again as in the *Odyssey*, both a private and a public story is concluded – the one by the burial of Patroklos and the funeral games, the other by the reconciliation with Priam and the burial of Hektor.

The symmetrical composition of scenes in the *Iliad* has been worked out in great detail by Sheppard and Myres and for speeches in the *Iliad* and the *Odyssey* by Myres.[1] I am doubtful whether the poet intended such precise correspondences as are found in their schematization, but they have certainly detected a basic principle of Homeric composition, and the parallel drawn by Myres with the procedure of Geometric vase-painters is fundamentally sound; many instances of balanced composition and some of symmetrical composition on a small scale have already been quoted. As in the *Odyssey*, there is a real corres-pondence between the beginning and the end of the *Iliad* – the quarrel with Agamemnon and the reconciliation with Priam – and both contain similar elements, in the first book a visit of Thetis to Achilles succeeded by a divine council and in the twenty-fourth book a divine council succeeded by a visit of Thetis to Achilles; a curious minor point[2] is that each divine council begins on the *twelfth* day and that the poem opens with a nine-day plague after Chryses' appeal and ends with a nine-day period before Hektor's funeral. Within this prologue and epilogue a correspondence

---

[1] Sheppard, *Pattern of the Iliad, passim*; Myres, cf. above p. 200, n.1.

[2] *Il.* 1, 493 = 24, 31; 1, 53 = 24, 784. On symmetrical chronology in both poems cf. Pfister, *Würzburger Jahrbücher*, 3 (1948), 141.

may be seen between the first duel of Menelaos and Paris (book 3) and the last duel of Hektor and Achilles (book 22), between Diomede's attack on Aeneas when Aphrodite and Apollo save him (book 5) and Achilles' attack on Aeneas when Poseidon saves him (book 20), between the duel of Hektor and Ajax (book 7) and the duel of Hektor and Patroklos (book 16): the Embassy to Achilles (book 9) is answered by his reconciliation with Agamemnon (book 19) and the parallel is marked by the striking personification of Ate in both passages, and between these two come the mission of Patroklos to Nestor (book 11) and the corresponding scene in which he is sent out to fight (book 16).

Several instances have already been given of the shaping of the narrative by the use of contrasts, pairs, and symmetry. A striking example is the climax, the duel between Achilles and Hektor. Beginning and end balance: at the beginning Priam and Hekabe appeal to Hektor not to fight, at the end Priam, Hekabe, and Andromache lament him. Hektor decides to stand, but then 'trembling captured him'. The pursuit of Hektor is in two sections; after the first Zeus decides in council that he will not save Hektor, after the second Zeus uses his scales. Then Athena persuades Hektor to stand. The duel itself begins and ends with a dialogue between Hektor and Achilles, and is in two parts, spear fight and sword fight. Afterwards Achilles decides to bury Patroklos before attacking Troy. The whole is therefore shaped thus:[1] A. Appeals. B. Hektor decides. C. Pursuit. D. Divine Council. C^1. Pursuit. D^1. Scales of Zeus. B^1. Hektor persuaded. E. Dialogue. F. Spear fight. F^1. Sword fight. E^1. Dialogue. B^2. Achilles decides. A^2. Laments. On this scale also the contrast between scenes of action (the pursuits and fights) and quiet scenes (appeals, laments, councils, and decisions) is clear. On the larger scale of the whole poem the long series of battles is punctuated by quieter interludes of which the most obvious are Helen on the walls of Troy (book 3), the peaceful scenes in Troy preluded by the meeting of Glaukos and Diomede (book 6), the Embassy to Achilles (book 9), the scene between Nestor, Machaon, and Patroklos (book 11), the deception of Zeus (book 14), the arms of Achilles (book 18), the reconciliation with Agamemnon (book 19).

The scenes on Olympos belong both to the static pattern and

[1] *Il.* 22, 32; 99; 136; 166; 188; 208; 226; 248; 273; 306; 337; 376; 405.

to the dynamic pattern, to the static pattern because they make a recurrent contrast with the action on the human level and to the dynamic pattern because they forecast a future stretch of action. Some of them, as has been already noted, are marked by late linguistic forms and they take their place with the speeches of command, exhortation, and advice in so far as they warn the reader of what is to come, and so bind the poem together into a unity. The various ways in which future action is prepared in the *Iliad* have been very carefully examined by Schadewaldt,[1] who rightly finds in them a powerful argument for accepting the poem as it now stands as a unity. He excepts the Doloneia, but the particular argument from preparation does not touch the Doloneia, since it is an isolated incident with little connexion backwards or forwards. In the accompanying tables I have only included preparation in the narrowest sense: orders, exhortation, advices, prophecies of the human characters, and statements about the future made by the gods or the poet; all the passages have late linguistic clusters except those with bracketed references. Even with this restriction the passages are sufficient to show what pains the last poet has taken to point out to his audience the future course of the action.

ILIAD

1.1–20	Prologue: Wrath of Achilles, arrival of Chryses.
1.493 f.	Zeus promises Thetis to give the Trojans victory (prepares Achaean defeats up to 9).
(2.694)	Catalogue: Myrmidons. Achilles mourning for Briseis 'but soon he will rise again' (prepares for 9, 16, 18).
3.448–461, 4.1 f.	Transition from Paris and Helen to Pandaros episode. Agamemnon demands restitution of Helen (then divine council).
6.77–101	Helenos advises Hektor to pray to Athena (prepares for quiet interlude).
(7.337)	Nestor advises building of Wall. Prepares for building, 7, 437, and attack on Wall in 12.
8.470	Zeus announces that Hektor will go on fighting until Achilles returns to the battle (general programme up to 18).
9.1–20	Transition from Trojan successes to Embassy.
9.60–78	Nestor advises posting of sentries and preparation of banquet for seniors.
96–113	Nestor advises embassy to Achilles.
225–246	Odysseus reports on Hektor's achievements and intentions (preparation for 15).

[1] *Iliasstudien*, 150 ff. (summing-up).

(11.186–194)	Zeus tells Hektor to avoid Agamemnon but when he is wounded to fight on until he comes to the ships.
11.596–606	Achilles sends Patroklos to Nestor ('and it was the beginning of disaster for him').
11.790–803	Nestor tells Patroklos to ask Achilles to send him into the battle (preparation for 16).
15.64–77	Zeus announces return of Patroklos to battle, death of Patroklos, death of Hektor (general programme to 22).
15.281–300	Thoas advises orderly retreat to ships.
(15.592–614)	The attack on the ships: the poet comments on Hektor's future (leads into hoplite passage and similes).
16.74–96	Achilles states the position of the Greeks and sends Patroklos into the battle.
17.183–214	Hektor puts on Achilles' arms and Zeus prophesies his death (preparation for 22).
17.248–255	Menelaos' call to fight for the body of Patroklos.
20.23–30	Zeus sends the gods into the battle (Xanthos is included among the gods because of the impending river battle).
21.520–30, 21.570–99	Transition from general battle to death of Hektor. Priam opens the gates. Agenor's diversion.
22.378–90	Achilles decides to bury Patroklos before attacking Troy (preparation for 23).
24.1–30	Transition to ransoming of Hektor. End of funeral. Maltreatment of Hektor. Council of the gods.

ODYSSEY

(1.1)	Prologue. Council of the gods (preparation for wanderings, mission of Telemachos, and return of Odysseus 1–4, 5, 9, 12, 13).
3.420	Nestor orders sacrifice.
(4.556)	Proteus tells of Odysseus on Calypso's island (preparation for 5).
(5.3f.)	Council of gods: Athena to send Telemachos home (preparation for 15). Hermes to send Odysseus to Phaeacia (preparation for 6–13).
6.255	Nausikaa's instructions to Odysseus (preparation for 7).
10.488	Circe's instructions (preparation for 11).
11.60	Elpenor's appeal (preparation for 12).
11.100	Teiresias on the cattle of the Sun and the suitors (preparation for 12, 13–22).
12.376	Sun's appeal to Zeus (preparation for shipwreck).
(13.125)	Poseidon's complaint to Zeus (ship to be turned to stone).
14.158	Odysseus prophesies his return and vengeance to Eumaios (preparation for 22).
14.174	Eumaios on ambush (preparation for 15).
16.267	Odysseus plans for Telemachos (preparation for 17, 18, 19).

17.152	Theoklymenos prophesies return of Odysseus.
17.468	Odysseus prays for the death of Antinoos (preparation for 22).
19.262	Odysseus (in disguise) recounts his wanderings and prophesies his return to Penelope.
(20.392)	The poet comments on the unlovely feast which Athena and Odysseus will make.
21.98	The poet comments that Antinoos will die first (preparation for 22).
21.153f.	Leodes' prophecy of death.
24.472	Council of the gods to stop the war.

5. PERFORMANCE

The *Iliad* and the *Odyssey* are organic unities, as Aristotle saw, and this fact is impressed on the hearer by the dynamic pattern. They also have a unity of the kind sought by the Geometric vase-painter, the static pattern formed by the interweaving of a large number of elements, which recur through the length of the poem either in the same form or in variations. They also, as we have seen, presuppose in the audience both knowledge and apprecia-tion of Greek mythology far beyond the stories which they actually tell. What occasions were there in the eighth century for which a highly educated audience could demand the composition of such poems and enjoy their diversified unity? The audience, the occasion, the manner of performance, the manner of com-position (oral or written), the relation of these poems to the Cyclic poems of which we have fragments, and finally the relation of the *Iliad* and *Odyssey* to each other – about all these we should like to have precise information but we can only make conjectures.

At least we have evidence for widespread pride in the heroic past, and this pride explains the demand for allusions to the whole range of mythology. The evidence has already been quoted:[1] the names of the kings, Hektor in Chios and Agamemnon in Kyme, the mythological scenes on Geometric pottery in Attica and Chios and possibly Ithaca and Ischia, the allusion to Nestor's posset on a cup in Ischia, the tripod in Thebes purporting to have been dedicated by Amphitryon, the cult of Mycenaean heroes in Pylos, Mycenae, Argos, Sikyon, Athens, Kephallenia, and Delos, the games in honour of Odysseus in Ithaca, the political manipulation of legend. It is possible that all of these things started before our *Iliad* and *Odyssey* reached the relevant places; it is certain that

[1] Cf. above pp. 137f.

Hektor of Chios and probable that Agamemnon of Kyme antedated our *Iliad*, and the games in Ithaca started at least in the ninth century. By the middle of the eighth century the demand for wide mythological allusion could be found all over the Greek world but particularly among the Ionians with their very ancient and very mixed ancestry.

Continuous recital is the only kind of performance which would make it possible for the audience to appreciate the complicated unity of these poems. Gilbert Murray[1] saw this long ago and suggested both the festival of the Panionia on Mount Mykale and the four-yearly festival at Delos as ancestors of the Athenian Panathenaea, at which we know the *Iliad* and *Odyssey* were recited by relays of rhapsodes. By such methods the *Iliad* could be recited in rather less than three days, possibly even in two, if the audience had the stamina of the audiences of the Athenian Dionysia. The solo singer, as we have seen,[2] would require at least fifteen two-hour sessions. Such a protracted performance would be quite possible for a story which was told in a straight line. But, unless all that has been written of Homer's technique is an illusion, no audience could perceive the subtle perfection of his art if they only heard a thousand lines at a time. For this reason alone recital by relays of bards at a festival must be assumed for the *Iliad* and the *Odyssey*, and the *Iliad* and the *Odyssey* are the only poems for which this need be assumed, since we know of no other poems of comparable complication.

We know little enough about these festivals. Wade-Gery[3] has pointed out that knowledge of a sacrifice to Poseidon Helikonios (presumably on the occasion of the Panionia) and knowledge of Ephesos are assumed in the *Iliad* and knowledge of the palm tree on Delos in the *Odyssey*. When Thucydides writes of the revival of the Delian festival in 424 and quotes the *Hymn to Apollo* as evidence of its very early musical contest, he compares the festival at Ephesos, which was still held in his own day. But we know nothing of any performance of the Homeric poems at Ephesos, and the ancient Asiatic mother goddess who became the Ephesian Artemis hardly seems a likely recipient for the *Iliad* or the *Odyssey*. If we pursue this question of the likely divine recipient, we might

---

[1] *Rise of the Greek Epic*[2], 209ff. cf. Wade-Gery, *Poet of the Iliad*, 14f.
[2] Cf. above p. 133.
[3] *Op. cit.*, 2f.; *Il.* 20, 403f.; 2, 459f.; *Od.* 6, 162f.; Thuc., III, 104.

further ask whether Apollo, who is always on the Trojan side, is likely to have been the original recipient of the *Iliad* or whether Poseidon, whose justifiable dislike of Odysseus is consistently thwarted in the *Odyssey*, is likely to have been the original recipient of that poem. On the other hand Poseidon is a figure of great dignity and power in the *Iliad* and is friendly to the Greeks, and in the *Odyssey* Nausikaa is twice compared to Artemis as well as to the Delian palm tree, and Odysseus' triumph was with Apollo's weapon on the day of Apollo's festival. Moreover, Odysseus' bow was the bow with which Eurytos challenged Apollo, his success is prophesied by Apollo's bird, Telemachos' growth to manhood is attributed to Apollo, the heralds bring the animals to be sacrificed to Apollo just before Penelope sets the suitors the ordeal of the bow; when Eurymachos fails to draw the bow, Antinoos suggests delaying the contest because of the feast of Apollo; finally Apollo grants Odysseus his prayer and he shoots Antinoos.[1] Thus the *Odyssey*, with its compliment to Artemis in the Nausikaa story and its emphasis on Apollo in the bow story, could very well have been designed for recitation at Delos, and the *Iliad* with its benevolent and magnificent Poseidon could very well have been designed for the Panionia at Mykale. Later (and before the time of Peisistratos) the *Iliad*, too, may have been performed at Delos, but it can hardly have been designed to honour a god who is continually unkind to the Greeks.

The argument then runs thus. The *Iliad* and *Odyssey* can both be dated to the eighth century; the *Iliad* refers to Helikonian Poseidon, the god of the Panionia, and treats him with reverence; the *Odyssey* refers to Delos, and Odysseus' triumph is due to Apollo. The artistic unity of both poems compels us to assume an original performance at a great festival by relay of rhapsodes, as they were performed at the Panathenaea from the sixth century onwards. Composition of the *Iliad* and *Odyssey* in Athens in the sixth century is unthinkable. Language, metre, subject-matter, and general atmosphere could not have been recreated 200 years later, when Greece in general and Athens more than anywhere else had advanced into a quite different world. The structure of the Homeric poems has a real analogy with the decoration of Geometric vases in the eighth century; from the sixth century we have a unique example of an Athenian mixing bowl decorated

---

[1] *Od.* 21, 32 (cf. 8, 224); 15, 525; 19, 86; 20, 276; 21, 258; 22, 7.

with a multitude of small scenes instead of one or two grand scenes, and the result is not an *Iliad* but an anthology of myth.[1] The recitals at the Panathenaea were, therefore, instituted not to display new poetry but to preserve heirlooms, the performance of which was desirable for political as well as poetical reasons. Before that we hear of contests of rhapsodes performing the Homeric epics at Sikyon, and they were evidently established well before the early sixth century.[2] These performances are clearly distinguished from the tragic choruses in honour of Adrastos and were recitations and not songs, but Herodotos does not tell us whether each competitor chose a different piece or whether they recited a Homeric epic in relays, as later at the Panathenaea. Earlier still and probably at the very end of the eighth century, Hesiod competed with a 'hymn' at the funeral games of Amphidamas at Chalkis; he crossed to Euboea from Aulis, 'where once the Achaeans waited for a storm and gathered a mighty army from holy Greece against Troy, land of fair women'. The allusion has suggested that Hesiod's hymn was a recitation based on his *Marriage of Helen* as preserved in the *Catalogue of Women*,[3] and later Greeks believed that he competed with Homer; this then may be early evidence for a contest of rhapsodes with individual compositions, and takes the rhapsode back into the eighth century.

Of the Panionia itself nothing is known except that it was a festival celebrated by the twelve cities. The festival at Delos was already flourishing in the mid-eighth century when the Messenians sent their choir to sing Doric hexameters composed by Eumelos of Corinth, and on the evidence of pottery Delos was an international meeting-place much earlier.[4] The Delian hymn to Apollo,[5] composed by a blind poet from Chios and sung by the Delian choir, on linguistic statistics would be dated between the *Odyssey* and Hesiod's *Works and Days*. The poet speaks of a musical contest and says that the Delian choir can sing songs composed in local dialects and rhythms. This must mean that in the eighth century the Delian festival admitted not only Epic Ionic hexameters from Chios and Doric hexameters from Corinth, but other

---

[1] The François vase in Florence, Beazley, *ABV*, 76.   [2] Hdt. 5, 67.

[3] Hesiod, *Op.* 650f. I owe the suggestion to P. Walcot in an unpublished dissertation, *Hesiod and the Boeotian Epic*, 68f.

[4] Eumelos: Pausanias, 4, 4, 1 (with 4, 33, 2); Dunbabin, *J.H.S.*, 68 (1948), 67. Pottery: Desborough, 153f.

[5] Homer, *Hymns*, 3, 1–178, cf. Wade-Gery in *Greek Poetry and Life*, 56f.

songs in local dialect and metre by poets who were the precursors of Terpander, Arion, Alcman, Sappho, and Alcaeus. All the evidence that we have quoted suggests a movement away from large-scale anonymous poetry in a common epic dialect and metre towards medium- or small-scale individual poetry in local dialect and increasingly in local metre. This again suggests that the recitals at the Panathenaea were instituted to preserve heirlooms. The poet of the Delian hymn, before he speaks of the Delian choir, only says that Apollo was honoured with contests of boxing, dancing, and singing. The contest of song may have included a contest of rhapsodes; but this is not specified, and we can only say that Delos provided a festival in the eighth century at which Homeric epic could have been performed by relays of rhapsodes. The facts then are these: first, the *Iliad* and the *Odyssey* were composed in the eighth century (and their architecture demands performance by relays of rhapsodes); secondly, they were performed by relays of rhapsodes from the sixth century in Athens; thirdly, everything that we know of the intervening period makes the composition of anonymous large-scale epics unlikely, and nothing that we know is inconsistent with the continued performance of the *Iliad* and *Odyssey* at the Panionia and at Delos and with the communication of them piecemeal to the rest of the Greek world by itinerant rhapsodes.

The artistic unity of the *Iliad* and the *Odyssey* compel us to assume continuous recital and, therefore, a team of reciters. What we hear in the poems themselves about the performance of poetry tells us nothing about the performance of the *Iliad* and the *Odyssey*. Neither the choir of Muses singing at the banquet of the gods nor the warrior singer in his hut nor the court poet of Phaeacia or Ithaca, singing to his lyre, could have performed an *Iliad* or *Odyssey* in its entirety so that its unity could be appreciated. But have we any evidence for saying when poetry was first recited instead of being sung? Plato's Ion certainly recited, and the rhapsode on an Athenian vase of the very early fifth century recites holding a stick in his right hand. A rather earlier reciter is shown on a black figured vase of the late sixth century.[1] Before that are the rhapsodes at Sikyon. The Greeks believed that the rhapsode

[1] Red figure vase, London, British Museum, E 270; Beazley, *ARV*, 122, no. 13; Wade-Gery, *op. cit.*, 31, fig. 2. Black figure vase, Otago Museum, E 48.226, Anderson, pl. 6b; Beazley, *ABV*, 386.

was so called because he held a *rhabdos*, a light stick like the one held by the reciter on the fifth-century vase, and this is the staff which the Muses gave to Hesiod when they breathed into him divine song.[1] If the Muses gave Hesiod a staff, they made him a reciter and not a singer; if they had wanted to make him a singer they would have given him a lyre like Archilochos.[2] Hesiod brings us nearly back to Homer, and there is no reason to suppose a change of practice between Homer and Hesiod. But perhaps the change of practice, the change from singing with a lyre to reciting with a staff, is not very old. Hesiod still speaks of himself as singing,[3] and the *Iliad* begins with an invocation to the goddess to sing of the wrath of Achilles; the *Odyssey* on the other hand requests the Muse to 'tell' and 'speak', but these words do not in themselves exclude song. It has been argued that the invocations in the *Iliad* and the *Odyssey* show that these poems are performing the function of sung poetry, which would mean that epic recitation was a new form of festival poetry, invented for the international festival.[4] Sung poetry is so natural to the Greeks that it is tempting to suppose that recitation originated in the need to have a long poem performed by a team.

But if we accept recitation by a team as the necessary condition for the correct performance of the *Iliad* and *Odyssey*, we are thereby committed to believing that the poems were reduced to writing before they were so recited. It is credible that a poet could compose orally a poem of this length and perform it as he composed it (although such composition would lack all the subtle unity of the Homeric epics). It is not credible that, as he composed orally, he could teach his team a poem of such length and that they could remember it. The most recent statement on the introduction of alphabetic writing dates this between 850 and 750.[5] Whether Linear B survived or not is, as we have seen, an open question. If it did survive, nevertheless the alphabet brought with it the

---

[1] Hesiod, *Theog.* 30. The actual derivation of the word *rhapsode* is still unclear. Cf. Patzer, *Hermes*, 80 (1952), 315; Else, *Hermes*, 85 (1957), 26f. I see no reason to believe that the word is not as old as the practice.

[2] Cf. Kontoleon, *AE*, 1952, 58. The story comes from a poem of Archilochos, of which the essential word *lyre* is preserved in the inscription (cf. *Lustrum*, 1 (1956), 102).

[3] *Op.* 659, 662; *Theog.* 34, etc.

[4] Koller, *Philologus*, 100 (1956), 200.

[5] Albright in *The Aegean and the Near East*, 162.

reduction of the number of signs by 75 per cent and an immense gain in precision; these changes must have enormously increased the speed both of writing and of reading. It is doubtful whether Linear B could have been read by anyone except the scribe, but the new alphabet could be read by the reciter himself. Poems of medium length were dictated to Eastern scribes, who used a syllabary, and the texts were used for recitation; but the process must have been extremely laborious, and the scribe was an essential link in the chain between poet and performance. I think we can be certain that whether Linear B survived or not the invention of alphabetic writing was a necessary condition for the composition and performance of the *Iliad* and *Odyssey*. If, as Wade-Gery suggests,[1] the poets themselves invented alphabetic writing (and if Linear B survived it is difficult to see what else needed this new and unique precision of recording), they thereby unwittingly ensured the death of the oral technique. Up to the time of the *Odyssey* the poets were still composing in the old manner and using the new linguistic developments both to adapt old formulae to new uses and to create new formulae; Hesiod is already beginning to break away from the old technique. If the invention of alphabetic writing is put at 850, it will have been invented by the great-grandfather of the poet of the *Iliad* (or his exact contemporary), when his grandfather was a very small boy. It does not seem unlikely that their poetry was recorded (and was available to members of the family) before the *Iliad* was composed, and teams of reciters may have already been reciting at the festivals by the time that Homer was born. Then the poet of the *Iliad* was the first person to exploit to the full the new methods of composition and production and the new occasion, the first person to write a poem which could only have its full effect when so produced.

Kakridis[2] has discussed this essential difference between the *Iliad* and the Cyclic epics. The chief points that he makes are these. The epic is the first form of chronicle writing and should, therefore, describe the events in the order in which they happened. If time presses, the poet can either leave the rest of such an epic for another day or can pick out a particular length of narrative for a particular occasion. Such a long epic is not necessarily a decadent form of the dramatic epic (the *Iliad*) but rather the necessary

[1] Wade-Gery, *Poet of the Iliad,* 11 f. [2] *Homeric Researches,* 91 f.

presupposition of the dramatic epic, as an intermediate stage between the short epic and the dramatic epic. We should, therefore, consider whether, when scenes are common to Homer and the epic cycle, Homer should invariably be regarded as the creator rather than the borrower. The particular instance which Kakridis then quotes is the likeness of various scenes in the *Iliad* to the *Aithiopis*, to which he gives priority. This problem has been discussed above, and I believe it is more probable that Arktinos remodelled the Penthesilea and Memnon story for the *Aithiopis* under the influence of the *Iliad*. The traditions about the Cyclic poets are not reliable enough to help us much.[1] Arktinos of Miletos, who wrote the *Aithiopis* and the *Sack of Troy*, was according to one authority a pupil of Homer, born 736–2, and according to another flourished 776–2. The fragments show three late forms in twelve lines but are far too short for statistics. Forty-five lines survive of the *Cypria*, and they show fourteen late forms, as high a proportion as Hesiod's *Works and Days*; the author, Stasinos, was said to be Homer's son-in-law. The little evidence that we have seems to confirm the tradition that the poems about the Trojan war of which fragments survive were written later than the *Iliad* and the *Odyssey*; but Kakridis' suggestion that long epics were written before the *Iliad* is valuable. In our terms it may be rephrased like this. Poets may have performed at the Panionia from an early date; they would have been oral singers, the same men in fact who sang in the houses of the kings and nobles. But the great festival was especially the occasion on which all the different strains of ancestry claimed by the present-day Ionians would be celebrated, and the siege of Troy would be sung as a joint Hellenic enterprise. But each individual performance would necessarily be short, and if there was any attempt to tell the story as a whole, the treatment by different poets of their allotted portion would vary considerably in spite of their common stock of inherited formulae. The invention of writing, let us say towards the end of the ninth century, made a greater uniformity of treatment possible; one poet provided a text which a team of rhapsodes recited. The poet himself, no doubt, was one of the reciters and the other reciters were themselves poets; but the cleavage between poet and performer had begun. The technique

[1] Sources are given by Allen in Oxford Text of Homer, vol. 5, under each epic.

of composition was unchanged because writing was only used for these comparatively rare great occasions. This is the kind of situation which must be assumed to provide an occasion for the genius, Homer, to exploit.

6. RELATION OF THE *ILIAD* TO THE *ODYSSEY*

One problem remains, the relation of the *Iliad* to the *Odyssey*. It is a problem which can be defined rather than solved. Antiquity was unanimous, but antiquity seems to have had little or no external information. The traditions about the earliest Cyclic poets in the generation after Homer probably contain an element of truth, and Arktinos and Stasinos may well have belonged to Homer's team of reciters. Their names are remembered because starting with Hesiod and ever afterwards poets advertised themselves. But nothing was remembered of them except their names, and the next name in the direct line of rhapsodes from the blind man in Chios, who wrote the Delian hymn, is Kynaithos of Chios at the end of the sixth century.[1] In fact at the moment when Hesiod started to be autobiographical the successors of Homer ceased to be interesting, whether they advertised themselves or not. Antiquity had therefore little, if any, external information about the poet or poets of the *Iliad* and the *Odyssey*. Comparison with the other surviving epics marked them out as the work of a genius for whom tradition provided the name Homer. The valid distinction, as Aristotle saw, was their superiority as compositions. But this does not by itself prove unity of authorship.

We are left with the kind of problem with which art historians are familiar, stylistic attribution. But stylistic attribution needs a considerable number of works, whereas we have only two, which may or may not be by the same man. Stylistic criteria (including the linguistic statistics which have proved so useful) certainly suggest that the *Iliad* and *Odyssey* form a group with the Delian hymn, from which the Cyclic epics and Hesiod (and the majority of the other hymns) can be clearly separated. Technical criteria – composition on the large scale, preparation of the audience, psychological commentary, typical scenes, use of similes etc. – do not distinguish the *Iliad* from the *Odyssey*. The elements which can be dated late – hoplite armament, modern geography, *polis*

[1] For the Homeridai see Wade-Gery, *op. cit.*, 19 ff.

organization etc. – do not preponderate more in one poem than the other, or rather their distribution is determined by the subject-matter; more is heard of hoplites in the *Iliad* because it is a war poem, and perhaps more of the *polis* in the *Odyssey* because its setting is the home and not the camp. It is often said that the *Odyssey* is ethically more advanced than the *Iliad*, but the material of the *Iliad* was far less tractable and the load of traditional divine and human behaviour was far heavier; the poet who retold the Trojan war story as a story of wrath and repentance (Agamemnon and Chryses, Achilles and Agamemnon, Achilles and Hektor) and commented on it through the mouth of Apollo[1] was no less bold or advanced a thinker than the poet who saw the story of the suitors as a parallel to the story of Aigisthos, the story of wilful folly leading to unnecessary suffering. To produce both poems in their present form a genius remodelled in a still living poetic language a mass of traditional stories, which went back to widely different Mycenaean origins: these had been sung and resung ever since in gradually changing language, which never-theless preserved many diverse formulae of extreme age; only comparatively recently rhapsodes may have started performing the Siege of Troy as a continuous story, and the story of Odysseus may also have been formed as a straight tale from the day he left Troy to the day he slew the suitors.

This history must be borne in mind when the question is asked whether the *Iliad* and the *Odyssey* are the work of one poet or two. Lesky[2] leaves both possibilities open but inclines to the latter. 'To see the *Iliad* and the *Odyssey* as poems of the maturity and old age of a single poet is not a sheer impossibility. . . . Yet it is much more reasonable to give the *Odyssey* to a poet who created this work about 700, a successor of Homer who followed in his tracks.' The last phrase is incompatible with Page's statement 'that the Odyssean poet lived in a region isolated from that in which the *Iliad* was composed'.[3] This gives a third possible view: the three possibilities are (a) one poet, (b) two poets, one follow-ing in the steps of the other, (c) two poets working in isolation. It may be impossible to decide between (a) and (b), but clearly no decision is necessary if (c) is true. Page has argued the extreme

[1] *Il.* 24, 33f. partic. 44–5.
[2] *Gesch. der. gr. Literatur*, 52. Cf. Heubeck, *Odysseedichter*.
[3] *The Homeric Odyssey*, 149.

case with great eloquence and wealth of vocabulary detail. His argument in brief is that the number both of old words and new words which occur in one poem but not in the other is so great that the two poems must have been composed and transmitted in separate regions of Hellas: the stream of the Greek epic divided at an early date in the dark ages. The total number of about 300 words which Page quotes to support the theory of isolation perhaps amounts to 3 per cent of the whole vocabulary and the total number of occurrences of these words to a far smaller percentage of the total occurrences, just over 0·6 per cent. The question is therefore whether so much weight can be put on such a small percentage of the vocabulary. We must ask first whether the other 97 per cent of the vocabulary is sufficiently accounted for by the theory that 'the stream of Greek Epic divided at an early date in the dark ages'. Words must be considered in their context, and the *Iliad* is tied to the *Odyssey* not merely by a large common element in vocabulary but by a multitude of identical lines and half lines.[1] The majority of these cannot be dated, but a cursory inspection of repetitions found in both poems showed thirty different lines, half lines, and formulae embodying contractions, irreducible genitives, or neglected digammas; they include the lines repeated in and after speeches of advice.[2] These common elements of the *Iliad* and the *Odyssey* cannot be earlier than 900; they belong to the last stage of heroic poetry, and prove that if the stream divided at all it cannot have divided until the last stages of heroic poetry.

If Page's list of words is examined, considerable subtractions will be found necessary. First no argument for isolation in space can be based on the small list of words which occur more frequently in one poem than the other. Secondly, words which only occur once must all be excluded; if a word occurs only once in one poem, there is no reason why it should occur at all in the other. This is a large class amounting to over 140 of the 300 words. Thirdly, I should also exclude a small number of lines which result from a recombination of elements known in the other poem, and a small number of words for which the other poem provides analogous words from the same root but no examples of the actual words themselves.

[1] Cf. W. Diehl, *die wörtlichen Bezeihungen zwischen Ilias und Odyssee*, Greifswald, 1938.   [2] Cf. above p. 258.

A much more interesting class is formed by the words which are closely related to the subject-matter of the two poems. Miss Gray's[1] careful examination of Homeric epithets for things helps us here. The *Odyssey* is a seafaring poem and the *Iliad* is a fighting poem, but in fact seafaring invades the *Iliad* (in the similes particularly) more than fighting invades the *Odyssey*. Thus all the main *Odyssey* sea formulae occur at least once in the *Iliad*; the *Iliad* has seven unique combinations of noun and epithet and the *Odyssey* has three, one of which, however, recurs three times (πολυκλύστῳ ἐνι πόντῳ), and is called in evidence by Page, but its absence from the *Iliad* proves nothing. Shields and helmets show the difference between the two poems more clearly: three noun epithet combinations describing shields are common to both poems; the *Iliad* has in addition thirty-one others; nine noun epithet combinations describing helmets are common to both poems; the *Iliad* has in addition twenty-three others. A considerable number of Page's *Iliad* words seem to me to fall into the general category of fighting words, which must be extended to cover not only weapons, war-horses, and wounds but also death in battle, tactical movement, and abuse of the enemy. It should also be noted that fighting words are much more likely to be transferred to other subjects in a fighting poem than in a seafaring poem.

Three instances should be quoted because Page evidently regards their absence from the *Odyssey* as good evidence for isolation. The first is the word *phlox* 'flame' and its cognates. Its use in the *Iliad* is almost confined to funeral pyres and metaphorically to the raging of battle. The *Odyssey* has no raging battles, and its only major funeral has *phlox* (Page excludes it presumably because he does not regard the twenty-fourth book as belonging to the *Odyssey*). It is a curious fact that the only ordinary fire in either poem which has a *phlox* is the fire which Patroklos lights to cook for the Embassy; and the line in which 'the fire burnt down and the flame stopped' is so like the description of Patroklos' funeral 'the burning fire was extinguished and the flame stopped' that Homer perhaps meant to make this meal ominous in the ears of his audience.[2] Secondly, Page wonders at

[1] Gray, *CQ*, 41 (1947), 109f.

[2] *Il.* 9, 212; 23, 228. On *phlox* see J. B. Hainsworth, *J.H.S.*, 78 (1958), forthcoming.

the absence of *poina, apoina* from the Revenge of Odysseus; *apoina* means ransom, and *poina* normally means compensation for murder. Neither is relevant to the suitors, but *poina* is used of the Cyclops' murder of Odysseus' sailors[1] (but again the line is beyond the limits of Page's *Odyssey*). The suitors' 'violence' demands 'vengeance', and these words belong to a different vocabulary which is not needed in the *Iliad*. Thirdly, the word for 'free' *eleutheros* is only used by Hektor of the deliverance of Troy; this word has no place in the *Odyssey*, which says nothing of Trojan hopes, but in return Penelope speaks of 'wicked Troy, unspeakable', a phrase that could only be used by one who was left at home, and therefore has no place in the *Iliad*.

A few other words, though they have nothing directly to do with fighting, belong to the subject-matter of the *Iliad* rather than the *Odyssey*: Artemis is 'noisy' when she appears in the *Iliad* to fight; Achilles (and a few other heroes) are 'dear to Zeus'; Ocean has 'great strength' as an antagonist; 'Come, go' seems to have originated with Iris, who does not appear in the *Odyssey*. Peculiar to the *Odyssey* subject-matter are the 'wiles' of wizards, the 'ponderings' and 'enduring spirit' of Odysseus, the 'grieving' and 'relaxed sleep' of Penelope, the suitors' 'biting their lips' in amazement at Telemachos' eloquence, the ominous 'utterance' of the woman grinding corn, and such homely words as 'bread', 'feast', 'sandal', and 'bed'. Together these words, which I should exclude as being dependent on the subject-matter of the poems, amount to 60 words occurring over 500 times.

A number of formulae and words remain for which the explanation is not so immediately obvious. Eight of the formulae are in the *Odyssey*, and seven in the *Iliad*. The maximum number of occurrences of any one of them is five: 'began words', in the *Odyssey*. It is a convenient line ending before an opening speech in a debate and corresponds to the much commoner 'spoke in answer' formula of the replies. A possible reason for its occurrence in the *Odyssey* rather than in the *Iliad* is that opening speeches in the *Iliad* are made by speakers whose names can occupy the end of the line: this is impossible for Telemachos, Arete, and Peisistratos, with whom this formula is used. Another *Odyssey* formula 'to her the word was wingless' is used once of Penelope and three times of Eurykleia; the situation, a woman receiving

[1] *Od.* 23, 312. Contrast *Od.* 1, 379.

information which she keeps to herself, is unknown in the *Iliad*. The twice repeated 'lovely Kalydon' in the *Iliad* may well come from an Aetolian poem, but could not recur in the *Odyssey* because Kalydon is not mentioned there. In fact, these rare formulae tell us nothing of the relation between the two poems.

The remaining individual words may be divided into abstract nouns and others. Of the others (twenty-two in the *Iliad* and six in the *Odyssey*) eight only occur twice and seven more only three times. Only one occurs ten times, and this total is only made by counting the noun *heǎnos* and adjective *heānos* together. This word is worth inspection: the adjective is twice applied to cloth used in Patroklos' funeral (the *Odyssey* has no such elaborate funerals), once to Achilles' unique tin greaves, and twice to Athena's peplos: the noun is used of the dress of Hera, Artemis, Helen (twice), and once in a simile, when Achilles compares Patroklos to a little girl tugging at her mother's dress. This must surely be a modern simile (though the noun itself is Mycenaean), so that Helen and the goddesses are dressed in the latest fashion, whereas in the *Odyssey* the traditional words have been kept for Penelope and Calypso. On the other hand, what may be an old form of the second person pronoun, τύνη, occurs six times in speeches in the *Iliad* but not in the *Odyssey*; it may well be a survival, but the contexts where it occurs – military abuse or orders; mother to son; Hermes to Priam – hardly recur in the *Odyssey*: Hermes could have spoken thus to Odysseus, but Penelope could not speak to Telemachos in the same tone as Thetis to Achilles or Hekabe to Hektor. Finally, where words that are common in later Greek occur in one poem and not in the other, words like 'pity' or 'hesitation' (each six times in the *Iliad*) or 'kick' (four times in the *Odyssey*), I doubt whether we can say more than that if the idea came up in the other poem, it did not come up at a moment when the line admitted a word of this particular shape and therefore the idea was put into other language. But it must be emphasized again that these individual words are a tiny class. The total vocabulary of the *Iliad* and the *Odyssey* contains about 9,000 words used about 180,000 times; not much weight can be put on 28 words occurring in all 107 times.

On the whole, considering the difference in subject-matter and the different and ancient linguistic traditions connected with the different subject-matter, the vocabularies of the two poems do not diverge sufficiently for us to be able to say that the writer of the *Odyssey* was unacquainted with the *Iliad*. Page, however, also makes a number of points about the relative dates of the poems. He quotes with approval Cauer's[1] judgement that the number of true abstracts is not only relatively but also absolutely greater in the *Odyssey* than in the *Iliad*, and regards this as a recent element. It is difficult to arrive at accurate figures because it is difficult to agree on which word is a true abstract. Cauer in the passage quoted by Page defines abstracts as denoting a mental process or state, but on the next page speaks of them as showing the development from purely concrete to rather more abstract thought, which is something quite different. Page gives figures for the number of abstracts ending in *-tys*, *-syne*, *-sis*, and *-ie*, but omits the number of occurrences for the last. I have worked on Krarup's[2] figures (with minor corrections) and arrive at approximately the same result where results can be compared; the totals for these four groups are (*a*) words common to *Iliad* and *Odyssey*, 33; (*b*) *Iliad* only, 53; (*c*) *Odyssey* only, 66; (*d*) *Iliad* occurrences, 162; (*e*) *Odyssey* occurrences, 177. On these figures the *Odyssey* shows an increase over the *Iliad* both in numbers of nouns and in the number of their occurrences. Krarup's last two tables show a rather different picture. The *Iliad* has 9 nouns in *-tes* used 74 times, the *Odyssey* 5 used 53 times; and in abstract nouns outside these classes the *Iliad* has 14 occurring 140 times and the *Odyssey* 22 occurring 116 times. The general position is undoubtedly true, that the *Odyssey* has more abstract nouns than the *Iliad* and if the disparity of length is taken into account uses them more often. But again the total number of occurrences is small. The disproportion between Krarup's last two lists and the rest is startling: in the last two lists the average number of occurrences of each word is over 9 in the *Iliad* and over 6 in the *Odyssey*; in the lists examined by Page the average number of occurrences is under 2. The old words which are firmly fixed in the epic language are those in Krarup's last two lists. The other lists contain a few common words: 'message', 'nemesis', 'truth', a few words specially appropriate to either poem 'man-slaying' (*Iliad*) and 'recklessness' (*Odyssey*);[3] these occur from six to eighteen times, but the majority of the rest only occur once.

[1] *Grundfragen*, 437 ff.   [2] *C. & M.*, 10 (1949), 1 f.
[3] *Atasthalie*, cf. D. M. Jones, *Ethical themes in the plot of the Odyssey*.

Many of them seem to be creations for the particular moment in the poem and never entered into ordinary speech, but the poet formed them on the analogy of ordinary words. Thus in the *-ie* group 'wisdom' is probably a common word, although it only appears once, but 'kindliness' would seem to be a new creation to define Patroklos, just as 'fierceness' is a new creation to define Hektor and Achilles.[1] It is true that the *Odyssey* has more of these words than the *Iliad*, but the poet is following in the footsteps of the *Iliad*, and it is doubtful whether he would have created poetic words on these lines and for these purposes without the *Iliad*.

Neither the use of abstract nouns nor the other two criteria analysed by Page,[2] the use of the short form of the dative plural in the first and second declension and the freedom to leave a vowel short before mute and liquid, dissociate the *Odyssey* from the *Iliad*; at most they show that the *Odyssey* is later than the *Iliad*; the developments in the *Odyssey* are not new but a further elaboration of tendencies already visible in the *Iliad*. It is interesting to compare the results of Porter's[3] careful and widely based analysis of the metre of the Homeric poems, Hesiod, the hymns and Callimachus. 'The *Iliad* and the *Odyssey* differ very little from each other in the 1,000-line samples examined in this paper. When compared with any of the other texts they present a common front. The differences between them are slight. . . . The evidence of the structure of the line strongly supports the unity, if not of authorship or of time, at least of style of the two poems.' Metre then joins the other criteria which testify to the close kinship of the two poems.

Enough has been said to show that the *Odyssey* was not composed in isolation from the *Iliad*. It is likely, as we have seen, that they were composed for two different festivals. Of their dates we can only say that the *Iliad* was not composed long if at all before 750 and the *Odyssey* was not composed long if at all after 720. Thus a maximum gap of thirty years between the completion dates of the two poems is possible. The definition of this gap will be determined by the view taken on the one hand of the advance represented by the *Odyssey* as compared to the *Iliad* and on the other of the speed with which Greek poets were moving towards contemporaneity and self-expression. My own inclination is to

[1] Cf. above p. 255.   [2] *The Homeric Odyssey*, 151.
[3] H. N. Porter, 'The Early Greek Hexameter', *Y.C.S.*, 42 (1951), 27.

make the gap as short as possible. Further than that I see no means of going. Poets only began to be interesting after the composition of the *Iliad* and the *Odyssey*: Hesiod and the blind man in Chios tell us of themselves and others tell us of Arktinos and Stasinos. In the *Iliad* and the *Odyssey* the author or authors do not appear, and the ancient lives of Homer tell us nothing useful about their composition. Our only view of the author or authors comes from the poems, and traditional poetry is essentially unrevealing. We may ask why the Greeks remembered a relationship between the older Homer and the younger Arktinos and Stasinos but forgot the relationship between the poet of the *Iliad* and the poet of the *Odyssey*. But such negative arguments count for little. We must admit that those who like to believe that the *Iliad* was the poem of Homer's maturity and the *Odyssey* the poem of his old age cannot be proved wrong.

9

CONCLUSION AND SUMMARY

Homer looks forward to classical Greece and backwards to the Mycenaean world. The Mycenaean world was a world of great palaces of which Mycenae itself, Tiryns near by, Pylos on the West coast, Thebes in Boeotia, and Knossos in Crete are the best known. Their treasures compare in kind with the treasures of the Egyptians and Hittites and of the inhabitants of Ugarit, and are themselves evidence of the international character of this civilization. The Mycenaean palaces were connected with this larger Eastern Aegean and Eastern civilization first, perhaps, chiefly through their contacts with Minoan Crete, but later directly. Minoan Crete itself had cross links with contemporary Eastern culture in art and architecture and possibly also in language.

The attempt to distinguish what the Greeks, wherever they came from, brought with them from what they found in Greece and borrowed from their neighbours seems to me less profitable than the attempt to form some picture of the Greek world when it had become literate at least to the extent of keeping records. We have the fullest records for Pylos in the thirteenth century, and tradition connects Pylos with Athens and through Athens with Ionia and Homer. The records only date from the destruction of the palace, but Mycenaean civilization in the area of Pylos can now be traced as far back as in Mycenae itself, so that the last palace had a great heritage behind it, a heritage of civilization, poetry, and art. For the fourteenth and thirteenth century the question of what the Greeks brought with them and what they found need not be asked; by that time they were well established as a flourishing civilization among flourishing civilizations. The Mycenaean kingdoms were sufficiently closely linked together to undertake a common expedition if necessary, and the King of Ahhiyawa could correspond with the King of the Hittites. Mycenaean establishments in Cyprus, Ugarit, Alalakh and elsewhere were open to literary and artistic ideas from the East, quite apart from what the Mycenaeans in Knossos must have absorbed from the Minoans. Traders may have been responsible for the loan words for clothing and spices; but princes, warriors, poets, and master craftsmen also journeyed between the Mycenaean world and the East, and their commerce was ideas and art forms.

The palace of Pylos was, therefore, one of a number of Mycenaean palaces which communicated not only with each other but also with Egypt, Syria, and Asia Minor, including Troy (until Troy was sacked). In spite of the differences of scale, landscape, types of manufacture, religion, and language many elements in life at Pylos would not strike a visitor from Asia Minor as strange: the palace itself with its costly furniture and precious objects of ivory, gold, silver, and lapis lazuli, gifts received and gifts to be dispensed, the archive room with its minute records of every department of life in war and peace, the divine King with his special estates and his Companions, partly military leaders and partly administrative officials, the wider circle of nobility who formed the chariotry and provided the mayors responsible to the palace for the surrounding towns and villages, which were centres for the craftsmen and land workers of the different districts. The King of Pylos sat on his throne 'tippling like an immortal'. The brightly coloured frescoes of his palace had as their subjects the griffins and lions, which gave him divine protection and symbolized his power (fig. 8), the seated goddess, who lived in his house and gave him instruction, the legend of the Siege, which his poets sang, and the divine singer, who was their patron (fig. 9). At the appointed times he caused offerings to be made to the gods, to Poseidon, Zeus, Hera, Hermes, and also, as we may assume, to Artemis, Demeter, and Dionysos. But he also made offerings to other powers who are less well known to us: to Peleia the dove goddess, to Posidaeia, who is perhaps a divine spring, to Iphimedeia, who is known from legend, to the 'thrice-hero' and 'the lord of the house', representatives of the mighty dead, who continued to send blessings to his people. The offerings, besides agricultural produce and precious objects, included men and women, who perhaps became 'slaves of god' and thus received instruction in various crafts.

The paintings, precious objects, and painted vases of the Mycenaean palaces strike us at first as realistic. This is partly due to the subject-matter, particularly to the amount of wild life depicted, partly to the abundant gay colour, and partly to the curved lines, which express so admirably volume and speed. Against this must be set not only the strong decorative sense of the vases painted in the so-called Palace Style, which becomes desiccated formalism in the later phases of Mycenaean art, but also the strong conventional element in the treatment of space which allowed the artist to tell the spectators far more than he could see. Gay colouring, decorative sense, and conventionalism (in the particular sense described) justify the use of the term Court style for the art of the Mycenaean palaces. Court style is a style conditioned by a court, in this case the court of a divine ruler, who had considerable military power. Court style is a term which can equally well be applied to poetry.

The evidence for Mycenaean poetry must be drawn from Mycenaean art, from the tablets, from survivals in Homer, and from the analogy of contemporary and earlier Eastern poetry. Art, besides telling us much about the subjects of poetry, shows various forms of song: the ecstatic dances of the nature ritual, which is naturally connected with Dionysos and a mother goddess, must have had accompanying song (fig. 13); and a particular kind of harvest chorus and dance is represented on the Harvester vase (fig. 16); hymns to the gods are attested by the lyre-player and three women in terracotta; the sacrifice to the mighty dead on the Hagia Triada sarcophagus (fig. 6) is accompanied by song; the god singing alone on his mountain (fig. 9) is the patron of solo singers, not only the court singer but also the warrior poet, like Achilles when he waits for the Embassy.

We are concerned here only with solo court poetry and primarily with solo court poetry in Pylos which is ancestral to Homer. The fact that Homer preserves noun epithet formulae for Mycenaean objects which had long gone out of use shows that Mycenaean poetry like Hittite poetry and Ugaritic poetry used formulae. To this we can now add the evidence of the tablets that such formulae as Telamonian Ajax were Mycenaean titles. Formula is a vague term covering many kinds of repetition such as divine titles, royal titles, official titles, cult refrains, operation orders, conventions of correspondence. All of these originate in the Court style; they were the suitable forms of expression in a Kingdom ruled by a warrior of divine status and occurred in all the second-millennium Kingdoms of which we know. In

Pylos too, they corresponded with the realities of court life; in Homer they are a poetical survival and they do not survive Homer. If this is true, why do they survive so long? Two probable reasons for survival are nostalgia for past glories and poetic convenience; they ceased when neither reason was any longer operative, when the audience wanted contemporary rather than backward-looking poetry and when poets and performers were able to exploit the possibilities of alphabetic writing. A third reason may be a new positive delight in this generalized form of expression, which corresponds to the painter's delight in Geometric patterns and schematized figures and disappeared before seventh-century individualization in art and poetry.

The Court style was convenient both for slow dictation into and for recitation from a difficult script such as Linear B (if it was used for poetry; and we have no evidence either way) or syllabic or alphabetical cuneiform. It was also convenient, as the analogy of later poetry shows, for oral poetry. In the second millennium the distinction between recited and oral poetry was probably a distinction of kind. Religious poetry, whether sung to the gods or to the mighty dead, was sung normally by choirs, and the text must have been fixed. The poetry sung by the solo singer at banquets was adapted to each particular occasion. The solo singer of the Pylos fresco (fig. 9), the lyre in the tomb of Menidi, and the evidence for early mishearing of poetic phrases allow us to admit the existence of Mycenaean oral poetry and to use the analogies provided so brilliantly by Milman Parry. Among the reasons for altering the song on a particular occasion must have been the arrival of a guest from within or even without the Mycenaean world, and court poetry was international in the double sense that its range included heroes from other Mycenaean kingdoms and that its poets could borrow stories from Eastern poetry. The siege story, which is attested by works of art from Knossos, Mycenae early and late, and Pylos, and in literature from Ugarit (to say nothing of recorded Babylonian, Egyptian, and other Eastern sieges), was the kind of story which could be sung in many different ways: it could be told of Thebes or Troy or any-where else; armament could be brought up to date; new heroes could be introduced or old heroes dropped; new colouring could be added from Eastern poetry – it could become a war to win a woman, or a hero could be remodelled to look like Gilgamesh.

Various qualities can be attributed to this Mycenaean poetry. Individual performances were short, but this does not exclude the serial story sung night after night: such a serial would, however, be unlikely to have any appreciable unity. No clear distinction was drawn between divine and human, dead and living, past and present, historical and fictional. The gods were, of course, the subject of songs which did not include humans: the Creation myth is the obvious example, but perhaps these songs belonged rather to the cult than the banquet. The King was given divine honours; his father at least and probably his grandfather were still given divine honours at the tomb; a goddess shared his house and a god was not very far back in his pedigree. His successes and failures in peace and war were attributed to the direct intervention of a god, which meant that in poetry he fought with gods and was helped by gods. The comparatively rare but still sufficient references to body-shield fighting in Homer show that older stories about older fighters were incorporated into the Trojan war story. Nestor's campaign against the Epeians seems to have been historical, but in it the twins Aktorione-Molione were miraculously saved by Poseidon. This can only mean that old stories were sung and resung, and that, although they were brought up to date, were attached to new historical events, and accepted new literary elements, the old names survived and preserved some of an earlier reality.

Much the most probable explanation of the mythological names on the tablets is that (with the exception of Iphimedeia who is already a goddess in Pylos) they were borne by men who were called after heroes of mythology. We can then believe that the siege story in fifteenth-century Knossos already had attackers with Greek names and defenders with Trojan names, that the story was elaborated for generations in the different Mycenaean kingdoms and was then given a new Eastern setting when Troy VII A was attacked by a great expedition under the leadership of the King of Mycenae. A new historical event was more likely to give rise to a modification of an old song than to a new song. If this is true, then many of the stories of Greek mythology go back beyond our earliest records, but these stories were continually remodelled to conform with changed conditions, to include imported incidents, or to have a new historical setting.

This curious blurring of the outlines between god and man,

past and present, fiction and reality, lost two of its conditions with the destruction of the Mycenaean palaces. The divine King, the link between god and man, went with his palace, and there was no reason to confuse the iron present with the golden past. The main facts are clear, however unclear the causes and the details may be. Between the middle of the thirteenth century and the end of the twelfth century disaster had overtaken not only the Mycenaean palaces from Iolkos in the North-east to Pylos in the South-west but also Troy, the Hittite capital, and Ugarit. The period which follows is one of isolation and poverty, with Athens, the one city which was not sacked, acting as a centre for refugees from the Peloponnese and Boeotia. The refugees from Mycenaean Greece took various routes to Asia Minor, which was remembered as a land where successful settlements had been made in the old days; in Samos and Miletos the Mycenaean settlements may have still existed when the refugees arrived, but their existence must have been tenuous and their memories dim. The main stream of migration to Ionia passed through Athens between the early eleventh and the late ninth centuries. The chief assumptions which I accepted in discussing this dark period were these. First, the Greek tradition that Mycenaeans from Pylos passed through Athens, where their kings reigned for a period, and then went on to found the cities of Ionia is in general true, and this Pylian-Attic strain was the dominant strain in the mixed cities of Ionia. Secondly, the settlement of Asia Minor was a long and difficult process, and fruitful contact with the East which could lead to borrowing of ideas, stories, or art forms is unlikely again until well on in the eighth century. Thirdly, the so-called Aeolic features in the language of the Homeric poems may be classified as (*a*) Mycenaean (i.e. the language of the tablets), (*b*) very early borrowings which may date from the Mycenaean age, (*c*) late borrowings from Aeolian speakers in the mixed cities of Ionia or from their Aeolic neighbours. Without startling new evidence from Aeolis itself the theory of an Aeolic stage in the development to Ionian epic is unlikely, and we are justified in regarding the Pylian-Attic strain as also the chief carrier of poetic tradition. Fourthly, the likenesses and divergences of stories which are common to the Homeric poems on one side of the Aegean and to Hesiod or Attic Geometric pottery on the other are best explained by the assumption that the streams of poetry had finally divided not very long before the eighth century, and therefore such stories can be used to form some picture of mainland poetry in the dark period (figs. 20–28).

An attempt must be made to assess this transition period. The Mycenaean palaces fit in the context of Eastern palaces of the second millennium; the *Iliad* and *Odyssey* already foreshadow archaic and classical Greece. Between lies the dark period – 'a chaos in which an old civilization is shattered into fragments, its laws set at naught, and that intricate web of normal expectation which forms the very essence of human society torn so often and so utterly by continued disappointment that at last there ceases to be any normal expectation at all'.[1] Out of chaos the new Greek world was born. Our only contemporary evidence is archaeological, and in this Attic pottery, in which the new style develops and by which it is carried over the Greek world, takes pride of place. Archaeology also proves the introduction of iron and cremation. Both allow us to say that in these respects at least (and we can add the use of the throwing-spear) the old stories were partially brought up to date by the poets; where it was convenient, the heroes dealt wounds that could only be dealt with iron swords, threw their spears instead of thrusting, and were cremated. This bringing up to date differed from the bringing up to date within the Mycenaean age itself in that, so far as we know, the settings and the characters remained fixed; the siege story was not attached to any city after Troy nor were new characters introduced. The old characters might behave in a new way, but this is normal anachronism, albeit on a large scale. So the division between past and present became clearer because the past was receding. Similarly the division between dead and living was sharpened. Cremation was not a new custom, but it suddenly became universal in Athens and places which had had contact with Athens. In Athens overcrowding and overseas uncertainty were probably the causes; but, however slow beliefs about the dead were to change and however much actual performances connected with inhumation were still carried out at cremations, cremation meant a sudden and complete severance of the dead from the living, whereas the great Mycenaean was believed to live on in his sealed tomb and bless his fellow countrymen at least until his body had decayed, a period of time neither known nor knowable.

[1] Gilbert Murray, *Rise of the Greek Epic*, 78.

The other division which was blurred in Mycenaean times was the division between god and man. Of course Homer preserves a great deal of the old relationship, yet it is possible to argue that the worlds of god and man are essentially separate in Homer, that the gods normally have to find an occasion to interfere with the doings of men, and that when they cause men to do things, the men were very often going to do these same things of their own volition.[1] In Homer we have the end of a development which leads on to lyric poetry. But this development started in the dark period. In the first place the King who lived on equal terms with the gods had gone with his palace. Even for Athens, which survived unsacked, though attacked and though swamped by refugees, archaeology and tradition provide just enough evidence to enable us to date in the eleventh century the change by which the King became a king and the goddess Athena received her own dwelling. Secondly, the essential change in the Trojan war story was made in the dark period, because the new story with divergences is common both to Homer and to Hesiod: the change by which the vassals of Agamemnon became the Suitors of Helen was the invention of a genius, who wanted to make the story intelligible to his contemporaries. What concerns us here is that the Trojan war became the 'will of Zeus'. It is arguable that this view that war is god's will is an adaptation of an old Eastern theme to the sack of the Mycenaean palaces, which in the *Iliad* Hera permits in return for permission to sack Troy. These are not gods who meet Kings on equal terms but gods who dispose of mankind as inferiors, whether to bring the age of heroes to an end (as in Hesiod) or to relieve the burden on Earth (as in the *Cypria*) or because of the wrath of Achilles (as in the *Iliad*).

The division between past and present, dead and living, gods and men was the work of the poets in the dark period. Homer added the everyday world in his similes so that gods, heroes, and men make three contrasted levels, but the third and lowest level is the addition of the last poet or poets. The principle of clear division, which seems to have been introduced into poetry in the dark period, is the principle which most obviously distinguishes Protogeometric pottery from Mycenaean pottery. Now the parts of vases were clearly defined, black areas were sharply contrasted

[1] Cf. Kullmann, *das Wirken der Götter in der Ilias, passim*. On the last, cf. Dodds, *The Greeks and the Irrational*, 5 f.

with reserved areas, and the structure of the vase was emphasized by pattern. The patterns themselves were arranged in complicated symmetry (figs. 29–30), and here again a parallel may be drawn with the kind of poetry which consists of the listing of parallel instances in parallel forms – catalogues, genealogies, songs of consolation and the rest, which have been with reason traced back into the dark period.

But a more important and more difficult question remains. Pottery was always a major art. Greek vases always showed great artistic and technical mastery. They were prized by the Greeks themselves and exported far beyond the boundaries of the Greek world. The revolution in the decoration of pottery is therefore likely to have corresponded to some spiritual revolution which took place in the dark period. At first figure scenes, animal life, and plant life were abandoned. The desiccation of the latest Mycenaean art may be decadence or it may be that a new view of the world was already arising. Certainly from the beginning of Protogeometric art there is no question of decadence; the new ornament was executed with mathematical precision and love. Moreover, the rare horses on Protogeometric vases and the figures which became common on later Geometric vases were executed with the same precise abstraction; only after the middle of the eighth century did the movement towards realism begin. With great hesitation I should like to suggest a parallel for this very precise and rational new art. Obviously it is an art stripped down to essentials just as life was stripped down to essentials with the collapse of the Mycenaean palaces. The essential here is perhaps a belief in human reason, in human capacity to reduce things to simple and clear patterns so that they become manageable – a purely human operation when all the mystery and magic of the Kings had failed. Seen like this, the Protogeometric vase-painter takes his place not only as the forerunner of later developments in art (ultimately the invention of perspective), mathematics, and philosophy but also as the colleague of the poet who sees life in similar rational and human terms. Again we are forced to argue back from Homer. Possibly we should find here the origin of his unromantic unmysterious view of the gods, who only differ from man in being deathless and ageless and strong.[1]

[1] Cf. the very interesting discussion by P. Chantraine in *Entretiens Hardt*, I, particularly 64f. Cf. also H. Fränkel, *Dichtung etc.*, 77.

This is a manageable way of thinking about the gods: within their own sphere and with their very different powers they yet behave like us. More clearly we may find in this new view the reason for the rejection of the ecstatic and magic elements in Mycenaean religion which link it to earlier religion. We know that ecstatic nature worship continued and Dionysos reconquered the Greek world in the seventh and sixth centuries; Homer glances at the god of Maenads and once compares Andromache to a maenad, but on the whole ecstasy and mystery is excluded, just as certain forms of magic and miracle were excluded – Althaia's fatal brand, Bellerophon's winged horse, Herakles' impenetrable skin. This very enlightened rationalist outlook was no doubt the possession of very few, but its consequences for the future were immense, and I think we may suppose that it originated in Athens in the dark period.

Thus partly bringing up to date, partly rethinking and re-forming, the poets of the dark period kept the old stories of the Mycenaean age alive and transported them by their various routes to the new settlements in the Eastern Aegean. They sang in the houses of the nobles and at the courts of kings, but the difference between an Iron Age king and an Iron Age noble was a slight difference of degree rather than a major difference of kind. The dominant strain was the Attic-Ionic strain, and the cities of Ionia gradually formed, consolidated, and enlarged the League, which had its common festival on the Mykale peninsula; but their origin was mixed, and they must always have demanded poetry which covered the range of their mixed ancestors, whether the poet was singing at their houses or at the festival on the Mykale peninsula or at the other great Ionian festival on Delos. Two conditions at least had to be realized before the *Iliad* and the *Odyssey* could be composed. The first was, quite simply, the achievement of some prosperity so that there was time and desire not only for the privileged aristocracy to hear the poets in their houses but for a much wider section of the population to hear them at the great festivals. This means that the great past was felt to be the heritage not only of the kings and nobles but also of the population as a whole and not only of that part of the population which could trace its descent back to the Mycenaeans but also of the Dorian cities who could not. Thus we find in the eighth century (and in some places still earlier) widely dispersed and varied phenomena testifying to Greek interests in the Mycenaean age: hero cults, games in honour of heroes, choruses in honour of heroes, kings called after heroes, forged dedications to heroes, manipulation of heroic legends to political ends. This was the atmosphere in which the large-scale epic was created, and it was created not as court poetry but as festival poetry, not as poetry for kings and nobles but as poetry for well-to-do citizens, who were beginning to achieve political importance because they formed the hoplite line in their cities. For them the hoplites were inserted into the old stories and their institutions were also included, particularly in the new long similes which reflected the everyday life of Ionia.

The second condition was the introduction of alphabetic writing, whether it was the invention of the poets themselves or not. Only alphabetic writing made the change possible from the short song of the solo singer to the prolonged recitation by a team of rhapsodes; only prolonged recitation made appreciation possible of the long and complicated unity of the *Iliad* and the *Odyssey*. How long a period we can assume for the performance of large-scale epics before the *Iliad* and the *Odyssey* depends on when we suppose the alphabet was introduced: a century would seem to be the absolute maximum, but the period may have been much less. If, in fact, syllabic writing had survived through the intervening centuries, the effect of the new script would have been felt very swiftly. If syllabic writing had been forgotten, then the new invention would have taken longer to master. Large-scale epic composed in chronological order was written for recitation by rhapsodes before the *Iliad* and the *Odyssey*, but Homer was the first to exploit the new form and the occasion to the full – the first and the last unless the *Odyssey* was not the work of the old poet but the work of an extremely gifted pupil. For these two poems prolonged recitation is a necessity if their involved unity is to be appreciated.

The Homeric epics are the supreme literary example of the kind of composition which is seen in the Attic Geometric vases by a few great painters about the middle of the eighth century.[1] Every possible device is used with consummate skill: withholding of the hero, alternation of quiet scenes and scenes of action, static symmetry of echoing scenes, dynamic pattern of preparation

[1] See particularly figs. 21–2, 35–6.

and suspense, massed similes, contrasted similes, echoing similes, typical scenes with variations. It cannot be chance that poetic compositions and artistic compositions of unique size and of parallel complexity, showing the same kind of system in reducing material to form, should appear at the same time. A very small number of geniuses in poetry and painting seized the moment when creations on this scale would be accepted. In both arts these geniuses were the heirs of a long tradition which stretches back through the dark period to the Mycenaean age: more specifically, if the argument of this book is accepted, both were the heirs of a Pylian-Attic tradition which had only finally diverged into an Ionian and a mainland stream a century or so before their birth. Their ancestors had together made the spiritual revolution which has been described and in which the beginnings of classical Greece can be seen. They themselves chose the first and the last moment at which art and poetry on this scale and dominated by these conceptions was possible. It was the first moment because only now had either Athens or Ionia the necessary wealth, and the last moment because, although the definition and clarity of Geometric art was never quite forgotten and although the *Iliad* and *Odyssey* continued to be recited in entirety at the festivals and swiftly spread over the Greek world in piecemeal recitations, the creative artists and poets of the next generation had quite different aims and met a different demand.

Figure scenes, as we have seen, dominated later Geometric vases more and more, and the figures became larger and more individual. Early in the seventh century the outline style superseded the silhouette, and the figures were often identified by inscriptions. Rectilinear ornament then gave place to curvilinear ornament and animals filled out. Gorgons, sphinxes, and sirens became common and important. Occasionally anonymity was broken and an artist signed his vase. We call the new style Orientalizing or Mycenaean renaissance, and both these titles have some justification. Poetry in the seventh century was no longer anonymous. The scale, style, and metre of the *Iliad* and *Odyssey* were all abandoned in poems which were short, individual, and emotional. If we now suspect that the beginnings of mystery religions and of Dionysiac ecstasy and revelry can be found in Mycenaean Greece, we shall speak of revival rather than creation or importation in the seventh century. But these dark growths had to win their way against the bright and sterilizing light of the Geometric spirit, if our interpretation of the spiritual revolution in the pre-Homeric period is right. Yet Homer is the link between the old and the new, partly because he was scrupulous in preserving the ancient elements of traditional poetry, partly because his sympathy was quick to observe and record the new. The theme of Homeric sympathy with the everyday life and aspirations of the common man has often been elaborated. It is a pointer to the future. Observation of everyday life is found chiefly in the similes, and long similes were probably the creation of the latest poets. They have at least three functions. In so far as they represent the Ionian present day they thrust the heroes further into the past and make them more magnificent. Sometimes similes, particularly those which belong to sets each developed from a single short comparison, are used to form a recurring pattern which holds a stretch of action together. Their third function looks forward to the future. Unlike all comparisons in earlier poetry, the long Homeric simile does not illustrate a single point but a number of points in the heroic situation which is to be apprehended by the audience; the poor woman weighing wool to make a living is a kind of working model of the swaying lines of battle in a desperate situation. Not only this type of comparison but also the inductive type ('like an oak or a poplar or a tall pine') and the proportional type ('But, Achilles, tame your great spirit . . . the gods themselves can be persuaded, whose excellence, honour, and strength is greater') can be found later in the Presocratic philosophers. Two essential elements in early Ionian philosophy were first the use of observation and secondly explanation of the unknown in terms of the known. Homer was their predecessor both as an accurate observer and in his use of everyday life to explain the unknown, in his case the heroic past. He was writing for an audience which in a century and a half would be ready for Thales.

We have noticed also the similes which illustrate psychological events, the special use of abstracts to describe emotions and psychological characteristics, and that a number of speeches of decision can be dated late. This effort to describe accurately mental events and characteristics points forward to the elegiac, iambic, and lyric poets of the seventh century and later, to Archilochos' address to his soul and to Sappho's description of her emotions, and further still to the heroes and heroines of tragedy. In the *Odyssey* the responsibility for disaster is laid firmly on Aigisthos by the gods, and a similar recklessness brought the suitors of Penelope to a similar disaster at the hands of Odysseus, who himself triumphs over all his misfortunes because his wisdom includes moral force besides cunning and resource. It is true that Homer preserves many ancient views of the gods: old Eastern stories of battles between the gods and of the gods' desire to destroy mankind, the special relationship between the Mycenaean god or goddess and the King and the corresponding relationship between the King and a hostile god, predestination and the spinning of fate, and the natural human desire to ascribe the unaccountable in many spheres of life to the gods or some particular god. These are all part of the tradition which he inherited or of the thought of his contemporaries. Hesiod himself provides parallel and incompatible accounts of the fall of man; we should not, therefore, expect a consistent theology from Homer. Yet in the *Iliad* as well as in the *Odyssey* human responsibility and divine justice are emphasized. The main story of the *Iliad* is the story of Agamemnon's wrath with Chryses and his folly in taking Briseis from Achilles, of Achilles' wrath with Agamemnon and his folly in refusing Agamemnon's apology, of Hektor's 'recklessness' in wearing the arms of Patroklos, of Achilles' wrath with Hektor and his reconciliation with Agamemnon, of his excessive vengeance on Hektor and his final reconciliation with Priam. This story of human responsibility is the central story into which the mass of traditional material, carrying with it traditional views of gods and men, is woven. Human passions are strong, and therefore Agamemnon calls Infatuation the daughter of Zeus; but human supplication is also strong, and Phoinix calls Prayers the daughters of Zeus. Homer knows that self-control is also a real force, and when Achilles unaccountably does not draw his sword against Agamemnon, he ascribes this restraint to the intervention of Athena. This view of life that man is responsible for his disasters if he fails to use restraint to govern his passions is described at the beginning of the *Iliad* as the Will of Zeus. It is Zeus' will that wrath should cause suffering. If this interpretation is right, the very old idea of god's will to destroy mankind has been given a new twist: Zeus' will is not directed to relieving pressure on the earth nor to ending the race of demigods and so separating mankind from the gods but to government of the world in accordance with the principles of justice. Thus before Hesiod, who must be regarded as an independent development of the same traditional poetry, Homer in Ionia was also concerned with the problems of divine government, human responsibility, and justice in the *polis*. Homer not only inherits a tradition which descends from the singers of Mycenaean palaces but is also the forerunner of archaic and classical Greece.

INDEX

299

1a PYLOS TABLET, TA 641

1b PYLOS TABLET, TN 996
(cf. pp. 13, 65, 111, 113)

2   IVORY WARRIOR, DELOS
(cf. pp. 27, 111, 139, 170)

3   LION HUNT DAGGER BLADE, MYCENAE
(cf. pp. 28, 57, 214)

4 STELE FROM SHAFT-GRAVE, MYCENAE
(cf. pp. 32, 57, 58, 126, 224)

5   SILVER SIEGE VASE, MYCENAE
(cf. pp. 32, 58, 214)

6　PAINTED SARCOPHAGUS, HAGIA TRIADA
(cf. pp. 35 f., 41 ff., 63, 109, 129, 202, 286)

7   WARRIOR VASE, MYCENAE
(cf. pp. 38, 40, 60, 94, 191, 195, 202)

8   GRIFFIN FRESCO, PYLOS (RECONSTRUCTION)
(cf. pp. 32, 39, 108, 285)

9   SINGER FRESCO, PYLOS (RECONSTRUCTION)
(cf. pp. 47, 63, 129, 285 ff.)

10   GODDESS AND WOMEN,
MYCENAE
(cf. p. 42 f.)

11   MAN LEADING TWO
WOMEN, ATHENS
(cf. p. 48)

12   MASK BETWEEN GOATS,
PHAISTOS
(cf. p. 50)

13   DANCE AND GODDESS,
ISOPATA
(cf. pp. 50f., 62, 286)

14 CHARIOT AND SEA MONSTER, ENKOMI
(cf. pp. 48, 127, 204)

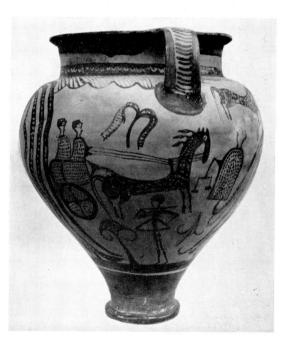

15 CHARIOT AND FIGURE WITH SCALES,
ENKOMI (cf. p. 49)

16 *a*, *b*, and *c* HARVESTER VASE, HAGIA TRIADA
(cf. pp. 50, 62, 214, 286)

17 MAN APPROACHING GODDESS, ARADIPPO (cf. p. 53)

18 CHARIOT AND PALACE, CURIUM (cf. p. 59)

19   THE BATTLE IN THE GLEN, MYCENAE
(cf. p. 58)

20   BATTLE FOR THE SHIPS, ATTIC
(cf. pp. 171f., 198, 203, 205, 224, 289)

21 FUNERAL, ATTIC
(cf. pp. 169, 172f., 196, 198, 200, 203ff., 289, 294)

22   FUNERAL AND CHARIOT RIDE, ATTIC
(cf. pp. 169, 172f., 199f., 203ff., 289, 294)

23 PARADE, FUNERAL, AND CHARIOT RACE,
ATTIC (cf. pp. 172, 174, 199, 203, 289)

24*a* GAMES AND MAN BETWEEN LIONS, ATTIC
(cf. pp. 174, 176, 289)

24*b* GAMES, ATTIC
(cf. pp. 174, 289)

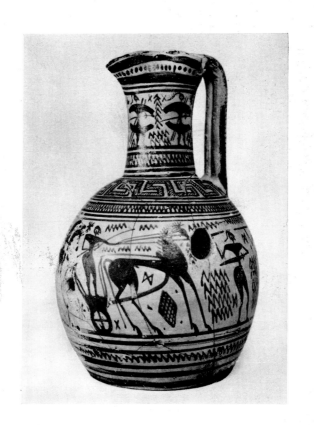

25*a* and *b*   NESTOR AND AKTORIONE-MOLIONE, ATTIC
(cf. pp. 175, 199, 203, 289)

26 MAN AND CENTAUR, ATTIC (cf. pp. 175, 199, 289)

27 HERAKLES AND STYMPHALIAN BIRDS,
ATTIC (cf. pp. 175, 289)

28*a* and *b* SHIPWRECK, ATTIC
(cf. pp. 176, 198, 205, 224, 289)

29, 30   ATTIC PROTOGEOMETRIC VASES
(cf. pp. 190, 191, 193, 196, 291 f.)

31, 32 ATTIC GEOMETRIC VASES
(cf. pp. 193, 196, 199)

33, 34 ATTIC GEOMETRIC VASES
(cf. pp. 194, 195, 199, 203)

35, 36   ATTIC GEOMETRIC VASES
(cf. pp. 197, 200, 294)

37   CRETAN BRONZE SHIELD
(cf. p. 213)

38   DETAIL OF NO. 34